THE FOUR HEAVENS

DAVID STUART

The Four Heavens

A NEW HISTORY OF THE ANCIENT MAYA

PRINCETON UNIVERSITY PRESS
PRINCETON AND OXFORD

Princeton University Press is proud to have partnered with Planeta for the co-publication of this edition in the Spanish language.

Published by Princeton University Press
41 William Street, Princeton, New Jersey 08540
99 Banbury Road, Oxford OX2 6JX

press.princeton.edu

GPSR Authorized Representative: Easy Access System Europe - Mustamäe tee 50, 10621 Tallinn, Estonia, gpsr.requests@easproject.com

ISBN 9780691213842
ISBN (e-book) 9780691280660

Library of Congress Control Number: 2025946266

British Library Cataloging-in-Publication Data is available

Editorial: Rob Tempio, Chloe Coy
Production Editorial: Elizabeth Byrd, Nathan Carr
Text and Jacket Design: Heather Hansen
Production: Erin Suydam
Publicity: Julia Haav (US), Alyssa Sanford (US), Carmen Jimenez (UK)
Copyeditor: Karin Kipp

Jacket Credit: © David Stuart. Illustration of K'awil, the animate force of lightning and of royal power, the basis of kingship and dynastic authority. The design comes from a painted vase from Xultun (ancient Baxwitz).

Endpapers Credit: © David Stuart. Drawing of Element 56 from La Corona, Guatemala.

Frontispiece Credit: © David Stuart. Drawing of Lintel 11 from Yaxchilan, Mexico.

This book has been composed in Arno Pro with Swear Display and Obviously

Printed in the United States of America

10 9 8 7 6 5 4 3 2 1

With love to my parents,
George Edwin Stuart and Gene Ann Strickland

u kahlay cab tu kinil lay tumen tz'iban lae, tumen lae kuchuc tu kin u meyah lay hunob lae, picil thanob lae, utial katabal u chi Maya uinicob uay yohelob bix zihanilob etz'lic cab uay ti peten lae.

This is the history of the world in those times, because it has been written down, because the time has not yet ended for making these books, these many words, so that Maya people may be asked if they know how they were born here in this country, when the land was founded.

THE BOOK OF CHILAM BALAM OF CHUMAYEL
CHUMAYEL, YUCATÁN, SIXTEENTH CENTURY

CONTENTS

LIST OF MAPS

FOREWORD

IN 1839, AFTER spending thirteen days exploring the Maya site of Copan in Honduras with his colleague, the artist Frederick Catherwood, the intrepid explorer John Lloyd Stephens wrote: "One thing I believe: its history is graven on its monuments. No Champollion has yet brought to them the energies of his inquiring mind. Who shall read them?" He continued on to say: "I cannot help believing that the ... hieroglyphics will yet be read. ... For centuries the hieroglyphics of Egypt were inscrutable, and, though not perhaps in our day, I feel persuaded that a key surer than that of the Rosetta stone will be discovered."

We are now at that point. We now have our Champollion(s), courtesy of David Stuart, author of this book, and those who have gone before him. We can finally read the hieroglyphs inscribed on the Maya monuments at Copan and elsewhere. John Lloyd Stephens was correct; they do indeed tell us their history ... and it is fascinating.

Readers of *The Four Heavens* are in for an unsurpassed intellectual treat: the story of the Maya as it has never been told before, courtesy of the advances made in our knowledge over just the past few decades—advances in which David Stuart has been a pioneer for virtually his entire life. It is exactly the type of manuscript that we had envisioned when we began this new series of books intended for readers fascinated by archaeology, from amateur enthusiasts and general readers to seasoned scholars looking for a compelling and state of the art synthesis.

David Stuart is arguably the leading Mayanist in the world. As the son of two Mayanist scholars, he essentially grew up on and around ancient Maya sites. As every ten-year-old does, he started to read scholarly works about the Maya, and by the age of thirteen, he began making contributions to the decipherment of Mayan hieroglyphics. He eventually became the youngest person ever to win a MacArthur Genius award, at the age of eighteen, for his decipherment work. This is quite literally the book he was raised to write.

This series, *Uncovering the Past,* was conceived back in 2019. During a conference keynote address, I challenged my archaeology colleagues to write more books and articles meant for the general public. I suggested that they could begin telling their stories, each in their own way, about what they had found on their excavations, or what they found interesting about the ancient world, or what they would want most people to know about a particular topic.

David Stuart has done exactly that, by bringing the Maya to life through his highly readable first-person storytelling and wonderful illustrations. This is indeed, as he says in the opening pages, a history of the Maya as it has never been told before. It reflects the most recent discoveries, the latest thinking, and the cutting-edge hypotheses that have recently revolutionized our thinking, including the contributions that he himself has made. We are extremely fortunate to be able to read and listen to the words of one of the preeminent Maya scholars of our generation.

Please dig into this volume and enjoy the journey into the past!

Eric H. Cline

PREFACE

ON A SPRING afternoon in 2012, I took an unexpected call from Guatemala, with exciting news of a discovery. My colleague Marcello Canuto, archaeologist at Tulane University, was working with his crew at a ruin called La Corona, and he had just driven for hours out of the jungle camp to get cell service and make the call. Once we were connected, I immediately could sense excitement in Marcello's voice. Just a couple of days earlier his crew had found twenty-two stone blocks with carved scenes and well-preserved hieroglyphs. I was a member of the project team, a specialist in reading Maya inscriptions, and in 1997 I had been part of the first expeditions to explore and document La Corona, new to archaeology at the time. Marcello's news was thrilling, and I was eager to read what these new texts had to say. With my semester of teaching at the University of Texas winding down, I made plans to fly down to Guatemala, cameras and clipboard in hand.

A few days later, driving along the muddy forested track into La Corona, I had little idea what I was about to encounter. After I dropped my bags at the camp, Marcello, project co-director Tomás Barrientos, and I excitedly ran straight to the dig site, down a winding jungle trail, all the while watched by a troop of spider monkeys in the trees above. The shallow excavations in front of a mound were being overseen by Tulane graduate student Jocelyne Ponce, who had found the stones just days earlier. There were the stones, all in a line, clearly a part of an ancient stairway on a building long ago collapsed. On closer inspection it was clear that the carved blocks were of many different styles, mixed up and taken in antiquity from other buildings. For reasons unknown, the ancient Maya had deconstructed several of La Corona's architectural monuments to create a mash-up of texts and images, each telling parts of a larger tale.

As I walked along the line of stones viewing them one by one, I saw long strings of hieroglyphs and portraits of kings and queens. Soon I was overwhelmed by the snippets of history I was reading. Each stone mentioned parts of a long and complex story of people who had lived in the seventh and eighth centuries CE:

> The first stone, lying slightly apart from the rest, recorded the death of a king named Yich'ahkk'ahk' ("Fire is his Claw"), on December 15, 697. I knew his name from other historical records, as a ruler of the powerful Kanul dynasty had lost a battle against his great enemy, the Mutul dynasty, in 695. I wondered: did Yich'ahkk'ahk' die because of his loss, or of his war wounds?
>
> The next block recorded the war and conquest of a place possibly called Ika', overseen by a man named K'inich Yaxk'uk'mo', aided by warriors from Calakmul. The name again was familiar, as the founder of the dynasty of far-off Copan, in what is today western Honduras. What was he doing mentioned here, in La Corona?
>
> The next stone bore a carved scene of a man seated on a throne, with bundles of tribute lying before him. The text was broken and incomplete, but I could make out another mention of a war, and the defeat of a lord named Numul Ahnchahk. The date was eroded, and the circumstances unclear, but the image of a seated lord with bundles of cloth and precious quetzal feather as tribute suggested a major transfer of riches.

There were several more inscribed stones resting in the dirt beyond these few, each placed side by side and each telling its own stand-alone segment of ancient history. It was clear that other blocks were missing, taken away by looters who had found La Corona decades ago, well before any archaeologists. They probably encountered this very building back in the 1960s, carting off numerous carved stones they saw on the surface and missing the line of stones Jocelyn found just below the ground. These stones quickly made their way into the art market, for sale in galleries in Zurich, Paris, and Brussels, others in New York, Boston, Los Angeles, and Mexico City. For decades I and other Mayanist scholars had studied these "homeless" carvings, wondering where they had come from. Some mystery site must have been their source, a place we came to call "Site Q" (Q for "question"). It wasn't until 1997, on our first expedition into La Corona, that I was able to help identify it as the source of the looted stones, having realized that yet other monument fragments left by the looters told parts of Site Q's history. La Corona was Site Q, and the newly discovered stones I was reading confirmed it, beyond all doubt.[1]

In the excavation trench, I moved along, eager to absorb what stories came next:

> The sixth block, dense with hieroglyphs, recorded the establishment of the Kanul dynasty at the site we call Calakmul, an event overseen by a great king named Yuknomch'en (the father of Yuknom Yich'ahk'k'ahk', mentioned on the first block). It went on to highlight the playing of a ritual ballgame between the local ruler of La Corona, a man named Sakmas, and the Kanul king, perhaps key stage in the cementing their new political relationship. Yuknomch'en's daughter would go on to marry Sakmas's son. This block's long inscription closed with a mention of how all this important history took place many centuries before the future close of the cycle of 13 bak'tuns, each a 400-year period. This would happen, it said, on December 24, 2012.
>
> The seventh and eighth blocks showed two men, dressed in finery and with headdresses, sitting on the floor playing a ball game. The inscription indicates that this was the very same game mentioned on the sixth block, between Sakmas of La Corona and Yuknomch'en of the Kanuls (Plate 1).
>
> The eighth block recorded the arrival to La Corona of a woman, Lady Tz'ihbwinik, princess of the Kanul court. She was the daughter of Yuknomch'en, sister of Yuknom Yich'ahkk'ahk', and soon to be the wife of the Sakmas's vengeful son. Calakmul found favor with the restoration La Corona's dynastic line.
>
> The tenth block recorded a ritual dance by the Sakmas's son on February 2, 681. His performance was called the "Green Feather Flute Dance."[2]

Each stone resting in the excavation trench told a previously unknown story or historical event. They were snippets of far longer narratives, with parts still missing here and there. Remarkably, some of the newly discovered blocks even matched ones that were in museums or private collections across the globe. I soon realized that the stone recording the "Green Feather Flute dance" joined with a similar inscribed block I had seen displayed in a living room in Boston back in the '90s. Together they told us that, months after the dance, an enemy was executed ("he died by the point of the stone") and then sixteen days later the king performed yet another ceremonial dance, on the calendar day that repeated that of world creation. With this one discovery in the field, several threads of Maya history could be woven together.

I use the exciting discoveries at La Corona to illustrate just how transformative a time this is for understanding Maya civilization. Its ancient history is in sharp focus as never before due to our newfound ability to read its hieroglyphs, what has been called "the last of the Great Decipherments."[3] I have been fortunate to be at the forefront of this effort and to be able to now read a detailed history that no archaeologist a century ago could have ever imagined. The story we can reconstruct extends back to about the second century CE, leaving us roughly six or seven centuries of royal narratives and insights into religion and philosophy. As a result, we know more about Classic Maya geopolitics circa 800 CE than we do about parts of early medieval Europe, say, around the same time. Theirs is the oldest written history anywhere in the Americas, reaching back to a period when Roman emperors and the Han Dynasty were at their height. It was then that Classic Maya civilization, building on a long foundation of predecessors, developed into a vibrant culture that lasted for centuries, adapting to new challenges, transforming, resisting, and lasting up to the present day.

The La Corona blocks give us tiny, isolated glimpses of a bigger narrative, and we will come across many more fragments of that larger history, each telling parts of a much longer tale of a civilization growing, forming connections, transforming, in conflict, and under stress. Admittedly we are only reading the voices of scribes and authors, members of numerous royal courts who were carefully maintaining the official narratives of their rulers and fellow court members. It is a biased and narrow voice of the elites, to be sure, but like the extant records from ancient Egypt or early China, it can provide a rich means to study aspects of the broader culture and its development over time. The ancient texts offer insights into a wider system of beliefs and lifeways that were shared among the broader population. And, importantly, they offer up a self-portrayal, indeed the oldest written account of events and actors from any place or culture in the Americas, reaching back more than two thousand years.

So this is a book of new history. Not a fresh retelling of an old story about the ancient past, but new in the sense that the people, places, and events related herein have been, until very recently, absent from any broad narratives of the ancient world. Put simply, the Americas have for too long been disregarded within the world's collective sense of its own deeper history. This book hopes it can help correct that skewed, stubborn, and incomplete picture. It presents the history of the ancient Maya in many of its complexities, amounting to the oldest written history we have from any region outside Europe, Africa, or Asia. It is my hope that the kings, queens, wars, and political maneuverings of fifteen centuries ago can begin to be incorporated into our emerging and ever-changing sense of what our world once was and who played a role in shaping it.

Maya history is long and detailed, and there is no way I can hope to present all that we think we know, from a field of research that is still quite young. Rather, this book reflects the strengths and weaknesses within my own personal perspective, grounded in over fifty years of working and living in the Maya world, straddling the ancient past and modern life. Many important places, events, and historical figures must be omitted for the sake of space and clarity, and those stories will be told in due time. Here I have chosen to offer my own take on Maya history as understood at this moment, emphasizing the grand sweep of the culture rather than a patchwork of kingdoms. As I hope will become clear, we are beginning to see a remarkable interconnectedness among ancient kingdoms and their individual storylines. It is a story that will no doubt change in its details and become more refined with time, as new sources and new discoveries come to light.

When the seeds of this book were first planted, two things nudged me to let the idea grow and develop. For one, there had not been a general history of the Maya for the public published in over two decades. My shelves are full of academic books about the ancient Maya, but they are mostly archaeological overviews, not so concerned with the framework of the history itself. Second, such historical accounts tend to be broken up into atomistic considerations of individual dynasties and sites. As I have come to understand more about the ancient Maya over the decades, it is clear that the story of the so-called "Classic" period, between roughly 150 and 900 CE, is not just localized bits but is rather of one piece, with the fates of kingdoms and dynasties integrated with one another. In the big scheme, it proves to be a complex interfamily drama, involving a dozen or so lineages who intermarried, fought, and strove to promote their special status in their world through the inscribed monuments we have today to study. So this is not a broad introduction to Maya archaeology. It is focused on certain places and people and above all attempts to reframe the Maya past as a very human story.

My telling ends with the invasion of the Spanish in the sixteenth century. Accounts of that time and of the ordeals of the colonial world have been told by many accomplished historians and anthropologists, focused on the different subregions of the Maya world, such as Yucatán, the Peten, or the Guatemalan highlands. But my treatment picks up elements of the story after 1800, with the initial explorations of Maya ruins, and how those small adventurous steps led to where we are today.

The book has four parts, reflecting in a way the Mesoamerican understanding of time, cosmology, and spatial balance—the center and the four quarters. Part I is "The World Revealed," or *paskab*, a Maya word that literally means "to open the earth." It is a phrase found in ancient texts in reference to the founding of new ceremonial plazas and spaces, a phenomenon that is conspicuous in the archaeological record of the earliest Maya. This section of the book reveals a new space of its own, beginning with the premise of what I call the Rupture—a significant break in the historical memory of the Maya after 900 CE, the collapse of the Classic period. The fall of many Maya states at that time accounted for much of this loss, so that by the time of the Spanish invasion, any awareness of the people and events of the Classic period was gone or mostly so. The first explorers and antiquarians who ventured into ruins had no idea who built them or any notion that they were occupied by the ancestors of the living Maya. It was a "rupture" of cultural memory, a cut-off in history with little parallel in the world. This situation provides a stepping stone for the presentation of the history we now know, recovered only in the past eighty or so years of scholarship. The revealing of a world also involves how the Maya began to form themselves into an early civilization; their emergence onto the scene from the depths of prehistory is another sort of revelation. The Maya of "prehistory," from the time before our records of dynasties and rulers, set the stage for everything that was to come.

Part II is "The Earth and Caves," where we begin our detailed historical narrative with a look at the dynasties of the Classic period and the social and political world they shaped and occupied. The Mayan word I use for this section is *kabch'en,* meaning a kingdom, territory, or realm. Here I lay out what we know of Maya politics and the culture of the elite courts. We will see how the rarified world of Maya kings and queens formed a culture unto itself as well as a highly interwoven social and political network of alliances and fractured relations. From the very beginning, war and revenge form a theme that runs through several chapters, especially as we examine the many clashes between the dynasties of Mutul (based at Tikal) and Kanul (at Dzibanche and Calakmul).

These rivalries play out further in Part III, "The Four Heavens" (*chante'chan),* which also serves as the book's title. This refers to the basic underlying structure of Maya cosmology, to the four "sides" or vectors of the sky, as determined by the daily and annual movements of the sun. (It is no accident that in the Mayan language of the hieroglyphs, *chan* means both "four" and "sky.") This four-part scheme included geopolitics as well. Starting in the seventh century, a handful of kings in the east, west, north, and south of the Maya world saw themselves as representatives of rainmaking deities at the four directions, the *Kalomte',* revealing a coherence to the wider Maya world. First, we will look at eastern kingdoms, the principal being Dzibanche, followed by the western, southern, and northern city-states. Our divvying up of kingdoms within such a cosmic layout is a good indication that the ancient Maya saw their world in some sense as a unified and idealized whole despite it also being politically balkanized, unstable, and embroiled in frequent conflict.

The chapters of Part IV look at the much-debated "collapse" in the ninth century and at its aftermath. Maya histories make no direct mention of the endings that befell the kingdoms and their courts, but the written sources show us a world in deep crisis leading up to that time, especially after 790 CE. The wars that had begun in the sixth century grew steadily, creating an unstable world where people often left their home sites, and their histories turn obscure. I therefore call this section "The Leaving," looking at how Maya culture during the last centuries before the arrival of the Spanish encapsulated a dynamic of movement, seeing the old replaced with new systems and arrangements. As the old, conflict-ridden political world of the Classic era fell apart many rejected the elite culture and the centers of power that weakly maintained it. They chose instead to participate in a cultural reset, finding new homes, new rulers, and new relationships with the surrounding world. We have long described this complex process as a "collapse," but this characterization tells only the initial part of the story, for it was more broadly an adaptation of life in the face of great change, involving many scales of migration in search of better options. For centuries, the Maya of the central lowlands had succeeded in forging a sustainable way of existence, but once there came a tipping point, exacerbated by environmental change and population pressure, they saw what no longer worked and remade themselves anew. It offers a historical lesson we should examine carefully.

In writing the historical chapters, with their steady emphasis on crownings, conquests, and shifting allegiances, I have wondered if some readers might find the details of names and dates a bit dry or tedious. But on reflection it occurred to me that the very existence of such detail is a key takeaway of this book and that we should celebrate our ability to peer into it. Maya sources are good at presenting us with "just the facts"—for example, that a certain royal individual died on October 25 in 726 CE, he was buried in his pyramid three days later on October 28, and a successor assumed the throne on January 7, 727. To have this sort of temporal resolution of events, down to the day, is extraordinary for any ancient history, as matter-of-fact as they might seem. We have a history to sift through that is extraordinarily detailed and still being revealed. This book represents my own attempt at sorting and distilling, and others in the future will do so in other ways through the refined methods of historical scholarship. We are still in the early stages.

Finally, a brief word is necessary on the spelling of Mayan words. I have chosen where possible to show the names of people and places are in the original language, Classic Mayan, unless otherwise indicated. There are still a few whose pronunciation is uncertain, and in those cases I have gone with names of references as used in the literature. In this era of rapid decipherment and refinement, however, some names are bound to change. What a few years ago was "the Kan kingdom" was changed later to "Kanal" and most recently "Kaanu'l." Here I simplify it and other words to "Kanul" for heightened readability. The writing of Classic Mayan words often entails a complex orthography, and here I have tried to simplify the forms of the words and names as much as possible, perhaps at times at the expense of linguistic precision. Also, the *x* we often see in Mayan words such as *ixik*, "woman," is pronounced as "sh" ("eesheek"). The insertion of an apostrophe in many words like *k'in* or *ch'ak* represents a glottal stop—a brief interruption in the flow of air before a vowel.

For the sake of brevity and accessibility, I have also at times chosen to abbreviate some lengthy royal names. For example, a ruler of Naranjo named K'ahktiliw Chanchahk is sometimes just "K'ahktiliw" following his initial mention. I am relieved to know that sometimes Maya scribes did the same thing when writing complex names. When an ancient name remains undeciphered or unknown, I will follow the convention of using the established nickname in the literature, usually a description of the name hieroglyph, as in "Scroll Serpent" or "Animal Skull." In time we will probably discover more accurate names for these historical actors. In general, my hope is that these thorny choices will make Maya history more open and accessible to the modern, nonspecialist reader.

As a child, living with my family in a small village of Coba, in Yucatán, I learned a good deal of the Yucatec Mayan language spoken there. I have since lost most of that slight conversational ability, replacing it with the particulars of sound and grammar from the ancient language of the inscriptions that I study and teach. In working at the decipherment of Maya hieroglyphs, I came to realize that many features of these two distantly removed languages are much the same. In a real sense, the words of the Maya live on.

PART I

Paskab

THE WORLD REVEALED

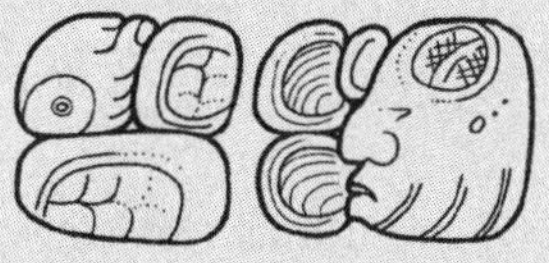

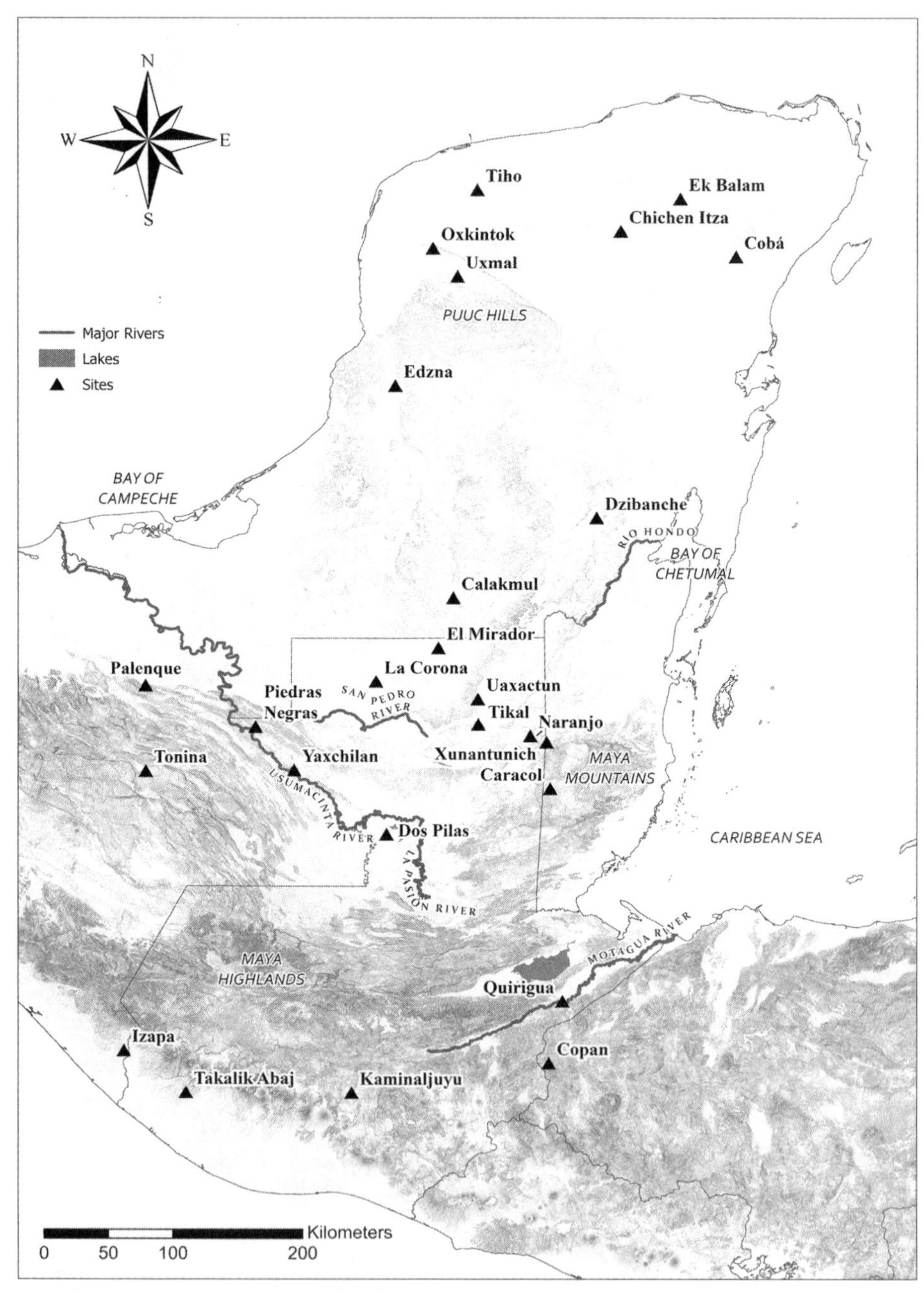

MAP 1. The Maya area with selected archaeological sites.

CHAPTER 1

Rupture

THE PEOPLE OF Baxwitz rapidly fled their city, never to return. A few remained here and there, determined to maintain a life among the emptied palaces, courtyards, and pyramids, but the elements soon took their toll, and nature began to reinhabit nearly every space of the city. Where once the din of music and voices echoed among the temples, there was only silence, replaced now and then by the chatter of parrots and the distant roars of howler monkeys. With the passing of many years, the main plaza began to be covered by shrubs and trees, growing amid the stone monuments that stood alone, bearing portraits of a long line of rulers. One of those large carved stones was newer than the others, erected not long before the end, showing a young king standing in full regalia, cradling the images of his patron gods (Figure 1.1). A date, inscribed on the stone's side, corresponded to our year 889. Within a few years, the great city of Baxwitz, once inhabited by kings, queens, merchants, and the images of deities, would be no more, covered in dense forest, with no one present to look upon the lonely king or to read of his triumphs.

Baxwitz, or "Hammerstone Hill," was the ancient name of a very old place we know today as Xultun, a large ancient city located in the remote forests of northern Guatemala. Its ruins and monuments were first seen

FIGURE 1.1. Stela 10 from Xultun, Guatemala. Dating to 889 and one of the latest carved portraits of a king from the Classic period, shortly before the city's abandonment. The current location of the stela is unknown. Composite photograph by Eric von Euw, courtesy Peabody Museum, Harvard University.

by archaeologists just over a century ago, in 1920, when the site was given the name Xultun ("End Stone") because of the very late monument mentioned, Stela 10, one of the very last we know from anywhere in the central Maya region. The city's original name was long lost until only a few years ago, when hieroglyphs on a painted vase revealed its name for the first time.[1] Today, wandering through its massive tree-covered pyramids and empty plazas is an eerie, even jarring experience of a "lost city," for it can't help but raise disquieting questions about our world. After all, our modern sense of place and community presumes a constancy of growth and expansion. The abandonment of a city or of many cities in a short time span is difficult to comprehend, on the face of it. But the Maya *did* leave many of their settlements and royal centers, and not just in the ninth century. Why? What could compel a group, community, or urban population that had adapted and thrived for centuries to reach a stopping point? If Maya archaeologists have learned anything after a century of pondering such questions, it is that the questions themselves often need to be carefully framed and considered, for it is obvious that the Maya didn't just disappear, as is so often lazily claimed. The five million speakers of Mayan languages who live today are obvious testament to this simple fact. Rather, it seems that the populations who had lived in and around Baxwitz and many other cities saw good reason to move away, seeking new places to live and new patterns of life. Through abandonment, as we will see, the Maya were trying to adapt to a rapidly changing world.

The crisis that confronted Baxwitz in the ninth century also played out in cities throughout the Maya region, many of which were also abandoned. (A few managed to change and even thrive.) It was not the "collapse" of a people, but the endgame of an old elite social system and of a political culture that drove it in previous centuries, during the Classic period (150–900 CE). Whatever problems and tensions led up to it had probably festered for decades, reaching a confluence of tipping points. What came after, alongside empty cities and displaced people, was a radical readjustment of an old social and political order. The long course of Maya civilization, as we will see, was full of similar convulsions and readjustments both large and small, from its earliest beginnings.

Once the city was abandoned, Baxwitz's royal history was largely forgotten, as were the chronicles of nearly all the ruling families of the Classic period. This is what I call the great "Rupture" of Maya historical knowledge—a profound break in the consciousness of the ancient past that occurred in various stages, brought on initially and most strongly when the institutions of Maya courtly life dissolved. The ninth-century landscape around Baxwitz was unstable, beset by violence, foreign meddling, and a constant movement of royal courts. New communities were eventually founded elsewhere, yet, as we will see, the refashioned societies that emerged circa 1100 or 1200 were very different from those of before, with new ruling lineages who felt little connection to the fragile legacies from the Classic era. Evidence suggests that after abandonment, the memories of Baxwitz and other royal courts were not maintained, much like the decaying cities themselves. The old glories of the kings and queens of the past apparently held little relevance for the newly founded Maya communities. I suspect that few if any of the old archives from Baxwitz even survived for long, if the later indigenous histories we know from Yucatán are anything to go on. This "Postclassic" era represented an important stage within the larger Maya story, but many of the Classic kingdoms were by this time ignored or forgotten, probably well before the arrival of the Spanish in the sixteenth century.

The most jarring crisis of all came with the Spanish invaders. Although the process of conquest took far longer and was more protracted in Yucatán and in Guatemala than in New Spain (central Mexico, essentially), much of the indigenous nobility was eventually erased or nearly so.[2] Hundreds of texts were lost, either through the active destruction by Spanish authorities or by the fragility of the materials on which they were written. Much of the loss came about through a long and concerted effort by Spanish authorities and landowners to exploit and "reduce" Maya communities and by the Catholic church to dismantle "idolatrous" beliefs. Maya communities struggled to exert both their independence and identities, always under immense pressure. It is a process that we can even trace up to the present day. Within decades, indigenous communities in Yucatán suffered large population declines, whether through disease or through mass flight to less populated regions to the south.[3]

Centuries of colonial rule took a heavy toll, wrenching Maya peoples away from what sense of history and rootedness they had left. A few documents were carefully copied from the old hieroglyphic books, but by the seventeenth century, few could read any ancient writings that might have been preserved in village archives, as the Spanish continued to establish their colonial hegemony. A sense of deeper history, so carefully maintained and recorded by the Maya over the earlier centuries, had disappeared. Seldom if ever in human experience has a civilization's past been so utterly wiped clean. The Rupture took hold.

"¿QUIÉN SABE?"

The first people to explore the ruins of the ancient cities were the Maya themselves, many no doubt the direct descendants of those who had built them centuries earlier. During the Postclassic era and into historical times, Maya would sometimes revisit the empty ancestral spaces, leaving offerings of incense. Later, in the colonial era, they wandered among the tree-covered pyramids and palaces, passing inscribed monuments covered in moss, often while hunting or tending to their nearby fields. The "old houses" were very old indeed, and some came to believe they were built by giants or gods of an earlier creation. The purely descriptive names they gave to some of these ancient places, with a few notable exceptions, point to this pervasive historical detachment: *Labna*, "Fallen Houses"; *Calakmul*, "Two Adjacent Mounds"; and *Tulum*, "The Wall." Near the town of Palenque, in the province of Chiapas, the local Maya paid regular visits to an especially impressive set of overgrown structures that included a palace, still well preserved next to a small cascading river (a wonderful watering spot then, just as it is today). They gave these the name *yototlum*, "houses of earth" (spelled in later sources as *Otolum*), yet were unaware that centuries before this was once the seat of a great kingdom ruled by the Bakel dynasty. Wandering their half-collapsed hallways and courtyards, the occasional hunter or other visitor would have easily sensed the continuing majesty of these remains, but maybe also with a hint of fear and unease. They were powerful and magical places, even in a state of long decay.

The foreign explorers who eventually visited the ruins—the priests, the soldiers, or an occasional antiquarian—were also left with a profound state of wonder. For all who gazed upon them, the tree-covered buildings seemed lost in time, with no one able to explain their presence or account for their existence. John Lloyd Stephens, the most famous nineteenth-century explorer of Maya ruins, was struck by this lack of historical knowledge even among the Indigenous people he encountered in his travels in 1839, concluding that it came from decades of Spanish oppression: "It is not strange that the present inhabitants, nine generations removed, without any written language, borne down by three centuries servitude, and toiling daily for a scanty subsistence, are alike ignorant and indifferent concerning the history of their ancestors, and the great cities lying in ruins under their eyes."[4] Here Stephens may well have overlooked a guarded sense of ancestral history among the Maya of his day, kept hidden from view, but his overall point rings true.[5] He and others could only tell that the ruins of the ancient city were very old, older than the arrival of the Spanish in the sixteenth century.

This was also an era of intense curiosity about ancient Egypt, which serves as a rough parallel to the questions Stephens and other early travelers asked in their travels through Mexico and Guatemala. Before the initial decipherment of Egyptian hieroglyphs by Jean François Champollion in 1820s, antiquarians had no detailed sense of Egyptian history and civilization, either. But there was one key difference. As mysterious as it was, ancient Egypt was still seen to be *Egyptian*, linked in some way to the detailed accounts of pharaohs of the Old Testament. By contrast, nearly all the ruined temples and palaces of Central America had long been stripped of any cultural or historical identity whatsoever. They were not even seen as "Maya" until only a little more than century ago, when some, including Stephens himself, made the bold suggestion that they had been built by the ancestors of the Indigenous communities who lived among them. In many ways, his experiences offer a good entry point in our own intellectual journey to find and reconstruct Maya history on a deeper timeline.

A prolific traveler and writer, Stephens had long been interested in ruins and ancient remains, and he had already published popular accounts of his travels in Egypt and Greece. The persistent stories of "lost cities" closer to home intrigued him. Vague reports referred to one place named Copan, located in the interior not far from where he landed. Another account of a "lost city" near a village named Palenque had been published in 1822, just a couple of decades before Stephens's journey (and the very same year of Champollion's decipherment).[6] Written decades earlier by Captain Antonio del Río, in 1787, it described stone palaces, large temples with rooms, and beautiful sculpted reliefs where "we seem to view the idolatry of the Phoenicians, the Greeks, and the Romans most strongly portrayed." News about Palenque's ruins had even gradually trickled into American newspapers in the years leading up to Stephens's trip, telling of "gigantic ruins of a race now vanished."[7] One 1833 report in *The Knickerbocker*, a prominent New York literary journal, was especially fanciful:

> It is now some four or five years, since a brief article went the rounds of the papers, stating that the ruins of an extensive city had been discovered in the interior of Mexico, which had been surrounded with a wall of vast circumference, and of regular hewn stone masonry. In the precincts of this American Babylon in ruins, were towers, temples, columns, arches, and massive fallen fragments of every form and size of dwellings, streets choked up with rubbish, and all the memorials of a city of great former populousness and splendor, of an architecture more resembling Greek and Roman remains, than those of the Incas, or Mexican princes.[8]

By this account, the ruins were far too impressive and elaborate to be the works of Indigenous people, hinting at a supposed European origin.

Stephens was levelheaded and skeptical of such outlandish claims and eager to see the ruins for himself. In 1839, he set sail to Central America from New York, in the company of his friend, the artist Frederick Catherwood. Stephens's recent appointment as a U.S. diplomat gave him a degree of cover and clout to travel freely in Guatemala, Chiapas, and Yucatán, areas still embroiled in varying states of civil war and rebellion—the lasting effects of Mexico's recent independence from Spain. Their travels in 1839 to 1840 took the two men across a rugged landscape of contrasts, from the dense jungles of Copan, through the high mountains of Guatemala, and eventually into the flat, scrub forest of northern Yucatán. This is what we loosely call the Maya area nowadays, and Stephens was struck by the similarities he saw at each ancient site they encountered. By the end of their long initial journey, he noted how the stone structures of Northern Yucatán resembled those far to the south and the also that the "hieroglyphics sculpted on stone ... beyond all question, bore the same type with those at Copan and Palenque."[9]

The first place on their itinerary was Copan, and Stephens wasn't prepared for the grandeur of its pyramids and sculptures. Stone monuments still stood in the dense forest, looking much as they did when first carved. The surrounding pyramids and courtyards were almost all collapsed and overgrown. Nothing had prepared him for a lost city built by a people completely unknown to history. "The tone which pervades the ruins is that of deep solemnity," Stephens wrote.[10] The age of the ruins and the identity of their builders were complete mysteries: "America, say historians, was peopled by savages; but savages never reared these structures, savages never carved these stones. We asked the Indians who made them, and the dull answer was 'quién sabe?,' "who knows?"[11] He and Catherwood were intrigued by the many hieroglyphs they saw carved on the stelae, and they surmised that these held Copan's story, long lost: "One thing I believe, that its history is graven upon its monuments. No Champollion has yet brought to them the energy of his enquiring mind. Who shall read them?"[12]

After surveying Copan, they forged onward through the Maya world, passing through the mountains of Guatemala and eventually reaching Chiapas, in today's southern Mexico. There they made the arduous descent of the Sierra Madre, determined to reach the ruins at Palenque. Upon seeing its magnificent buildings, many still standing (Figure 1.2), Stephens couldn't refrain from reflecting on the utter mystery that surrounded the surreal, tree-covered ruins: "In the romance of the world's history nothing ever impressed me more forcibly than the

FIGURE 1.2. Engraving from 1840 by Frederick Catherwood of "Casa no. 1" at Palenque, today known as the Temple of the Inscriptions.

spectacle of this once great and lovely city, overturned, desolate, and lost; discovered by accident, overgrown with trees for miles around, and without even a name to distinguish it."[13] Like Copan, Palenque was also a complete blank slate. The ignorance regarding the ruins' builders mirrored a pervasive attitude in North America during Stephens's era, when the deeper Indigenous past of North America was still invisible or else simply ignored. It is no coincidence that the 1830s and '40s, when his books were published, were among the most active years in the forced exterminations of Native Americans in the young United States. The Indian Removal Act of 1830 and the formation of Manifest Destiny, a term coined in 1845, expressed an erasure of "Indian" identity and culture, asserting their status as utterly detached from history or place. The newer nation-states of Mexico and Guatemala attempted to assert liberal-minded policies of indigenous assimilation, but demographics stymied any actual plans of action. Outside centralized capitals—Mexico City, Mérida, or Guatemala City—rural areas were isolated and mostly populated by Indigenous communities. When not advocating for their exploitation as indentured labor, systems of governance mostly ignored *los indios* in the hinterlands, including many peoples throughout the region. They were simply seen by outsiders as a people without history.

THE MAYA WORLD

Stephens never used the word "Maya" to describe the culture that built the mysterious ruins. In his day, the term was used only to refer to the native language spoken in Yucatán, and its meaning changed and expanded over the ensuing decades. Accounts from the sixteenth century strongly suggest that "Maya" was originally a geographical term, roughly corresponding to the northern part of Yucatán. As one key source of the time put it, "Maya" was "the proper name of this land (Yucatán)." I suspect there may even be a few ancient hieroglyphs from the Classic period spelling this same place name, written as a combination of the words *may*, "young deer," and *ha'*, "water" (Figure 1.3).[14] The people of the region were *ah maya*, "one who is from Maya." In the centuries before the Spanish invasion, the large, fortified capital of this northern region was Mayapan, the "Wall (Fortress) of Maya." During the turmoil of the colonial era, Spanish speakers began to use "Maya" in a broader sense, as a collective term for native inhabitants and for the language they spoke, known today as Yucatec (originally *maya t'an*, "the language of Maya"). In all these cases, Maya still referred to the place, people, and language of the northern regions, never to regions to the south or to the speakers of closely related languages. All of this changed in the nineteenth century. As scholars began to study the "Maya language" of Yucatán, they saw that it was clearly related to those spoken in highland Guatemala and Chiapas. Classed together, they all came to be known collectively as the "Maya-Quiche stock" and eventually as "Mayan languages." Archaeology began to come

FIGURE 1.3. Possible hieroglyph of the regional place name *Maya'* (**MAY-HA'**). Drawing by the author.

of age in the late nineteenth century, too, and the related peoples of the ancient landscape quickly fell under the same "Maya" label, even at distant sites such as Palenque and Copan, whose local Indigenous inhabitants had never even heard the term. Noting in 1895 that the ancient inscriptions from Copan, Palenque, and Chichen Itza were the same, J. T. Goodman was among the first to apply the word "Maya" in a collective sense to all the ancient monuments, employing, as he put it, "a broad racial appellation."[15]

Out of necessity, archaeologists soon adopted the broader cultural label, and by the early twentieth century, "Maya" was used to refer to the ancient civilization in a larger sense. This also solidified the once radical idea that the ancient ruins were built by the ancestors of the region's Indigenous inhabitants. Still, the name reflects the inescapable bias toward the region and people of Yucatán, the place once called Maya in the early days of research. It was there, as Stephens saw, that the ties between history and ancient remains were most evident, where the language was most strongly documented. As a result, all related languages have long been grouped together as the "Mayan" family. In only recent years, many speakers of Mayan languages both in and outside Yucatán have adopted this collective sense of identity, identifying themselves too as "Maya."

The Maya region is a large and varied landscape surrounded by seas and mountains. It encompasses the Yucatán Peninsula and areas south, crossing the borders of what is today eastern Mexico, Guatemala, Belize, and parts of Honduras and El Salvador. It forms the easternmost part of a broad cultural area known as Mesoamerica, home to several different but related peoples and civilizations, the names of which may be familiar—Olmec, Zapotec, Mixtec, Huastec, Aztec, and so on. The Maya closely interacted with many of these diverse groups over the course of time, and together they forged several common Mesoamerican traditions, ideas, and lifeways. Some of these distinctive aspects of culture resonate to the present day, given the central role Indigenous life still plays throughout the region. The traditional foodways of Mesoamerica, for example, form the basis of Mexican cuisine and the language we use to refer to it. ("Cacao," "avocado," "tomato," "chili," and "tamale" are all Indigenous Mesoamerican words.) The great variety of ethnicities and languages all relied on maize-based agriculture, which helped give rise to very old, shared ideas about cosmology, religion, and the understandings about the ways of the world. The earliest Mesoamerican art style, often called "Olmec," developed quickly after 1200 BCE and spread throughout the region from what is now west Mexico to Honduras, reflecting a new and influential religious ideology. The maize god, revealingly, was a central theme in its early iconography. Out of this early understanding of the cosmos also emerged a calendar system, a divination cycle of 260 days, shared by all later Mesoamerican peoples, including the Maya and the Aztecs. Remarkably, in some remote communities of Mexico and Guatemala, this same calendar survived the onslaught of the Spanish invasion and is still being used.

The Maya of northern Yucatán were probably the first Mesoamericans who Europeans ever saw. They were astounded at the richness of the area on their first encounter with it in 1517 (and probably during slightly earlier voyages from Cuba and the Caribbean, now lost to history). In his gripping first-person memoir, the soldier Bernal Díaz de Castillo, who participated in several of these early expeditions along the coast, expressed the surprise he and his companions felt at seeing large towns with masonry buildings and painted temples. The Maya were also highly organized in their fierce resistance to the strange newcomers. Near the town of Champoton, on the west coast of the peninsula, Díaz de Castillo recounted a battle where the Maya forces "killed over fifty six of our soldiers and wounded all of the rest."[16] It was in another coastal settlement where the same expedition, under the leadership of Juan de Grijalva, received news of very rich kingdoms far to the west called *Colhua* and *México*, places that would later be revealed to be the centers of Aztec civilization. Back in Cuba, Hernán Cortés heard of tales from the survivors of Grijalva's wounded expedition and quickly started to make plans of his own. Cortés later encountered belligerent Maya armies in 1519 during his brazen journey westward. He quickly opted to bypass many of them as he made his way along the coast and into the interior of Mexico. These resistance efforts were a taste of things to come, and Yucatán remained an unconquered land for many more decades.

The people who Cortés and Díaz de Castillo encountered on the northern coast were speakers of the language we call Yucatec. The

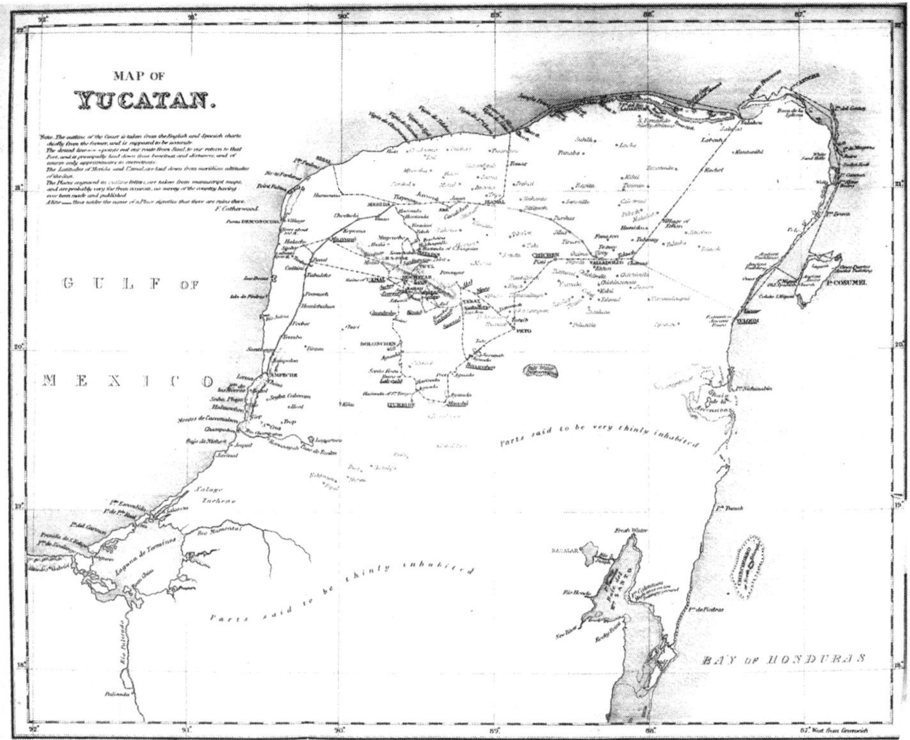

FIGURE 1.4. Map of Yucatán by John Lloyd Stephens, 1843, with "parts said to be thinly inhabited."

southern lowlands, where most of our ancient history plays out, was home to other Mayan languages, including another large linguistic subgroup called Ch'olan, with several varieties. If we imagine a bifurcation of the entire peninsula into northern and southern zones, very roughly where the northernmost border of Guatemala now runs east-west, Yucatecan speakers generally occupied areas to its north, and Ch'olan speakers to its south (see Figure 1.4). As recent research has shown, the sounds and grammatical structure encoded in the ancient hieroglyphic inscriptions are clearly Ch'olan and closely related to a now-extinct language called Ch'olti', which was once spoken along most of the southern edge of the lowlands. Its closest living relative, the Ch'orti' language, is spoken today in the eastern highlands of Guatemala by roughly 20,000 people and highly endangered. The ancient language we read in the glyphs we call "Classic Mayan," with its own grammatical rules and phonological features.[17] I find it remarkable and heartening that many of the words we read in the ancient inscriptions can still be heard today, spoken in the towns, villages, and cities throughout Mexico, Belize, and Guatemala.[18]

THE FIRST BRIDGE

By 1841, after visiting Copan, Palenque, and scores of other ancient sites, Stephens was convinced that the ruins must be the handiwork of the ancestors of the region's present-day inhabitants, the Maya. This was not the prevailing idea among U.S. and European antiquarians at the time, as we have seen. Stephens had good intuition about archaeology, however, and to bolster his suspicions, he also sought out as much historical context as he could, especially in northwest Yucatán, where Maya populations were large and old documents were still found here and there, giving hints of a deeper Indigenous past. He heard of one erudite historian living in the capital, Mérida, named Juan Pío Pérez, "the best Maya scholar in Yucatán, and . . . distinguished in the same degree for the investigation and study of all matters tending to elucidate the history of the ancient Indians."[19] Stephens tracked Pío Pérez down and quickly befriended him. Together they pored over many old colonial documents written in the Mayan language, which Pío Pérez had carefully collected and transcribed. For Stephens, the old writings were a revelation.

Juan Pío Pérez stands out for me as the singular hero of nineteenth-century Maya research. He was responsible for strengthening what tenuous threads existed between ancient and post-invasion Maya history. Born in 1798 in Mérida, he grew up speaking the Yucatec Mayan language, heard everywhere in those days on the quiet streets and in refined households of the city. As a young man, he acquired a passion for politics, in an era of fervent revolution and nationalism. Soon he was active in promoting the independence of Yucatán from Mexico, and he strove to create a separate political and cultural identity for the region, rooted in part in local Maya culture and history and in the study of the ancient sites. Pío Pérez pursued his main interest in history and language by seeking out the old manuscripts and documents kept in the archives of various small towns, many already centuries old and in deteriorating condition. Many of these were written in Yucatec, and they included medicinal guides, books of history and prophecy, and chronicles that revealed ancient modes of time and timekeeping. Some even had faint traces of old hieroglyphic writing, copied and recopied over generations. Pío Pérez carefully copied what he could of these precious records, and by the end of the 1830s, he had made concordances among many of them, realizing that many of the native histories derived from a common source, an older record of Yucatec Maya history long lost (Figure 1.5). These diverse manuscripts, some copied from an earlier prototype, would collectively come to be known as *The Books of Chilam Balam,* named for an obscure native prophet (a *chilam*) and historian who may have lived in the sixteenth century. In these eclectic documents, Indigenous scribes, well trained in alphabetic writing, had also recorded much of what they could about the old ways and about esoteric knowledge while also adapting to a new and fraught world of Spanish domination. The books thus reveal a world of changing Maya identity, of communities that by the eighteenth century were living and negotiating between two worlds.[20]

In the same years after the conquest, many Spanish friars had begun to write down other accounts of native history, as well as documents on the language and "idolatry" of the people. Some newly arrived priests were fascinated by the esoterica of Maya culture and religion of that time and preserved many aspects of language in dictionaries and other writings. Pío Pérez eagerly collected some of these sources, and these are the documents Stephens saw on his visit to Mérida, leaving him excited and intrigued. They revealed not only an Indigenous Maya history but also the sense of a deeper past that seemed to vaguely connect to the ruins he visited and carefully documented, including the great city of Uxmal.

Progress in these fledgling years of research was far slower than it could have been due to a series of unfortunate setbacks. Stephens died of malaria in Panama in 1852 at only forty-eight years old. Two years later, Catherwood perished at sea in the horrific *S.S. Arctic* disaster at age fifty-five.[21] And in 1859, Pío Pérez died, never having published the

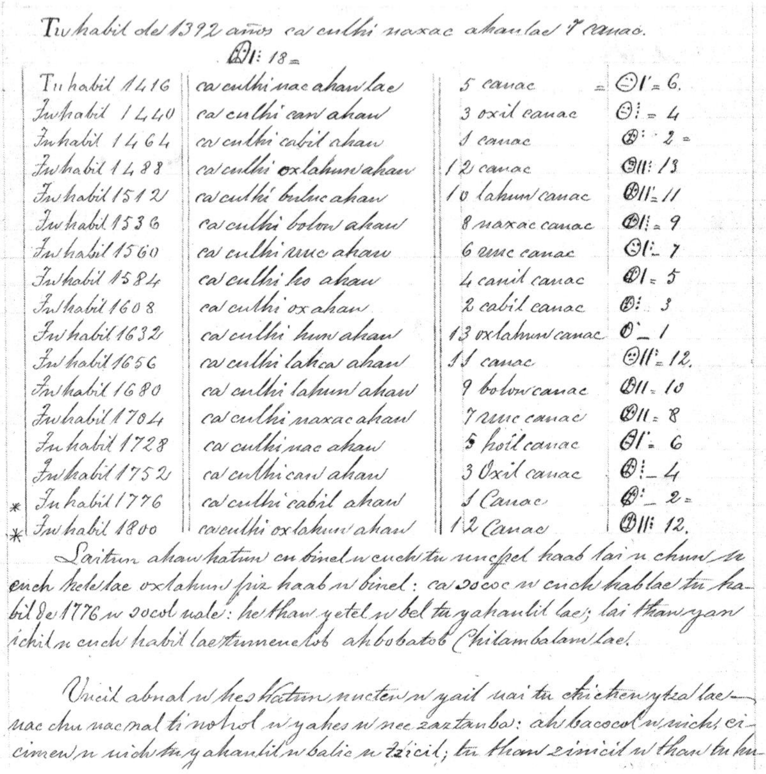
Tu habil de 1392 años ca culhi uaxac ahau lae 7 canac.
18 =

Tu habil 1416	ca culhi uac ahau lae	5 canac	= 6.
Tu habil 1440	ca culhi can ahau	3 oxil canac	= 4
Tu habil 1464	ca culhi cabil ahau	1 canac	2 =
Tu habil 1488	ca culhi oxlahun ahau	12 canac	13
Tu habil 1512	ca culhi buluc ahau	10 lahun canac	= 11
Tu habil 1536	ca culhi bolon ahau	8 uaxac canac	= 9
Tu habil 1560	ca culhi uuc ahau	6 uuc canac	7
Tu habil 1584	ca culhi ho ahau	4 canil canac	= 5
Tu habil 1608	ca culhi ox ahau	2 cabil canac	3
Tu habil 1632	ca culhi hun ahau	13 oxlahun canac	1
Tu habil 1656	ca culhi lahca ahau	11 canac	= 12.
Tu habil 1680	ca culhi lahun ahau	9 bolon canac	= 10
Tu habil 1704	ca culhi uaxac ahau	7 uuc canac	= 8
Tu habil 1728	ca culhi uac ahau	5 hoil canac	= 6
Tu habil 1752	ca culhi can ahau	3 Oxil canac	4
* Tu habil 1776	ca culhi cabil ahau	1 Canac	2 =
* Tu habil 1800	ca culhi oxlahun ahau	12 Canac	12.

Laitun ahau katun cu binel u cuch tu uucpel haab lai u chun u cuch katunlae oxlahun piz haab u binel: ca dzococ u cuch hablae tu habil de 1776 u docol uale: he than yetel u bel tu yahaulil lae; lai than yan ichil u cuch habil lae tumenelob ahbobatob Chilambalam lae.

Uucil abnal u hes katun, nucten u yail uai tu chichen ytzal lae uac chu uac nal ti nohol u yahes u nee zaztanba: ah bacocol u uich, cicimen u uich tu yahaulil u balic u tzicil; tu than zinicil u than tu ku-

FIGURE 1.5. The last Maya hieroglyphs. Page 79v from the *Codex Pérez*, an 1877 copy of a Maya history of Yucatán. The hieroglyphs at right designate a sequence of twenty-year k'atun periods (6 Ahau, 4 Ahau, etc.). Courtesy of Princeton University Library.

bulk of his own scholarship. So passed a traumatic seven years for the nascent field of Maya studies. Still, the connected legacies of these three friends—a New York lawyer, an English artist, and a Yucatecan historian and intellectual—established a range of new disciplines in the Maya world: archaeology, exploration, linguistics, and historiography. They made it clear for all that the Maya had indeed built the ruins at some point in the remote past. And it is impossible to overstate Pío Pérez's contribution in presenting a rudimentary working knowledge of the ancient calendar, at least as it existed in Yucatán after the invasion. In short, the three laid the firm foundations for all serious study of the ancient Maya and their history. Their collective efforts linked an ancient civilization to a modern people and therefore represent a first stage in bridging the massive gap of knowledge between the present and the past. In a real sense, Maya archaeology was born out of their meeting in Mérida in 1841.

Pío Pérez and Stephens did not live long enough to see the revelation of the most important early source of all, a sixteenth-century compendium of history and cultural facts known as the *Relación de las Cosas de Yucatán*, ascribed to an early Franciscan bishop of Yucatán, Diego de Landa. First composed around 1566, it survived only as an incomplete and somewhat mangled copy that was found in Madrid in 1862 and published soon thereafter.[22] Landa's *Relación* is full of information about the Maya culture of Yucatán at the time of the invasion, including a lengthy summary of its Indigenous history, with mentions of rulers and lineages who were said to have dwelled in the old cities of Uxmal and Chichen Itza. Unlike later generations, Landa and many of his contemporaries on the ground in Yucatán could easily acknowledge the historical and cultural connection between the native people and the ancient sites. If only later chroniclers and historians had known of Landa's book and of his direct assertions that the buildings of Uxmal and elsewhere "were built by a race of Indians," then the ignorance that worked to cement the Rupture in historical awareness would surely have been less pronounced. Still, it is significant that even for Landa, the origins of the much older, massive ruins at Izamal and still visible in Mérida remained truly mysterious, "so old," as Landa states, "that there is no memory of their founders." Today we know that Izamal's pyramids date to the Late Preclassic and Early Classic periods, constructed nearly fifteen centuries before Landa wrote these words. Even at the time of the conquest, breaks with the deeper layers of the Maya past were evident.[23]

A gap existed in geography as well. At the time of Stephens's journeys, large areas to the south of Yucatán and Campeche remained in dense forest and were "said to be thinly inhabited," as he noted in his own map of 1843 (see Figure 1.4). Only the regions around Mérida and Campeche are shown as densely populated. Earlier maps similarly depict the interior of the Yucatán Peninsula as empty terrain, *despoblado* ("depopulated"), or else represent the lower peninsula as strangely compressed and reduced in area. The skewed emptiness of interior Yucatán and northern Guatemala reflects the ignorance among the cartographers of those times, but I suspect it also points to an important underlying truth: that, over the centuries, the region had experienced a vast demographic displacement. This was probably the result of a protracted series of changes, beginning with the political collapses of the ninth century, followed by social and political reshufflings of the Postclassic period and then in turn by two and a half centuries of Spanish rule. By 1600 or 1700, the only inhabitants of the forested interior lived in small villages or in scattered fortified hamlets, clustered near the few rivers and lakes. These Maya were intentionally far from colonial or Mexican control, and they were ready to pick up and move farther into the *selva* at a moment's notice.[24]

Less than a thousand years earlier, this sparsely inhabited region had been the population center of the Maya world, replete with cities, towns, hamlets, agricultural fields, and roadways. The very middle of the Yucatán peninsula, what we call the Peten region, was once home to scores of ancient kingdoms and regal courts, including many that feature prominently throughout our newly reconstructed narratives of dynastic history. Stephens, Catherwood, and other explorers of the mid-1800s had naturally focused their attention on the more populated zones of the Maya area, in what is now Honduras, Chiapas, and northern Yucatán, completely unaware of many ancient cities that remained still out of reach within the expansive forest, where water was often scarce. They had heard rumors of other lost cities, but their limited time and exhaustion after two long years of arduous travel made further exploration impractical (not to mention the already overwhelming amount new information they had in hand). It is remarkable to think that these men who laid the foundations for Maya archaeology never even knew the existence of many places that proved to be key players in the narrative arc of Maya history—sites such as Tikal, Calakmul, Dzibanche, Naranjo, Caracol, and El Mirador. These would be found and explored years later in the nearly unpopulated areas of the Peten. If nothing else, this stark contrast in the history of population settlement within the Maya area points to the long-term movement of people in the deeper past.

It would be natural to ascribe this depopulation of the ancient Maya heartland to the brutalities that defined the colonial era. After all, diseases such as smallpox wiped out whole communities in the centuries immediately following the conquest of central Mexico, Yucatán, and Guatemala. But the profound effect of epidemic disease was never the whole story. In fact, big changes had already occurred in the Maya landscape long before Spanish ships ever appeared on the eastern horizon. Archaeological surveys demonstrate that the Peten region and the adjacent central areas of the peninsula experienced drastic demographic losses at the end of the Classic period, some six centuries earlier. As disruptive as the colonial experience was, Maya demography was never very stable to begin with, and people had been on the move a very long time, leaving large areas of the region far emptier than they once were. The historian Nancy Farriss, writing about the high degree of mobility of people in the colonial era, noted how "the lowland Maya seem to have been uncommonly restless for a people described as sedentary." As we will see, I suspect that this is not just a pattern of the later colonial era but a broader trend in Maya demography. It might even be seen as a strategy of adaptation that goes back thousands of years. In this scenario, settlements and even cities were not very permanent solutions to human life, resource exploitation, or political power.[25] The movements around 800 or 900 CE were instrumental in forming the Rupture of history I describe. In moving away, many Maya after the Classic period also lost core aspects of elite historical memory, putting some distance between themselves and an ancient history that, after a few generations, apparently held little relevance.

In this way, we see how "the Rupture" in history was made up of numerous smaller rifts and losses of knowledge, spread out over many centuries. The collapse and abandonment of many Late Preclassic cities around 100 CE were surely a significant disruption. So also was the break at the end of the Classic period a thousand years later, setting in motion a more systemic "collapse" of history. The Postclassic world that emerged after 900 CE had its own complex dynamics, emphasizing a new wave of foreign elites and their different symbols of royal power. Even though more recent, the history of people and events from 900 to 1500 is far less visible to us than what came before, known only from fragmented histories written after the conquest.

Did people of that time retain memories of the previous Classic world or keep written records of that ancient history? It is difficult to know, especially since the hieroglyphic books that contained history were tossed or else actively sought out and destroyed (see Plate 2). Historical books were seen in the years following the invasion, as Spanish chroniclers make clear. Pedro Sánchez de Aguilar stated that "in these (books) they painted in colors the count of their years, the wars, the epidemics, hurricanes, inundations, famines and other events." A few Spanish friars in Yucatán even learned the ancient hieroglyphs. One *oidor* (judge) in Yucatán named Tomás López Medel noted: "A kind of letters of characters which the inhabitants of this province (of Yucatán) use were taught to me. They draw in arabesques and by means of them they set down their affairs and their histories."[26] Bishop Landa wrote his now-famous description of old books he found in 1562, during his inquisition at the newly founded Franciscan mission at the town of Mani, the seat of the Maya rulers who had allied themselves with the new foreigners in the recent conquest of Yucatán: "These people also make use of certain characters or letters, with which they wrote in their books their ancient matters and their sciences, and by these and by drawings and by certain signs in these drawings they understood their affairs and made others understand and taught them. We found a large number of these books in these characters and, as they contained nothing in which there was not to be seen superstition and lies of the devil, we burned them all, which they regretted to an amazing degree and which caused them great affliction."[27] Landa's characterization of old books used in science and in teaching is enticing, giving a valuable hint of what once existed. His account is also horrific in its dismissive, matter-of-fact statement of their quick destruction. Were these books of truly ancient history? All we can say for certain is that the narratives of the Maya past that survived the early colonial era go back only so far. To my eye, they say nothing of the glories of the Classic period.

Much later in the colonial era, this break in historical knowledge led to more cultural isolation and exploitation for the Maya. The disconnection from ancient, historical narratives served the interests of Enlightenment politicians and intellectuals who strove to erase or assimilate Indigenous language and culture in all its aspects, even centuries after the invasion. It is not difficult to connect several modern misconceptions to these old tropes, including the widespread popular idea that ancient ruins must have been built with the aid of outsiders and not by ambitious and creative people. Even prominent scholars in the early days of Maya research, such as Sir J. Eric S. Thompson, referred to the ancient Maya as "a strange people which unaccountably had disappeared from the stage of history."[28] It is little wonder then that the Maya came to be constantly exoticized and made remote, a quintessentially "mysterious" and unknowable people of the ancient world. This idea has been reinforced time and time again in books, films, and other popular media, up to the present day.

ARCHAEOLOGY BEGINS

Maya archaeology emerged in the later decades of the nineteenth century, picking up where Pío Pérez and Stephens left off. Those early years were concerned mostly with a basic, straightforward question: Just how old were the ruins at Copan, Palenque, and Chichen Itza, if they were indeed Maya in origin? One early explorer who helped answer this was Alfred Maudslay, an Englishman who was intent on documenting the pyramids and sculptures seen by Stephens and Catherwood. Maudslay came to his task in the 1880s with an exciting new technology—the glass plate camera—as well as a knowledge of how to make molds of ancient sculptures. These he used to make plaster casts back in England (an early kind of "3D printing"). During several expeditions, he undertook careful, scientific surveys and records of everything he saw (Figure 1.6). Still, he wondered why many of the ancient cities were utterly absent from the early written histories that the Spanish had made of the same region. The implication is that they must have already been long abandoned, unknown to the various Spanish missionaries and soldiers (including Cortés himself) who traveled nearby. As Maudslay logically concluded,

FIGURE 1.6. A view of Tikal's Central Plaza in 1882, by Alfred P. Maudslay. © The Trustees of the British Museum.

"Although it is not yet possible to trace the various stages which must have marked the evolution of the art which culminated in Copan and Palenque, it is not difficult to show that a great gap exists between the remains of those centres of ancient culture and the ruins of towns known to have been inhabited at the time of the Spanish invasion." Maudslay made the simple but important observation that Palenque, Copan, and other great ruins were already old, lost to history even by the sixteenth century. While recognizing the sites as belonging to a broader Maya tradition, Maudslay had started to get a sense of the Rupture I have described—the marked distance and loss between the Classic period and the Spanish arrival.[29]

It was in the decades before the decipherment that various writers filled the historical void by crafting at times bizarre, even cringe-worthy narratives about Maya civilization. One idea that took hold in those years was that the ancient monuments were only records of arcane calendrics and astronomy and bore no written history at all. Even Maudslay, writing in 1899, remarked on the quantity of calendrical records in the texts of Palenque and Copan, suggesting that "it was more than doubtful if the inscriptions when fully deciphered will yield us much direct information of a historical nature." This opinion, so wrongheaded in retrospect, was influential and held firm within Maya studies for decades. In 1940, the most prominent Maya archaeologist of the day, Sylvanus Morley, asserted that "the ancient Maya indubitably recorded their history but not in the stone inscriptions."[30] To him the ancient texts "deal exclusively with the counting of time in one way or another."[31] At the end of his remarkable career as a field archaeologist and promoter of Maya studies, Morley penned a book called *The Ancient Maya*, one of the very first general works on the civilization and one that vividly bridged the ancient sites and the modern people—in my view, the work's most important legacy. Of course, Morley has absolutely no inkling of the historical narratives we will be looking at throughout this book.

Nor did the great Mayanist scholar J. Eric S. Thompson, who trained as an archaeologist and developed an intense interest in hieroglyphs. In 1954, he produced his landmark work, *The Rise and Fall of Maya Civilization*, one of the first wide-ranging narratives on the subject.[32] In the years leading up to Thompson's book, discoveries of "lost" Maya cities in the dense jungles of the region had captured the popular imagination, and *Rise and Fall* provided one of the few accessible treatments of an exciting and quickly changing subject. In fact, his *Rise and Fall* appeared at a truly pivotal time in Maya studies, at a transition from one conceptual paradigm to another. Before the early 1950s, the ancient Maya were very much romanticized as a culture, idealized by Thompson and other writers as quintessential noble savages living in remote cities in the jungle. Their impersonal rulers and priests were thought to have been more interested in esoteric knowledge than the concerns of the real world. The common people were largely ignored due to their relative inconspicuousness among the towering temple-pyramids and palaces of ruins such as Tikal and Copan. They were a culture that eked out a fragile existence in the unforgiving rainforest, building cities and refined monuments, but who would disappear into oblivion.

Thompson seemed even more adamant is his view of the Maya as a peaceful people, bent toward intellectual pursuits and unconcerned with their own history. Much like his friend Morley, he flatly denied any presence of written history: "These texts, to the best of our knowledge, contain no glorification of ruler or recital of conquest, such as are customary on the monuments of other peoples. Instead, they are an impersonal record of steps in the search for the truth, as the Maya saw it, that is the whole philosophy of time with its interlocking cycles of divine influences."[33] Thompson and some of his contemporaries were wrong in such characterizations, yet they still exerted a profound influence and helped give rise to a popular myth that Maya elites (and, by extension, the culture overall) were somehow different or exotic. The ancient Maya soon became characterized as odd stargazers, obsessed with the mechanics of time's passage, with little interest or engagement in worldly affairs. Based on these preconceptions, the supposed disappearance of the ancient Maya seemed fitting, in a way, seen as a sign of some inability to adapt in the face of external pressures or as an indication of their essential otherness. At least by the early twentieth century, the ancient inhabitants of Copan and Palenque were finally recognized by all as ancestors of the living Maya. Still, despite Morley's and Thompson's brilliant contributions and scholarly erudition, they dismissed the very existence of an ancient history for the Maya, and in this regard their outlook was not too far removed from the "blank slate" that confronted the first explorers of the Maya world a century earlier. The Rupture remained. Still, there were indications of great changes on the horizon. In one ironic twist, Thompson published his *Rise and Fall* in 1954, just when a revolution was brewing in our awareness of the ancient Maya, brought on eventually by the decipherment of the hieroglyphs.[34] The Rupture was being mended at long last.

CHAPTER 2

Reading

OUR ABILITY TO read any ancient script is a remarkable, almost magical gift, conjuring up the voices and thoughts of those who wrote in the remote past. Perhaps this is an obvious thing to reflect on, yet we should still pause to consider the miracle by which words can be communicated across cultures and over the great span of time. Reading an ancient script allows us to know the names of long-lost people and places and to learn of events we could have no knowledge of otherwise. Receiving ancient words for the first time is a thrill unlike any other, and as the writer Andrew Robinson has mentioned, "a successful decipherment of a major script carries a whiff of glamour or immortality about it, seldom found in the world of academic scholarship."[1] Of course, the most famous such breakthrough was the decipherment of Egyptian hieroglyphs in the early nineteenth century. Another great decipherment took place in the mid-twentieth century when Alice Kober made the first initial steps in deciphering Linear B script of Archaic Greece. Her foundational insights allowed for Michael Ventris's final breakthrough in early 1953.[2] From these brilliant scholars we might think that the decipherment of an obscure script happens in a singular "eureka" moment, followed by a rapid flood of translation. This is not always the case, however. In fact, the decipherment of Maya hieroglyphs was a drawn-out process, involving steady, incremental advances over the course of a century and involving many contributors: philologists, archaeologists, linguists, and art historians. Several breakthroughs were more important than others, but there was never one moment that marked a turning point from illegibility and legibility.

The real decipherment of an ancient writing system takes time. With Maya writing, early progress came in fits and starts from the late nineteenth century up to the present. The most dramatic advances came only recently during the 1980s and '90s, in what might be considered the "golden age" of Maya decipherment. It was in those years that we went from reading about 20 to 30 percent of Maya texts in their original language (a generous estimate) to reading about 80 percent by 2000 and today. It is fair to say that Maya script is now deciphered. But the ability to read most of the texts is just the beginning of a much longer and richer cultural journey. Analyzing, absorbing, and processing the myriad historical and cultural details within ancient Maya texts is as daunting as the decipherment, if not more so. This will take a great deal of work in future decades.

It is no small irony that the initial spark that led to the twentieth-century decipherment came from Bishop Landa, the Spanish friar who was responsible for the burning of numerous hieroglyphic books. In 1860, a copy of his *Relación de las Cosas de Yucatán* appeared in the library of the Royal Academy of History in Madrid, discovered by the French priest and scholar of ancient Mexican history Charles Étienne Brasseur de Bourbourg (Figure 2.1). Brasseur quickly saw that the manuscript was a gold mine of information on Yucatán's history, language, and culture from the time of the Spanish invasion. Landa's text contained long descriptions of the native Maya calendar and of festivals, gods, and rituals. It also contained a single page with crude drawings of hieroglyphs, each glossed by a letter ("a," for example) or a combination of two letters ("cu"). This is what Landa described as "their a, b, c," never once thinking that the Maya writing system could be anything but an alphabet (it is not). Landa noted that the "ponderousness" of the signs made them difficult to use, and "already they do not use at all these characters

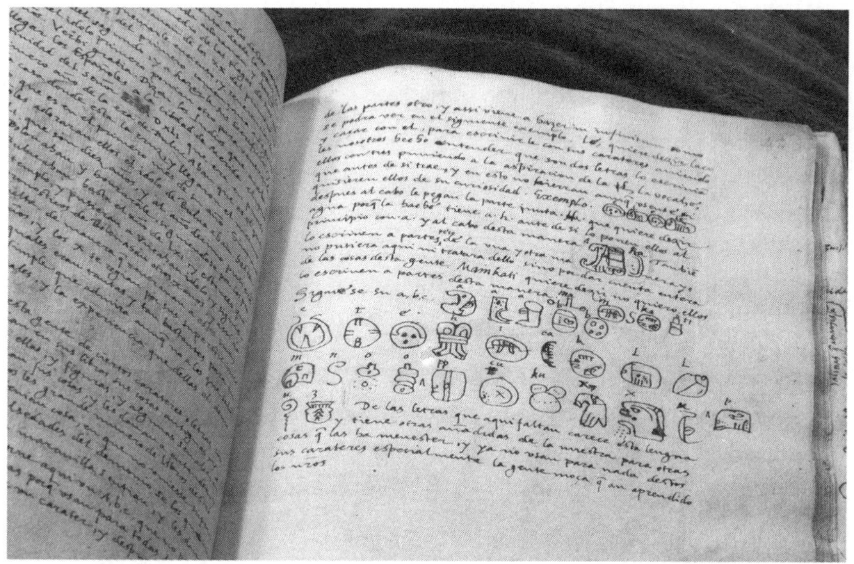

no pusiera aqui mi tratara dello sino por dar cuenta entera
de las cosas desta gente. Mamkati quiere dezir no quiero, ellos
lo escriuen a partes desta manera.

Siguese su a,b,c.

De las letras que aqui faltan carece esta lengua
y tiene otras añadidas de la nuestra para otras
cosas q las ha menester, y ya no usan para nada destos
sus carateres especialmente la gente moça q an aprendido

FIGURE 2.1. Page from the Landa *Relación* manuscript, showing Mayan "letters" and the "abc." Photograph by Harri Ketunnen.

of theirs, especially the young people who have learned ours." Clearly Landa did not understand the system, and it appears that his Maya informant, probably a Maya nobleman named Gaspar Antonio Chi, became utterly confused and frustrated by what Landa was asking. When Landa prompted him to write the word for "water," *ha'*, Chi wrote three signs, which we now know to read as **a-che-a**, the *sounds* of the pronunciation of "h-a" in Spanish. In answer to another apparent prompt from Landa, an exasperated Chi wrote a sentence, **ma-i-ni-k'a-ti**, for *ma' ink'ati*, "I don't want to." The drawings of those glyphs shines out from the page as a wonderful testament to Maya colonial resistance.

Soon after its discovery and publication, the Landa manuscript was celebrated as the potential codebook for cracking the glyphs. Not realizing that the "letters" were something else entirely, scholars only met dead ends, however, and some even posited that Landa's array of signs was an outright fabrication. Even so, one influential anthropologist, the American philologist Daniel Brinton, anticipated later breakthroughs when he reasoned that the "abc" might hide the true nature of the script. As he wrote in 1879:

> My later reading has led me to doubt whether Landa's alphabet is really an alphabet in the proper sense of the term, that is, representing elementary sounds of the language by written characters. It appears more likely that the figures he gives represent compound sounds, syllabic or partly so, and that they are but fragments of a large repertory of phonetic signs, never reduced to the elements of sound, used by the Mayas of that age. He evidently very positively considered them phonetic and not ideographic, and he could not have been mistaken on such a point, I should suppose. In his endeavor to arrange them according to the analogy of the Latin alphabet, he obscured their real purport, and I think we should reject the whole of his theory of their use in this manner.[3]

Here Brinton rightly surmised that some Maya glyphs might be "syllabic." He is imprecise about what he exactly means by this, but his simple statement turned out to be very prescient and absolutely correct. Oddly, no one at the time took Brinton up on this proposal or attempted to tease out any possibilities of syllabic writing and how it might be structured. Without the follow-up, one of the earliest and most perceptive insights about the nature of the glyphs turned out to be a quick dead end, completely forgotten.

Another turning point toward decipherment came just one year after the publication of Landa's *Relación* when, in 1865, the German scholar Ernst Förstemann accepted a new appointment as the head librarian at the Royal Public Library in Dresden. This was a fortuitous career move, for soon Förstemann grew fascinated with the strange manuscript now under his care, with its paintings of strange figures, numbers, and hieroglyphs. This we know today as the *Dresden Codex*, the finest of all the ancient Maya books (see Plate 2). Using Landa's clues and his own great intuition, Förstemann studied the manuscript in depth, and from its pages he was able to reconstruct the basic mechanics of the Maya calendar, including the days, the months, and especially the so-called "Long Count" system. The latter, he recognized, was a sequence of five numbers, each standing for multiples of units of time, either a "year" of 360 days (*hab*) or a day (*k'in*) (see Appendix B). Some decades later, using Maudslay's photographs, he was able to recognize the same date in glyphs in the much more ancient monuments at Palenque, Copan, and elsewhere.

LANDA'S "LETTERS"

The cracking of the calendar proved to be a windfall for Maya studies. Now there was a working *chronology*, a means of seeing which dates at certain sites were earlier or later than others. As we will see, these inscribed dates would later provide the framework for placing historical events in their proper time frame, but that would only be realized after many decades. For the time being, scholars could delve into Maya inscriptions and "read" their Long Count dates, listing them in tables and tallies. Why was there no progress on other fronts in reading the glyphs? Everything seemed to be about the calendar, or at least that was all that anyone could read, and chronology drove the field. Here we ought to remember that Maya studies was a still a new and small field, and the discovery of new sites and new dates were enough to occupy the inquisitive minds of Morley and other early Mayanists. Also, we shouldn't underestimate the disruptions caused by the two world wars. Between 1914 and 1945, the countries that had once been the hotbeds of Maya epigraphic study—the United States, France, and Germany—were at war, and only a few scholars found the time to examine the strange writings from ancient Central America.[4]

In 1952, a Russian philologist named Yuri Knorosov published a short article positing that Maya hieroglyphs were indeed phonetic. Knorosov had no background in Maya archaeology, but he was well versed in Egyptian hieroglyphs, cuneiform, and other ancient scripts of the Old World. When he saw Maya writing for the first time, he intuited that it was ripe for further study and patterning out. Publications that included the three ancient books known at the time, as well as a dictionary of Yucatec Mayan, gave Knorosov the minimal raw materials he needed. He also took close notice of the Landa manuscript and its supposed "abc," with crude drawings of signs corresponding to "*letras*" (letters). Like Brinton long before, Knorosov suggested that the *letras* were not alphabetic elements at all but in fact misrepresentations of syllables. In fact, looking at Landa's chart of signs, he saw that some had alphabetical glosses such as "b" or "h" whereas others had glosses like "ca" and "cu"—a clue that something else was at work. Landa himself was inconsistent in his description of "the writing of the indians," describing them in one moment as letters, elsewhere as "caractares," but in at least one place as "silibas." Knorosov took these descriptions as clues to a more complex picture. He reasoned (much as Brinton had) that Landa had misunderstood the actual nature of the script, producing a contradictory and messy description of its nature. He posited that the elements of writing in Landa's table were indeed purely phonetic in nature and probably consonant-vowel combinations, the "cu," "ca," and "lu" being more accurate than other glosses. For almost a century up to that point, numerous Maya scholars had attempted to forge a general decipherment based on the supposition that a single sign corresponded to a single word, holding an intrinsic semantic value (what we call a logogram). Those ideas were in no way mistaken, for there were hundreds of such signs in the script. What Knorosov recognized was the existence of another category of sign that represented pure sound, a consonant-vowel (CV) syllable. These syllables would be combined to spell words, as in **ku-tzu**, for *kutz*, "turkey," **tzu-lu**, for *tzul*, "dog" (Figure 2.2). The proposed readings corresponded well with the accompanying pictures he saw in the *Dresden Codex* and *Madrid Codex*: **ku-tzu** above a picture of a turkey and **tzu-lu** above that of a dog. These text-image connections provided the key semantic controls by which Knorosov could build a tight, mutually reinforced argument. As it turned out, the script was composed of both logograms and phonetic signs, and the linguistic decipherment of Maya writing had reached a new level of sophistication, at least in its potential.[5]

At first, Knorosov's approach looked productive, but also it was not completely new. Brinton had long before seen through the "alphabet," concluding that the signs might be syllables, and in 1933, the American linguist Benjamin Lee

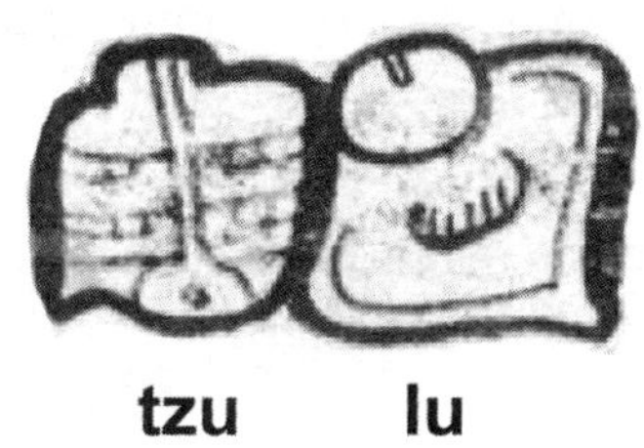

FIGURE 2.2. The hieroglyph *tzul*, "dog," from the *Dresden Codex*. Note the **lu** sign's faint resemblance to one of the "l" signs in Landa's alphabet.

Whorf had suggested the same. Like Knorosov, Whorf had used Landa's list as a point of departure, noting the odd insertion of probable syllabic signs among the various "alphabetic" characters. In one particularly important observation, he noted that Landa's "ma" and "ca" signs appeared in various examples of a glyph for a month in the Maya calendar named *Mak*. He made the simple point that the glyph "may be read **ma-ka**"—again a perfectly accurate analysis by today's standards. Alfred Tozzer, the great Maya scholar at Harvard in the 1930s and '40s, noted that Whorf was on to something, stating that he dared "to reopen the phonetic question" in a paper that "may open up a vista for further investigations along the trail which he has blazed."[6] In retrospect, Whorf's idea stands as an important, isolated breakthrough, yet, once again, no one followed it up. His musings about other glyph readings were very off-base, as it turned out, leaving him open to biting criticism from Thompson.

Knorosov's approach was much more comprehensive and on firmer ground, but still it failed to establish any quick inroad toward a larger decipherment of the system. Such an assessment may come as a surprise, for Knorosov is today often heralded as *the* singular decipherer of the script. In truth, he could read several words and word sequences in the painted books but never any whole texts. By 1963, he produced a sign catalog of both syllables and logograms comprising 540 total elements. Looking back from what we know today, we can see that Knorosov was correct in identifying forty-one of those signs, resulting in an accuracy of only less than 10 percent—a huge leap nonetheless. Later, Knorosov went on to publish whole "translations" of text passages, but the majority of these were, in retrospect, completely wrongheaded. He never was able to make any progress in reading the texts on the Classic-era monuments or on the inscribed vases. Something was still missing in the overall decipherment.[7]

THE NAMES

In 1952, the very year that Knorosov had published his first article, an archaeological discovery in Palenque rocked the Maya world, which would ultimately set the stage for the recognition of ancient Maya history. This was in the pyramid known as the Temple of the Inscriptions, an imposing, well-preserved building named for the three inscribed tablets placed on the rear walls of its upper shrine, containing a total of 620 hieroglyphs. When Stephens saw these over a century earlier, he was impressed by the length of the narrative, clearly to him "the real written records of a lost people." He went on to make a very important and prescient point regarding the long inscription on the walls: "The hieroglyphics are the same as were found at Copan and Quirigua. The intermediate country is now occupied by races of Indians speaking many different languages, and entirely unintelligible to each other; but there is room for the belief that the whole of this country was once occupied by the same race, speaking the same language, or, at least, having the same written characters."[8] Standing within the temple, Stephens had his first inkling of the remarkable consistency and standardization across the ancient Maya culture. What Stephens could not know, of course, is that the lengthy text on the tablets celebrated the life and times of a great Maya king, named K'inich Janabpakal (or Pakal for short). As we will see, his story forms an anchor for our larger account of Maya history in the seventh century CE.

Work at the temple began in 1949, overseen by Alberto Ruz Lhuillier, a French-Cuban archaeologist who was tasked by Mexico to preserve Palenque's deteriorating monuments. Ruz was eager to consolidate the deteriorating buildings and learn something about the time depth of the Palenque as a whole, thinking that the large pyramid might hold many earlier layers, providing a much-needed baseline for understanding Palenque's ceramic chronology and long-term development. Ruz found that the pyramid and its discernable phases represented only a short time frame, however, pointing to a single major construction during the Late Classic. The last known date recorded in the tablets (those were readable) corresponded to 692, and this seemed to him a good estimate of the time in which it was built.

After clearing the interior of the upper temple, Ruz turned his attention to a curious feature in the floor of the rear room—a large flagstone with six pairs of carefully drilled holes, each filled by a single stone plug.

He also noticed that the wall of the temple continued below the flagstone, indicating something beneath. He had the plugs removed, allowing for the slab to be lifted, whereupon Ruz and his laborers were confronted with dense rubble and clay fill, and they dug farther until they reached a series of steps. Naturally Ruz set about clearing them, and it soon became evident that it was the top of a stairwell that penetrated down into the body of the pyramid. The stairs did not seem to end, and the hard work of clearing the heavy debris took three long years, until June 1952, when the stairs reached an ancient floor nearly at the same level as the temple plaza outside. Densely constructed walls still lay ahead, but once they were cleared, the space turned out to be an unassuming corridor, along with some small offerings and a crude crypt with six skeletons—but clearly not the main point of the stairwell. The chamber raised many questions in the minds of Ruz and his crew. "Was that all?"[9]

One of the Maya crewmembers working in the deep tunnel was named Juan Chablé, from the town of Oxkutzcab, Yucatán. A stone mason by training, he worked with Ruz to oversee much of the reconstruction and consolidation being planned for Palenque's structures. Over time he had developed a keen eye and a practical sense of archaeology and its methods.

It was Chablé, in fact, who discovered the great Palenque tomb. In the bottom of the stairwell, he had noticed that a section of the wall was set in an odd triangular pattern, which he showed to Ruz and the others. Removing the mortar and the rocks around them, they revealed a large triangular stone set into the wall, clearly a door. This was carefully pivoted on its vertical axis to reveal enough of an opening to look through. Ruz took a bare light bulb and peered within, startled by a huge chamber and, at first, the sparkling pinpoints of light reflected by the crystalline limestone within. When his eyes adjusted, he could see a huge carved slab placed horizontally and stucco figures on the walls. At first, he assumed the slab was an altar, but it was later revealed to be a sarcophagus, holding the skeleton of "a great chief of Palenque," his name unknown (Figure 2.3).

For the young field of Maya studies at the time, the ramifications of the Ruz's discovery are difficult to overstate. Here was an elaborate

FIGURE 2.3. The Tomb of K'inich Janabpakal, Palenque. Photograph by the author.

chamber devoted to the celebration of an authority figure of some sort, a "great chief" from the Classic period. Never had Maya archaeology encountered such evidence of a single individual's importance. The discovery also soon gave rise to a small but important breakthrough in the decipherment of the hieroglyphs. This came thanks to one of Ruz's colleagues also working in Palenque, a German expatriate named Heinrich Berlin, who had quickly become enchanted by ancient Mesoamerica and Maya archaeology. Berlin had accompanied Ruz's team to Palenque several years earlier and, like so many others, soon was intrigued by the site's intricate hieroglyphic inscriptions. Berlin would have been one

FIGURE 2.4. Two ancestral figures on the side of the Palenque sarcophagus, showing the mother (left) and father (right) of K'inich Janabpakal. Drawing by the author.

of the first people to see the imagery of the tomb and its sarcophagus, including the lengthy text around the edges of the upper slab, as well as the carvings on the sides, with their beautiful images of bejeweled men and women emerging from the earth as fruiting trees.

Berlin soon studied the images and hieroglyphs and saw a few key patterns. For one, there were paired hieroglyphs next to the tree-like figures, and he made the very reasonable guess that these must be labels, probably personal names (Figure 2.4). This was a simple, almost obvious insight, but never had the name of a historical individual been recognized in a Maya inscription, making it a radical idea. Berlin was able to find examples of the very same names in the inscription carved on the sarcophagus lid, each in association with a different date. Berlin's simple proposals, set in motion by the opening of the Palenque tomb in 1952, set the stage for a series of even further breakthroughs. By the 1980s, it ultimately led to the full phonetic reading of the name of the tomb's occupant: K'inich Janabpakal. We will tell more of his story in ensuing chapters.

Another breakthrough came a few years later, in 1960, in a single academic paper that transformed Maya research forever. This was from a brilliant artist and scholar named Tatiana Proskouriakoff, a specialist in the study of Maya art and architecture. Over time she had seriated the styles of Maya sculptures, playing close attention to their dates and to the patterns of how visual motifs changed over time. From this work, she recognized that the dates inscribed on the monuments of one site, Piedras Negras, revealed an especially interesting pattern. The city's stelae were arranged in discrete clusters, placed in the plazas before various pyramids, each member of a group erected within a relatively short span of time, every five years or so. The span of each set of monuments never exceeded a reasonable human lifetime. The first date inscribed in each set, the "initial date," was accompanied by a particular glyph representing the upturned head of a reptile or amphibian. Another date came two or three decades later in middle of the span (more or less) and showed a bowtie knot element. There was also a final date in each monument cluster, with a glyph that showed a bird's wing, among other signs. This followed the initial date of the subsequent set. Proskouriakoff reasoned that these events were the births, accessions, and deaths of individual rulers—the lords of Piedras Negras—and she was able to tentatively point to their names, following up on Berlin's ideas. There were seven complete series of monuments in all, spanning two hundred years and corresponding to the lifespans of seven people. Her elegant paper relied on the teasing out of mathematical patterns, and in doing so she had recognized an ancient dynasty.[10]

Proskouriakoff then took a systematic look at the inscriptions of other sites, where she found many of the same patterns. Sequences of rulers in different lineages or dynasties were apparent across much of the Maya world, and the outlines of ancient Maya history were at last emerging, only a few years after Morley, Thompson, and others had summarily rejected the idea that history was anywhere to be found in the inscriptions (texts they could not yet read). Proskouriakoff had overturned the old paradigm. Thompson, often quite stubborn in his views, quickly acknowledged her discovery. Writing a decade later, he called her observations "the most significant achievement" of recent scholarship.[11] Still, throughout the rest of his career, Thompson continued where he seems to have felt most comfortable, with the esoterica and romanticism

FIGURE 2.5. The hieroglyph for *chuk*, "tie up," in the *Dresden Codex* and on Yaxchilan, Lintel 16. Photograph courtesy of the Trustees of the British Museum.

of Maya religion and philosophy. History, with its messy reflection of the human condition, was too difficult for the idealistic Thompson to embrace, and in the second edition of his book from 1966, he acknowledged no need for "painting over the former picture and starting again."

Proskouriakoff never collaborated with Knorosov, but she was well aware of his work on the phonetic nature of Maya script (unlike other Mayanists in the West, she could read his articles in full, in her native Russian language), and she quietly accepted his proposals.[12] Their mutual contributions and approaches to decipherment converged in the reading of one hieroglyph that appeared in the *Dresden Codex*, which Knorosov read as **chu-ka,** *chuk*, "to captured, tie-up."[13] Sure enough, this appeared in the *Dresden* above the picture of the storm god Chahk bound like a war prisoner. Proskouriakoff recognized the very same glyph in her studies of the newly revealed historical texts at Yaxchilan, where it accompanied the images of warriors with bound captives (Figure 2.5). This link represented a meeting of language and history, and by the late 1960s, a new, more integrated approach to the interpretation of the glyphs had begun to take hold.[14] This was also a time when many new sites were found through survey and exploration and many new inscriptions—the raw material for any new decipherments—were discovered and recorded. This was thanks largely to the explorer and photographer Ian Graham, who beginning around 1962 devoted much of his life to recording Maya texts in the remote forests of Guatemala and Mexico.[15] By the mid-1970s, hundreds of never-before-seen inscriptions were available for scholars to study, not only on stone monuments but also on the hundreds of ceramics that began to appear in museum and private collections in those years. The main person behind the documentation of Maya ceramics was Justin Kerr, who developed a "roll-out" method for photographing cylindrical vessels. Like Graham's efforts, Kerr's database was essential to the eventual decipherment of the ancient script.[16]

By the late 1970s, it seemed that Maya history was well on its way to being cracked open. The advances came rapidly, as a new generation of scholars appeared on the scene inspired by the new possibilities. Representing the new synergy was an informal working group focused on the art and inscriptions of Palenque. Peter Mathews, Linda Schele, and Floyd Lounsbury, all new to Maya studies, led the way. In 1973, Mathews and Schele presented their new detailed overview of the dynasty of Palenque, building on the initial work of Berlin and others. It jump-started an intense period of interest and a new type of collaborative teamwork in Maya epigraphy, especially in the United States. But appearances were deceptive. Knowledge of a wider history remained patchy, with little indication of any deep connections between important centers of the Classic period. We had a dynasty at Tikal and another at Palenque, but how did they ever relate to one another? How were these royal lineages arranged, and were there hierarchies among them? Was Maya power ever centralized in any way, with major kingdoms dominating others? Political organization became a major question and point of debate in those years and throughout the 1980s.

Barriers to a full decipherment still held despite the progress of the 1970s. Numerous signs remained unread, as either syllables or word signs, and any larger grammatical system that underlay the texts was still opaque. In the late 1970s, we could identify names (i.e., "Ruler 2) or event glyphs ("death") but still not necessarily *read* them. Why the hindrances? I believe that much of the problem was the same one that had held back Whorf, Knorosov, and other would-be decipherers—an inadequate understanding of the visual system behind the script. That is, scholars still were not sure of many of the orthographic principles behind how signs looked, what variants they had, and how they could combine with one another. Many signs were rare, even unique-looking, and therefore almost impossible to analyze in terms of what was known. The forms of certain glyphs, even in, say, the personal names of various historical figures identified by Proskouriakoff, seemed overly complicated.

This is where my own experiences in decipherment began to take shape. I had entered the world of archaeology in the late 1970s while still young, having absorbed a fascination of hieroglyphs from my two parents, both archaeologists, artists, and writers. During expeditions to Yucatán, the Stuart family would spend months in remote Maya towns and nearby archaeological sites, where I sometimes saw real glyphs carved onto stone monuments lying about the jungle. We lived a rustic life in those summers, and the passing days were punctuated by my father's exciting finds—new sites to map, new monuments unearthed in the area. I vividly recall one afternoon in 1975 when my father was called away from our thatched house to help excavate a new discovery. The top of a massive stone stela had been found, bearing an inscription and the record of the date of November 29, 780 CE. (My encounter with the new stones at La Corona brought back the thrill I saw in my own father's face when he saw the Coba stela.) What of the other glyphs? I asked him. They couldn't be read, he told me. The elegant, cartoonish designs fascinated my young mind, and I wanted to know all about them. At the time, in our field house, the only inroad I had available were a couple of impenetrable books, where I could understand little. For me, it was far more interesting (and fun) to copy whatever intricate drawings of glyphs I could find and get a sense of their visual forms. From that moment, living among the Maya and hearing their language being spoken around me, I was completely hooked.

By the early 1980s, I found myself working with Schele, Lounsbury, and Mathews on the ongoing studies of Palenque's texts. I also struck up a close collaboration with Stephen Houston and Karl Taube, then graduate students at Yale. It was in those years that we came to realize that Maya hieroglyphs were a complex visual system that disguised a rather simple underlying structure. It became clear not only that a given basic sign, such as a word sign or a syllable, *could* assume a great variety visual forms but also that this variation was part of the system in the first place. Any given element of the script could be freely replaced by many others that were functionally equivalent. Not only were there three or four **ma** signs, let's say, but there were a few ways of writing a given word, such as *ajaw*, for "ruler, king" (Figure 2.6). We had good indications of such "allography" in past decades, but now it was clear that this variety was baked deeply into the script, in such a way that we always had been expecting its use and appearance. Through a careful study of tightly controlled contexts—say, personal names or parallel passages—these various ways of writing the same thing soon revealed themselves. The system broke open, mostly in the mid- to late 1980s.[17]

Once the larger system was visible, the texts could begin to be read—verbs and nouns, actions and subjects, adjectives and adverbs, grammatical forms, and narrative structures. The phonetic controls of the decipherment allowed us to narrow down the language of the Classic texts to a particular subgroup of Mayan known as Ch'olan Mayan. The members of this group (Ch'ol, Chontal, Ch'orti', and Ch'olti') were spoken in the southern Maya lowlands, spanning an area from Tabasco on the Gulf Coast to the southeastern Peten, and up into the mountains of the eastern Guatemalan highlands. This region corresponds well with the

FIGURE 2.6. Three hieroglyphs for *ajaw*, "lord, noble." Drawings by the author.

area where we find many of the major sites of Classic Maya civilization, especially those who participated in the tight networks of interaction and conflict that form the history of this book. The linguistic connection now reveals that the hieroglyphic writing system was invented by speakers of a Ch'olan language. The ancient language of the glyphs we call "Classic Mayan," and it was a lingua franca used throughout the region, helping bind the many polities and kingdoms through a common elite language and means of communication. Classic Mayan language reflects an old tradition, it seems, and it probably emerged along with other elements of a prestige culture that formed in the southern lowlands during the Preclassic era, spreading from there to other regions.[18]

With the original language at last before us, the Maya writing system can now be said to be deciphered. We can read most texts we encounter, whether at archaeological sites, newly excavated in the field, in museum galleries or storerooms, or in old photographic archives. These are the sources that give us the deep texture and nuance of ancient Maya culture and history, and much remains to be done. Each year there are new inscriptions found in excavations, whether on a stone monument or on some portable object, and it is fair to say that each text gives us something we have never seen before.

A CULTURE OF WRITING

The origins of the writing system can be traced back to the Middle Preclassic era, probably well before 400 BCE. By this stage, the lowland Maya had forged a distinctive visual culture alongside ambitious expressions in architecture and urban planning. The new art movement spread rapidly across the lowlands, built on the firm foundations of what Olmec artisans had produced throughout much of Mesoamerica in previous centuries. And as a part of this artistic culture, the Maya also developed a system of writing, merging standardized visual elements with the words and sounds of language. It is among the most beautiful scripts in the ancient world, and it would persist for well over two thousand years until the arrival of the Spanish.

The first evidence of this system appears around 300 BCE, and by then it already looks highly developed, with centuries of history already behind it. The discovery of these first hieroglyphs came only recently from small fragments of painted plaster walls at San Bartolo, Guatemala. One of the larger inscribed fragments shows the written calendar date "7 Deer" (7 Manik') in the 260-day calendar known as the *tzolk'in* ("the order of the days"). Other pieces show elements familiar from later Maya script. Examples of the very same writing system appear between 300 BCE and 100 CE here and throughout the lowlands, up into Yucatán and even as far south as the Guatemalan highlands and Pacific piedmont region, at sites such as Takalik Abaj and Kaminaljuyu. No doubt excavations in the future will reveal even earlier examples of Maya script, showing its widespread use and development in the Preclassic.[19]

At the height of its use in the Classic period, the hieroglyphic script appears in many places associated with elite households and courts, and on a wide variety of objects: stone monuments, ceramic vessels, buildings, cave walls, jewelry, shells, crafting tools, bones, and masks, among many other luxury items. Any durable surface seems to have been written on by scribes at one point or another. As might be expected, most extant Maya texts are on stone, placed in architectural settings around palaces and temples, usually in the form of upright stelae. Their inscriptions indicate that they were usually erected to commemorate rituals occurring with the passing of major cycles of the calendar. The rulers who oversaw such rites are named, as might be some essential background information on their reign or other aspects of their personal stories. Over time, we see how inscriptions in public places grew in narrative scope, often recounting remarkably detailed narratives of people, places, and events. And near the end of the Classic period, we see a pronounced uptick in the records of war between Maya cities, indicating important cultural shifts that may have had fatal consequences for Classic society.

The literature now at hand, in an original Mayan voice, reflects the interests and concerns of the times in which they were written. Records of ritual performances, of dynastic events, and of interactions among kingdoms were the mainstay of the formal inscriptions, and their natures changed somewhat over time. We also see differences in literate practice on smaller, more intimate objects that were inscribed with dedicatory texts, labeling their owners. If we only had books, we no doubt also could see differences in how they also changed over time, with perhaps different topics of emphasis over time. Here it is perhaps worth noting that the four extant books that all date from the Postclassic era (after 1000 CE) contain no history at all. I suspect that this may reflect the initial stages of the Great Rupture in those times, when Classic history was beginning to be forgotten or at least not maintained. Historical texts must have been an emphasis of the Classic archives, of course.

No Mayan word exists in the ancient texts that easily translates to our idea of "history." But if we look at some Mayan languages today, we find something close to it in the word *k'ah*, "to remember." This was used in some post-invasion documents relating to the record of past events. Also important and revealing is the word *tzol*, meaning "to order, align," used to form many terms connected to timekeeping. All things have their proper arrangement and place relative to one another, whether the furrows of a cornfield, the offerings on a ceremonial altar, or the words spoken to convey their proper meaning. These fall under the concept of *tzol*, "ordering," and events past and present—history itself—derive their significance through their proper placement in a larger scheme. More broadly, the word can mean "to recount, explain, translate." I am intrigued especially by a term that appears in modern Yucatec Mayan, *tzolan beeh*, "ordered path," which can also be translated as "history." The idea here is that the recounting of events in one's life experience—one's "road"—involves a proper ordering just like everything else—time, work, and ritual life. I suspect that in ancient times *tzol* carried similar meanings. In fact, one hieroglyph that introduces formal historical dates at the beginning of a historical account likely proclaims the term *tzol-haab*, meaning "the ordering (or recounting) of the Years." The ordering of time and of life presents a sense of "history" that comes close to our own definition, relating events of the past and making them relevant for the present day.

As in much of the ancient world, written Maya history recounts the events and actors of elite society. Texts were produced within a courtly world and for its own members. The bulk of the monumental texts focuses on ceremonial topics, especially the commemoration of important cycles in the Long Count calendar. Typically, a stela might be dedicated on such an occasion, carved with a ruler's portrait and with an inscription that says something about the ceremonies on that day. Sometimes we find long texts on the public monuments, when scribes desired to insert some sort of backstory, including biographical details of the people who performed in the rituals—dates of crowning, birth, important wars, records of parentage, and so forth. We also find verbose texts carved in stone in more direct architectural settings—doorjambs, door lintels, temple steps, and so on. And here there was often space to include great more detail. The greatest example of "long history" can be found on the massive Hieroglyph Stairway at Copan, Honduras, presented on the face of a large pyramid in the center of the site. Every riser of every step, sixty-two in all, is carved with a string of hieroglyphs. As we will explore in more detail, the stairway presents a grand summary of Copan's dynastic history, spanning the reigns of fifteen kings over the course of nearly four hundred years.[20]

Each city-state, or *kabch'en,* emphasized its own dynastic affairs, so that the representation of history was mostly local and inward-looking. But there are also many intriguing overlaps and references to foreign rulers, marriage alliances, and wars, allowing us to cross-reference many of the actors and events. What emerges from this more integrated perspective is an internally consistent historical record covering most of the southern Maya lowlands. It expresses a coherent literary culture as well as a tight, mutually reinforced network of knowledge and interaction among ruling families. Records of events also tended to be highly episodic, highlighting a single event here and another event there without necessarily specifying the connection between them. Clearly the ancient readers were meant to be in the know, supplying some of that necessary context that we lack today. This can sometimes hinder our reconstruction of detailed narratives. For instance, a typical historical record might relate how a ruler performed a ceremony on a certain day, perhaps at a certain place. It might also give that ritual performance some historical context by relating it to past events—the ruler's accession to the throne so many years and days beforehand or recent wars and so on. Maya history is written in this piecemeal and patchy way, and we are left to carefully make inferences where we can. Formal texts were designed to be official records of history as it happened, placing events in their proper historical and religious context as the Classic Maya saw it.

A typical historical account from the Classic period emphasizes these underlying connections between human events and cosmic structures. Stela 36 from Piedras Negras provides one example (Figure 2.7). Dedicated in 667 CE, it was erected by the local king named Xokmo'chahk to mark his oversight of a station or "period ending" in the so-called Long Count calendar. These moments came every five or ten years, when it was custom for a dynast to set up a large stone monument to celebrate the occasion. Stela 36's text opens with a lengthy register of a date using several different calendrical cycles, including what we call the Long Count, the Calendar Round, and the Lunar Calendar (see Appendix B). We transcribe this single day as 9.10.6.5.9 8 Muluc 2 Zip, corresponding to our April 13, 639. On that day, Xokmo'chahk assumed the throne as the Holy Lord of the Yokib dynasty, twenty-eight years before the stela was erected. The rest of the text notes that he had been born forty-one years before the stela's dedication, on May 23, 626 (9.9.13.4.1 6 Imix 19 Zotz'). The upshot of it all is to mark the important new station in the count of cosmic time and Xokmo'chahk's two main life events (birth and crowning) in relationship to that singular moment. The underlying message is that the king shepherded the end of one time cycle and the beginning of another.[21]

Apart from formal stone inscriptions, a great many other written texts come to us from ceramic vessels, either painted or carved (Plate 7). These were everywhere in ancient Maya courts, used in everyday contexts and in more formal ritual occasions, inscribed with the names of their owners and often with a mention of their function. A typical vase from the Classic period might say, "It is his drinking cup for cacao" or "It is her plate" with the name to follow. Others are a bit more intimate and mundane: "It is his hand-washing cup" or "It is her face-paint container." Many of these objects were buried with their owners, whereas others we often find disposed of in elite trash dumps. Other ceramics bear elaborate paintings of

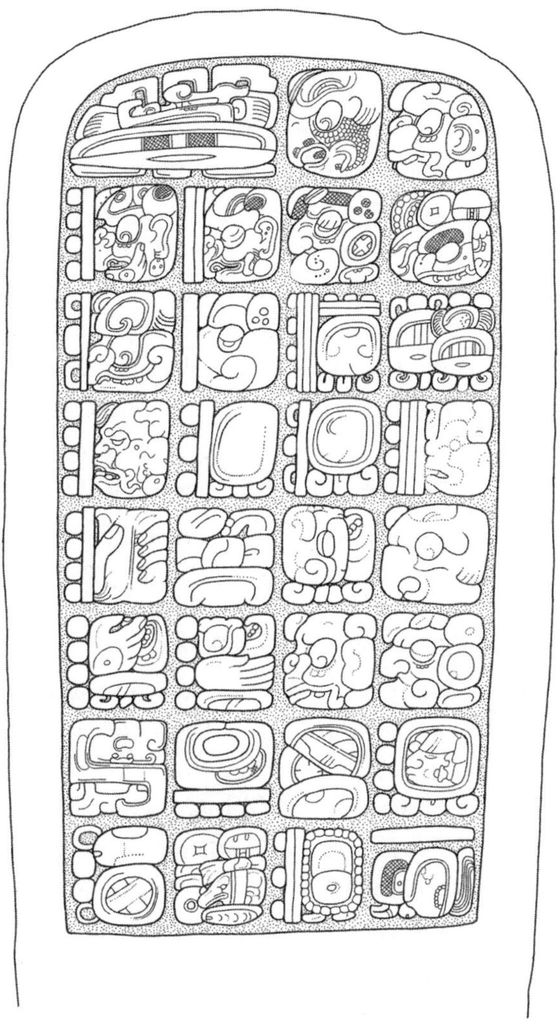

FIGURE 2.7. Stela 36 from Piedras Negras. Drawing by the author.

historical scenes or images from epic myth, much like we see on ancient Greek vases.

Sadly, many of the sources we rely on have been ripped away from their original contexts, illicitly excavated from remote sites and sold into the art market. In the 1960s and '70s, especially, many ruins in northern Guatemala and southern Mexico were raided and despoiled before they could be studied by archaeologists, La Corona ("Site Q") being a famous case. Another sad story involves ancient Baxwitz, the ruins we know today as Xultun, where looters carted off many beautiful ceramics they found within the city's tombs and burials. So absurdly "rich" was Xultun that the looters gave the site their own name: *El Delirio*, "Place of Delirium." And at the ruins of El Peru-Waka', first encountered by oil prospectors from the United States in the early 1970s, several beautifully carved monuments were sawn into pieces and carted off on muleback, making their way eventually to museums in Cleveland, Fort Worth, and Budapest. Looters also targeted ruined buildings wherever they could find them, trenching and tunneling in search of elaborately painted ceramics and jade. (Ironically, many of the first looters learned their "trade" having been employed by archaeologists on field projects at Uaxactun and Tikal.) These sad vestiges of carvings and ceramics often hold texts with key historical references, and in many cases, we can use these clues to reconstruct their places of origin, even to identify the very spot where they were stolen.

Many thousands of books existed during the Classic period, holding all sorts of records and accounts—mythic cycles of gods and ancestors, dynastic lists, records of wars and conquests, tribute lists, and tallies of gifts received by the courts. Each kingdom would have had its own library and archive, none of which survive today. Only four books, including the *Dresden Codex*, have come down to us from the Postclassic era, three collected by Spanish invaders as exotic curios and sent back to European archives. Another was found in the 1960s in a dry cave in southern Mexico, probably not far from Palenque. While no books survive from the earlier Classic period, one recent discovery gives us a hint of what they would have looked like, from the early ninth century CE. In 2017, while excavating in a plaza at the site of Baking Pot, Belize, archaeologist Julie Hogarth and her team found a smashed ceramic vase, seemingly left on the surface around the time of the site's abandonment in the ninth century. We call this remarkable vessel the "Komkom Vase," named after an ancient place cited in its numerous beautiful hieroglyphs. The calligraphic lines stand out on a white background, replicating the look of a page or pages from an ancient book (Figure 2.8). When we look at the dense

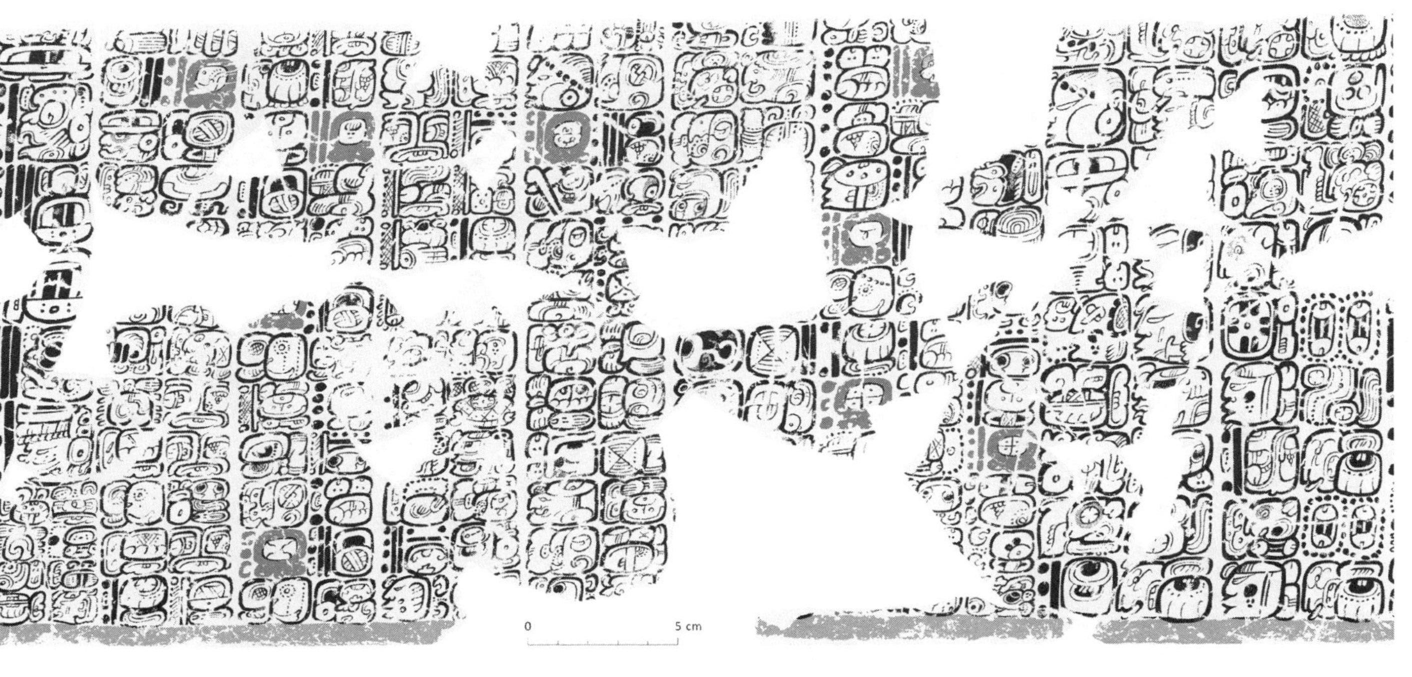

FIGURE 2.8. The painted text of the Komkom Vase. Drawing by Christophe Helmke.

text, we can easily imagine how it was copied from a few pages of an ancient historical manuscript, as my colleague Christophe Helmke has noted. And in this case, it *is* a glimpse of history. The vase's text recounts a complex story of war and political disruption, of towns burning and of lords fleeing their palaces in the face of conquest. Its narrative offers a remarkable window into the violent landscape of the ninth century CE in the decades that immediately led up to the Classic collapse.[22]

CHAPTER 3

Dawning

THE EARLIEST STRANDS of knowable Maya history coincide with the arrival of the Classic period, roughly around 100 to 200 CE, when several dynasties and elite courts suddenly appear on the scene. Our awareness of that early history comes from the retrospective accounts of Maya scribes who lived centuries later and who, from time to time, had something to say about the beginnings of their own social and political world. These scant records, while spotty and incomplete, set the stage for the more detailed history to come, hinging on the complex and ever-shifting relations among the major ruling families. The faint origin stories about these Classic period dynasties are in no way the beginnings of Maya culture and politics, however. For a thousand or so years leading up to this time, during the long "Preclassic," civilization itself rapidly took shape. While nearly invisible to us from a historical standpoint, the Preclassic was a precocious era that saw the exponential growth of populations, the rapid development of urban sites and monumentality, the perfection of new intensive agricultural techniques, and the standardization of the hallmarks that define Maya visual culture, including its art and iconography. And for reasons we will still do not quite fathom, this early "predynastic" iteration of Maya civilization underwent a collapse and transformation of its own. Major cities were abandoned and even in ruins by 200 CE, ushering in a new "dynastic" era that we call the Classic period. Whereas the historical accounts of that earlier time are cloudy and vague at best, archaeology has revealed an astonishing civilization of its own, a time when farmers, priests, and rulers shaped the world around them in ways that resonated for centuries. For the later Classic Maya, what we call the Preclassic was the stuff of legend.

In the early twentieth century, archaeologists had only a rough idea of the time depth of Maya civilization, as serious, deep excavations began in the central lowlands. One noteworthy day of discovery was May 5, 1916, when Sylvanus Morley, the pioneering archaeologist we met in the previous chapter, was guided to an unexplored ruin known to the local *chicle*-gatherers as Bambonal, in the deep rainforest of northern Guatemala. Over the years, Morley had canvassed the remote region in search of carved monuments with hieroglyphic inscriptions, and he was most interested in looking for the ancient dates recorded on them. As he explored the many tree-covered temples and plazas of this new ruin, Morley's team came upon many stone monuments still standing and bearing traces of sculpture. Several of the stelae had what he was looking for—legible dates written in the Long Count. Two stones stood out, to Morley's shock and delight. On one he read the date 8.16.0.0.0 (357 CE) and on another 8.14.5.12.16 (323 CE). These were far older than any inscribed dates Morley had ever seen, falling in the remote "cycle eight." In his excitement, Morley named the new site Uaxactun, Yucatec Mayan for "eight stone." World War I prevented further exploration, but with the war's end, Morley planned a follow-up expedition. Soon Uaxactun became the focus of one of the first excavation projects in the Maya lowlands. As Morley wrote, "no other site now known would probably shed more light on the beginnings of the Old Empire (Morley's term for the Classic period) than Uaxactun, where all the earliest surely deciphered monuments have been found."[1]

The monuments were indeed early, but Morley could not have imagined that this exciting new site offered only a superficial idea of Maya cultural development overall. Only in the past few decades, archaeological research on many fronts has pushed the beginnings of the Maya much further in time, far earlier than the dates Morley saw. The study of the very earliest Maya is itself a remarkable story that has transformed our view of the Mesoamerican cultures and undercut many assumptions about how civilizations in general develop, including many I absorbed as a young archaeologist in graduate school. So we will begin our historical journey seeking out evidence for the very early peoples who inhabited the later Maya world, in very remote times, scores of centuries before the existence of glyphs and knowable kings.

REMOTE BEGINNINGS

How does an archaeologist detect the beginnings of "civilization"? The earliest remains of any culture are, by definition, the most difficult to access and analyze, lying deep in the ground and underneath newer remains. As we "dig backward," going further back in time, the evidence naturally tends to be scantier, less well preserved, and always, it seems, discovered late in the arduous process, after years or decades of previous work. This makes the evidence of early cultural development notoriously hard to make out, subject to different interpretations, and therefore in some ways found in the eye of the beholder. Archaeologists sometimes do not even know what they are looking for until they are confronted with a complete surprise, much as Morley was on his first visit to Uaxactun. We must keep in mind that archaeology in general is always a science of constant surprise, which is not too surprising, given the remarkable capabilities and creativity of our ancestors.

Historians and anthropologists have long used the presence of urbanism (cities) as one obvious box to check in defining what a "civilization" is. (*Civitas*, Latin for "city," is even the basis of the word.) But here we run up against a few problems and problematic assumptions. What is a city? Is it defined by the scale of monuments? Layout? Evidence of dense demographic settlement? The use of writing? All of these have their caveats. Large temples and other structures can occur very early, predating the cities and large towns that may eventually surround them. And the presence of writing, while important, need not be a prerequisite for sophisticated recordkeeping. Put simply, we find it increasingly difficult to offer a simple definition of what a "civilization" is. And perhaps it does not really matter in the end. It is probably best that we do not assume much or pre-categorize such features and patterns before we encounter them.

Now that a century of intensive Maya archaeology has revealed a long-lasting culture with numerous phases, punctuated by periods of rises and collapses (yes, more than one), we must ask the simple yet difficult question: Where did it all come from? People, many of them ancestors of the Maya, had already lived on the landscape for 15,000 years at the very least, adapting to their environment, living off the land, and expanding their presence. Then, starting around 1500 BCE, there was a sudden shift toward something different: a more settled life in small villages, with horticulture and the careful management of staple foods. Alongside this came, within only a few generations, an ideological turn, where the scale and ambitions of cultural expression burst forth. So what changed? Somehow, in ways we are still striving to understand, the Maya aspired to create their own environment in their own religious terms, building on the ideas and lessons they had learned over countless centuries. Perhaps in the end, "civilization" is that pivot point where people in numbers, once settled with a sense of place, are finally able to fashion their own worlds for themselves. Art and expression are a fundamental part of that universal human process.[2]

Up to this point, people had already lived for thousands of years on the Yucatán Peninsula, long before any recognizable "Maya" culture ever appeared. Most archaeological research naturally focuses on the more visible and obvious remains of the Preclassic and Classic periods, leaving only scant notice of these very early populations. Still, several sites in Yucatán and in Highland Guatemala show distinctive projectile points in association with carbon dates, indicating a clear presence of hunters and gatherers before 10,000 years ago. In the shallow, rocky terrain of Yucatán it has been especially challenging to encounter such early evidence, but there is surely much more to be found, especially in the caves and shelters of the karstic terrain.[3]

The "Archaic" period, a vast span of time between about 10,000 and 2,000 BCE, saw people living in many different regions of Mesoamerica, active in adapting to a warming climate and to a host of varied environments where they busily extracted resources. Gradually, these scattered populations developed new technologies, including an ability to cultivate wild maize and other important food plants. Much of the evidence for these developments comes from outside the Maya region, including the early efforts to cultivate and domesticate maize, which we can best trace in highland Mexico and along the Gulf and Pacific coastal regions. Archaic populations in the Maya lowlands began to live mostly within the dense neotropical forests that had developed there in a world that must have presented many unique challenges but that was also teeming with resources. One can imagine how attractive some of the larger rivers and lakes of the southern lowlands must have been in that time, as relatively open spaces with constant access to fish and fresh water. Those who managed to live in Yucatán or the Peten prior to 5000 BCE did so by hunting, gathering, and even with the rudimentary cultivation of fish, maize, and other key food resources.[4]

Over the millennia, the geology of the Maya region determined many aspects of human settlement. The terrain is quite young, in the grand scheme of the earth's evolution. Most of the Yucatán Peninsula was formed during the Paleocene, following the catastrophic impact sixty-five million years ago that resulted in the Chicxulub crater. The uplift of the ancient seabed created limestone layers that form the substance and surface of the region, always visible and exposed, with relatively little topsoil. The solubility of the young rock led to the rapid formation of caves and sinkholes, or *cenotes* (from the Yucatec Mayan word *tz'onot*). In the northern part of the peninsula, where surface water was scarce, these became vital for human survival. The limestone was especially porous near the edges of the ancient impact crater, creating a "ring of cenotes" around which we find a great many important ancient sites (Plate 3). The distribution of such features across the karstic landscape determined patterns of human placement and interaction from the beginning and continues to do so to this day. In this way, we can draw a direct line from the asteroid impact that killed the large dinosaurs and the environment in which parts of civilization grew and developed. Nearly everywhere, the integrated nature of limestone and the water beneath it and around it created the elemental foundations for Maya life.

In ancient art, we see water represented in animate form by the fantastical creature we call the Water Serpent, a dragon-like beast adorned with waterlilies (Figure 3.1a). It resided in the primordial sea out of which the stony earth arose during world creation. The essential stoniness of the karstic landscape left its own lasting mark on Maya culture and religion. Stone, or *tun,* was, like water, an animate substance endowed with its own spirit and persona (Figure 3.1b). Among some modern-day Maya of Yucatán, large limestone boulders in the forest are seen as living entities (still called *tun*) whose spirits dwell among the many inhabitants of the forest.[5] The many carved limestone monuments of Maya civilization—upright stelae and table-like altars—took on much of their meaning by virtue of their substance as *tuns.* These could exemplify the substance of the earth or the piled stones of a cornfield and could also serve a more abstract purpose as material expressions of time, specifically the year. This juxtaposition of stone, the hardest substance of the world, with time, an abstract structure for life and experience, provided a dualistic idea that was the heart of Maya thought. In ancient Maya art, stones often appear with large, snarling faces resembling that of Chahk, the storm deity, whose stone axe and hammerstone could strike the clouds to produce thunderous rain (Figure 3.1c). Chahk's ever-present axe emerged in the Classic period as a symbol if its own, *k'awil,* "force," a symbol of kingship and of the underlying power of regeneration.[6]

Stone had its obvious practical uses, though it was not initially used much as a building material. (In the neotropics, houses are far more practical when made of wood and thatch.) Rather, early populations of the lowlands would have been especially attracted to the many chert outcrops in the interior limestone uplands, essential resources for tool production and especially in crafting the axes needed for clearing the forest.[7] Later, limestone proved most important (as its name suggests) in the eventual production of calcium oxide, a crucial material with numerous practical applications. In food production, lime was essential in the cooking and preparation of maize in a process known as nixtamalization. This drastically increased maize's nutritional value and allowed

FIGURE 3.1. Animate elements of the Maya world: water (*ha'*), stone (*tun*), and thunderous storms (*chahk*). Drawings by the author.

it to become a staple of the Maya and Mesoamerican diet. In the later Preclassic period, the Maya also quickly adopted the use of lime in the making of plaster, realizing its ability as surfacing over walls and floors and, ultimately, as a sculpting material on a monumental scale. The limestone pervading the Maya world allowed for the monumental ambitions of the civilization.[8]

At the beginning, those who lived in and amid the stony terrain made good use of the natural cavities and shelter formations within the mountains. Recent excavations at two rock shelters in Belize add compelling evidence about various populations during the Archaic, including perhaps the earliest identifiable ancestors of the historical Maya. The two remote sites, named Mayahak Cab Pek and Saki Tzul, revealed over fifty human burials under the natural feature, the earliest of which dates between seven thousand and eight thousand years ago—remarkably early in the harsh tropical environment. The study of stable isotopes in the teeth of these skeletons tells us something of their diets, including the types of plant foods they were reliant on during their lifetimes. The earliest skeletons, spanning about five millennia from 7600 BCE to 2700 BCE, show a consistent reliance on forest plants and resources, pointing to a life of foraging. A remarkable pattern emerges in the later samples, though, where maize can be seen entering the diets between 3000 and 2000 BCE. The analysis of the DNA of these same skeletons shows that they have a close genetic relationship with populations to the south, where we know maize was domesticated earlier than in the Maya region. This raises the intriguing possibility that migrant populations, still small, entered the lowlands region from the south in Central America, bringing maize alongside a familiar life of mixed foraging. Whatever the case, maize became a true staple by about the middle of the second millennium BCE, when it was farmed throughout much of the region.[9] These early cultivators of maize in the highlands and lowlands of the peninsula, it would seem, were among the first archaeologically visible Maya populations, and by 1500 BCE they were well in place, occupying a diverse, resource-rich, and challenging landscape.[10]

Living in numerous scattered small settlements, the early Maya adapted new ideas, ceramic technologies, and techniques of early agriculture. They are known collectively as people of the "Pre-Mamom," referring to the time period that spans about 1200 to 700 BCE and before the well-defined "Mamom" ceramic phase that followed. This may well have been the most transformative time in all of Maya prehistory, when, over just five rapid centuries or so, we see the transition from impermanent settlements, horticulture, and foraging to permanent hamlets and villages, intensive agricultural practices, and a newfound attention to artistic expression and collective identity. Given the continuities we see over this time of rapid transformation and growth, we have good reason to think that these were indeed Maya people and probably speakers of Yucatecan and Ch'olan Mayan languages.

The foragers and early horticulturalists of Pre-Mamom times were small and scattered, mostly semi-mobile groups. Some settlements near the central lakes of the Peten and elsewhere may even have been year-round, subsisting on more ambitious farming methods and fishing. Given the ecological variation in the lowlands, it is no surprise that small communities were at any given time more nomadic than others, with small populations settling in a more permanent way along rivers and lakes, relying on fishing and hunting along with their modest agricultural practices. Maize cropping existed on a modest scale and may already have been cultivated in some regions for several centuries, alongside other important food crops such as manioc. It may well be that diets at this time in the central lowlands were even more varied than we find in later periods.

Before 1000 BCE, we see a widespread adoption of ceramic technology in the lowlands, which clarifies the archaeological picture greatly. This correlates with a rapid increase in more permanent settlements and a need for food and water storage, building on earlier practices.[11] The very first ceramics from the Pre-Mamom era are sometimes classified with names such as "Eb," "Xe," "Cunil," or "Buenavista," depending on their findspots. (Different excavation projects develop their own systems of ordering pottery types, and many of course overlap with one another.) Similarities among the different wares from Belize and central and southern Guatemala show some degree of contact among these populations, even if small regional differences point to more local "tribal" arrangements. Archaeologists still debate what the formal variations and discrete groups signify—are these different ceramic traditions reflections of different ethnicities or languages, for example? But most agree that these are "homegrown" ceramics, not indications of outsiders moving into the Maya area.[12]

With only meager physical evidence of residential buildings, it is difficult to know how these small communities organized themselves socially and politically. Among the best studied of such sites is Cuello, an early village site in northern Belize, which was initially occupied around 1200 BCE.[13] By 1000 BCE, we also begin to discern signs of a status hierarchy among people, indicated by burials of a few select individuals who had access to precious materials, including jade and other precious stones. Not all settlements of this era were the same. If we were able to fly over the Maya landscape around this time, we probably would look down on a variety of settlement types in the landscape below, much of it covered by forest but also with clear evidence of human modification of the terrain—felled trees, villages and hamlets of various sizes and densities, agricultural projects large and small, and, even still, impermanent foraging camps. Status differences emerged in a world of diverse lifeways. Some Maya of the time were ambitious in designing architectural forms that expressed novel ideas about community identity, cosmic forces, and agricultural cycles—the foundations of a powerful religious worldview spurred by rapid social and economic changes. The synergy between the observed cycles of the sun and the advent of new means of subsistence led in turn to new concepts of human agency and authority, setting the stage for the true beginnings of Maya civilization as we know it.

FIGURE 3.2. *Jun Ixim* (One Maize Kernel), the embodiment of primordial maize. Drawing by the author.

There is no better example of these coalescing ideas than to consider maize itself, and not just as a staple crop. The cultigen came to play a central role in the early development of Mesoamerican religion and cosmology for reasons that may seem obvious but that still bear close consideration. It assumed an animate, corporeal form in mythology (several, actually), and its initial, primordial form was called "First Maize Kernel," *Jun Ixim*, represented in Classic-period art as a beautiful, slender young man with jade jewels and flowing quetzal feathers on his head—visual metaphors of an upright maize plant (Figure 3.2). In later Maya myths of the *Popol Vuh*, we read how humanity was forged from maize after several false starts with mud, wood, and other unstable materials. This narrative of creation acknowledges a fundamental truth, in a way, that civilization in Mesoamerica truly was a by-product of maize. It is probably no accident that the ancient Maya hieroglyph for "person" (*winik*) incorporated maize imagery in its visual form. Similar ideas about the transmutation of human flesh and maize dough are basic to Mesoamerican metaphysics.[14]

OPENING THE EARTH, REVEALING THE SKY

The ever-present connections between the Maya and the rest of Mesoamerica were developed early on through contacts with an important culture we generally call "Olmec," closely associated with the beginnings of complex political organization and a broader Mesoamerican ideology and identity. We find Olmec art and monuments mostly with sites to the west of the Maya area, in what is today southern Veracruz and Tabasco, at major sites such as San Lorenzo, La Venta, and Tres Zapotes. Monumental stone heads are one conspicuous hallmark of Olmec sculpture, but many other types of sculpture emerged in the Middle Preclassic, including 3D figural sculptures, finely crafted ceramics, polished jades (imported from the Maya region), and innovative architectural designs. As archaeologists continued to study these early sites and materials in the mid-twentieth century, a common "horizon" of Olmec art and material culture was perceived across southern Mexico, Guatemala, and

Honduras, including nearly all the Maya area, fostering a good deal of debate about what such evidence really represents. Were the Olmec a people? A fashionable style of art? An innovative ideology? All of these are true to varying extents. Whatever the case, the major sites we label as Olmec were clearly places where elites adopted conspicuous expressions of high culture, representing themselves and ideas of religion and cosmology in a novel, systematic way. Sculpture and high-end ceramics were decorated with a sophisticated and highly abstract iconographic system, where maize and an animate Maize God comprise one of the most important themes. Polished jade emerged as one of the most important of the precious commodities, used as jewelry or shaped into axe-like "celts" that were placed in cached offerings. These were perhaps seen as symbolic maize cobs, but, in later Maya terms, these were also the instruments of Chahk, the storm god, and of his power and a generative force.[15]

San Lorenzo, less than two hundred miles west of the Maya area, was especially impressive and precocious in its day. It emerged as the principal regional center of the Olmec around 1300 BCE. The main site sits on a natural rise surrounded by rivers and swamps. The terrain was heavily modified, leveled, and filled in to create a "ceremonial center" well over fifty hectares in size, with numerous platforms and other forms of earthen architecture. Some even consider it to be the first Mesoamerican "state," although whether that word applies is a matter of debate. By 1000 BCE, San Lorenzo no longer was a major regional power, and its collapse, if we can call it that, seems to have set the stage for the rise other regional centers and new power structures that extended into the Maya region.[16]

Some have thought the Olmec to be Mesoamerica's "mother culture," giving rise to the art and complex culture that would soon emerge in the Maya area and beyond. Yet the rapidity with which Olmec culture appears throughout Mesoamerica points to a more complex dynamic among regions and centers that seem to have been in constant communication. From 1200 to 1000 BCE, elites in the highlands and lowlands of Mesoamerica, including the Maya region, seem to have "gelled" in some manner, participating in shared conceptions of cosmology and high culture. San Lorenzo and the Gulf Coast region may have been one of several driving forces behind that development. The early Maya were clearly part of a complex mesh of cultures, whether we call them Olmec or something else. I prefer not to see this as foreign influence, but rather as the early Maya elites buying into an important idea of "high culture," probably in association with early powerful community leaders who were seeking the fashionable trappings and symbols of religious and political prestige. And the early Maya in turn exerted a considerable influence in their own right, especially during the subsequent centuries of the Preclassic. After 300 BCE, the precocious Maya, like the earlier Olmec, were instrumental in the spread of ideology and "high culture" throughout much of Mesoamerica.

It is not surprising, then, that the most dramatic evidence of communal religious and political activity comes from the western edge of the Maya world, where early Maya communities had long been engaged in intensive contact with the Olmec and other early Mesoamerican cultures. Here, several large river systems thread their ways northward toward the southern edge of the Gulf of Mexico, bridging the Olmec "heartland" to the Maya lowlands to the east. Unlike the stony plains of Yucatán, this was a lush, water-filled environment, close to both mountains and sea and full of valuable natural resources. In the past few years, my colleagues Takeshi Inomata and Daniela Triadan examined lidar surveys of the area, finding numerous large and important sites with massive, carefully planned earthworks.[17] Their sheer size and great age have stunned the archaeological community. The largest is named Aguada Fénix (Figure 3.3). Like many other sites in the area, we see immense rectangular plazas and pyramids, mostly earthen constructions, all dating to about 1000–800 BCE. This would make it comparable in time to some of the first pre-Mamom settlements we can find in the central Maya lowlands, a short distance to the east. A rectangular platform defines the main construction at Aguada Fénix and is astounding in size, about 1,400 meters in length and 400 meters wide. That would be about fourteen football fields in overall length. Upon this raised flattened area were built various small mounds regularly placed in geometric patterns. Canals and causeways radiate out from this central location. In volume, the Aguada Fénix platform is 2,800,000 cubic meters in size—the largest artificial construction in all of ancient Mesoamerica from any era.

FIGURE 3.3. Lidar image of the monumental platform at Aguada Fénix, Mexico. Courtesy of Takeshi Inomata, University of Arizona.

Clearly, this discovery shows how huge, monumental constructions can appear very suddenly and near the beginning of complex social and political organization, not as an outcome of them.[18]

At the very center of the Aguada Fénix platform is a distinctive arrangement of structures known to Mayanists as an "E Group." This consists of a single platform and an adjacent elongated eastern structure. (Their name derives from their initial identification at the architectural complex known as "Group E" at Uaxactun in the 1920s.) E Groups appear at numerous Middle Preclassic sites, well beyond Tabasco. Their origin may lie in earlier monumental architecture at the Olmec center of San Lorenzo, but the Maya adopted this as a preferred architectural plan from the outset. Other examples of E Groups of about the same age as Aguada Fénix appear in the Peten region, and I suspect others of the same age will be recognized in the coming decades. One very early example was also identified by Inomata and Triadan in their important fieldwork at Ceibal, on the Río Pasión in Guatemala. There they excavated into deep layers underneath a Classic-period plaza, revealing one of the earliest examples of monumental architecture known in the central Maya area, an earth and clay platform a few meters high that was clearly also a small E Group, dating to about 900 BCE.[19]

Like the central Peten, the lowlands farther to the north also saw key developments in the Middle Preclassic, with settlements as early and as complex as sites farther south in the Peten. Centers such as Xocnaceh, Poxila, Yaxhom, Yaxuna, Edzna, and Santa Rosa Xtampak emerged with remarkable suddenness around 800–600 BCE, all with the monumental architecture including, in a few instances, other ambitious E Groups.[20] Some of these early sites cluster in the very northwest part of the peninsula, where water was only obtainable in *cenotes*, the natural sinkholes and caverns that provided access to the shallow water table of the region. As we have seen, these water wells had been vital to the human presence in the area since Paleolithic times; now they were key in providing water for incipient communities, permanent settlements, and their growing populations. Cenotes were sacred places, too, not surprisingly, and the most impressive of all was the centerpiece of the religious and political center at Chichen Itza during the Classic and Postclassic periods.[21]

Given their early, widespread use, E Groups can be reasonably considered a hallmark of Middle and Late Preclassic architecture and site planning, the "earliest recognizable form of public and ritual space in the Maya lowlands."[22] As we see at Cival, Yaxnohcah, and Yaxuna—three representative sites spread across the entire peninsula—E Group complexes were often the very first architectural monuments to be built at a given location, constructed atop exposed bedrock, around which villages and cities ultimately grew.[23] At Cival, in the eastern Peten, we find compelling evidence of a much larger effort to create an open expanse out of the jungle, flattening out a limestone hilltop to open up a ceremonial space and an E Group, around 800 BCE. Cival's public works project involved the removal of "only" 1.4 million cubic meters of fill, about half of Aguada Fénix, but still stunning in its scale.[24] These two communal efforts, roughly contemporaneous, represent a related vision of creating new ritual space, radically modifying an existing landscape in the process. As far as we know, nothing like Aguada Fénix had ever been attempted before in the Maya region. The effort to design and build on such a scale would have required a careful coordination of human labor, with hundreds if not thousands of people involved. And at about 900 BCE, this occurred centuries before we can really speak of any true "state-level" society in the region. Here we should remember that permanent villages had only existed in the central lowlands for a few centuries, and intensive maize agriculture was still a relatively recent development in the area as well. Inomata believes that Aguada Fénix may have been conceived and built even before permanent populations resided in the area. I suspect that the evidence of permanence is very hard to see in the archaeological record, but his overall point is cogent and remarkable nonetheless—that the platform of Aguada Fénix and others very similar to it, all supporting E Group plazas, date to a time when Maya civilization was just beginning, when agriculture was new and later power structures were not yet formed.

Ever since they were first studied, E Groups have been recognized for their astronomical function, as built-up observation points for viewing the eastern horizon, tracking the risings of the sun and other celestial bodies over the course of the year. The elongated eastern structure creates a regular "horizon" that can be viewed from the western platform. Recent studies of the orientation of the earliest known E Groups atop the platforms of Aguada Fénix and related sites show that the early Maya there were keenly interested in the 260-day calendar, one of the hallmarks of later Mesoamerican calendrics.[25] It is no accident that the earliest date glyph from the Maya area was recovered at the modest E Group from San Bartolo, the initial construction beneath the architectural complex that would eventually house the elaborate paintings from a few centuries later (Figure 3.4).[26] It was also at an E Group at Uaxactun where the Early Classic Maya later erected some of the first known monuments commemorating the k'atun stations of the Long Count calendar, including the very stelae that caught the attention of Sylvanus Morley in 1916. The primary purpose of E Groups would seem to be as "time temples," conceived as cosmological center points and

FIGURE 3.4. The small E Group of the Xbalanque complex, San Bartolo, ca. 300 BCE. Reconstruction by Heather Hurst, courtesy of the artist.

places of world renewal. Many were no longer used by the end of the Middle Preclassic (after about 400–300 BCE), but they were maintained elsewhere, well into the Classic period, apparently as places of deep historical and religious identity.

As my colleague James Doyle notes, very early E Groups may also represent efforts to forge community cohesion and a sense of political identity. The complexes were built as large, open-air plazas and were no doubt places for the congregations of large numbers of people. Their connections to seasonality and to agriculture have led Travis Stanton and David Freidel to call E Groups "maize theaters," which I think gets to their central significance in the origins of complex Maya lifeways.[27] The clearing and leveling of such spaces was, in a meaningful way, an extension on the arduous task of preparing an agricultural plot or *milpa*, what the Maya called a *kol* or *chol*. For many present-day Maya, cornfields were sacred spaces in their own right, square-shaped microcosms where cycles of growth and decay replicated the rhythms and cadences of time and the cosmos.[28] It is no doubt significant that agricultural themes permeate the elite religious ceremonies of the later Classic era, especially those centered on the renewal of time and the "replanting" of the periods of the so-called Long Count. E Groups and their plazas were the center points of these ideas, as metaphorical planting places where the cosmos itself could be engaged with and revived when the proper time came. For me, these immense efforts to create artificial landscapes and new vistas, whether by building upward above the canopy or by leveling forested hilltops, represent something akin to a new religious zeal that emerged on the heels of great changes in population and subsistence technology. The Maya were compelled to see the sky and its constant patterns of movement. This arose from the natural realization that their nascent social fabric hinged on time and the cycles of the day, the month, the year, and the higher orders of time.

Pondering these first monumental efforts, I am reminded of an expression we find written in the histories of the later Classic era. Several hieroglyphic texts of the Late Classic include tantalizing records of the founding of ceremonial spaces and plazas, with one noting a long sequence of them at different times in the deep past, usually separated by a generation or two. The situation suggests a regular pattern of establishing new ritual centers over time, something like the place-making we find in the archaeological record, both in the deep Preclassic and in later history. In the texts, such events are called *paskab*, "ground-opening" or "ground-clearing." One inscription from Pomona, Tabasco (close to Aguada Fénix, in fact), dates to 700 CE and lists several *paskab* events spaced over a few centuries, each at different places and overseen by rulers of the same long-lived court named Pakbul. I suspect that each event refers to a new plaza complex being built and constructed, a new "earth-clearing." The word *paskab* also has another important meaning of "dawn, sunrise," highlighting a different sense that the earth and the world could be opened and revealed daily. Given that the very first E Groups at Aguada Fénix, Ceibal, and other Middle Preclassic centers were built out of newly cleared forest and oriented toward the rising sun, I have to wonder if they represent the first examples of the *paskab* events we know from the Classic period, uniting concepts of "clearing" and "dawning" in early plazas and monumental architecture.[29]

Other monumental constructions and observatories of the region were abandoned before about 700 BCE, after two or three hundred years of use, for reasons still unclear. Their cessation evokes the numerous "collapses" we see later in Maya history and perhaps the first widespread example of a phenomenon involving the termination of a place or of a network of places. It is a fascinating and important pattern we will address in more detail, but suffice it to say that we will encounter other endpoints and abandonments many times and on many scales. These include the abandonment of many Late Preclassic urban areas around 100 CE, followed by the more famous collapse of cities in the ninth century CE. All these major episodes are separated by several centuries, and it seems to be a cyclical pattern that plays out in the long span of Maya history.

While historically obscure, the precocious architectural monuments of the Middle Preclassic reveal how calendars played a fundamental role in the early development of Mesoamerican civilization. The 260-day cycle that all Mesoamerican cultures share may have been invented around this time (and in this region), as Inomata and his colleagues propose, and I wonder if the Long Count calendar made of k'atuns and bak'tuns was also developed in this era. We have no direct evidence of its use before the first century BCE, but the numbers of the system might betray an awareness and accommodation for deep history and for the cycles that determined it. While impossible to know with assurance, could it be relevant that the 400-year bak'tun period that ended at 5.0.0.0.0 occurred in 1142 BCE, around the beginning of monumental sites in the Maya region? Or that the following bak'tun took place in 747 BCE, as the Maya were transitioning into new settlements and ways of building in the central lowlands? Or that the next bak'tun of 7.0.0.0.0 came with the rise of the Late Preclassic centers in the Peten? These are provocative questions, for they imply that the cyclicality that is embedded in Maya time somehow resonated with the sociopolitical world "on the ground," with the rises and falls over the long span of Maya civilization. As we will see, the same intriguing pattern may have been at work in the later Classic period, which faced its own abrupt end soon after the passing of another bak'tun (10.0.0.0.0) in the early ninth century CE.[30]

THE FIRST CITIES

After 600 BCE, these quick developmental trends continued into the Mamom period, marked by a region-tradition of ceramics and monumental architecture with its own distinctive forms and styles. Hundreds of sites developed rapidly in this Middle Preclassic era and across the entire landscape, showing that a cohesive Maya civilization, with its associated religious and political institutions and ideas, had now taken hold. In some select sites, vast areas were cleared, leveled, and terraformed, preparing the ground for monumental constructions that arose quickly, employing collective efforts, careful designs, and close coordination. While there is some heterogeneity to these early centers, they share several features. Many are designed with a purpose that clearly revolves around celestial observation and timekeeping, focused on the eastern horizon and the daily track of the sun and other moving bodies. The early Maya, now fully engaged and expert in the cycles of agriculture, were keen to formalize the rhythms and cycles of time into the fabric of their religion and worldview. I suspect that the massive changes reflect the existence of a powerful and exciting new ideology, a movement that involved the first codification of the cycles and rhythms of the cornfields into a more formalized Mesoamerican cosmology. At this time, the ritual calendars we know from later Maya culture developed their rhythm and complexity, and when institutions of the priesthood and esoteric knowledge assumed their first shape as something beyond the local. These religious specialists who oversaw the design of E Groups and other ambitious projects had to coordinate many people and resources to do so, and there is good reason to believe that these individuals were the distant precursors of the nobles and rulers who oversaw the later Maya world of history. As the Preclassic era continued into its later phase, the Late Preclassic, we begin to see these individuals take on a more visible role in art and architecture, as leaders within a highly complex and sociopolitical order.

The communities of the Middle Preclassic represent an expanding network of places and social groups, all of whom were keen to maintain connection through trade and an agreed sense of "cultural self." Here we have the first coalescence of elite Maya culture, and its presence spread widely throughout the lowlands. Ceramic types were widely shared among regions, and new waves of monumental construction began to take hold in both the central Peten and Yucatán. It was a widespread "boom" in new monumental construction, site planning, and design involving many major regional centers.[31] In the central region, the ruins at Nakbe stand out as particularly impressive, with many large architectural monuments clustered in three major groups, all linked by causeways. One of these ancient roads connects Nakbe to its neighbor, El Mirador, thirteen kilometers to the northwest, which we will see was an even more dominant center during the Late Preclassic. All these sites were built in the stony, karstic uplands, nestled among many low-lying areas known as *bajos*, probably seasonal lakes and swamps in ancient times. Understandably, the residents of Nakbe and other Middle Preclassic centers preferred to settle on the well-drained rocky high ground adjacent to these wetland environments, found throughout much of northern Peten and in southern Campeche. Unlike today, where access to water remains a constant challenge, this was a fertile environment once rich in agricultural potential and food resources, a desirable spot that attracted large populations through the Middle and Late Preclassic. We might consider this raised, wet terrain in the center of the peninsula as one type of "Maya heartland," a place where the civilization thrived and coalesced in its earliest centuries of existence.

After 700 BCE, Nakbe's planners erected large masonry platforms, some as high as eighteen meters. The site's overall plan represents a different vision from the earlier centers of Tabasco, such as Aguada Fénix, whose major platforms exhibited a more pronounced and rigid north–south orientation. Nakbe's clustered groups of architecture in contrast seem more organically placed around natural hillocks in an east–west arrangement, including its large E Group (also eastward looking). Significantly, Nakbe's early stone structures show the pervasive use of clay and thick lime plaster as a surface for monumental architecture. As we will soon see, the discovery of plaster represented a transformative technological leap forward, another result of living on an earth made of limestone.

Another tantalizing site of the Middle Preclassic has also only been recently reported, named Nixtun Ch'ich' (Plate 4). Located on the western shore of Lake Peten Itzá, just a short boat ride from the island of Tayasal (the center of Itzá power up to the end of the seventeenth century). Nixtun Ch'ich's beginnings are old indeed, predating the Mamom period. Around 800 BCE, we see its rapid and dramatic transformation from a village to a civic-ceremonial center, carefully planned and involving an impressive amount of labor and coordination. Today the site appears as numerous grassy mounds on a cattle ranch, and systematic surveys have revealed a densely packed arrangement of platforms and structures within a dense, grid-like plan. This layout is unique in the Maya world, although it shows some intriguing similarities to the rigid alignment seen in structures alongside Aguada Fénix and similar early architectural complexes.[32] A ball court and three E Groups are easily visible in the maps and lidar imagery, indicating the site's importance as a civic-ceremonial locale. Intriguingly, its three E groups are again all arranged on a single east–west axis (94 degrees 7′ from true north) that dominates the entire city's plan, with considerable symmetry in the features to the north and south of this principal line. Also found along this axis is a large artificial sunken area, thought by its excavators to be another key element of the city's ritual landscape, possibly as a ceremonial sinkhole, a "cave-like portal to a watery underworld."[33]

Nixtun Ch'ich' must have been an attractive place for settlement, given its setting on the breezy shoreline of the largest water feature of the central Maya lowlands. And it lasted for many centuries, well into the Late Preclassic era, before it was abandoned, like so many other precocious sites. Two thousand years later, the ruins of Nixtun Ch'ich' became the site of ceremonial veneration during the Late Postclassic. It is tempting to think that Nixtun Ch'ich' may have been the ancestral locale for later historical kingdoms of the Lake Peten Itza region, such as the Classic court of Ik'a' and the Itza' of the Postclassic.

The momentous leveling off and construction at Nitin Ch'ich' around 800 BCE can be interpreted as yet another example of a massive "public works" project, maybe similar in broad outline to what we see happening in Aguada Fénix and other sites where "place-making" appears to have been a prime motivation. As we have seen, another significant example is Cival, to the east of Nixtun Ch'ich'. It was another Mamom (Middle Preclassic) center where we find massive earth-moving in action, clearly with the intention of clearing and making space for people and monumental architecture. Around 800–700 BCE, a small natural hill was chosen for this new center, leveled and filled in to create a

500-square-meter "mesa," with an E Group complex in its center. Like that of Nixtun Ch'ich', Cival's plan also shows a strong alignment along an east–west axis, no doubt oriented toward sunrises and sunsets. A similar complex of similar age has also been documented at nearby Nakum, and there are no doubt others to be found.

EL MIRADOR

Around 300 BCE, we begin to see the development of larger urban sites with massive architectural designs and perhaps even a "state-level" political organization. These transformations were not unique to the Maya. Formative Mesoamerica had long been a breeding ground for civilization in many regions, seeing the rapid growth of Olmec centers in the Isthmus of Tehuantepec and of Zapotec civilization in the Valley of Oaxaca. The lowland Maya nevertheless stand out from the crowd, I think, given the rapidity and scale of the changes we see over these six or seven centuries—the blink of an eye in historical or archaeological terms. We should remind ourselves that during this short span, Maya culture developed out of a semi-sedentary existence into what can reasonably be described as a type of urban cosmopolitanism, from building small clusters of houses here and there to the construction of imposing, sky-reaching monuments to gods and ancestors (Figure 3.5). Along the way the basic outlines of Maya civilization, including its elite political institutions, art, power structures, and cosmology, fell into place. Still, the Late Preclassic remains very much ahistorical for us, known only through its visible archaeological remains and by our own extrapolations back from the Classic period that came directly after.

The most impressive of all Late Preclassic Maya centers was El Mirador, not far from its slightly earlier predecessor, Nakbe. The archaeological site and its architecture are so large that it is difficult to excavate deeply or thoroughly. From what we can discern after several decades of investigation and surveys, by about 300–200 BCE, El Mirador succeeded its close neighbor Nakbe as the dominant regional center and perhaps the largest city of its time in all of Mesoamerica.

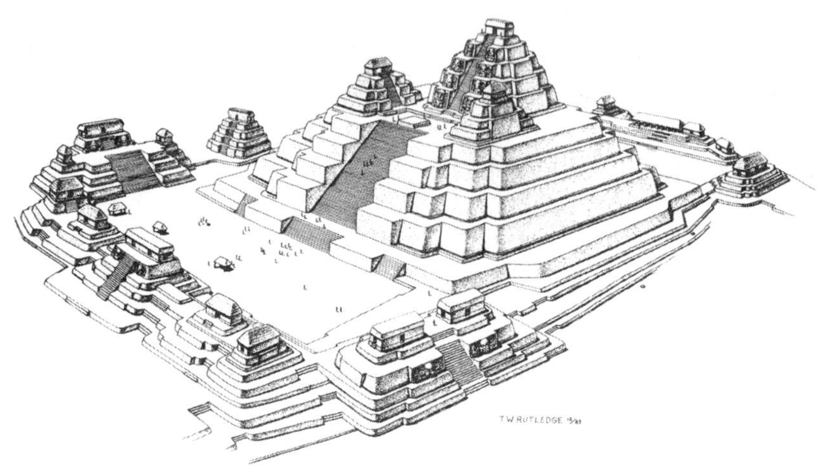

FIGURE 3.5. Reconstruction view of the El Tigre temple complex at El Mirador, Guatemala, ca. 100 BCE. Drawing by Terry Rutledge, courtesy of Richard Hansen.

During the Late Preclassic, El Mirador became the hub of a regional network of major sites connected by wide causeways, many crossing what were once lush wetlands. The region defined by the causeways is immense, situated at the very center of the entire Yucatán Peninsula (Map 2).

Two major architectural groups define the eastern and western parts of El Mirador, the largest being the Danta complex, consisting of a large plaza, another E Group, and stepped terraces that reach a pyramid standing over seventy meters (200 feet) above the surrounding terrain. Endless buildings, most untouched by archaeologists, run for kilometers in all directions. It is an awe-inspiring place, immense even as a tree-covered ruin today. In its heyday, around 100 BCE or so, its Danta architectural complex would have been one of the largest monumental constructions anywhere in the world. No other place in all of Mesoamerica was comparable in size and dramatic presentation, not even the great city of Teotihuacan, which was still in the early centuries of its own long development. Indeed, it is possible that El Mirador and other imposing precocious Maya centers were inspirations for Teotihuacan's own sense of monumental scale, which emerged generations later, well after 100 CE. Most of El Mirador's fuller, deeper development remains obscure, buried under meters and meters of construction, awaiting archaeological investigation. But its roots surely go well back to Mamom times and even earlier.[34]

At El Mirador and at other Late Preclassic centers, we see the emergence of triadic temples—typically a prominent pyramid with a principal shrine at its top flanked by two other smaller structures facing one another, forming a patio or courtyard with one open end. The function of these arrangements is unclear, but it is likely that they reflect a great interest in the meaning of the number three in early religion and cosmology. We see this more clearly indicated in later sources, where Late Classic temples symbolized the three realms of the cosmos—the sky, the earth, and the underworld—and the divine ancestors and patron deities who inhabited those realms. It is possible that the triadic groups in Preclassic architecture show the early stages of this same quintessentially Maya cosmology.

There are seven or more causeways that radiate out of El Mirador head out toward distant "islands" with ancient settlement and monumental buildings, forming a large regional network of closely connected centers (Map 2). Nakbe itself stands at the end of one prominent roadway heading south. The longest of all the roads runs fifteen kilometers southward to the ruins of Tintal and then another fifteen kilometers from there to a newly discovered site called Balamnal. All these sites have impressive E Groups and triadic complexes. The area covered by El Mirador and its road network is close to 2,000 square kilometers—roughly that of Japan's Tokyo Prefecture today (of course, with a far less dense population).[35] The western part of "greater" El Mirador is dominated by low-lying *bajos,* or what were probably seasonal lakes or swamps in Preclassic times, while karstic uplands lie to the east. El Mirador and Tintal are both situated along the transition zone between these areas, taking advantage of water resources and developing sophisticated irrigation methods for intensive agriculture. Unlike today, it must have been a lush, watery world.

Its sheer size and presence on the landscape leave little doubt that El Mirador was a true "center"—the capital of *something.* We probably will

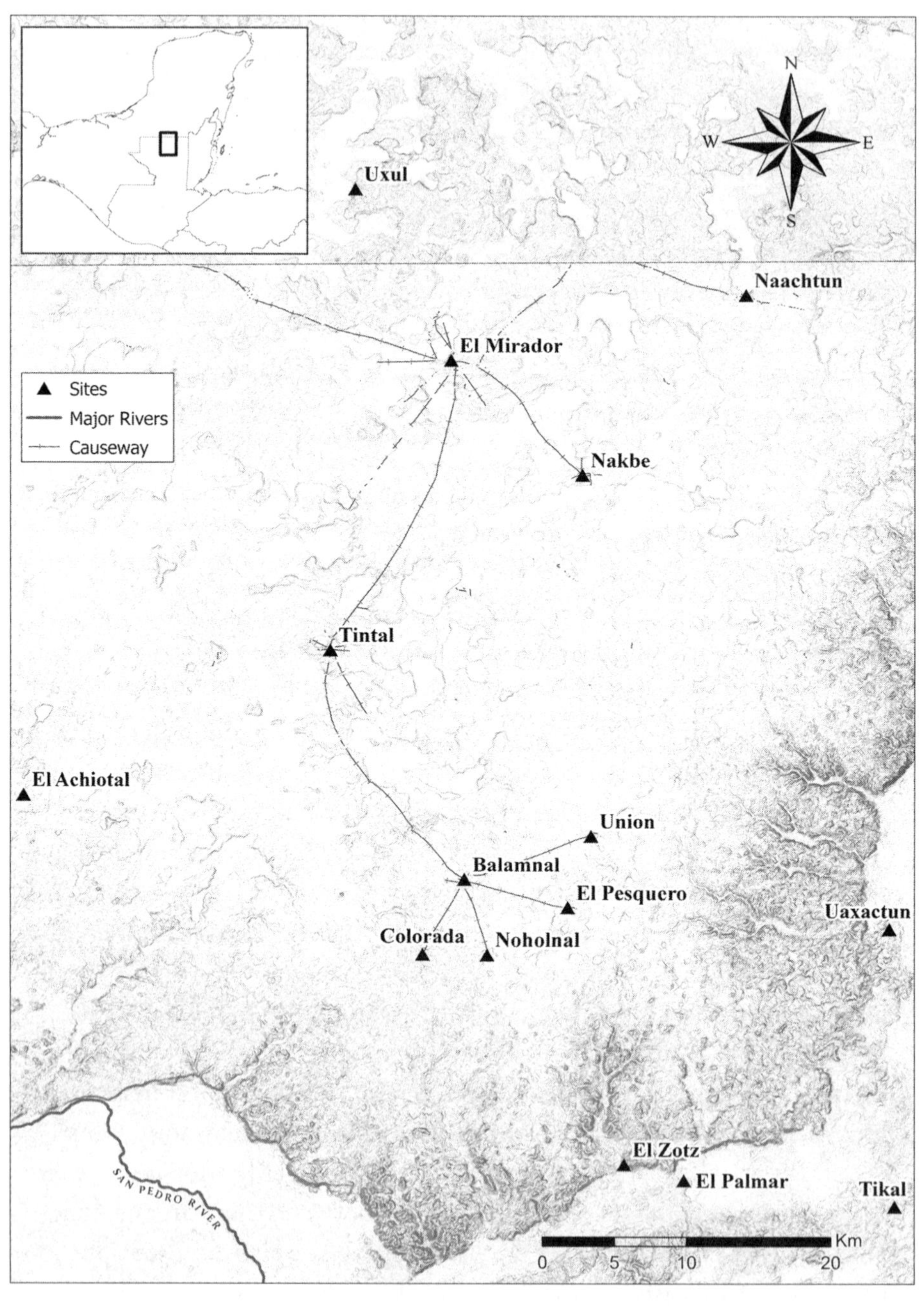

MAP 2. The causeway network of El Mirador, Late Preclassic era (ca. 100 BCE).

never know the details of its political and social structure, however, faced with the lack of history that surrounds the ruins today. (Then again, we long assumed this was the case for the Classic period.) A few sculpted monuments have been found among the plazas and pyramids, but these bear no discernable dates nor any legible texts. We can only surmise that after 300 BCE, it was a religious and political locale of great influence. It is likely that the major nearby centers such as Nakbe and Tintal were powerful centers in their own right, yet they were tethered by roadways to the more centralized place of El Mirador. The construction of any one of these sites, and of the roads that connected them, required a tremendous amount of labor investment and time as well as close coordination. And like the large public works projects that we see in the Middle Preclassic, we can surmise that this labor involved contributions of many diverse people, social units, and extended kin groups within the wider community.

Were there "kings" at El Mirador? Possibly, but as mentioned earlier, whatever sort of centralized power existed there in the Late Preclassic, it seems different from what came a few centuries later, when the rhetoric of public-facing art was centered on historical rulers. There surely were rulers of some sort within the network of El Mirador, presumably members of a closely knit class of elites who were perhaps closely related. They may have been *ajaws,* to use the Maya term for someone of high rank, but "kings" or "queens" may be too strong a word. It was the greatest of the early Maya states, yet it remains hard to gauge just how far its power and influence extended beyond its surroundings, in the karstic uplands and *bajos* of the central peninsula.[36]

The ideological cohesion among El Mirador and its contemporaries is noteworthy. We see this through a unified visual culture, with its codified iconography and early uses of hieroglyphic writing, which was well established by this time. This need not imply a large-scale centralized political system, however. During the Late Classic, nearly a thousand years later, the political landscape was terribly fragmented and in constant conflict, yet we still see a surprising amount of ideological and cultural cohesion among those elite courts, probably because many were all closely related by family, as we will see. The art and messaging of the Late Preclassic were even more standardized, with remarkably consistent forms of ceramics, architectural forms, plaster masks, and iconography. It would be difficult to read too much into this in terms of political structure and the centralization of authority. There were many rulers and many centers of power, with El Mirador standing out in its scale and ambition. And the El Mirador region was not the only center of political influence and power during the Late Preclassic. The entire Maya lowlands were dotted with significant sites exhibiting large, monumental architecture in the very same style, some probably regional centers or even political capitals.

El Mirador, Tintal, Nakbe, and several other Preclassic sites in the central region were later reoccupied, after centuries of abandonment. Elite households dating to the Late Classic, after 600 CE, have been found at these locations, representing ruling lineages who perhaps wanted to establish a connection with the grandeur of what were even then ancient ruins, some already a thousand years old. I suspect that these pilgrims were descendants of the original inhabitants of those places, but we cannot be sure. They constructed large residences and courtyards adjacent to the old monuments and refurbished some of the old temples for their own ceremonies. By and large, they did not construct their own separate temples. Many of these elites were buried in these small "places" or residences, often with some of the finest ceramics of the Late Classic period, known widely as "codex style."[37] Most of these were looted in the 1960s and '70s, but they may provide fascinating clues about the history and political identity of the region in the far deeper past.

One of these Late Classic nobles was a man named Yopat Bahlam, who in the eighth century ruled over a community established among the ruins of Nakbe. His name appears on several ceramic sherds recovered there and on several looted whole vessels in the codex style, all bearing his name and titles. He nearly always takes the honorific *k'uhul 'chatahn' winik*, "the holy man of 'Chatahn.'" (The reading of the "Chatahn" glyph is still problematic, so we use it only as a term of reference here.) Chatahn was a polity of importance in very early Maya history—its first mention comes around 200–300 CE—but we have a hard time placing it in space and time. Its mentions cluster around this same area of northern Peten, in texts on ceramics recovered from Nakbe and El Mirador, but also with mentions at nearby Calakmul, Uxul, and El Achiotal. While all date to the Classic period, there is a sense of great antiquity to "Chatahn" based on the places where the name occurs. I and others have even considered the possibility that it was the name of a place or of a dynasty that existed before the rise of the great Classic cities. It is indeed tempting to see "Chatahn" (however we eventually decipher it) as the name of the polity that was associated with ancient El Mirador and its network, but, again, we lack the contemporary sources to confirm this.[38]

To the north, in Yucatán, other major Late Preclassic centers also emerged and influenced their neighbors, and some may have even rivaled El Mirador (only two hundred miles to the south) in power and significance. After the demise of earlier major centers of the Middle Preclassic, such as Xocnaceh and Poxila, the political and ritual landscape of the region rearranged itself, and new centers emerged as key players around 200 BCE. Among them were Ake, Dzilam, and Izamal, located not far from the northern coast. All shared a distinctive style of megalithic architecture.[39] Izamal is today a charming town of colonial buildings, churches, and large, ancient pyramids. During the Late Preclassic and Early Classic periods, Izamal stood out as one of the largest urban sites of the north, its stone architecture rivaling that of El Mirador in scale. It maintained a special place in the Maya world for centuries thereafter, and today the many stages of its rich archaeology and history can be taken in all at once, layered one atop another. Later chronicles tell us that before the Spanish invasion, Izamal had been one of the most important pilgrimage centers for the Maya of Yucatán, its name originally being *Itzamnail*, "Place of Itzamna," named for the celestial creator deity. Later the Franciscan order chose Izamal as its own center of authority and religious pilgrimage, appropriating the ancient center for the new cult of the Virgin Mary, still venerated today as the patron saint of Yucatán. The huge monastery dominates the town today, built atop an immense masonry platform that dates to the Late Preclassic, with even earlier foundations. It is likely that Izamal was one of the great early Maya centers of Yucatán, and to see its importance in early colonial history is remarkable. Alongside the historical and cultural ruptures of the Maya past, Izamal shows there was there was functional continuity as well.

THE FOUR DIRECTIONS

Our awareness of Preclassic Maya religion and ideology was given a surprising boost in 2001, with the discovery of the magnificent wall paintings at San Bartolo, a remote site located also in northern Guatemala, well east of El Mirador.[40] At the time, it was a place completely new to archaeologists, although (as is usually the case) it had long been known to local chicleros, loggers, and, inevitably, the looters who probed its pyramids in search of tombs. An archaeological project began there in 2003 to find out more. Tunneling over the ensuing years revealed a richly painted room of nine by four meters with stunning imagery and iconography (Plate 5). These scenes represented numerous vignettes of Maya creation mythology, and they anticipate many of the characters and themes we know well from the later Classic period. The room was not a temple shrine but rather an open and accessible chamber at ground level behind the pyramid and probably meant to be viewed by anyone standing outside in one of the five window-like doors. We suspect it was a place where people could see and ponder the narratives of world creation without entering the small, cramped shrines above. Our current thinking is that the mural chamber was painted between 100 BCE and the year 0, perhaps in anticipation of a major calendrical event.

Two painted walls were found still in place, while two others had been intentionally bashed in by the ancient Maya when they made a new construction. Several years of digging brought out over seven thousand fragments of plaster bearing remains of the mural program. Further excavations into the pyramid also revealed another surprise: very early evidence of writing. The mural paintings contain several short lines of hieroglyphs that clearly label some of the actors and deities portrayed. They look to be names and titles, and while often difficult to read, one or two fragments of texts clearly show early versions of the sign for *ajaw*, "ruler, noble person." This is a direct indication that there were individuals of high rank in Preclassic society, confirming our long-held suspicions about the rise of hierarchy and rulership in this period.

The main mural chamber displays a fully developed style of art, clearly the end result of centuries of development and refinement. Enough is preserved to show a gorgeous array of mythical figures and endless fine details—the Maize God, a turtle in primordial waters, or human babies bursting forth from a bottle gourd (probably representing the creation of humanity). One of the main protagonists of the mural's iconographic program is the fantastical bird we call the "Principal Bird Deity," represented several times throughout the narrative scene (Figure 3.6). It has a large wingspan, a prominent tail, and the distinctive facial markings of a celestial god. Its talons are massive, and its crest-like head suggests that it may have been inspired by the harpy eagle, the largest avian predator of the neotropical Americas. On one of its wings, we often see the symbol for sun, and on the other the symbol for night. The deity's ancient Maya name was perhaps Yax Kokaj Mut (cited in later historical sources), and there is little doubt that this great bird is an animated representation of the sunlit sky and perhaps an early version of the solar eagle found in many indigenous American

FIGURE 3.6. The Principal Bird Deity, symbol of the radiant sky. Late Preclassic and Late Classic images. Drawings by Heather Hurst and the author.

stories of world creation. On one of the walls, the bird descends from the sky and then alights on four trees, each associated with a world direction. The theme is the establishment of the four quarters of space and of time, the so-called year-bearers of the Mesoamerican solar year. The great eagle is a foundational figure of Maya and Mesoamerican myth, and its image is found in much of Late Preclassic art. Apart from San Bartolo, we see its representation in a great many architectural masks, with examples known from Nakbe, Cival, and Cerros in coastal Belize. Eventually, for the Maya, the great bird would become a symbol of the kingship during the later Classic period.

Another prominent figure in the mural's narrative is a person, clearly a ruler, who sits perched atop a high scaffold, approached by a caped man holding up an elaborate headdress. It is an unmistakable scene of crowning, a motif that appears again centuries later in the stone monuments of the Classic period and surely a good indication that rulership and authority were well in place by the first century BCE. Still, the nature of power depicted at San Bartolo may have been a bit different from what we know from the later Classic period. The named kings and queens from those later dynasties tended to trace their own dynastic origins a few centuries back to the period that came *after* the Late Preclassic, around the second or third century CE. Whereas some speculate that all the basic outlines of Classic kingship were developed in the Late Preclassic, I prefer to see more of a disjunction between the two periods, with the Preclassic as essentially a "pre-dynastic" era. Authority figures were well in place, surely, and they would have played central roles in the planning and operation of the massive civic ceremonial "parks" such as Aguada Fénix, Cival, and El Mirador. The art and visual culture of the time nevertheless indicates that these early *ajaws* were not the protagonists of such ritual but perhaps the facilitators. Instead, we see in Preclassic iconography a consistent emphasis outward and upward, to the celestial deities, the Maize God, Chahk, and other animate forces of nature. It was a cosmologically oriented religion already centuries old by the Late Preclassic, rooted in the earlier transformations of the first towns and temples. I suspect that this conservative arrangement could not easily accommodate the changes in individual authority and rulership that came centuries later, as *ajaws* took center stage. The San Bartolo murals place rulers within a wider scheme of creation and cosmology, but the human ruler still seems a rather minor participant in the whole mix. The impetus of later Classic period politics and ideology, and the history that played out after 200 CE, was the very different idea that individual rulers and their lineages were themselves the embodiments of natural forces and had the ability to act upon them. The rulers we know from later Maya history were very much seen as cosmic agents who could embody and replicate the actions and patterns of the deities who created and renewed the world. Among other transformations, the Late Preclassic represents a centuries-long era where this arrangement was being tested and negotiated, as rulers themselves were increasingly celebrated as the main protagonists of ritual and cosmological events. For me, the murals of San Bartolo and other Late Preclassic artworks signal this melding of political and religious themes and, given what came later, perhaps even an emerging tension between them.

Like other buildings of the time, the pyramid of San Bartolo resembled a series of stacked terraces with a central staircase on one side, all covered in thick plaster. Flanking the steps were large masks richly modeled and painted. Its facade was also richly decorated in modeled stucco. We find this architectural design template throughout the Maya lowlands during the Late Preclassic and fairly standardized in its overall form. Many terrace masks are three or four meters in height, truly monumental artworks on their own. What was the purpose or message? It is difficult to say, but we can reasonably think that they served to identify gods or ancestors associated with their respective buildings. In a well-preserved example from Calakmul, the upper facade shows Chahk, the rain deity, descending from the horizontal band of the heavens (Figure 3.7). The platform below was faced with large masks representing the Maize God, whose face emerges from the open mouth of a turtle, representing the earth. Some seem almost hieroglyphic in their composition, pointing to their possible roles as conveying the proper names of these mythic or historical characters. (Hints of this come from later parallels in the Classic period.) It seems miraculous that such plaster artworks are ever preserved, but in fact they are common, and more seem to be discovered with each new excavation. For

FIGURE 3.7. Virtual reconstruction of Structure II-C, Calakmul, north facade. The upper register represents the storm god Chahk, flanked by descending lightning bolts. The two heads below represent the Maize God within the earth. Digital reconstruction by Benjamin Esqueda Lazo de la Vega and Daniel Salazar Lama.

this we owe our thanks to Maya architects, who would routinely build on earlier edifices. As they developed and changed over time, Maya buildings became "layer cakes" of construction that would preserve early versions of temples and their painted plaster decorations, often showing remarkable detail. These ancient techniques provide a boon to archaeologists today, who when digging or tunneling can track construction histories of a single location over many centuries, if not millennia. Each steep, terraced pyramid developed after 400 BCE or so represented an artificial mountain, or *witz*. In building them on large foundation platforms and around spacious plazas, Maya architects created their own sacred landscapes of symbolic mountains, valleys and cornfields.

HINTS OF PRECLASSIC HISTORY

In Izamal, Yucatán, a few blocks to the north of the great sixteenth-century monastery with its Preclassic foundation, lies another great ancient construction, much more exposed and noticeable as an ancient

Maya pyramid. No church stands atop it. This has been known from colonial times as the pyramid of K'inich K'ak'mo, a name usually interpreted to be an alternate name for the Maya sun god, K'inich Ajaw. I suspect, however, that it may hold a tantalizing clue of local pre-conquest history. The name clearly incorporates the honorific term K'inich, "solar," but the other elements sound very much like royal names we know from deeper Maya history. Here I am thinking of K'inich Yaxk'uk'mo' of Copan or K'inich Ahkalmo'nahb of Palenque, among many others. K'inich K'ak'mo' means "Solar Fire-Macaw," and the form of the name suggests that it derives from a historical figure from Izamal's very deep past.[41] The pyramid's connection to a remote historical person, perhaps a local ruler of the Classic period or even earlier, is pure speculation on my part, but I have to wonder if it reflects a long-term memory of the ancient city and a ruler. Perhaps he is buried there, deep in the upper pyramid. (It has never been tunneled or deeply probed.) Alternatively, the name may also point to the pyramid once being a place of ancestral veneration to an illustrious historical figure of the past. Izamal provides a tantalizing hint that even in the colonial period of the sixteenth century, elements of deeper history were in the consciousness of the local Maya, living in a major pilgrimage center with pyramids and platforms that were already nearly two thousand years old.

Ancestor worship was a key practice within Maya religion, and it is through its lens that we see hints of other historical people who were venerated centuries after their lives. One recent archaeological find from Uaxactun indicates that ancestor worship was well in place in the Late Preclassic, setting the foundations for what was to come. In 2016, archaeologists were probing a Preclassic temple complex and discovered a modest ritual deposit or "cache" set into the plaza floor in front of a pyramid. It was a small offering consisting of ceramic bowls and ceremonial implements and dating to about 0–100 CE, so close to the end of the Late Preclassic.[42] But unique among the things they found was a stone awl-like device, carved with a curious human figure. The smooth shaft of the object was incised with a band of hieroglyphs, all in an early style. The text describes the offering itself, including the phrase "it is raised up," a term of dedication. But most importantly it provides a series of names, basically a list of people. Each name is preceded by the revealing title *mam*, "grandfather, elder, ancestor," probably as an honorific expression, "Elder So-and-So." The three listed names remain hard to read, but there can be little doubt that they refer to a triad of revered ancestors, pointing to the offering perhaps being dedicated to their memory. It is possibly no accident that the dedicatory offering where this awl-like object was found was a large triadic compound typical of much Late Preclassic architecture. The glyphs offer an important clue as to the "elders" or gods venerated in that locale.

Mentions of royal ancestors continued in the later Classic period as well, alluding to people and events very deep in time, back to the Late Preclassic. These are rare, however, just a handful of inauguration dates or citations of "first kings" who seem very remote figures, even at the time the Classic-era texts were written. They reveal how later Maya had a keen sense of their own deep history, which must have been written in far more detail in their screen-fold books. We can easily imagine "antiquarian libraries" in Classic times, with old manuscripts carefully preserved and passed down over the generations, much as we know from medieval Europe, the Near East, or China. The oldest and most famous manuscript from the ancient Maya, the *Dresden Codex,* was collected in the early 1500s but was painted about four centuries earlier, a testimony to the Maya fascination with maintaining records and the written word. It is hardly a stretch to think that around 800 CE, say, similar antiquarian books were kept, some quite ancient, copied and recopied by meticulous scribes. These would have been the raw materials for preserving and conveying the deepest awareness of Maya history.

At Tikal, one of the major players in the history of Classic times, we find artworks and inscriptions that mention an illustrious ancestor named of Sakhixmut ("White Jaguar Bird") (Figure 3.8, left). He was a ruler of mythical history, described as a "Holy Lord of Mutul." This is the same royal emblem title held by the later Tikal kings from Classic history, indicating that Sakhixmut was considered an ancient "king," even in the eighth century CE. What is odd is that the dates that Tikal's scribes gave to him seem fantastical, the stuff of myth. He reportedly celebrated a great station of the Maya calendar—a rare ending of the bak'tun cycle (5.0.0.0.0)—on December 9, 1143 BCE. On that day, "he raised the stone," describing the dedication of a monument and, perhaps in a mythological sense, an event in the earth's creation. But he also celebrated other stations in the calendar, dedicating ceremonial stones in 456 BCE and 157 BCE. Like Methuselah of the Old Testament, Sakhixmut's life is said to have spanned nearly one thousand years. His retrospective chronology is couched squarely in myth, but the numbers themselves reveal something about Maya ideas of history and prehistory. For example, it is significant that Sakhixmut's very first event fell in 1143 BCE, which corresponds reasonably well to the initial appearance of major monumental constructions in the Maya lowlands and to the transformative time when we see the first substantial, permanent villages. I am tempted to think that the Tikal historians who wrote about Sakhixmut in the eighth century were recalling the name of a remembered figure of that time, lost in Tikal's "real history" yet real nonetheless.[43]

Another very ancient person we read about comes from Palenque, named Ukohkanchan ("Snake's Spine") (Figure 3.8, right). There he is cited in the beautifully sculpted tablet that was housed in the Temple of the Cross, dedicated in 692 CE. The inscription cites many of the ancestors of Palenque's royal house, named Bakel, the first of whom was Ukohkanchan. The chronology of the text makes clear that he was crowned as king over sixteen centuries earlier, in 966 BCE, at the age of twenty-six. The tablet goes on to cite the names of other Palenque rulers, all leading up to the contemporary king K'inich Kanbahlam, who commissioned and dedicated the temple. Other Palenque kings mention Ukohkanchan as well, citing him as a foundational figure.[44]

FIGURE 3.8. Two names from early mythic history: Sakhixmut of the Mutul dynasty (left) and Ukohkanchan of the Bakel dynasty (right). Drawings by the author.

As with Sakhixmut of Tikal, my guess is that Ukohkanchan of Palenque was a real historical person. There is no question that the scribes of the seventh century saw Ukohkanchan as having one foot in myth and another in history, for in the narrative of the Tablet of the Cross he occupies a transitional role between the patron gods who lived in the far deeper past, and the earliest kings whose dynasty was founded in the fourth century CE. (The historical dynasty of Bakel began then with a man named K'uk'bahlam.) Ukohkanchan was of legendary history, a category we should perhaps define carefully in contrast to the history of memory and of precise recordkeeping, even if the lines were blurred by the ancient Maya themselves. And like his Tikal counterpart, Ukohkanchan's timing in the tenth century BCE would put him roughly around the time of the first monumental sites. They are the first discernable people of importance in "history," and they surely were connected to the major changes we see archaeologically for the same era, including the rise of monumentality, elite status, and a highly standardized art and script. The emerging lords—it again may be a stretch to call them "kings"—were actors in an increasingly complex political world about which we know very little. They likely saw themselves as participants within the broader cosmological and solar themes we see in ceremonial architecture, such as the all-important E Groups, focused on the cyclicality of days and years.

By the Late Preclassic, such public spaces became political stages for the displays of ritual power, often centered on ideas of ancestral veneration, resurrection, and rebirth. This all helped set the stage for a new dynastic ideology that would develop in later centuries during the Classic period, where individual rulers expanded their roles as active agents of cosmological renewal and change, displaying their rituals on sculpted monuments for all to see. In the Preclassic, there is no contemporary history of such people, and compared to the later Classic period, it seems to have been a highly impersonal world. If the art and monuments are anything to go on, the Preclassic was also a time showing a remarkable unity of purpose, from place to place and region to region. This sense of relative cultural unity during the Late Preclassic is conveyed by a regularity in architectural design and planning, at least when compared to the more checkered, balkanized political system we see later. The plans and layouts of its cities adhere to a certain deep-seated rigidity, focused on the monumental scale of sacred architecture, the clustering of temples in well-defined "cells" and groups, and the straight-line alignments of massive causeways. Its artistic production was remarkably cohesive in its vision and scope as well, and indeed it is nearly impossible to see much difference in the architectural styles among various disparate sites. Similarly, the pottery of the Late Preclassic (the Chicanel sphere, which postdates Mamom) seems highly regular from place to place in the central area, with only a few regional variations found among sites in Belize and the rest of the Peten.

What does this imply? Without any historical perspective, all we can discern is an elite world that was highly unified, reflecting a tightly bound intellectual culture. This does not necessarily imply any large-scale political unification. My sense is that the sheer number of Preclassic sites with massive temple shrines and monumental architecture reflects the many lords and rulers who all bought into a similar ideology, sharing an expression of elite identity within an extremely close network of people and places. The predynastic idea of kingship, if it existed as such, was different from what we would later see in the Classic period. In this I draw a somewhat different conclusion than my colleagues David Freidel and Linda Schele, who a few decades ago argued that the beginnings sacred kingship were visible in the messaging and in the specialized iconography of Late Preclassic architecture. Whereas they preferred to see continuity in the institution of Maya kingship from the Preclassic to the Classic, I see a subtle disjunction indicating that the political structures of the two eras were different. The iconography of deities and cosmological structures was surprisingly unchanging, it is true, but dynasts themselves were not featured in a conspicuous way as part of that sacred context until around 100–200 CE. This is not to say there were no rulers, but that the expression of sacred power focuses constantly on the sun, the sky, forces of nature. The ancestors seem to be the real and primary actors within that mix.

THE EARLY COLLAPSE

The demise of many Late Preclassic centers occurred around 100–200 CE, marking a major systemic collapse of a political order some six or seven centuries before the more famous fall of the Classic Maya. Major construction ceased at cities both large and small, including at El Mirador, Nakbe, San Bartolo, and others, and they were unable to sustain their populations. After the cessation of major construction, small populations continued to live at many of these places, including El Mirador, but the "downtown" areas of the cities were largely abandoned. At sites outside the El Mirador network, such as Uaxactun and Tikal, we may see a smoother transition into the Classic period, with more direct historical continuities. The differences in how early Maya cities faced the challenges of their time are not easy to explain, but they could be partially understood by different local environments and access to resources.

Water, as always, seems to have been key. I think it significant that a large watery vignette showing herons and other freshwater fauna decorates one of the major structures of El Mirador, perhaps showing something of the environment that once surrounded it (Plate 6). Paleo-environmental studies show that water access was an important problem for many of the early cities of the central zone. By 200 CE, the lush wetlands and lakes adjacent to El Mirador and Tintal had dried up, becoming seasonal swamps—the *bajos* we see today. This was probably due to extensive soil erosion and overexploitation of the water by local populations. (Even today, lack of reliable water around this region presents a major challenge for archaeological projects.) The change may have been due to intensive deforestation during the Late Preclassic as well as a drier climate overall and the feedback loop between these two individual factors. The central region that holds the most impressive Late Preclassic remains, and the densest early populations, was also perhaps one of the most fragile and vulnerable natural environments in the region, where human impact had the most detrimental effects.[45]

Maya history is punctuated with similar cycles of occupation and abandonment, on both local and widespread scales. We should recall that long before the burst of urban activity after 500 BCE, the great platforms and gathering spaces of Tabasco also had been left to the elements, having served their own purpose before about 800 BCE. The gargantuan structures at Aguada Fénix and Buenavista lasted no more than two or three centuries in their own day before abandonment. Our terminology remains inadequate for characterizing that very first iteration of Maya culture, but we might think of those places as representative of a "Pre-Preclassic," a first wave of activity along a sequence of many rises and falls to come. Understanding the end and collapse of the Preclassic, while difficult, may well have involved similar dynamics, a Maya sense of civilizational "shelf life" we will examine near the end of this book as we take a closer look at how Classic Maya culture ended and transformed in the ninth century CE. For now, we should simply acknowledge that there was never one such "collapse" in Maya history, but that it came and went over the course of deep history, each followed by a partial reconfiguration of politics, art, and society.

The social and demographic rupture at the end of the Preclassic, while still obscure for us, influenced the later Maya ideas surrounding the cadences of history and its cycles, instilling a long-term awareness of how whole communities and cities could come and go. Many of the first dynastic centers of the Classic era arose not far from abandoned places that must have been understood as old yet still within historical memory. I would imagine that such a juxtaposition gave the early Maya a keen sense of their own deep past, of beginnings and ends, and of how communities could have their own lifespans. From this backdrop, the elites of the very Early Classic were eager to move ahead with a new ideology, embracing change and cyclicity as part of a new notion of how people and societies should maintain themselves. The Preclassic era instilled a strong underlying foundation for the later Maya, including a strong sense of history, with narratives of creation, foundation, and involving ancestral forebears who would long be evoked and celebrated, if imperfectly remembered, by their descendants.

Another idea that I take from the long view is the profound influence of the early Maya on their later Mesoamerican neighbors. Eager as they were to adopt new technologies and ways of subsistence after 1500 BCE, they were not always just passive recipients of culture emanating from the "Olmec," as some offspring of a "mother culture." Rather, my sense is that the early Maya were proactive participants and innovators on a larger network of ideas, ideologies, and practices that gave shape to Mesoamerica from the first centuries after 1200 BCE. Throughout the Middle and Late Preclassic, the lowland Maya were one of several cultures that contributed to the religious ideas that would later permeate the art and iconography of early rulership, even beyond the confines of the Maya world. The 260-day calendar may well have been one of these innovations that spread far and wide.

We see this at Izapa, for example, an important early site located far from the lowlands, in what is today southern Chiapas, on in the piedmont area of the Pacific coast. From about 200 BCE to 100 CE, its many stone monuments show the strong influence of what I take to be essentially lowland Maya art and iconography. Other important centers of the southern highlands of piedmont are similar in this regard, including Takalik Abaj and Kaminaljuyu. These were diverse places linguistically, not so solidly "Maya" in the sense of the lowland centers we have been discussing. Nevertheless, for a time, each of these important southern sites adopted for their own purposes a powerful visual ideology whose roots seem to have been in the Maya lowlands, forged in the Middle and Late Preclassic. Later Mesoamerican cultures in the Isthmus region, in Oaxaca, and in highland central Mexico expressed their own visual cultures, always indirectly aware of their eastern Maya neighbors and the cultural weight of history that surrounded them. Even as late as the fourteenth and fifteenth centuries, the Aztecs, who were always eager to couch themselves as an inheritor of a deep Mesoamerican past, developed an art and visual culture that channeled many of the same powerful sacred images, architectural forms, and religious ideas. Some of these we can track directly back to the Maya region. It might not always be a direct line of influence, but there is an old Maya legacy that left a long imprint on Mesoamerica's larger story.

PART II

Kabch'en

THE EARTH AND CAVES

CHAPTER 4

Dynasties

THE END OF the Preclassic saw the demise of many great centers of the old order, especially those in the uplands of the central Peten region, adjacent to the *bajos*, as well as in small, fertile valleys of southern Yucatán. Soon afterward, around 100 CE, there emerged a new political landscape with many smaller communities and, it seems, more dispersed centers of elite settlement than we once saw in the central Peten. And whereas there was once a noticeable "impersonality" in the complex art and iconography of the Late Preclassic, the art of the new era began to focus on new themes and on the powerful roles of individual rulers. By 200 CE, a new and vibrant flavor of Maya culture blossomed in the wake of El Mirador and its contemporaries, at places such as Uaxactun and Tikal, among others. Through the scattered monuments of this early time, and especially from later retrospective accounts, we can finally identify individual historical actors and the seats of power where they ruled. This was the beginning of what we call the "Classic" period, a time of regrouping and reformulation as a new elite culture came on the scene, expanded its influence, and set in motion many aspects of Maya civilization over the course of the next five or six hundred years.

We should keep in mind that this was an era of intense change and transformation throughout Mesoamerica, not just in the Maya region. In the distant highlands of central Mexico, Teotihuacan cemented its role as the behemoth urban space of Mesoamerica, its massive Sun and Moon pyramids constructed by 100–200 CE. It's no stretch of the imagination to see the changes in the Maya world connected in some way to those radical transformations in politics, economics, and society at Teotihuacan. The elite of Teotihuacan were clearly aware of the early Maya during this Preclassic-Classic transition, as revealed by ritual artifacts that have been found at the great highland city. The recognition was mutual, with rulers of Maya cities clearly aware of the emerging power and influence of Teotihuacan. In fact, it was in the third century that we begin to see strong archaeological evidence of Maya elites actually living in Teotihuacan, in the form of polychrome ceramics, jade, and other artifacts.[1] While our understanding of the early years of this long-distance relationship remains spotty and very incomplete, I suspect that the changes and convulsions of the Maya lowlands around 100 CE had some direct relationship with the quick rise of Teotihuacan as a majestic power and place of influence in highland Mesoamerica. Just a bit later, by the fourth century, we will see how Teotihuacan's rulers inserted themselves into the local politics of Uaxactun and Tikal in a very direct way.

The new arrangement of centers after 100 CE revolved around the emergence of several dynasties, probably mixing and coexisting with more established elite networks reaching back into the Preclassic. These powerful families did not emerge sui generis, out of nothing, and many probably had roots that could be traced back centuries to the old power structures. But the diversity of elites and their smaller centers in the Early Classic suggest that some powerful families were new, having gained power in the wake of the Late Preclassic collapse. The old and new elite lineages forged a novel system of political and social institutions, establishing the elite culture we know so well from the written sources of the Classic period. Or, perhaps better said, this was the time when such things are first visible to us, given the dramatic breakout of inscribed monuments that was soon to come.

Whereas several Preclassic centers were abandoned, at least temporarily, other communities managed to adapt to a rapidly changing landscape of the Early Classic, maintaining their traditional status as significant places of political power. Uaxactun was one such locale, as were also Naranjo and Calakmul, among others. (These sites will emerge as major players in later history.) Why some centers continued while others did not remains a puzzle, although, as mentioned earlier, a changing environment and the drying of the *bajos* were probably factors. If anything, this mixture of abandonment and continuity points to the deeper pattern of demographic and political adaptability throughout Maya history—a key topic of discussion to which we will return in our final chapter. All in all, we can envision the beginning of the Classic period as one of several "resets" along the greater Maya story, one in which the place of dynastic history and rulership becomes much more visible and assumes center stage.

Clues about politics and society during this transitional time are few. Hints of a change include an increased visibility of individual rulers on stelae, sometimes accompanied with text that provides names and honorific titles. One we have mentioned, *ajaw*, "ruler, noble," becomes especially prominent as a general term for anyone of authority and high rank. We find it cited alongside formal portraits of kingly ritual, showing historical individuals blended with elements of myth and religious iconography. One well-preserved example is the so-called Hauberg Stela, a small monument probably dating to the second or third century CE, probably from northern Guatemala. It shows a standing figure accompanied by a long hieroglyphic text, recounting the "first penance," or blood sacrifice, of an early prince or nobleman who has fused his identity with that of a solar deity (Figure 4.1). A new honorific title also appears in these Early Classic sources: *k'uhulajaw*, or "godly lord." We might interpret this as a title for a new sort of divine kingship, but it more likely specifies a role in which individual figures drew their political authority from their proximity and intimate connections to divine forces. This is certainly the message conveyed by the Hauberg Stela, whose text includes the earliest known example of this title. Unlike the nonpersonal representations of the Preclassic, rulers were now moving front and center in the art, shown as agents on the cosmic stage. This ideology began to crystalize into a new and energetic idea of power

FIGURE 4.1. The Hauberg Stela, showing a young ruler or prince in the guise of a deity. Drawing by Franco Rossi.

adopted by many ruling lineages that coexisted throughout the central lowlands. The new idea of kingship was one of several political, demographic, and religious developments that we can begin to discern in the earliest detailed history.[2]

It all played out in a political landscape less centralized than what we perceive during the Late Preclassic, in the time of El Mirador's apparent dominance over much of the Peten. To be cautious, this impression may arise from the lack of any historical context for that earlier era, making it seem more uniform in a way. All we can say with assurance is that a newly formulated dynastic culture emerged with the start of the Classic period, consisting of a network of power centers or regimes both large and small, many coalescing around the central Peten and the sites of Uaxactun and Tikal. Along with a new narrative focus on individual rulers, there arose a vibrant courtly and artistic culture, building on the old, established aesthetic foundations of the Preclassic. The arts and culture that had been forged during the Middle and Late Preclassic now merged with a more intimate, smaller-scale refinement. Architects of the Early Classic were no longer concerned with building on a massive scale, designing buildings that tended to be smaller elite households and palaces or modest modifications of earlier structures. Along the same lines, individual artisans, closely tied to the political networks of the time, seem to have adopted a newfound freedom to express their own designs, often with staggeringly creative results. This was true especially for elite ceramic wares, which after about 200 CE became awash in complex linework and iconography. These prized dishes held cacao beverages, tamales, and other foods, and the large size of some may point to the importance of feasting in forging connections among the new elites of the time. The new dynasties and elite lineages that emerged in this era had strong ties, and their close interactions and family connections set the stage for the narrative histories we read in later centuries.

RULERS OF MYTH AND HISTORY

As mentioned in the last chapter, several dynasties of the Classic period traced their origins to mythologized rulers of the deep past, some maybe based on real historical figures. At Arroyo de Piedra, a small site in southwestern Peten, one ruler noted that he was "the 65th in the sequence" of local lords, all associated with a kingdom on the shores of Lake Petexbatun. Needless to say, this line of kings must reach very far back in time. (For comparison, Japan's imperial line today recognizes 101 historical monarchs, reaching back nearly 1,500 years.) If we conservatively give this eight to ten centuries, we reach back in the Late Preclassic. If we take this record at face value, it points to the oldest dynasty from anywhere in Maya history.[3]

But here we are on shaky ground, with the near-impossible task of teasing apart myth from history. In terms of narrative, the Maya never saw much of a meaningful distinction between the two. To illustrate the fusion, we can turn to the inscriptions from the city of Naranjo (Sa'al), a large and important *kabch'en* (kingdom) of the Preclassic and Classic periods. One inscription from there dates to 593 CE and mentions a mythic hero, Ik'mihin, who was enthroned over 21,000 years earlier. Curiously, another Naranjo inscription mentions the same primordial founder in connection with a date 896,000 years in the past. These are contradictory sets of information, of course, and couched in purely mythic time. To complicate things further, a well-known historical king of Naranjo named K'ahk'tiliw Chanchahk (born in 688 CE) was designated as "the thirty-sixth successor" of Ik'mihin. Might this be a reliable historical statement? Perhaps. Given real lifespans and times on the throne, we should expect so many "successors" to cover something like eight or nine centuries. Still, time spans of 21,000 or 896,000 years associated with a single ancestral name reveal that the Classic Maya saw their dynastic "founders" as people of a mythic time, even sometimes as gods (*k'uh*). This leads me to suspect that Ik'mihin was a real person from remote history, hearkening back to a Late Preclassic era where temporal distance was already a bit blurry, subject to telescoping and contortion to fit the needs of narratives in later times. We need not take these records too literally, in other words, yet they probably reflect some degree of historical truth. If nothing else, these long narrative reaches into deep time show us how Maya historians looked back into the Preclassic. The foundations of many royal houses occurred around this time, with others emerging a few centuries later in the beginning of Classic era.[4]

A noticeable switch toward history and the new dynastic arrangements came in the first and second centuries CE, according to several later historical records. One noticeable hint of this comes from Pusilha, Belize, in a later inscription that looks back to the k'atun ending 8.2.0.0.0 (81 CE), although the nature of the event itself is obscure. At the site of Pol Box, close to Dzibanche and the seat of the Kanul kingdom, we read of a foundational episode event that took place a bit later in 141 CE. The specifics are unclear, but one suspects it may allude to the founding of the Kanul dynasty itself in the region.[5] Another prominent retrospective episode occurs on the k'atun ending at 8.6.0.0.0 (156 CE). Three different inscriptions at Copan and Pusilha (again) mention this one date as a distant historical remembrance, centuries in the past, yet some sort of foundational event. Clearly it had wide, regional significance to later Maya historians, but we know precious little about this episode, except for the tantalizing names of an ancient place. Both the 81 CE and 159 calendar cycles were said to have been commemorated at a place named Chihcha'. We have been unable to identify this name with any known archaeological site, and it is mentioned at a great many places, including Palenque, Copan, Tikal, and Dzibanche. The elusive Chihcha', wherever it was, may have held a special place in the deep historical consciousness of the Kanul dynasty, one of the great royal houses of the Classic period.[6]

One personal name stands out among these tantalizing remembrances of the mid-second century. According to several texts, the protagonist behind the events of 141 and 159 was "Foliated Ahau," using a nickname to describe his unreadable name glyph. Far from being a local dynast, he seems to have held singular importance as an early king, recognized by numerous later courts and royal families. Like other protagonists of retrospective dynastic history, he eventually assumed semi-mythic status, a personification of rulership in later centuries. His beautifully carved portrait may appear on a shell recovered from a Classic-era tomb at Dzibanche—the seat of the Kanuls (Figure 4.2). I suspect that many of the very early dynastic narratives of the Classic period pertain more to this eastern area than to the central Peten or to the El Mirador region.

Foliated Ahau occupies a foundational role like that of another murky figure from early history, named Uxyophun. He was another venerated

FIGURE 4.2. Portrait of an early Maya king from a carved shell, Dzibanche. Drawing by the author.

ancestor who emerged as a symbol of authority and early kingship, and it is possible that their identities were merged over time, if not the same from the outset. As an early historical figure, Uxyophun may have been viewed retrospectively as an initiator of the political order that lasted throughout much of the Classic period. A Palenque king in the eighth century displayed himself as a reincarnation of Uxyophun, implying in a complex narrative that the mythologized ruler was the embodiment of royal paper-cloth headbands and kingly attire—the idea of a "crown" personified. Clearly, the geographical spread of Uxyophun's mentions, from Palenque to Copan, and his deep mythological significance suggest that he was instrumental in the creation of Classic Maya kingship as we know it from later history, the embodiment of the idea of kingship itself.[7]

TIKAL AND UAXACTUN

Among the first dynastic names we can trace in Maya sources is Yax Ehbxok, named in Tikal's inscriptions as the founder of the local ruling line of Mutul (Figure 4.3). While there were more distant ancestral figures such as Sakhixmut, Yax Ehbxok seems to be the first in the sequence of historical rulers. Even though we lack any contemporary records of his reign, we can place him at the very remote beginnings of the Classic period. Unlike some other names we have considered up to now, there's little doubt he was a real person.[8] And thanks to the Maya interest in numbers, we know from later records that the kings and queens of the Classic era were placed in a precise sequential order, using Yax Ehbxok as the starting point. The great ruler Jasaw Chank'awil was his "twenty-sixth successor," his son Yik'in Chank'awil the twenty-seventh, and so on. With Yax Ehbxok as "the first," we can roughly surmise from the average span of average reigns that he lived no earlier than the first or second century CE.[9] The communities of Tikal and Uaxactun are significantly older, going back into the Middle Preclassic, so we might interpret Yax Ehbxok and similar founders of his time as representative of a new, Classic political dynastic order.[10]

Tikal's dynasty may have taken its name, Mutul, from an older place. This is suggested by the name sometimes used to refer to Tikal in ancient times, Yaxmutul, meaning "New Mutul," perhaps implying that some original Mutul was located elsewhere. Whatever the case, by Yax Ehbxok's time, Tikal was the center of a new and vibrant Classic kingdom, building on its old roots as a Late Preclassic center. His burial spot may have been excavated at Tikal, deep within the North Acropolis. The beginnings of this architectural complex can be traced even earlier to the Late Preclassic when it was conceived as a familiar-looking Triadic Group. By the first and second century CE, this transformed into an ever-growing series of ancestral shrines, many housing tombs. The earliest was Burial 85, found deep

FIGURE 4.3. Name hieroglyph of Yax Ehbxok (left), founder of the Mutul dynasty, and Mutul emblem title (right). Drawings by the author.

within the very center of the complex by the explorers of the University of Pennsylvania, who were surprised by its early ceramics found within. They suggested a date around 150 CE, which would fit around the time of Yax Ehbxok. (The identification of it as his burial, while compelling, is purely circumstantial.) Resting on a bundle of bones was an extraordinary greenstone mask representing the face of a ruler. Across his forehead was the paper-cloth band of Jun Ajaw, adorned on its form with an abstracted representation of a maize flower. This is one of the earliest representations we have of the Maya "crown" called *sakhun*, which came to be an important symbol of elite status. Its connection to maize can be traced centuries earlier to the iconography of the Olmec, who featured images of the animate maize god in jade and other prized objects. In Maya mythology this headbanded figure retained a somewhat different mythological role as Jun Ajaw, the headband twin and hunter who was another model of rulership. Burial 48's jade portrait wearing such a headband is a revealing sign of a new ideology, of the arrival of kings and dynasties in Maya history.

There were several other early Tikal kings after Yax Ehbxok, mostly lost to history. (The founder's name appears several times in the later sources; others' not so much.) But we can discern over the next couple of centuries how Tikal's power and influence rose quickly and may even have surpassed that of Uaxactun after 250–300 CE. It was at this time that Tikal expanded its own massive early E Group complex known as the Mundo Perdido, located a short distance from the North Acropolis. It far surpassed Uaxactun's E Group in size, and at 300 CE it would have been among the largest architectural monuments anywhere in the Maya region. As we will see in the next chapter, the two great early centers were also engaged in a military conflict in the late fourth century, perhaps a sign of a rivalry that had a deeper history we will never know.

Uaxactun and Tikal are where we also find the earliest inscribed monuments bearing legible dates, in keeping with Morley's early realization.[11] Inscriptions from there provide our first contemporaneous written history as well, relating events and actors of the time they were written. The only such monuments we can securely date are those with actual dates written on them—Stela 29 from Tikal is the earliest, with a record of July 9, 292. Uaxactun's Stela 9 bears a date for February 25,

333 CE. Neither of these are period endings, the all-important stations of the Long Count calendar. Rather they are "odd dates" that stand out for being unremarkable in terms of the calendar itself; they may well mark important historical occasions, such as the crowning of early kings. The Uaxactun stelae come from the E Group identified by archaeologists in the 1920s, the penultimate phase of which was built probably around 150 CE or so.[12] With its observatory and nearby triadic platform, it was clearly following a very old pattern of sacred and communal architecture, and soon stelae were added to the complex, bearing portraits and hieroglyphic texts that identified them as markers of time's passage.

Another important early Mutul ruler from this era was a queen who governed at Tikal in the early fourth century named Lady Unenbahlam (Lady Infant Jaguar). She is said to have "replanted" the twenty-year k'atun cycle in 317 CE (8.14.0.0.0). Lady Unenbahlam is perhaps the earliest woman we know from all of Maya history and first of several great queens who left their mark on local dynasties throughout the lowlands. We know very little about her, but she was an illustrious figure, celebrated by rulers of later generations. And there are hints in other Tikal sources that she was the mother of one of the most famous kings of early Tikal, Chaktokich'ahk, who we will see plays a central role in the most important historical event of the Early Classic period, some sixty years after her calendar celebration.

DYNASTIC VASES

Tikal and Uaxactun, while in many ways more precocious and active than their neighbors, were not isolated. Glimpses of early kings also appear in the later historical annals of other smaller sites, again pointing to the first and second centuries as a widespread time of renewal and dynastic foundation in the wake of the Preclassic abandonments. Naranjo, to the east of Tikal, was one of these major political players, and its early kings seem to go back to this time. And we have already seen inklings of early kingship farther to the north, in the area that would be the center of the Kanul kingdom.

After 300 CE, there were many coeval dynasties in the Classic period. No firm count is possible, but between that time and 900 CE, we can discern more than thirty individual royal lines, what we can call individual "dynasties." These were lineages with patrilineal inheritance into the status of k'uhulajaw, usually passing directly from father to son, but not always so. In a few cases, we even have official king lists that directly tell us who was who in a particular dynasty; far more often we are left with a more patchwork assortment of texts from which we painstakingly reconstruct the names and dates of royal families at a given site. This process of checking dates and the appearance of personal names was pioneered by Tatiana Proskouriakoff in her groundbreaking study of the "Series" rulers at Piedras Negras, or ancient Yokib. As a result of decades of research, we have long dynastic tallies at some ancient polities and short or highly fragmented lists at others.

One very important king list that survives from the Classic period appears on a series of twelve inscribed vases, all painted with a sequence of dates, names, and royal titles (Plate 7). These so-called "Dynastic Vases" were produced around the same time in the seventh century and seem to come from the region ruled by the Kanul dynasty during the Late Classic era.[13] The vase with the most complete list gives nineteen names in all, each with a date and an event that read *ch'am k'awil,* loosely understood as "he takes power." And each name also takes a distinctive title we call an "emblem glyph." As described earlier, these are royal titles that label rulers the lord or k'uhulajaw of a particular place, dynasty, or royal court. Each ruler of the Dynastic Vases takes the so-called "snake emblem" for the Kanul, the royal house that dominated much of the history of the Classic era. Taken together, the texts provide us with the names and partial dates of nineteen rulers of the Kanul dynasty, leading up to a king we know as "Scroll Serpent" (a working nickname for now).

At first, it would seem a boon to the study of Classic Maya history—a king list for one of the most powerful of Maya dynasties—but for many years, there were problems in its study. For one, the dates are all shown in a format that is not very precise in time. (Any such date can repeat every fifty-two years). Moreover, only some of the names looked familiar from the monuments we associated with Kanul history, and some established names seem to be missing. Who were the others? Where did all the names fit in history? Without a firm anchor, it was thought for a time that these names might represent a list of legendary rulers from a deeper past, perhaps from the Preclassic. Recent studies by Simon Martin have clarified the situation. Through the study of newly found inscriptions, he was able to see that some names had alternate versions and that matches could be made between more names than was originally supposed. What had looked like "extra" names may involve the inclusion of "corulers," which we know existed in some Late Classic Maya polities. For example, two brothers apparently ruled together at Palenque in the eighth century, each as a k'uhulajaw, with the elder of higher rank than his younger brother. The last of the nineteen names on the vases, "Scroll Serpent," can securely be linked to the Kanul ruler of the same name who we find mentioned in texts at several sites and who reigned after 583 CE. With this anchor, we can surmise that the king list takes us back to the very beginnings of the Classic period. The very first name in the list, a person apparently named "Skyraiser," seems best placed around the year 180 CE (at the latest), in the same century we see the emergence of Classic dynasties elsewhere (Figure 4.4).[14]

FIGURE 4.4. Name of "Skyraiser" with his Kanul emblem. From vessel K6751, Kerr Database. Drawing by the author.

EMBLEMS, COURTS, AND TOWNS

Like Mutul and Kanul, other Maya dynasties had their own proper names, like the various royal houses of medieval or renaissance Europe. Their glyphs are what we often call "emblems," first recognized by the Mayanist Heinrich Berlin in 1958. Some forty or so different emblems have been identified so far in the inscriptions. Tikal's dynasty was *Mutul,* that of Dzibanche and Calakmul was *Kanul,* Yaxchilan's was *Pa'chan,* Palenque's was *Bakel,* and so on. A high-ranking nobleman of a kingdom would be an *ajaw* of that courtly institution, as in *Pa'chan Ajaw*, "the Noble of Pa'chan." A noblewoman's version of such a title would add the feminine prefix *ix* in front, as in *Ix Pa'chan Ajaw*, "Noblelady of Pa'chan." A young prince could bear the title *Ch'ok Pa'chan Ajaw*, a "Young Noble of Pa'chan." Most of the emblems we know from Maya history were used to write the common title for rulers that we have already mentioned—*k'uhulajaw*, a "godly lord" who had special connections to divine beings or who could embody them on ritual occasions.

Typically, dynasties were connected to kabch'ens, or locations on the map, as we would expect, but we also see that they could shift and move about over the course of history. At times, contemporaneous rulers of different sites shared a single emblem title, probably as claimants to a single dynastic line. On other rare occasions, we see a single ruler claiming a connection to more than one emblem, as a lord of this-and-that dynasty. The pattern reflects the messiness of dynastic politics and family dynamics over time, as we will see in detail.

We should be careful to keep in mind that the dynastic names we see in "emblems" are not always the same as kabch'ens, or territorial realms. The latter are far more rooted in location and a sense of place, as we have seen, whereas dynasties could be less grounded, their centers of activity moving from place to place through history. Still, names and labels for place and court did overlap.

Let us look more closely at the name Pa'chan to illustrate some of these overlaps and distinctions. Pa'chan was a dynastic court or "house" first and foremost, referring to the royal family associated with the large and beautiful site known today as Yaxchilan, located on the Usumacinta River. For much of its history, Pa'chan was the seat of an actively militaristic regime led by several important figures in the Late Classic, including the belligerent usurper named Yaxun Bahlam ("Cotinga Jaguar"), who reigned from 752–768 CE. For much of the Classic period, Yaxun Bahlam and other Pa'chan kings were engaged in a prolonged conflict with their rival at the court of Yokib, at what we know today as Piedras Negras, a couple of days' distance downstream. Yaxchilan's sculptors commemorated these and other details of history and ceremony in numerous artworks throughout the city, adorning buildings with sculpted door lintels and steps in addition to the more customary stelae and altars located in the plazas. From these well-preserved monuments, we have images and texts that provide a particularly detailed picture of the ritual life, including numerous records of dance, period ending ceremonies, and the presentation of war captives.

Yaxchilan's earlier royal history was written in a series of inscriptions carved into the doorways of one small, unremarkable structure in the site's lower plaza, known as Structure 12. Pieces of these inscribed stones were visible to several early explorers and archaeologists, and later analysis revealed them to be portions of a long king list, enumerating the first ten rulers of the Pa'chan dynasty ("the fifth seated lord was., the sixth seated lord was..."). While not as long as the Dynastic Vases of Kanul history, the lintels of Structure 12 are just as important for reconstructing its early dynasty. I recall studying portions of this king list in my earlier days as a Mayanist, frustrated that the one portion with the first four names of the king list was still missing. All we had was the fifth to the tenth rulers, the last being a man named K'inich Tatab Jol, who assumed the throne in 526 CE. Fortunately, excavations at Yaxchilan in the early 1980s finally revealed a door lintel carved with the first part of the list, all the glyphs perfectly preserved. I was very excited to see it in 1983, shortly after its discovery, and thrilled to read off the names of Pa'chan's first rulers: Yopat Bahlam, Kahkaj Bahlam, Yaxun Bahlam, and Yax Xukub Jol. All of them bore the title *Pa'chan Ajaw*, "Pa'chan Lord." I quickly made a drawing and circulated it among my colleagues (Figure 4.5). We finally had the missing piece, and it helped anchor Pa'chan among the best-known of Maya courts, at least in terms of its dynastic history.[15]

The timing of Pa'chan's first ruler, Yopat Bahlam, raises a thorny question. His precise dates in history remain vague, but we might be able to place his accession in the year 359 CE. We have no contemporary records of this at Yaxchilan, for everything we know about the first eight or so rulers comes from later, retrospective accounts, including the king list of Structure 12. In fact, the earliest contemporaneous date from anywhere in Yaxchilan comes only a little earlier, in 514 CE, when the ninth ruler of the Pa'chan court celebrated the k'atun ending on

FIGURE 4.5. Yaxchilan, Lintel 11, recording the beginnings of the Pa'chan dynasty. Drawing by the author.

9.4.0.0.0. What I find interesting is that the very same k'atun date is cited as a starting point for other major polities of the west, including Piedras Negras and Palenque. Something obscure happened in 514 to "kick-start" the politics of the western region. The early sixth century comes late, far after the initial rulers we know from Tikal and other Early Classic courts, leading us to conclude that Classic Maya dynasties are not all of the same age and time depth. I suspect that these western latecomers are timed in connection to political changes happening between Teotihuacan and the Maya region, which we will explore in the next chapter. So the question immediately comes to mind: Where were the Pa'chan kings before 514? Were they at Yaxchilan but quiet in their building programs and erection of monuments? Perhaps. But there is another likelihood in my mind. As we will see throughout the various historical narratives, Maya elites and the courts they inhabited were mobile to a surprising degree, often picking up and moving about the landscape after a few generations. Much of Maya royal history involves such movement and the founding of new seats of authority in new places, sometimes over great distances.

I suspect that Pa'chan's earlier rulers originated elsewhere, with roots in the central Peten region. One telling clue for this comes from the use of the same name *Pa'chan* as the local emblem at a distant site named El Zotz, located close to Tikal in the central region. It seems that a seat of the Pa'chan dynasty or a branch of it also thrived there, running parallel somehow with the rulers at Yaxchilan. El Zotz is a much earlier site with deeper roots in the Preclassic and Early Classic, so we suspect it may have been the "original" Pa'chan. Nearby is a heavily fortified center that dates to the fourth century, when political changes were happening rapidly in the central Peten. Because of this instability, a branch of the Pa'chan lineage may have split off and moved westward to the Usumacinta River to form a new seat and base of operations, in the area Yokib had long dominated. My suspicion is that Yopat Bahlam of Yaxchilan was from El Zotz, establishing his own dynastic outpost in the Early Classic, in or around 359, in a turbulent era in the Peten.

One inscription from the reign of Yaxchilan's most prominent ruler, Shield Jaguar, the father of Yaxun Bahlam, offers an even more interesting clue into the deeper historical origins of his dynasty. He took the throne at Yaxchilan in the year 681 and perished in 742 after a very long and eventful sixty-year reign. As one text tells us, Shield Jaguar was "the fifteenth in the line of Pa'chan" at Yaxchilan, founded by Yopat Bahlam. But he was also the twenty-seventh in the line of another founder from a more distant era, with a different emblem title altogether (difficult to read yet distinct). Subsequent rulers of Yaxchilan take both emblems, proving that some kings could claim membership in two royal houses. In this respect, Maya dynasties and royal families probably operated a bit like the royal houses of the European Renaissance, at times touting multiple connections and cross-cutting lines of descent.[16] Rather than being place names, emblems specify the royal lines of succession, named dynasties, and they could at times fissure and break into various coeval branches, even having rival claimants.

Our sense that there was some internal structure or arrangement among the many Classic dynasties came into sharp focus with the discovery of an altar that simply lists several k'uhulajaws associated with different kingdoms. These were probably the "main" dynasties and royal houses at the time it was carved, sometime in the mid-eighth century. Among the royal emblem titles we can recognize in the damaged text, carved on the perimeter of the circular stone, are those of "Chatahn" (the first listed), Kanul (Dzibanche and Calakmul), Mutul (Tikal), Bakel (Palenque), and Ik'a' (Tayasal).[17] There were perhaps originally thirteen such royal titles listed, corresponding to the sacred Maya number that was a fundamental structure of both space and time. It is a tantalizing hint of the ways that Maya kingdoms saw themselves on a cosmological stage, and it clearly anticipates some historical accounts we know from much later in Maya history, after the time of European contact. Writing in the seventeenth century, the Spanish priest Avendaño y Loyola noted how the structure of Maya history was reflected in geopolitics, with the ages of the calendar "divided into thirteen parts, which divide this kingdom of Yucatán and each with its idol, priest and prophecy."[18]

Emblems were the principal organizational units for elite society, and their patterns of use allow us to reconstruct Maya history beyond the details of individual rulers and other actors. It is all from a dynastic viewpoint, of course, and so we lack endless amounts of information about the social and political lives of others who operated below them at various levels. Still, the labels such as Kanul, Mutul, or Pa'chan represent more than elite lineages. Affiliated with them and included in each local elite network were numerous offices and subordinate roles: provincial rulers, religious specialists, scribes, artisans, calendar priests, and so on. Many were members of the extended royal families, especially in the later centuries of Maya history, when any individual dynasty would have many inheritors, or claimants of elite status. The economic support for such a large political and social enterprise presumably had far-reaching effects. The k'uhulajaw and his immediate family oversaw complex systems of economic patronage that helped define some of these broader social relationships, solidifying a sense of community and identity.

EARTH AND CAVE

Beyond the dynasties, there were the communal and territorial units over which the k'uhulajaw ruled at any given time—what we usually describe as "kingdoms" or "city-states." The ancient Maya used the word *kabch'en* to refer to these fundamental geopolitical units, as we have seen. Given how loaded our own terms like "state" can be and how Mayanists still debate the nature of Maya geopolitics, I will use *kabch'en* to refer to the individual polities large and small that existed in the Classic period. This ancient word is made from two nouns, *kab*, "earth," and *ch'en*, "cave," sometimes reducible to just *ch'en*, "cave." The pairing of words conveys the idea that a "territory" incorporates both the ground (*kab*) and the nether regions in the earth's interior (*ch'en*). Throughout ancient times and up to the present day, caves are highly important places strongly associated with community identity and ceremonialism. In Classic times, an "earth-cave" was a territorial unit associated with a particular royal court. Pa'chan was one of many prominent kabch'ens, as were others across the Maya landscape.

I see the kabch'en as similar to the ancient Greek idea of *polis*, a city-state and community with a strong sense of identity relative to others. And the polis, like kabch'en, could encompass a wide variety of scales and internal arrangements, perhaps even at times as groupings of political units. It is notoriously difficult to define in any straightforward way.

One attractive parallel might be to the sociopolitical scene in Yucatán at the time of the conquest and throughout the colonial period. There, towns and their affiliated lands were called *kah*, probably based on the same word *kab* that forms the beginning of *kabch'en*. The historian of early colonial Yucatán Matthew Restall notes that *kah* was a close-knit and well-defined geographical settlement but also included the fields and agricultural plots that existed off on the edges, sometimes many miles away.[19] This idea resonates with what we understand of ancient Maya sites, composed of a nucleus of imposing buildings and elite spaces but with more sparsely oriented centers in the surrounding terrain. A kabch'en was a land that was *conceptually* centralized as a place of identity, but perhaps not so condensed in terms of its presence on the landscape. Because they were often rooted to a particular place, dynastic emblems could often overlap with the idea of a kabch'en, but again it is best to think of the latter as more of a territorial entity, a town or community. Later in Mesoamerican history, the Aztecs arranged themselves in highland Mexico using a very similar idea called the *altepetl*, "water-and-mountain." This has been various defined as a "town" or "city-state," so it approximates what a kabch'en was for the Classic Maya, as a nucleus of social connections, politics, and economics.[20]

Maya dynastic centers are good examples of what is described as low-density urbanism, a common model for community and settlement throughout much of ancient Mesoamerica.[21] Typically, around the core areas of public and ritual architecture were irregular and dispersed clusters of settlements, as revealed by the foundations of houses, patio groups, and sometimes smaller ceremonial structures. Some clusters look very much like "neighborhoods," and particularly well-defined clusters may correspond to extended kin groups associated, at varying levels, with the activities of the royal court. Agricultural plots and extensive gardens often existed within even the very densely populated areas, much like we see in Maya towns in present-day Yucatán. Extensive agricultural terracing is especially visible in the regions of many sites such as Caracol and Dzibanche. This dynamic of integrated land use was a strategy for sustainability that we can trace back to the Preclassic. It was successful for a long time, clearly, but it also was susceptible to stresses as populations grew exponentially throughout the Classic period.[22]

We are accustomed to seeing our modern cities as ever-growing and expanding over time, yet so many ancient Maya centers had their own lifespans, founded and abandoned sometimes after only a few generations and often with surprising intentionality. Some inscriptions and indigenous histories suggest that this could be closely tied to ideas to prophecy and predetermination. One good example of this comes from Copan, one of the great Maya centers whose main ceremonial precinct was established in the early fifth century and then abandoned in the ninth century. Not coincidentally, I think, this is the span of the period of the Maya calendar known as a bak'tun, or, as the ancient Maya would put it, the span from 9.0.0.0.0 to 10.0.0.0.0. We know people lived at Copan before and after, but the vibrant history of the place as a political and ceremonial center was confined to this four-hundred-year period when sixteen rulers of the local dynasty ruled. All are portrayed on a famous stone monument at the site, Altar Q, carved during the reign of its last known king. Four rulers are shown on each side of a square altar that represents the four-sided cosmos, emphasizing history as balance and symmetry. The message is a "closed system," a finite idea of succession that could not easily incorporate a seventeenth ruler. After the death of the sixteenth ruler, Yaxpasaj Chanyopat, the royal family and court abandoned Copan's central acropolis, at just about the time of the bak'tun's turn in 830 CE.

We will return to Altar Q, and similar evidence at other sites when we confront the thorny and complex problem of the ninth-century collapse. The point to keep in mind for now is that the end of the dynastic system in the ninth century may have involved, at times, a sense of predestination, or at least an idea that communities and even political arrangements had a finite existence. Dynastic politics shows us that radical change and adjustment can be integral to the system, not always working against it. It is an old pattern we can even trace to the beginnings of Maya settlement in the Middle Preclassic, originating in the idea of sustainability, and the movement and adaptation were essential for survival. These dynamics of Maya history are little explored as yet, but as internal factors I think they lie at the heart of understanding the cadence of change and even the greater trajectory of Mesoamerican civilization over the long term.

TIME, KINGSHIP, AND MAIZE

Maya history was an extension and expression of cosmology and therefore highly cyclical in its structure. Episodes in recorded history were often framed as events on a larger universal stage, as extensions of primordial events and divine actors that took place in the era of "deep time." The defeat of an enemy might be shown as a reenactment of the "axing" of a foe by the storm god Chahk, now embodied by the victorious king. The marriage and arrival of a princess to an allied court might be couched in the same language as the appearance of a new moon—that is, the arrival of the moon itself in the lunar calendar. The crowning of a king—the placement of a great feathered headdress—was seen to be the figurative descent of a great celestial bird from the sky, alighting upon the head of the new ruler. Death was understood to be a cosmic happening as well, as the entrance of the deceased on the path of the sun and other celestial bodies that rise and set. There was little to distinguish the happenings of royal families from mythic events or even from the regular and repeating mechanisms of cosmology.

The kabch'en, or political territory, was also an idealized concept of community and place conceived according to the cosmological ideal, reflecting the essential order of the universe. Courts, towns, and temple precincts were all microcosms, with the ruler and elites at their conceptual heart. Physically, the highest-ranking rulers and their courtly members lived and worked amid the palatial structures at the centers of the kabch'en, adjacent to imposing ritual architecture. Other nobles and elite seem to have lived a little farther afield, in more rural "estates" where they probably maintained some degree of oversight over agricultural production and other activities.[23] This integration of urban and agricultural space is reflected too, I think, in Maya political ideology. To be a Maya ruler was to be a religious actor, a central player within a larger cosmological order. This is revealed to us through artworks that make explicit reference to narratives of ancient gods and their royal descendants. As mentioned earlier, kings were embodiments of a mythic hero called Jun Ajaw, "One Lord," a primordial forest hunter and farmer. In fact, the common title *ajaw* derives from the word *aj-aw*, "one who sows." One epic story that we have recently begun to reconstruct centers on Jun Ajaw and his shooting of a bejeweled Principal Bird Deity, eagle-like Yax Kokaj Mut, who embodied the sky and heavenly light. Jun Ajaw's hunting of Yax Kokaj Mut and the latter's descent from heaven symbolized the appearance of jade and wealth on the earth, providing a mythical grounding for the status and regalia of rulership and elite society.

One deity associated with rulership is K'awil, embodying several abstract concepts associated of power, wealth, and sustenance. His image is found everywhere in Maya sculpture and ceramics, recognizable by his elongated forehead pierced by a flaming axe blade (Figure 4.6). His fanged face and reptilian scales point to his strong connection to snakes, but he is usually shown with a human body, wearing the jade jewels of a ruler. K'awil probably originated as the animation of the stone axe wielded by the storm god Chahk, as we have seen, who used it to strike the clouds to make thunder and rain, much like Thor's hammer. On stone monuments, rulers are often shown holding a K'awil axe-scepter, clearly evoking Chahk's power

FIGURE 4.6. K'awil, the animate essence of power and force. Drawing by the author.

as both a rainmaker and vanquisher. In time, K'awil became a symbol of rulership and of "force" incarnate (*k'aw,* from which the name is derived, means "to force through"), swirled in divine essence and embodying a constellation of associations centered on royal power and authority.

In later representations, we find images of K'awil surrounded by food, in the form of maize kernels and bundles of cacao beans, as if he was the patron deity of fine eating. Throughout Maya history, K'awil emerged as a central icon among the many symbols the elite used to represent their own controlling role in society, as the human representatives of divine influence on earth. To show this fundamental connection, rulers and various high-ranking lords would engage in an important ritual called *tzak k'awil,* "to conjure K'awil" (Figure 4.7 and Plate 13). This occurred on important calendar stations, accessions, or anniversaries. The rite probably involved bloodletting, an offering of divine essence of the body and to one's ancestors. As "cosmic" actors, kings, queens, and other elites were charged with the essential role of communicating and manifesting powerful deities and ancestors, embodying and "performing" as those beings, and managing and curating the flow of time itself. Throughout the ancient ideology, the powers of K'awil permeated the intertwined realms of ritual, society, and politics.

We have seen how time and its ritual maintenance were central concerns of Maya builders and theologians from almost the very beginning. The carefully planned orientations of E Groups at Aguada Fénix and other Middle Preclassic sites, oriented to the eastern horizon, tracked the movements of the sun over the course of the year. Another key interval was the interval of 260 days (thirteen times twenty days), a basic divinatory and agricultural calendar shared by all Mesoamericans. While often described as a purely ritual construct, it too may have a natural basis. Today, the Ch'orti' Maya of Guatemala maintain the 260-day interval as the time between maize planting and harvesting, before the onset of the dry winter season. It is also roughly nine months, the period of human gestation (maize and humans being grown and created on parallel timelines). This was embedded within the 365-day solar year and gave time its other natural cadence. It is no coincidence that the word for "year," *haab,* derived from the word for "rain" and "water,"

FIGURE 4.7. Ruler manifesting the spirit of K'awil, the animate symbol of power and authority. Lacanha, Panel 1. Drawing by the author.

ha'—the rainy season. The sacred calendar that defines so much about ancient Maya cosmology and religion was based on this essential unit, which can refer to either the 365-day solar year or to another "vague year" of 360 days. The latter was a ritual year that formed the basis of the immense Long Count calendar, with its base-20 exponential system—20 haabs (that is, a k'atun), 400 haabs, 8,000 haabs, and so on. The Long Count also had its origins in the Preclassic, although it is difficult to pinpoint when it was first used; the earliest examples of the Long Count appear just outside the Maya region, in the Isthmus of Tehuantepec region, and in El Salvador in the first century BCE. Whatever the case, rulers were the overseers of these cycles and the rites that marked their stations.

The presentation of individual rulers in the Classic period reflected a changing ideology that increasingly placed the k'uhulajaw within the matrix of cosmology and of time itself. Maize agriculture and the associated complex of deities provided one important framework for these notions of sacred kingship—a connection that, again, surely had its origins in the religious ideas of the Preclassic, when E-Groups were ubiquitous and the structures of sacred time were first sketched out.[24] The texts and imagery of the Classic period bear this out in very direct ways. Rulers were constantly concerned with maize and ritual metaphors surrounding agricultural work, which were extended to operate on a cosmic scale. For the k'uhulajaw, periods of time were in a sense "crops," requiring proactive maintenance and periodic renewal. When the new dynastic flavor of Maya authority appeared on the scene in the Classic period, it tapped into an old, well-established system of ideas, highlighting the role of an individual king or queen as agent and "sower." Through the calendar, rulers of the Classic period performed their essential ritual tasks of renewing time on a variety of scales.

This religious duty of kingship was the preeminent topic of concern in public religious texts from the third to the ninth centuries. The stations of the years and their higher multiples were usually marked through the erection of stelae, outdoor stone monuments. Whereas farmers worked the fields, Maya rulers took on the responsibility of "growing" and sustaining the seasons that allowed agriculture to exist in the first place. Not only did the title *ajaw* originate as a word meaning "sower," it was also the name of the day in the 260-day calendar on which time itself was always renewed or "replanted," as the inscriptions explicitly describe it.[25] A great many inscriptions use this wording to describe the principal act of the ruler on the specified day. For example, the ruler of Tikal who reigned in the year 376 oversaw the period ending date of 8.17.0.0.0, which fell on October 21. On that day, "he replanted the seventeenth k'atun." The clear implication is that he was actively engendering time itself.[26] The stelae that marked these important occasions were called *lakamtun,* "wide stones," and hundreds are still visible today in numerous Maya ruins, many still standing upright after sixteen or so centuries. They first appeared in the lowlands in the first centuries CE, placed in plazas of E Groups and similar spaces. Related to the public use of stelae was a change in the way writing was used and displayed. Whereas during the Late Preclassic, hieroglyphs had been small-scale, confined to intimate contexts of wall paintings or small portable objects, in the Early Classic, they came to adorn the stelae, expanding the role of script in the public presentation of rulership and its underlying messaging (Plate 8).

Lakamtuns were so fundamental in Classic Maya art and kingship that we should look a bit further into their history and meaning. Evidence suggests that their early inspiration can be found in the small greenstone "celts" used as ceremonial objects throughout the Preclassic. Early celts sometimes bear images of ancestors and rulers, with accompanying short texts, looking like miniature stelae. These portable objects originated, in turn, as far back as the Middle Preclassic, when they were also often placed as ritual offerings in plazas and E Groups. For the Olmec, highly polished celts were stone representations of maize cobs, "planted" in the earth in ceremonies for the dedication or foundation of ritual spaces. The stone stelae "planted" in plazas in the Preclassic and Classic eras channeled the same idea, marking the passage of time and the rites rulers performed to maintain its continuance. This was a key proposition within the ideology undergirding kingship, first fully developed in the early years of the Classic period. Through their representation on stelae, Maya dynasts were, in a ritual and metaphorical sense, agriculturalists. The many stelae erected in a courtyard or plaza point to such spaces as being replicas of cornfields, with many "planted" stones representing the cycles of time.[27]

DYNASTY, LITERACY, AND VERACITY

The task of composing and designing the monumental records of these rites fell to the scribes and sculptors of the royal courts, the artisans known collectively as *itz'at*. Each center or court had one or more scribes, or *ajtz'ihb*, "one who writes, paints," and they were sometimes closely related to the royal families. In fact, for the elite culture that emerged at the beginning of the Classic period, literacy was a defining cultural expression, an ability that conveyed status and social connectivity. This synergy between political culture and the written word is the basis for how we know what we know of ancient Maya history. People, events, marriages, wars, and rituals had to be written in stone for posterity and made visible to others. This is another important difference from the Preclassic era that came before and the Postclassic era that came later, when elite literacy and the expression of the written form were far more restricted and less prominent. The scribes were therefore at the center of courtly life, responsible for everyday recordkeeping as well as the crafting of various inscribed goods such as vessels and jewelry, important commodities in the elite exchange system between polities. Some scribes also would have had important roles as *ajk'in*, "diviners" ("those who 'do days'"), who would interpret ritual and calendrical almanacs much like the day-keepers of today's Maya highlands.[28]

Artists of the court often signed their names to paintings and sculptures. These signatures, at times numbering as many as eleven or twelve on a single carved monument, suggest that literacy was a matter of pride and distinction in Maya society. Most scribes and sculptors that we know of were men, but two or three women bear titles that suggest that they were painters or scribes as well. Working closely with the rulers of their respective communities, these itz'at and ajtz'ihb would have crafted very specific messages through inscribed objects and monuments, documenting local affairs and also keeping track of histories among their contemporaries. Beyond just writing and painting, they were keepers of knowledge, perhaps educators, and specialists in various esoteric aspects of religion and science.

The sculptors and artisans who worked within the royal courts were often of noble birth or otherwise closely integrated into the cultures of the royal houses, where aesthetic production was so central to the presentation of being elite. Among the different courts and dynasties, there developed an intricate economy based on the gifting and the exchange of fine goods, helping cement the political and family connections among them. These included carved and painted ceramics, jade jewelry, and textiles, among many other high-end commodities. The tradition of lavishly painted vases, adorned with complex designs, iconography, and hieroglyphic writing, appeared around 200 CE in the central lowlands, and it grew in time into one of the great traditions of ancient Maya art. By the Late Classic, vessels for food and cacao drinks displayed intricate scenes of mythology, political events, and snapshots of courtly life. (The Dynastic Vases discussed earlier are of this era.) Often these were inscribed with the names of their patrons ("here is so-and-so's drinking cup"), and when traded and gifted, they became material expressions of diplomacy. For the elites, labeled jewels and fancy possessions were a means of documenting the interconnectedness among high society.

As official accounts, should we question the veracity of the historical texts? Were the inscriptions "just" the boastful records of kings and queens, a form of ancient propaganda? This question has been asked by many archaeologists over the last decades, especially in the years when the decipherment rapidly progressed after the 1970s. One prominent archaeologist even bristled at the notion that the written sources left to us by the Maya could even be seen as history "in our terms," being far from objective and so elite-focused.[29] I faced this debate head-on in the 1980s, just as I was getting my first training in archaeology. In my early twenties, I worked on the archaeological project at the wondrous ruins of Copan, Honduras, where the threads of archaeology and epigraphy began to be interwoven in innovative and revealing ways. A few of the many archaeologists and students working with me at the time were adamant that the hieroglyphs was hardly important for the broader study of Maya society and cultural evolution. History was simply outside their sense of "real" archaeology as a science and "not objective."

My response to such an outlook is to ask a simple question: Is it not important to know what the ancient Maya had to say about themselves and their own world, even if biased? For me, the beauty of the newly readable texts lay in their ability to give us unique access to their own words and what they felt worthy to communicate in stone for perpetuity. These were Maya voices, after all—rulers, court members, priests—speaking to our imperfect ears across thirteen centuries. Still, the methods and assumptions that had informed Maya archaeology in its early decades were not comfortable with the inclusion of history, and academic debate lasted throughout much of the 1980s and '90s. Despite some consternation, the Copan excavations in those years started to frame their approach and data in the light of the local dynastic history, knowing which ruler built which monuments and pyramid and realizing that records of war and conquest were vital to understanding patterns we could see in the physical archaeological record.

As a graduate student, I joined another field project at Dos Pilas, Guatemala, where my close colleague Stephen Houston had worked for several years. Though a small site by comparison, Dos Pilas was interesting from its many inscriptions, revealing that its court had some close family ties to Tikal. The written history also made clear that it was also in ongoing conflicts with many of its closer neighbors. A few years earlier, Houston had documented a series of hastily built defensive walls around the main sector of Dos Pilas, transforming what had been a ceremonial plaza into a citadel, a place of desperate defense.

Here the history and the archaeology pointed in the same direction, giving a deeper context to the physical remains of the site. Interpreting both together provided a new richness by replicating the innovations we had experimented with at Copan, seeing archaeology and epigraphy as complementary sets of information, not necessarily in conflict. Many field projects in the Maya area have since followed these same trends. Today, major excavations routinely integrate dynastic history into a more holistic picture, a particular type of "historical archaeology" that few scholars would have imagined fifty or sixty years ago.[30]

The underlying strength of the Maya sources is not their "objectivity" but rather their internal consistency across time and space. Details of dynastic history at one site are often echoed elsewhere, showing an adherence to a single, larger narrative. Even when different kingdoms were in conflict and when their respective histories featured local events, the larger arc of Maya history is consistent in its presentation, skewed and elite-focused as it clearly is. I see this coherence as a direct reflection of the intensive interactions that always existed among city-states, or kabch'ens, and of a network that was forged over centuries of royal intermarriage and interconnectedness. In a sense, the events and actors we can reconstruct from the ancient written sources form the history of a large, very extended social unit. The events we can read from the Classic period, from about 150 to 850 CE, reflect the mutual interdependence that existed among royal courts, even when in conflict. The inscriptions are therefore of supreme relevance for understanding just what happened at the end and how Maya civilization changed and adapted over the long term.

This is what lies at the heart of our larger story. The sources from the Classic period, meticulously recorded by scribes, commemorate the exploits of the royal families and paint a vivid picture of a tightly knit political culture that spanned roughly seven centuries, emerging from a "predynastic" era and then rapidly disintegrating for reasons we will explore in more detail. About two dozen of these dynasties developed alongside each other, maintaining close relationships over many generations, even amid war and conflict. Their interconnected lives unraveled quickly between 800 and 900 CE, followed by centuries of silence. Apart from a few lineages that may have persisted into the world of the Postclassic, the regal families of the Classic era seem to have disintegrated in a short span of time, leaving little to no trace in the later historical consciousness. This was the Rupture that represented the loss and forgetting of that closely knit elite world. The reasons behind its eventual demise are, I believe, partly visible in the historical narratives we can now read, at long last.

CHAPTER 5

Arrivals

IN 1960, ARCHAEOLOGISTS tunneled deep into an ancient temple at Tikal, Guatemala, and made a great discovery. They were investigating the early construction phases of the pyramid when they encountered a buried stela bearing a long, almost perfectly preserved royal portrait and hieroglyphic inscription. This was the same year Proskouriakoff published her historical discoveries on Piedras Negras, and the small community of Maya archaeologists was quickly becoming aware of an exciting new paradigm—that history might be teased out of such inscriptions. Proskouriakoff was soon sent photographs of the new monument, designated as Stela 31 (Figure 5.1). Building on her earlier methods in recognizing personal names and sequences of rulers, she would come to realize that Stela 31 was the single greatest source for the study of Maya history during the Early Classic period, before the fifth century CE, holding ramifications that went far beyond Tikal itself.

Before the discovery, the University of Pennsylvania's Tikal project had already spent several years excavating beneath the site's North Acropolis, a dense cluster of pyramids facing south toward the city's central plaza. The dig had revealed layer upon layer of architectural development reaching back to the Middle Preclassic, even to the foundation of the

FIGURE 5.1. Tikal, Stela 31. Photograph by the author.

city itself. And within these layers were many Classic period tombs, deep within the floors and terraces of the pyramids. As we now know, the North Acropolis was likely a central place of ancestor worship, with shrines built to honor the dynasts of the Mutul royal court. By 1960 the Penn project had deeply trenched and tunneled throughout this mass of stonework, plaster, and fill. The project director, Edwin Shook, had worked at Uaxactun and had ample experience with field excavation and the peculiarities of Maya architecture. When he came upon one buried temple in the North Acropolis, Structure 5D-33-2nd, he was reminded of a similar building he had excavated at Uaxactun, which had enclosed a buried stela. Thinking there might be something similar at Tikal, he instructed his workmen to tunnel into the temple's chamber. Sure enough they came upon a large stela, broken and slightly charred by ritual fire, yet covered in a beautiful relief of a ruler with two standing figures on the sides. The back of the monument was carved with one of the longest inscriptions ever found. Shook was delighted and noted with great satisfaction that both buried monuments he found at Uaxactun and Tikal bore the very same date, 445 CE.[1]

Stela 31 offers a gold mine of historical information about early Tikal, by far the most detailed and important source we have of that era. It relates a series of period ending celebrations by rulers who reigned before 445, including those mentioned in the previous chapter, Lady Unen Bahlam and Chaktokich'ahk.[2] One event in particular stands out in importance within the long narrative—something that happened on January 16, 378, involving a few newly introduced actors and protagonists. This was the most important day of the Early Classic, what we call the "Entrada" ("Entrance" in Spanish). It involved the arrival to Tikal of a powerful group of outsiders from Teotihuacan, in central Mexico, and what amounted to a hostile takeover of the local Mutul dynasty. Thanks to Stela 31 and other sources discovered since, we can even glean a little bit about the obscure history of that great highland city.

TEOTIHUACAN

Teotihuacan is an outlier among ancient Mesoamerican cities. Located a short distance outside Mexico City, it was a civilization onto itself, with massive temple pyramids, streets and plazas, and a distinctive, abstracted art style. It was a vast place, overwhelming in its scale and monumentality. A wide, straight avenue known as the Street of the Dead runs north–south through the heart of the city, ending at the Pyramid of the Moon. To the east of the avenue is the immense Pyramid of the Sun (as the later Aztecs called it), which seems to have been dedicated to the ancient Teotihuacan god of fire. The latticework of the city's streets was arranged in grid fashion, with elaborate apartment compounds and specialized craft workshops producing ceramics, obsidian, mica, and other commodities. At its height around 400–500 CE, it probably housed over 100,000 people. Still, without a firm grounding in history, Teotihuacan remains a place of intense mystery, even after decades of intensive archaeological work.

We cannot be sure even what language was spoken by its builders and inhabitants. Nor are we sure what system (or systems) of governance it once had. To some, the "impersonal" nature of its art suggests something far different than the dynastic culture of the ancient Maya. And the relative "good life" of its inhabitants has been taken by some scholars as an indication of Teotihuacan's experimentation with more egalitarian social and political arrangements, with a lack of a rigid hierarchy.

The city has even been interpreted as a Mesoamerican utopia without a central ruler or authoritative structure. I doubt this was the case, for reasons we will see, for it seems a simplistic and idealized accounting of what was clearly a very complex urban society. The apparent rigidity and hyperorganization reflected in Teotihuacan's plan could equally be interpreted as evidence for a centralized organization and of the presence of some powerful authority. Unfortunately, Teotihuacan has left no written history—a gap that makes questions of politics and governance especially difficult to address. I agree with an alternate view, offered by another group of scholars who have worked at Teotihuacan, that sees better evidence for rulership and of expansive militarism, at least for a time during the city's later history.[3]

What most researchers can agree on is that Teotihuacan experienced its own important political and demographic changes over the course of its history. This suggests that any one model of Teotihuacan's governance may only account for part of the site's story. The most pronounced change came around 300–350 CE, when we see evidence of the "canceling" of some important monuments and the construction of new ones, pointing to a new political arrangement. Mural paintings and images on ceramics reflect a new emphasis on militarism, and one of the earlier grand monuments of the city, the Feathered Serpent Pyramid, was partially demolished. Authority and power became more centralized, and people from throughout Mesoamerica came to settle at Teotihuacan in great numbers—including elite Maya from the Peten.[4]

We also find indications of Teotihuacan's growing influence throughout much of Mesoamerica. Its clear presence appears in the sculpture and ceramics of the Gulf Coast of Veracruz, on the Pacific Coast of the Isthmus of Tehuantepec, and in the valley of Oaxaca. One place of exceptional importance to Teotihuacan was the volcanic regions of what is now Guatemala, on the southern edges of the Maya world. The focal point here was Kaminaljuyu, located in modern Guatemala City, where elites clearly used Teotihuacan as a model in the design of their adobe-walled buildings and in the forms of their ceramics. These may have been trading enclaves, military outposts, or places serving combinations of these and other roles. Cacao was of special interest to Teotihuacan; one of the city's distinctive ceramic forms, the lidded cylinder tripod, was probably made especially for holding cacao drink, a staple of elite households throughout Mesoamerica, and only grown in the tropical lowlands.

Within this complex Mesoamerican matrix, the strongest evidence of Teotihuacan influence comes from the lowland Maya area. The art of Tikal, Uaxactun, and other Maya centers makes it clear that there were strong Teotihuacan contacts during the Early Classic, if not earlier. A deep interaction existed between the two cultures that probably went back centuries, even toward the end of the Preclassic period, when Teotihuacan experienced its own sudden "boom" in urban planning on a vast scale. Triadic arrangements of pyramids and even the imposing scales of the Moon and Sun pyramids suggest an awareness of early Maya monumental architecture from central Peten. It may be that Teotihuacan's sense of monumentality and urban scale was inspired in some way by Preclassic Maya precedents.

There is intriguing evidence that Maya peoples from Peten were living at Teotihuacan in the fourth and fifth centuries CE. Painted Maya pottery that was probably made at Tikal has been found near the so-called "Merchant's Barrio" to the east of Teotihuacan's main temples, among other material remains that point to an impressive number of Maya residents. One tomb dating to about 350 CE excavated in the Pyramid of the Moon contains the remains of two apparently Maya individuals adorned with jade jewels.[5] Even more conspicuous evidence of a major Maya presence at Teotihuacan is the recent discoveries at the Plaza of the Columns, at the heart of the city. There my colleague Nawa Sugiyama and her team have uncovered many fragments of a painted wall, clearly made by a Maya artist and representing figures of Maya myth. Nearby were found the smashed remains of numerous ceramic vessels, beautifully decorated by Maya artisans, representing the Maize God as an enthroned ruler. When I first viewed these pottery fragments in the field lab at Teotihuacan, I was stunned by their mastery and Maya "look."[6] The same excavations in the Plaza of the Columns have also uncovered evidence of a mass sacrifice, around the same time that the ceramics and the wall paintings were intentionally destroyed. The study of these deposits is ongoing, and the identities of the victims remain uncertain for now, but preliminary estimates place the destructive episode in the early fourth century. Before this, elite materials in the form of jade, shells, and other exotic materials point to long-lasting trade and interaction with the Maya region. But things changed around 350 CE or so. This curious pattern is surely relevant for understanding the backstory of the events of 378 and what led up to Teotihuacan's interference in Maya politics at that time.

Were there rulers or kings at Teotihuacan? I believe so, for a few reasons. One indirect clue is the overwhelming sense of rigidity in the layout and design of the city itself, suggesting a place that was tightly controlled and maintained over the centuries. The militarism emphasized in its art and archaeology also seems to point to a centralized authority of some sort. But these are only impressions. The best direct evidence of Teotihuacan's rulership and governance comes from Maya written records, especially those of Tikal. From these we can infer a very complex relationship between the regions that developed and changed over time. These Maya narratives center on one man who I believe was a ruler of Teotihuacan, perhaps even one of the most influential figures of ancient world history. We know him as "Spearthrower Owl," a long-standing nickname for a name that might more accurately translate as "Eagle Striker." His remarkable history can be pieced together from various sources at Tikal, including the all-important Stela 31.[7]

THE TAKEOVER

Stela 31's tally of early kings includes the name Chaktokich'ahk, the ruler who oversaw the great k'atun ending on 8.17.0.0.0, in 376. On that occasion, he reenacted the creation of the world by "raising a stone" (a stela), like his many illustrious ancestors. In a piece of remarkable luck, the very monument from 376 was discovered in the early 1980s at Tikal, broken and cached within the fill of Tikal's immense E Group complex (Plate 8). We will recall that there was a long association of E Group complexes with such time-marker stones, so we can assume with confidence that Chaktokich'ahk had erected this stone, known as Stela 39, somewhere in the outdoor plaza of the complex. While we only have the lower half of the original, the monument is one of the most beautiful known from the Early Classic, showing an intricately carved portrait of Chaktokich'ahk—or at least his legs (Plate 8). He stands above a prone and bearded captive, bearing a distinctive name, perhaps readable as Tz'akab Ti. In a fascinating insight, my colleagues Dmitri Beliaev and Alexander Safranov have found this same name on a monument at nearby Uaxactun, referring to the local ruler who reigned there in 357, nineteen years before the dedication of the Tikal monument. The implication seems clear: Chaktokich'ahk of Tikal captured the ruler of Uaxactun sometime in that span, pointing to a rivalry between the two early centers, separated by only twenty-three kilometers. This militaristic portrait celebrates the earliest known war in Maya history, and it helps us frame the changing relationship between these two centers over subsequent centuries.

After the mention of Chaktokich'ahk's great k'atun ending of 376, Stela 31 goes on to highlight the "Entrada" event of January 16, 378, when Teotihuacan's ruler inserted himself directly into Tikal's affairs and into the political culture of the Peten Maya. The nature of this event was first realized by Proskouriakoff, who noticed the very same date recorded on another stela at Uaxactun—an intriguing link between two sites that had been at war leading up to this moment. On the face of that stela, we see an image of a striding Teotihuacan warrior holding an obsidian "sword"—a distinctive weapon from highland Mexico (Figure 5.2). Based on its association with the image, Proskouriakoff surmised that this event must have been a key moment of interaction between Teotihuacan and the Maya, and perhaps the start of an intensive period of contact during the Early Classic, as also reflected in elite ceramics and art styles. Proskouriakoff called this an "arrival" of foreigners. Little did she know that this is precisely how Maya scribes described it as well.

FIGURE 5.2. Uaxactun, Stela 5, showing a foreign warrior. Drawing by Ian Graham.

Years after she wrote about her speculations, I found myself looking over these same Tikal and Uaxactun texts and was stunned to realize that a hieroglyph used to describe the event reads *huliiy*, "he arrived here." As was so often the case, Proskouriakoff was right. I also noticed that the relevant passage on Stela 31 went on to mention that Tikal's king, Chaktokich'ahk, died on the very same day. Not only was January 16, 378, an arrival of "foreigners," it saw the violent overturning of Tikal's king.[8]

The person who "arrived" in 378 was a transformational figure named Sihyajk'ahk' ("Fire Is Born") (Figure 5.3). Many inscriptions in the region mention him, accentuating his great importance in early Maya politics and history. According to numerous references, he was a *kalomte'*, a title reserved for the most powerful rulers, especially at Tikal, the seat of the Mutul dynasty, and Dzibanche, ruled by the lords of Kanul. (After 650 or so, it came to be adopted by allies of these expansionistic realms and for overlords who rule over hegemonies and multiple courts.) Just who was Sihyajk'ahk'? This still stands as one of the most important questions of Maya history and archaeology. Another title he takes in the Stela 31 text is revealing: *ochk'in k'awil,* which translates as "the western authority." (*K'awil,* in addition to being an animate idea of kingship, has the more abstracted meaning of "power.") Another text that refers to the Entrada, found painted on a palace wall at the site of La Sufricaya, a good distance from Tikal, notes that January 16, 378, was when "the k'awil arrived at Tikal." Clearly Sihyajk'ahk' was a person of supreme importance, a ruler himself in some sense, and he is said to have been from the west. Revealingly, he is never described as being from a particular Maya kingdom.

FIGURE 5.3. The name of Sihyajk'ahk'. Drawing by the author.

We can zero in on the Entrada and Sihyajk'ahk' in even more detail. Three inscriptions from El Peru-Waka', located to the west of Tikal, also mention Sihyajk'ahk', and in one of them, we find an intriguing detail about his travels toward Tikal. According to Stela 15, Sihyajk'ahk' "arrived here" (at El Peru-Waka', that is) on January 8, 378, eight days before his momentous arrival to Tikal. Seldom can we track the movement of individuals so precisely, but the implication here is clear—Sihyajk'ahk' and his companions passed through El Peru-Waka' on their way to depose the king of Tikal, moving from the west to east. The "west" title for Sihyajk'ahk' makes sense, and he presumably came from some place even farther westward. It is interesting to note that the El Peru-Waka' stela was dedicated much later in 416 CE by a local ruler named K'inich Balam, who had reigned for many years. His own inauguration took place shortly after Sihyajk'ahk's disruptive intrusion into Maya politics, and we might assume he was a local Maya ally of the newly arrived outsiders.

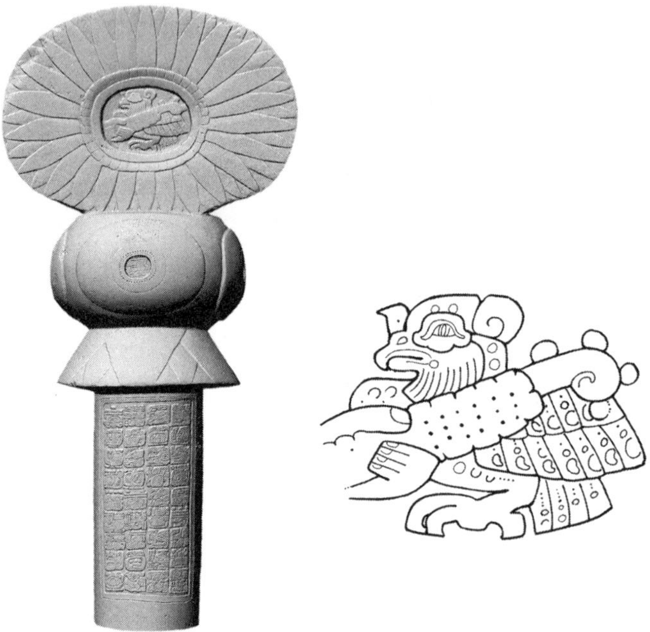

FIGURE 5.4. The Marcador of Tikal and the name Spearthrower Owl. Image courtesy of the Corpus of Maya Hieroglyphic Inscriptions, Peabody Museum, Harvard University, copyright President and Fellows of Harvard College. Drawing by the author.

The best source for understanding the nature of the Entrada is another Tikal inscription known as "The Marcador" (Spanish for "marker" due to its resemblance to a supposed ballcourt marker found at Teotihuacan) (Figure 5.4). This small, unusual sculpture, vaguely resembling a popsicle in form, was erected in the center of a patio in an elite residential compound in Tikal's southern sector. It may represent an upright spear or a dart topped by a circular shield, thus a visual a pairing of the two symbolic weapons of war and conquest. A long hieroglyphic text carved on the shaft of the stone provides us with further information about the Entrada and its participants. The text begins with a record of the Entrada in 378: "Sihyajk'ahk' arrived ... to Mutul (Tikal)." From there we read of an event called "cave-entering" (*och ch'en*), a term for a military defeat and conquest. Tikal was on the receiving end of this attack. This agrees with the mention that Chaktokich'ahk met his demise on the very same day, confirming that Sihyajk'ahk' was responsible for a takeover of Tikal's dynastic system. On the Marcador another person is brought into the story, the same Spearthrower Owl mentioned earlier. He is named as some sort of "companion" in the arrival, evidently someone who operated above the fray, not directly with Sihyajk'ahk'. On the other side, we read that the Marcador itself was erected in 416 CE—thirty-eight years after the Entrada—and that it represents the weapons and shield "owned" by Spearthrower Owl. To accentuate the personal connection, Spearthrower Owl's name is emblazoned on the rosette at the top of the Marcador sculpture (Figure 5.4). The Marcador's text harkens back to the day when Spearthrower Owl was crowned ("encircled in the kingship") in the year 374, four years before the arrival. He was not a ruler within the dynasty of Tikal, so where did he rule?[9]

Mayanists have been wrestling with the identity of Spearthrower Owl ever since his name was first identified and associated with Teotihuacan imagery.[10] For those who study the inscriptions, there can be little doubt that he was an unusually important king, of even higher rank than Sihyajk'ahk'. Not only does he occasionally take the title of hegemonic rulers, Kalomte', but he is also called a "West Kalomte'," probably referring to his place of origin in highland central Mexico. Other descriptive titles that he bears include "the fourth lord in the succession" and "the lord of the five (snowy?) mountains." Considering these and other points, the logical conclusion is that Spearthrower Owl was a powerful ruler based at Teotihuacan and likely the true power behind the conquest of Tikal in 378. His agent and representative was Sihyajk'ahk', probably a Maya ally of Spearthrower Owl who was directly responsible for Tikal's overthrow.

The idea of a named ruler at Teotihuacan, cited in Maya inscriptions of Tikal and elsewhere, has proved controversial. It casts us directly into the long-standing debates about the nature of governance at Teotihuacan and whether it was ever ruled in a centralized way or whether there was some system of joint rulership or even a more "egalitarian" culture where there was little distinction in social rank among its inhabitants. The lack of historical texts at Teotihuacan has always added to the uncertainty and even to the air of mystery surrounding that great

FIGURE 5.5. Yaxnunayin, ruler of Tikal and son of Spearthrower Owl. Drawing by William R. Coe.

highland city. Still, I feel that the details we read in Maya history can now help resolve part of this old debate. Given the close economic and political connections we know existed between these regions, it should not be surprising that powerful people of highland Mexico might be mentioned in the Maya inscriptions from time to time. There may even be emblematic representations of the name of Spearthrower Owl in the art of Teotihuacan, adding a new layer of evidence to the debate.[11]

While a distant king, Spearthrower Owl played a very direct role in Tikal's royal family. Among the many details provided by Stela 31, we read that he was the father of a youth named Yaxnunayin, who would quickly be appointed as Tikal's ruler in 379, over a year and a half after the conquest by Sihyajk'ahk'. Portraits of Yaxnunayin at Tikal show him in the distinctive garb of a Teotihuacan warrior, including a feline helmet, an atlatl (spear thrower), and a rectangular shield (Figure 5.5). He was installed at Tikal under the watchful eye of Sihyajk'ahk', who remained, it seems, the true power behind the throne. There are even strong indications that Yaxnunayin had traveled from highland Mexico and was a toddler when he became Tikal's new king, with Sihyajk'ahk' as regent. The picture that emerges from all of this is that Spearthrower Owl, the ruler of Teotihuacan, oversaw the conquest of Tikal, using Sihyajk'ahk' to head his military force and to oversee the installation of his own young son as the new king.

Clearly there are many details of this narrative that we still do not know, and the conquest of 378 must have had a very complex backstory. What was it all about, and what was Spearthrower Owl's previous connection to the Mutul dynasty? Here we should also ask: Who was the mother? We do not have her name clearly recorded, but there are a few things we can surmise about her. For one, given Yaxnunayin's very young age upon enthronement, she may have played an important role in the movements and machinations leading up to the Entrada and to the overthrow of Chaktokich'ahk. If Yaxnunayin came from distant Teotihuacan, where his father ruled, it is logical to think that she would have traveled with her young son. My guess in all of this is that she must have been someone of considerable importance and probably of Tikal's royal family or at least had some pedigree within the local dynasty. This would have ensured Yaxnunayin's claim to rulership as a Mutul lord and his inclusion by later kings as a significant dynastic ancestor. While speculative, it raises the strong likelihood that the Entrada episode, while a clash of cultures in one sense, had its origins in a conflict among strongly connected elites, some of whom were even intermarried. Part of me wonders, in fact, if we are looking at a long-distance family feud. Let us recall that Spearthrower Owl himself assumed the throne in 374, only a few years before the Entrada, suggesting a quick decision to take down Chaktokich'ahk once he was in power in order to install his own son as king.

The question we must ask again is why? Why would Teotihuacan have such a pressing interest in the affairs of a Maya center more than seven hundred miles away? What was behind the family feud, if we can characterize it that way? This will long remain a murky issue, I am afraid. What strikes me, however, is the importance of other sites besides Tikal in this story. El Peru-Waka' was a stopover for Sihyajk'ahk' and possibly an ally. And Uaxactun was an even more powerful Maya participant in the effort to overthrow Tikal. Its Stela 5 seems to happily commemorate the arrival of Sihyajk'ahk' to Tikal, and its own ruler nearly two decades later calls himself a vassal of Sihyajk'ahk'. This makes sense, given that before 378 Uaxactun had been an enemy of Tikal and its ruler had been captured by

Chaktokich'ahk. Spearthrower Owl and Sihyajk'ahk' had their Maya supporters, therefore, who were probably happy to see Tikal's ruler deposed. That man had many enemies, including possibly his own family members, before his sudden fall.

As regent and local authority, Sihyajk'ahk's political influence went far beyond the confines of Tikal and its Mutul dynasty. Almost immediately after establishing his new seat of power, Sihyajk'ahk' set out to create a network of influence over several other courts in the surrounding central area. Some of these may have been subservient to Tikal before 378 and quickly absorbed into a new political order. Other places such as El Peru-Waka', as we have seen, may have been old allies that had helped Sihyajk'ahk' and his forces quickly penetrate the region, all working in close coordination against Chaktokich'ahk. Whatever the case, his new hegemony based at Tikal covered a good deal of territory by the end of the fourth century, encompassing centers to the east and north and perhaps in other regions. Tellingly, Sihyajk'ahk's name appears in loose block form in a jumbled stairway inscription far to the north in present-day Mexico, at the ruins of El Resbalon near Dzibanche and affiliated with the Kanul dynasty. Sites in that region show intriguing iconographic allusions to Teotihuacan in the Early Classic as well, but we lack the detailed historical narratives as yet to contextualize them. It remains possible that Sihyajk'ahk's new political order reached much further that the incomplete written record indicates. This may prove of importance, for we will soon see how Maya politics during the Late Classic period was dominated by a protracted conflict between Tikal's Mutul dynasty and the lords of Kanul, based at Dzibanche. I wonder if this isolated mention of Sihyajk'ahk' in Kanul territory points to his own political connections in that region to the northeast of Tikal. Did Sihyajk'ahk's far-flung operations somehow help set the stage of that much later rivalry?

Discoveries since the 1990s have continued to flesh out Teotihuacan's intense presence in the Maya area during the Early Classic. Several years ago, excavations at a small center called La Sufricaya, mentioned earlier, revealed some telling new clues about the era. This site was already known to have some inscribed monuments roughly from the late fourth century, attracting the attention of my colleague Francisco Estrada-Belli and his team. There they found that looters, in search of elite burials, had trenched into a large platform or acropolis that once supported several public buildings. These illicit excavations revealed interior walls with remains of a mural painting, which were then excavated and documented starting in 2001 (a situation reminiscent of the discovery of the San Bartolo murals, found the very same year). The varied paintings were remarkable for their unusual style. One was a large panel portraying many armed warriors, each seated in a grid-like "cell." Their garments and weapons indicate that they are foreigners from highland Mexico. Most intriguing was a painted text from an adjacent chamber. This commemorated the construction of the rooms atop the platform, with the date January 16, 379 CE—precisely one year after the Entrada itself. The common date might be seen as a coincidence, but the painted glyphs go on to prove it is intentional, stating: "364 days earlier, the *k'awil* ('authority') arrived to Tikal." Sihyajk'ahk' is not named directly, but text and its associated paintings make clear that the La Sufricaya complex was built in the wake of the Entrada, as a commemoration of it. For me, the most important aspect of the find is the painted depiction of the many warriors—a good indication that the Entrada was not just the story of a handful of individuals but a strong-armed intrusion into the Maya world. La Sufricaya was not a Tikal satellite but a distinct kingdom in the Early Classic, which indicates how the Entrada was an event of regional import when it happened, with distant repercussions.[12]

Another surprising find came in 2022. Excavations at El Peru-Waka' led by Olivia Navarro-Farr unearthed a sculpted monument, intentionally broken and buried deep in the fill of later temple construction (a typical situation in recovering Preclassic or Early Classic materials, as we have learned). It depicts a standing warrior in Teotihuacan regalia, facing forward and holding a rectangular shield and an atlatl spear thrower. The inscription tells us that the stone dates to 435, at the turn of the great four-hundred-year bak'tun cycle 9.0.0.0.0, and that "fifty-seven years before, Sihyajk'ahk' arrived at Tikal." After decades, the arrival was still seen as a great turning point in history. The warrior on the front is a recently crowned local king, possibly a successor to K'inich Bahlam, who was eager to couch the bak'tun's turn in terms of Teotihuacan's persistent ongoing political and religious influence. The monument states that his accession to the throne, three years earlier, was "witnessed by Spearthrower Owl, Lord of Tikal."[13]

This last statement, added almost as an afterthought to the stela's narrative, was especially interesting. Spearthrower Owl "saw" the accession ceremony at El Peru-Waka'? He was a "Lord of Tikal"? On initial glance, all this seemed to throw a wrench into earlier interpretations. But does it? Maya texts often use the phrase "he witnesses" as a statement of royal sanctioning, of approval of a ceremony by a deceased ancestor or some other distant authority. On the very same stela, in fact, a number of local lords "witness" the ceremony at the bak'tun, present in a way, but not physically. The "Tikal Lord" title for Spearthrower Owl was intriguing, if only for the fact that we already know Tikal had its own ruler in office at this time. Yaxnunayin's son, named Sihyaj Chank'awil, assumed the Tikal throne sometime before 436 and erected his own monument to the occasion. For now, I consider the best interpretation of the evidence as an instance of ancient Maya name-dropping by the new El Peru-Waka' ruler. His seating in office was sanctioned by the great Spearthrower Owl, who was then on his own throne at Teotihuacan for fifty-eight years. His revealing title "Tikal Lord" probably refers to the geographical base of his political authority of the central Peten.

Yet another new find comes from Tikal itself. Just a few years ago, new lidar imagery of Tikal revealed the contours of the ancient city and its surroundings with incredible detail. Looking over the results, my colleague Stephen Houston noticed a large pyramid and a plaza located just south of the Mundo Perdido complex, features that did not show up on the old maps of Tikal from fifty years ago. On the surface these seemed like an unassuming area of low mounds, barely visible to anyone who walks the nearby jungle trails. This was adjacent to the very same area where a chance excavation in the 1980s led to the discovery of the Marcador, along with well-preserved structures and courtyards buried meters under the surface, all dating to between 350 and 450 CE. What's more, the large pyramid and plaza vaguely resemble an architectural design familiar from Teotihuacan and specifically the so-called "Ciudadela" ("Citadel") architectural complex of the great Mexican city. The Tikal excavations are continuing, but we already have a clear picture that this area of Tikal was the center of Teotihuacan's presence in the city. Hundreds of fragments of ritual censers were recovered bearing Teotihuacan designs Some dates from its earlier phases suggest it was in use well before 378, again pointing to a deep and close interaction between the two cities in earlier generations.[14]

Teotihuacan's militaristic agents and allies had developed a new system of political rule for the central Maya area, centered at Tikal but resonant among numerous nearby courts and kingdoms. Once in place this situation lasted, I suspect, for no more than fifty or sixty years or so, corresponding roughly to the time of Spearthrower Owl's own reign and his far-flung efforts at military adventurism. It was a culmination of what had been a longer era of close interaction between the two regions, when mutual awareness, trade systems, and family ties were established and maintained. I suspect that Tikal and Chaktokich'ahk himself may have interfered with whatever order had existed before 378 and became a target of Spearthrower Owl's enmity. Whatever the case, the Teotihuacan ruler, newly crowned in 374, took it upon himself to play a direct role in overseeing the politics of the Maya world, using Sihyajk'ahk' as his principal agent. Spearthrower Owl happened to outlive all the other players in this drama, passing away when his grandson Sihyaj Chank'awil eventually became Tikal's ruler, and as the tight political network established by Sihyajk'ahk' began to weaken.

Sihyaj Chank'awil used Stela 31 not only to document his pedigree among the old dynasts of Tikal, probably through his grandmother, but also to celebrate his foreign grandfather, who died only a few years before. When dedicated in 445, the monument was, in a way, an elegant political balancing act in artistic form. On the one hand, it shows how Sihyaj Chank'awil took pains to reassert a decidedly Maya identity in his monuments, even attempting to reach back to pre-Entrada days as an era of political inspiration. Even the defeated Chaktokich'ahk's name appears as part of official history. On the sculpture's front, however, he is shown holding aloft a headdress bearing the name of Spearthrower

Owl, perhaps a gesture of veneration and ancestor worship. Clearly, the messaging of Sihyaj Chank'awil's political art is to acknowledge both his Maya and Teotihuacan ancestry and to reconcile these earlier factions within his own dynasty.

The reign of the next Tikal king, K'ankitam, sees considerable change and even a rejection of Teotihuacan's local influence. He came to the throne in 458, soon after the death of his father, Sihyaj Chank'awil.[15] Kankitam's initial stela is very much in the mode of Stela 31, dedicated more than twenty years earlier, but soon we see a radical change. Rather suddenly, his monuments become less complex iconographically, smaller and more modest in their scale and design. His portraits are no longer dense with the symbols of ancestry, and the texts are much shorter, with little narrative structure to speak of. Here we may see a rejection of the "old art," which was quite conservative and baroque in its way. Gone also are any allusions to Teotihuacan and highland Mexico. Around this time, too, Teotihuacan's old enclave at Tikal was purposefully buried under massive amounts of soil and architectural fill, an effort that required considerable labor, essentially "erasing" those complexes from Tikal's urban landscape. This included covering the large elite residential complex where the Marcador had stood as a testament to the political change brought on by Sihyajk'ahk's conquest many decades earlier. Teotihuacan's local center of operations was not just demolished or repurposed; it was interred, much as if it was the body of a defunct ruler. We cannot be certain why so much effort was expended to terminate or cancel lived space, but it may be no coincidence that it came not long after Spearthrower Owl's death in 439. The passing of such a long-lived and consequential ruler would have certainly affected the political arrangement between the two cities. The record of his death comes near the end of the narrative on Stela 31, giving closure to that monument's long narrative of dynastic ritual and political change. By this point, it seems that the history of the Entrada and of Teotihuacan's intrusive presence was remembered as "old times," with the names of Yaxnunayin and Spearthrower Owl included among the long list of the new king's illustrious ancestors.

Elite material culture at Tikal and its region changed too. Gone now were the copies of Teotihuacan ceramics, as new local styles and traditions emerged, especially with polychrome pottery. New regional styles came to the fore, whereas most Early Classic pottery before 450 was far more homogenous across the lowlands (an adherence to tradition that goes very far back into the Preclassic period). And while Early Classic kingdoms had been very innovative and creative when it came to various *types* of elite objects within this visual world of conformity—inscribed mirrors, celts, carved shells and bones, cache vessels, and so on—we see by the end of the fifth century a more intense desire to create local ways of producing goods. Regional styles and types of objects were emerging as the norm. This is probably a reflection of a larger dissipation of earlier power structures, now far less centralized than they once had been.

TEOTIHUACAN'S LEGACY

In central Mexico, Teotihuacan itself was entering a time of turmoil, leading up to its eventual collapse. ("Collapse" was never just a Maya phenomenon in Mesoamerican history.)[16] According to the best understanding of Teotihuacan's chronology (there are no written dates there), the city suffered a social and political breakdown between 550 and 650 CE, when populations left the urban area and, ultimately, major monumental buildings were intentionally burned and abandoned. At least one hundred buildings in the central zone were intentionally burned and sculptures smashed in what has been described as "the Big Fire." By the end of the so-called Metepec phase at Teotihuacan, the city was a shell of its former self, its institutions and power structures largely gone.

Teotihuacan's sudden change in fortune must have resonated far and wide throughout Mesoamerica. Its effect on Maya history and politics is difficult to gauge, however, and no Maya inscription makes mention of it. Still, it is worth noting that the great city's end came a little more than a century after the death of Spearthrower Owl. Did a period of instability after his long, expansionistic reign contribute to the Teotihuacan's ill fortune? We have little evidence of a direct cause beyond the charred remnants of architecture. Populations continued to live at Teotihuacan amid the ruins of the city, many of them migrants from elsewhere. However we choose to interpret the cancelation of Teotihuacan's presence at Tikal after 450 or so, it seems reasonable to think that it had an indirect connection to events that would befall the city itself a century or so later.

Tikal's protracted encounter with Teotihuacan, involving alliance, close kinship bonds, and conflict, left strong marks on the Maya political world. Tikal's rulers were eager to reassert a Maya identity, but eventually, in later histories, they would also hearken back to the great military power of Mexico, adopting the symbols and ideologies of war for their own local purposes. The Entrada of 378 was remembered for centuries and cited in later histories as a transformative political event, not necessarily in a negative light. Throughout the Classic period and well into the ninth century, the k'uhulajaws of Tikal, Copan, and other Maya polities were eager to evoke the militaristic symbols and messaging of central Mexico, viewing themselves as the rightful successors of Teotihuacan's political ideology, even after its collapse.

After 650, it is common to see Maya lords dressed in the regalia of Teotihuacan, a direct yet nostalgic allusion to a time when political and military power was consolidated in the Peten (Figure 5.6). One might think it a risky way to represent one's power, given Teotihuacan's own precarious situation and downward trajectory. Whatever the precise historical context, the complicated dynamic reflects something at the heart of the Maya rationale in the use of outside symbols. Teotihuacan's constant resurrection within Maya political art seems designed to channel an ideology rooted in the most influential military event in Maya history. It was not about Teotihuacan's current capabilities as an expansionistic military power but about what the great highland city had once been. Maya kings appropriated a foreign legacy for their own ends, much the way the symbols of ancient Rome found new meanings among much later military regimes, even quite close to our own time. Some Maya dynasts were direct descendants of Teotihuacan's own ruler, so making such claims of authority in the wake of Teotihuacan's collapse was in no way an overreach or exaggeration. Maya dynasts saw themselves as inheritors of a great cultural legacy and were happy to make good use of it.[17]

FIGURE 5.6. A stela from Dos Pilas, showing the local ruler as a warrior in Teotihuacan regalia. Photograph by the author.

Numerous kingdoms of the Late Classic period were keen to trace their prestige and even dynastic origins back to this era and to the glory of central Mexico's great city. One of the most famous sculptures from the Classic period, now in the British Museum, provides us with a vivid example of how Teotihuacan continued to exert its importance in later Maya royal art. Lintel 25 from Yaxchilan shows a beautiful, sinuous serpent with its mouth wide open, out of which emerges a warrior holding a shield and a small spear or dart (Plate 13). He wears a round, balloon-like headdress, and his face is fronted by a mask representing the Teotihuacan storm god (details we see also in the stela in Figure 5.6). The deified warrior and serpent rise above a kneeling woman, who holds a bowl of sacrificial implements and presents the warrior with a ceremonial headband, like her own. Were it not for the hieroglyphic text written above the scene, we would have a difficult time interpreting it, and in fact it has often been misunderstood to be the fantastical "vision" of a shamanic ritual. This is not quite accurate. According to the text, the occasion is the inauguration of the Yaxchilan's ruler Shield Jaguar, the lord of the Pa'chan dynasty. The text tells us that as part of that event he is magically conjuring a deity who is the spirit or power (*k'awil*) of warfare. The serpent-warrior is explicitly presented as "of Teotihuacan" and can be taken to be the animate essence of military prowess. It is also, I think, an image of the newly crowned king who assumes that divine identity of an ancestor upon his inauguration, embodying the sacred duties of war. Shield Jaguar may not have been directly descended from Teotihuacan, like the kings of Mutul, but as a new Maya king, he was nevertheless eager to tout a foreign pedigree to bolster his own political and religious messaging.

No other Maya site does more to channel a Teotihuacan legacy than Copan, far to the southeast in what is now western Honduras. The site we see today, with its many pyramids and elaborate sculptures, was established by Maya elites who came from the Peten shortly after 400 CE. Why this was done is not at all clear. The beginnings of this distant "cultural outpost" can be traced specifically to one early Copan king who forged his own strong relations with Teotihuacan and perhaps with Spearthrower Owl himself. That legacy would exert a remarkable influence on the city and its design over the course of four centuries.

The buildings in Copan's imposing main acropolis date mostly to the eighth century, but its beginnings can be traced to some four centuries earlier, as a modest elite household or compound built alongside the Copan River, nestled in a beautiful mountain valley. Communities of farmers and local elites had occupied the Copan valley for centuries, and the newcomers established their modest palatial complex right in the river's floodplain, clearly with ambitions in mind. The main figure behind this new settlement was a ruler named K'inich Yaxk'uk'mo'. According to the voluminous history left to us by Copan's later scribes, he was the first in the line of a royal court perhaps called *Xukpi*. Throughout the span of four centuries, up to the very latest monuments, Yaxk'uk'mo' was celebrated as a singular heroic ancestor, the founder and embodiment of a long-lasting royal family. Many of the site's impressive temples in the acropolis we see today were dedicated to him in one way or another.[18]

The founder was in place at Copan by 416, when it is said that he "raised a stone" in celebration of a k'atun ending. The initial spark of his political and religious authority came a bit later in 426, when Yaxk'uk'mo' participated in an inauguration ceremony *at* Teotihuacan, on a building that the Maya called the *Winte'nah*, perhaps, as some argue, the Sun Pyramid. Wherever it was, he "received k'awil" at that place, using a familiar expression we have encountered in records of the Entrada and elsewhere. Spearthrower Owl was still alive at this time, and it seems probable that Yaxk'uk'mo' assumed his new role under the eye of the Teotihuacan ruler, his close ally. Six months later, he arrived back at Copan, described in familiar terms as when "the western k'awil arrived." In the case of Copan, Teotihuacan was instrumental in the establishment of a new dynastic center, and this connection was remembered for centuries. Even at the end of the Classic period, nearly two centuries after Teotihuacan's collapse, the ancient city in Mexico still had a grip on the Maya imagination and on its own view of history.[19]

The intrusive power play instigated by Teotihuacan was a flashpoint in a long relationship between the elites of the two regions, and it had a lasting effect on Maya history. Teotihuacan's own early ambitions to construct terraced artificial mountains—that is, great pyramids—may have been inspired by earlier "predynastic" monuments in the distant Maya lowlands, at sites such as El Mirador. After 100 CE, when Maya dynasties came on the scene at Tikal and elsewhere, there developed a mutual interest between central Mexico and the Maya region and even the forging of close family relationships among elites. Teotihuacan's own political changes took place around 350 or so, when Spearthrower Owl was ruling, expansionistic militarism took hold, and new populations arrived from different parts of southern Mesoamerica. As we've seen, a new ruling structure may have even planted the seeds of instability and conflict, leading up to the collapse around 550.

It's no coincidence that the sixth century was also the very time when many other people and places in Maya history begin to emerge from obscurity, as more and more sources come into play. From here, historical narratives include actors and events from a variety of kingdoms, going well beyond a handful of Early Classic sites in the central Peten. With the break from Teotihuacan, we begin to see how Maya politics played out even more vividly as a complex network of kabch'ens and k'uhulajaws, subject to ever-changing alliances and conflicts. Tikal and its Mutul dynasty continued to rise as a dominant player, as did its rival Dzibanche and its Kanul dynasty. Indeed, these two kingdoms would emerge in the sixth century as the principal players within a continuous rivalry that extended across the lowlands. Their fraught relationship shaped the larger narrative arc of ancient Maya history. There were many other "arrivals" to come, each bringing a transformation in politics and in the social lives of the nobility.

CHAPTER 6

Expansions

GREAT CHANGES CAME in the century that followed Teotihuacan's meddling in Maya politics. After about 450 CE, the Mutul dynasty at Tikal entered an extended period of relative quiet, no longer for us the main focal point of Maya history, as other cities and actors emerged as important players in dynastic politics. Tikal itself experienced an internal change as well, perhaps even a rejection of the political art and rhetoric of the previous century. By the later years of Kankitam's rule, Tikal's stelae become smaller and much more modest in appearance, and afterward, from 500 on, the city's record becomes more broken and scattered, resulting in large gaps in our sense of history. Even major building programs ceased, and in some cases long stretches of time came when no monuments were erected.[1] This turbulent time came to be called the "Maya Hiatus" and has been the subject of a good deal of debate. Back in the 1950s and 1960s, before the decipherment, many archaeologists sensed and pondered this broken legacy of the sixth century. Was it a symptom of Tikal's weak rulership and internal dynastic struggles or a direct effect of some outside conquest? Was it even local to Tikal or a phenomenon more widespread in the central region? In my view, either-or questions such as these fall short and fail to frame the issue completely. I believe that the "Hiatus" reflected all these things, as we will explore in this chapter, namely the unstable dynamics within royal families coupled with the pressures of external regional conflict.

During the 1970s, before the historical context was well understood, archaeologist Gordon Willey had speculated that the Hiatus was a "rehearsal" for the systemic collapse that came three centuries later, asserting that the study of each phenomenon might shed light on the other.[2] His general idea turned out to be prescient. The same political and ideological stresses that led to the instabilities at Tikal and elsewhere—warfare primarily among them—turned out to have close parallels within the more extensive crisis that would come three or so centuries later. As we have already seen with early patterns in Maya history, "dark ages" came and went with a great deal of regularity, as communities and city-states underwent constant adjustments and adaptions in a landscape beset by conflict. Willey was right, I think, to look at the Hiatus for clues about what befell Maya civilization on a greater scale after 800, for many of the same factors were at play, as we will see.

Tikal's fate in the sixth century had much to do with a renewed cycles of warfare and conflict that arose in the wake of Teotihuacan's waning influence in the Maya area. The problems come into focus during the reign of Kankitam's son, Chaktokich'ahk II, who reigned as early as 486. His name should be familiar, resurrecting that of the Mutul king who was defeated and perhaps sacrificed ("entering the water") by Sihyajk'ahk' at the moment of the Entrada in 378. The reuse of the name seems strategic, hearkening back to the pre-Entrada days, before the time of Spearthrower Owl. (The Teotihuacan ruler, now long deceased, was Chaktokich'ahk's great-great-grandfather, we should recall.) We know little about the new Chaktokich'ahk's life and times, except that he waged a war of conquest against a site (still unidentified) that a century earlier was part of Sihyajk'ahk's network of client kingdoms. This seems a good indication that the old order had broken down. The Tikal stela that bears this record, the eroded Stela 10, portrays the younger Chaktokich'ahk standing above a prone captive, repeating a familiar pose.

The only other detail we know of Chaktokich'ahk II was that he died on July 25, 508. What is striking is not the obscure circumstance of his death but rather where it was recorded—on a small, inscribed altar stone from the far-off site of Tonina, in the mountains of present-day Mexico and near the western frontier of the Maya world. There it is part of an inscription that tallied several royal deaths that had occurred across the Maya world in the years leading up to the k'atun ending of 514 CE (9.4.0.0.0), naming kings from a variety of places, listed one after another. This one sculpture gives us a valuable insight into the scope and awareness that Maya scribes had of their own times, recording the events of different kingdoms far beyond their own territories. For the Tonina scribe, the death of Chaktokich'ahk II from Tikal was worthy of official note in a public text. (Maya kingdoms were very aware of each other.) Fourteen days after the king's death, his high-ranking warrior (*yajawte'*), named Ajbahlamt'ul, suffered his own setback, captured by the Pa'chan dynasty at Yaxchilan. This may represent another western war waged by Chaktokich'ahk II, and he may have died as part of this military campaign far from home. Whatever the case, we come away with the sense that the first decades of the sixth century were another important turning point, a moment when Tikal's fortunes took a turn for the worse. The troubles may be signaled also by the rise in 511 of a six-year-old queen, Lady Yopk'in, to Tikal's throne. Her age suggests she was a daughter of Chaktokich'ahk II, but we are unsure of her background or the circumstances leading up to her accession.[3]

Tikal now entered a cloudy era, just as the k'atun ending of 514 (9.4.0.0.0) came and went. For the next century and a half, we have only scattered and incomplete records and actors and not much beyond a few names here and there. The central region seems to have been highly unstable both socially and politically, as indicated by the rise of many secondary sites around Tikal and the construction of fortifications around many of them. Tikal and its immediate neighbors were surrounded with an ambitious defensive system composed of ditches and ramparts, some dating to the sixth century. This era of conflict and turbulence in the central Peten corresponds to the rapid rise of a new kingdom located to the northeast, at a place and royal house called Kanul ("Place of Snakes"). Mentioned several times already, its importance has only emerged from obscurity in recent years. Before 500 CE it began to exert its own political muscle, perhaps as it sensed the waning of Teotihuacan's power in the central lowlands. The Kanul dynasty emerged soon thereafter as the greatest power in the region, with its kings among the most powerful figures of ancient Maya history.

SEEKING THE "PLACE OF SNAKES"

Kanul was probably the ancient place name for an immense ruin we know today as Dzibanche ("Inscribed Wood"), located in the southern part of Quintana Roo state in Mexico. It once sat within a large fertile region dense with ancient urban settlement and ceremonial complexes, surrounded by irrigated fields and terraced hillsides.[4] Dzibanche was the largest among several sites concentrated in the region, all comprising the Kanul polity, among them Kinichna, Tutil, Pol Box, and El Resbalón. Also near Dzibanche is a very large Late Preclassic center named Ichkabal, perhaps the "original" Kanul from previous centuries, and connected to the latter by an ancient road. In chapter 3, we first encountered Kanul as a possible home for one of the earliest rulers we know in Maya history, Uxyophun, or "Foliated Ahau," who is associated in later records with the date 156 CE. Whatever the case, we know that the Kanul dynasty arose in this region and was a significant player in regional affairs from almost the very beginning of history.

Our awareness of Kanul, or the "Snake Kingdom" as it is sometimes called, is only somewhat recent, and it remained unknown to archaeologists and epigraphers until the 1980s. In fact, its identification offers an interesting backstory of decipherment and detective work that began in those years, only a few decades ago. Back then a pressing question facing archaeologists and epigraphers centered on the identification of an enigmatic emblem glyph, or court name, that appeared in many Maya texts. Its sign represented a toothy snake's head, and the glyph clearly named an important place in Maya politics and history that was difficult to associate with any site (Figure 6.1; see also Figure 4.4). One difficulty was its appearance at several places, including Tikal, Copan Palenque, and

Yaxchilan. Where then was its true "home" on the archaeological landscape? At Copan, it was mentioned alongside the emblems of Tikal, Copan, and Palenque and in association with glyphs for the four cardinal directions of Maya cosmology. The snake emblem seems to be the northern place among the four. But where? In the early 1970s, the archaeologist Joyce Marcus proposed that it might be Calakmul, the immense ruin in Campeche not far north of the Guatemala-Mexico border. It was an intriguing idea yet hard to confirm at the time. The numerous monuments of Calakmul were in a terrible state of preservation, barely legible aside from a handful of dates and some scattered historical names. For a time, we called the snake glyph the "Calakmul emblem," but we still were not sure.[5]

FIGURE 6.1. The hieroglyph for Kanul. Drawing by the author.

Other finds from those years added a couple of false leads. One came from a large, well-preserved stela purchased by the Cleveland Museum of Art, bearing the portrait of a regal woman known today as "Lady Kabel" (a princess of the Kanuls, as we later learned) (see Figure 7.4). Its text displays an example of the same snake emblem, but no one was sure from where this magnificent sculpture was looted. The first scholar to publish on it in the early 1970s agreed with Marcus, tentatively suggesting Calakmul as its place of origin, based on stylistic connections.[6] Several years later, another clue emerged when the explorer Ian Graham found discarded remains of a sawn stela at El Peru-Waka', left behind by looters. Graham matched these discarded pieces with the portions of the stela in Cleveland, establishing its place of origin. This naturally led to the conclusion that the snake emblem must refer to El Peru-Waka', not Calakmul. Adding to the confusion, just a short time later, a true emblem for El Peru-Waka' and its rulers was discovered by Stephen Houston, casting firm doubt on the entire snake–El Peru-Waka' connection. (The snake was a foreign reference at El Peru-Waka', as it turned out.) Back to square one, or at least to Calakmul.[7] Around that same time, several looted stones appeared in art galleries and various collections in the United States, Mexico, and Europe. These recounted the details of an as-yet-unknown dynasty and again from a place no one could identify. This mystery location came to be called "Site Q," and the snake emblem appeared on a couple of those blocks as well. If the snake was not the emblem for Calakmul or for El Peru-Waka', it must be the emblem of this obscure lost city, or so we thought.

Happily, at long last, the confirmation of Calakmul came from a close analysis of how place names are recorded in Maya inscriptions. In the late 1980s, my colleague Stephen Houston and I first identified the existence of actual place names in Maya texts—names like Lakamha' for what we today call Palenque or Yax Mutul for what we know as Tikal. While sorting out those names, we were able to associate two places, Chihknahb and Uxte'tuun, with the snake emblem itself. Neither of these corresponded to any of the supposed candidates for "Site Q," but they did appear in some inscription fragments that came from Calakmul itself. The original identification of the snake emblem with Calakmul looked to be correct after all.

But this was not the end of the puzzle. Also in the 1990s, archaeologist Enrique Nalda began an intensive program of archaeological investigations at Dzibanche, the first ever attempted since the site's discovery in 1927. It indeed proved to be a huge ancient city—among the largest of the Maya area—but sparse on carved monuments. However, in one of his excavations, Nalda found the Stairway of the Captives, with its powerful images of images of bound, tortured prisoners. When epigrapher Erik Velazquez first showed me the stones at Dzibanche in 2003, I was amazed when he pointed out to me the snake emblem glyph repeatedly accompanying the name of an early king. Clearly the situation was more complicated than we had thought.

Today we understand that the snake emblem was a court name used at *both* Dzibanche and Calakmul and that the two massive centers were politically connected over the course of the Classic period. As we've discussed earlier, we now know that emblems like the snake specify a courtly name or designation and that this moved over the course of history. And there is ample evidence, too, that especially powerful royal courts could have more than one base of operations, even at the same time. This was especially true during times of intensive military hostilities among rival cities. In a general way, the pattern reflects the frequent mobility of even the most powerful of Maya royal courts.[8]

Kanul probably began as the actual place name of Dzibanche, where it appears as a hieroglyph before anywhere else. Later, the name came to be extended to the local dynasty that originated in the region during the Late Preclassic or very early years of the Classic era. The many years it took to tease out this complex pattern reminds us how we often work with misguided assumptions or incomplete questions, even over decades of investigation. As it turned out in the end, the "Snake" was never a single place at all but the name of a royal house with different bases of operation at different times of history. During the Classic period, Dzibanche and Calakmul were its "seats," sometimes working separately as dual centers of political authority for the Kanul family. Like some motifs in Maya art and iconography, the Kanul kingdom was a snake with two heads.

KANUL'S DYNASTY

In chapter 4, we mentioned an intriguing king list that names many Kanul rulers and their accession dates, including a founder who most likely dates to the second century CE. Some archaeologists have tried to push the Kanul kingdom even further back in time, associating it with the Late Preclassic and with El Mirador in particular. Given the lack of history at those "predynastic" sites, the evidence for such a connection is lacking, however. I see Kanul's historical roots as lying closer to Dzibanche or with the massive pyramids at the nearby Preclassic site of Ichkabal, located near the present-day town of Bacalar. Another intriguing clue comes from another ruin called Pol Box, close to Dzibanche, where one stela recalls an event in 141 CE when some sort of foundational event seems to have occurred, perhaps in connection with the enigmatic Uxyophun or "Foliated Ahau." It leads me to wonder if this same region of southern Quintana Roo played a special role in the rise of the early dynasties of the Classic period.[9]

Later on, after 450–500 CE, the Kanuls indicated their own intimate connections to central Mexico and to Teotihuacan. Several of Dzibanche's large pyramids, dating to about 500 CE, directly evoke Teotihuacan in their design and adornments, perhaps even more overtly than we see at Tikal. One tall structure at Tutil (a part of Dzibanche) was a religious shrine evidently dedicated to a deity of Teotihuacan, representing a feline with a war helmet grasping the torches of a sacred fire. And as mentioned earlier, an inscription from the nearby site of El Resbalon may even mention Sihyajk'ahk', suggesting a direct role in the dramas of the earlier Entrada and the political climate it created. From these clues, I suspect that future discoveries will reveal that Kanul was more than a bystander in that story of Tikal's conquest in 378, given Kanul's continued rivalry with Tikal in later years. Without more written sources, it remains impossible for us to know for certain. Still, the timing of these overt references to central Mexico suggests that Kanul's rulers were set on expansion, consciously trying to fill the political void left in the wake of Teotihuacan's exit from the Tikal-Uaxactun region, appropriating their role as a hegemonic power in the central lowlands.

Kanul's rulers at the very least chose to take advantage of an unstable situation, and their ambitions, whether old or new, seem to have set in motion a great many conflicts that played out over the next two centuries. We will encounter the details of this rivalry between the Kanul and Mutul dynasties throughout the ensuing chapters, but here I would like to frame that long-term pattern of discord by suggesting that it was, at its heart, a rivalry between Maya communities speaking different languages. Historically and going back many centuries, the northern half of the peninsula was populated by speakers of Yucatec Mayan. To the south, roughly below the borders that modern Mexico shares with Guatemala and Belize, historical sources from the early colonial era indicate that the Ch'olan Mayan languages were dominant. This is where the Maya script must have initially developed, for the language of the hieroglyphs was also Ch'olan, going back to the Late Preclassic period. This linguistic connection traveled with the script itself, so that Ch'olan was adopted as a formal lingua franca in inscriptions for all lowland elites, including those in Yucatán. (Tellingly, the inscriptions of late Chichen Itza, are

FIGURE 6.2. Carved step block from Dzibanche, showing bound prisoner. Photograph by the author.

Ch'olan, not Yucatec.) And this is why the name Kanul is interesting. In spelling the word *kan*, "snake," the emblem hieroglyph constantly displays a snake's head with an extra sign attached in front, the phonetic element **ka-**. (Observant readers can find this same sign included in Landa's notorious "alphabet.") This tells a reader to pronounce the word as *kan*. This is revealing, I think, for the Ch'olan Mayan pronunciation of the word for "snake" is quite different—*chan*—also clearly attested in the ancient texts. This all may seem a fine point of phonetics, but the takeaway here is that Kanul is, in origin, a Yucatecan name, spelled as such by elite scribes who used a system that seems Ch'olan in its origin and overall usage. At the end of the Classic period, we will see how the Kanul elite may have migrated northward into Campeche and Yucatán, perhaps solidifying an old historical and linguistic affiliation.

The expansionism of Kanul's early kings is on full display on the Dzibanche captive stairway, probably dating to sometime in the late fifth century (Figure 6.2). The steps were composed of at least twenty-one stone blocks carved in relief with the portraits of bound, miserable prisoners. All are shown on their knees, bent over, contorted, or prone on the ground. They've been stripped of their finery, their hair unkempt, many clearly shouting or groaning in pain. As one ascended or descended the steps, one "stepped" atop the captives' bodies, just as we see on stelae at Tikal. The prisoners are clearly elites, all named in the accompanying captions with dates and highlighted events such as "he was tied up" or "his town was conquered." While fragmentary, the accompanying glyphs tell us that they were all the prisoners of the Kanul ruler named Yuknomch'en, which we can perhaps translate as something like "the Shaker of Cities." There can be little doubt that these captives represent prisoners taken in a series of his military campaigns. It is an extraordinary document of outward-looking conquest, and in its time it must have seemed unusually direct and assertive as a historical record. No previous Maya monuments had ever highlighted the narrative of conquest and capture so overtly or in so much detail. Yuknomch'en was very innovative in his self-presentation as a great conqueror and power player. And it all set the stage for the intense wars we see waged throughout the rest of the Classic period. It cannot be a coincidence that over a century after the Dzibanche steps were carved, a later Kanul king based at Calakmul decided to use the same name Yuknomch'en, as he embarked on his own campaign of conquest and expansionism, a second "Shaker of Cities."[10]

As the historical records increase in number and clarity, we see that the next important Kanul figure from this early period was named Tunk'abhix, who ruled from before 520 up to about 550.[11] Mentioned in the histories of several distant kingdoms, he may be the most influential ruler to emerge in Maya history after the death of Spearthrower Owl. One illustration of his political outreach comes from a remarkable altar-like stone now housed in the Dallas Museum of Art, originally from the ruins of La Corona, or in ancient times as Saknikte' (Figure 6.3). Its ornate design shows us two royal women facing one another, surrounded by a lengthy text and complex religious and cosmological imagery. The carving was dedicated much later, around 721 CE, to commemorate the arrival and marriage of a Kanul woman into the local dynasty. This is the woman shown on the left, standing before a small stool-like throne. On the right we have the portrait of Lady Nahek', an earlier Kanul woman who had similarly married into the Saknikte' royal line some two centuries before, in the year 520. She is named in the text as the daughter of Tunk'abhix. The point of this narrative was to link the arrivals of these two Kanul princesses separated by two hundred years,

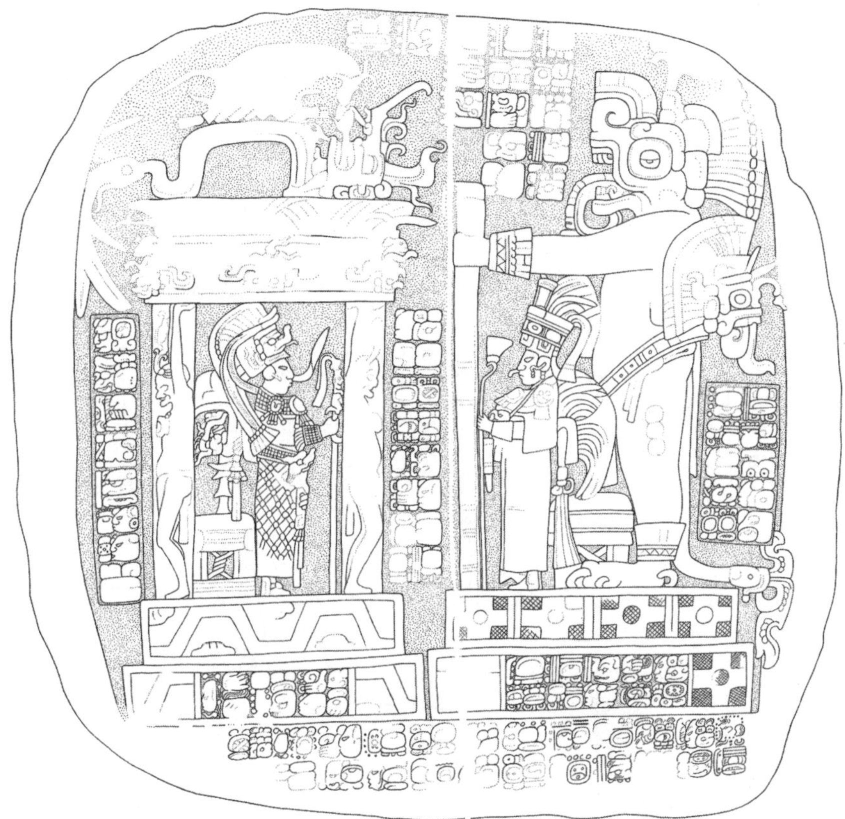

FIGURE 6.3. Two Kanul queens at La Corona, from La Corona, Panel 6. Drawing by the author.

as mirror images of one another, like-in-kind events that perpetuated a key historical and family relationship.

The La Corona altar highlights the importance of such arranged marriages as a strategy in Maya politics and alliance-building. Over generations, the local dynasty of Saknikte' was linked by marriage to the much more powerful Kanul lords. The Kanul dynasty used this same method to great effect throughout the centuries of the Classic period, when many of its princesses were married into several foreign courts. As we will see, a number of important women in history, such as Lady K'abel or Lady Wakjalam Chanlem, provided many of the essential family bonds among elite lineages.[12]

FIGURE 6.4. Ajnumsaj, king of Naranjo. Naranjo, Stela 47. Drawing by Alexandre Tokovinine.

THE TRUSTED ALLY

Tunk'abhix continued his far-flung efforts at alliance-building when he oversaw the installation of a vassal ruler at the kingdom of Sa'al, known today as the site of Naranjo, in the eastern Peten of northern Guatemala.

This occurred on May 5, 546. Naranjo was already an old city and a consistent player in many historical narratives of the Classic period, many of which we will trace throughout later chapters. Its new king and Kanul ally was named Ajnumsaj Chank'inich, the thirty-fifth ruler in a long dynastic line with roots in the Late Preclassic (Figure 6.4). We know only a little of Naranjo's history before this, save for a king named Natz' Chanahk, who ruled soon after the Entrada in 435, perhaps as a vassal of Sihyajk'ahk'. In the Early Classic, Naranjo seems to have entered a marriage alliance with the Mutul dynasty at Tikal; at least there are hints of a close dynastic connection between the two lineages before 500, well before they developed a protracted animosity that would play out in later centuries.[13]

Ajnumsaj was very young, perhaps even a child, when Tunk'abhix oversaw his crowning as the king of Naranjo. We lack the date of his birth, yet we can infer his young age knowing that his reign would last *at least* sixty-nine years, up to his death around 615. This would make him one of the longest-lasting monarchs from world history. His installment as a youth by a foreign power bears a striking resemblance to the other boy-king we have seen so far in Maya history, Yaxnunayin who had been crowned at Tikal in 379 when also a very young child, then under the authority of Sihyajk'ahk'. Perhaps Tunk'abhix was modeling his newer network of vassals on a template that had held sway over the Peten a century and a half earlier. Whatever his exact age, Ajnumsaj's enthronement under Tunk'abhix jump-started Naranjo's political fortunes, and its king would emerge as a major political and military actor in his own right, overseeing his own regional conquests and system of client kings, nested within the larger one. Two sources drive home this point. In 596, fifty years into his reign, we read that there was "the 'mountain-ing' of heads and the 'lake-ing' of blood," probably in connection with the refurbishment of a local temple at Naranjo. This poetic expression refers to the mass sacrifice and creation of a figurative "landscape" of hill and lakes out of the executed bodies of Naranjo's enemies. Ajnumsaj's regional power-playing also comes across at the ruins of Holmul, a large site twenty kilometers distant. There excavations revealed a well-preserved stucco facade of a building, with iconography and a hieroglyphic text celebrating a local ruler named Tzab Chanyopat, possibly buried within and shown in the center of the facade sitting atop a cosmic mountain, a "king of the hill" (Plate 9). The accompanying text cites a woman, possibly his wife, who was the daughter of Ajnumsaj, and the Holmul ruler is then called the "vassal lord of the Kanul Ajaw." Here we have good evidence of a nested hierarchy, with Naranjo's ruler helping forge Kanul's network of client kingdoms through the marriage of his own daughter. (A similar episode will occur in Naranjo's later history, as we will see, with the marriage of a foreign princess into its own dynasty.)[14]

This intriguing Holmul inscription also makes a tangential reference to, of all things, the Teotihuacan entrada. Tzab Chanyopat is named as the "fifth successor" in the line of the *winte'nah,* the lineage house associated with Teotihuacan and its system rule in the fourth century, probably about two centuries earlier. We know that Holmul had been a part of that same powerful network established under Sihyajkahk', so it seems Teotihuacan's political and symbolic legacy remained strong. Tzab Chanyopat represented himself not only as a vassal of Kanul and Naranjo but as an inheritor of that earlier role. The implication here seems to be that, through Ajnumsaj and others, Kanul's kings were attempting to re-create the sort of centralized political hegemony that had existed two hundred years before. It seems to bolster the idea that Kanul's rulers strove to establish Dzibanche as the inheritor of Teotihuacan's old regional dominance.

The later chronicles of Naranjo celebrate Ajnumsaj as a heroic figure and model king. He was a loyal ally under four successive Kanul kings, as one inscription takes special care to mention.[15] His very long reign ended in 615, also bringing an end to a long era of local political stability in the eastern Peten. Afterward came a hiatus of Naranjo's own, with a decades-long cessation of monuments and a silent historical record. Ajnumsaj's immediate successor is unknown. Something at the time jarred Naranjo's court, eventually disrupting even the long-standing alliance with Kanul's kings. So dramatic was the cut-off, in fact, that we might entertain the possibility that Naranjo soon suffered a political takeover from the Mutul dynasty at Tikal (an old family relation, we should recall). Fifteen years into Naranjo's "dark age," Naranjo found itself aligned *against* the Kanuls and even the target of a military campaign from its former overlords. To put this switch of allegiance in perspective, we need to take a wider view of the political landscape in the late sixth and early seventh centuries, which turns out to be an unusually dramatic period in wider Maya history, illustrating the fickle nature of Maya political relations.

TIKAL'S DEFEAT AND REVIVAL

In 550, an important new Kanul ruler appeared, with the impressive name K'ahk'uti'ch'ich' ("Fire Is the Mouth of Blood"), whose existence we only discovered in the past few years.[16] While only cited in only a handful of sources, he was also engaged in his own far-flung alliances and the strengthening of Dzibanche's hegemony toward the south. In 556, he oversaw the installation of a new ruler at El Peru-Waka', west of Tikal, signaling an encroachment from another direction.[17] The king's name was also recently discovered in an inscription on a temple facade at the remote site named Chochkitam, in far northeast Guatemala. There he also oversaw the installation of yet another local king, perhaps in 568.[18] Such small, piecemeal clues tell us that by the mid-500s, successive Kanul rulers had formed a far-reaching political network, stretching across the Peten and reaching to both the west and east of Tikal in a pincer-like motion.

K'ahk'uti'ch'ich's reach toward the west was perhaps a reaction to resurgent efforts by the Mutul king of the time, who was exerting his own control over at least one distant ally and client. In 553, just three years before Kanul's installation of a new ruler at El Peru-Waka', a Mutul ruler named Yax Ehbxok K'inich oversaw the installation of its own client at the site of Caracol, the vast, important city far to the southwest in the mountains of present-day Belize.[19] Its ancient name was Uxwitza', "Three-Mountains-Waters," and it had already been another important actor in Maya politics for a long time and during the Early Classic. The new Tikal ally at Caracol was named Yajawte' K'inich, and he reigned for several eventful decades until 599, a rough contemporary of Ajnumsaj of Naranjo.

Caracol will prove to have its own complex role in the shifting political alliances of the Classic period, even as an important Kanul ally, but here in the mid-500s, it was subject to a Mutul king, at least for a time. This may have been a prime motivator for K'ahk'uti'ch'ich' to press forward, solidifying Kanul's alliances and expanding them in new directions.

Adding to these political complexities (and also reflecting our patchy sources), it is possible that the Mutul court was in some way fractured during this unstable time, with different factions and centers of authority. A brief statement from an inscribed vessel excavated at Uaxactun appears to cite a Mutul king of this era as the "vassal" (*yajaw*) of K'ahk'uti'ch'ich', the king of Kanul.[20] If we take this statement at face value, it points to an even more dramatic scene of Kanul's political dominance than we ever realized. The overall situation is hard to reconstruct from such a brief mention, and we may be dealing with rival claimants or some "rogue" noble of Mutul who opted to ally himself with Kanul while another was making expansionistic moves toward Caracol. Perhaps he was the contemporary of Yax Ehbxok K'inich, another claimant to the Mutul throne, in 553.

K'ahk'uti'ch'ich' didn't reign very long past the year 556, and a new Kanul ruler took over by 561. We refer to him with the nickname "Sky Witness" (his full hieroglyphic name remains unreadable), and he left an even more important and lasting mark on Maya political history. His presence on the political landscape was equally if not more expansive, now involving cities and polities with an even farther geographical spread from Dzibanche. Several distant kingdoms cite his name as a person of authority, ranging from the site of Yo'okop in northern Quintana Roo to Palenque on the western edges of the Maya world and to Caracol in what is now Belize. As we will explore in chapter 10, Sky Witness may have been instrumental in establishing a new queen as a vassal at the great northern center of Coba in 569. The unusual length of his rule is another good indication of his power and influence. Nearly four decades into his reign, in 599, Sky Witness is said to have conquered the Palenque, only a few years before the birth of its most famous king, K'inich Janabpakal. Perhaps at no other point in Maya history do we see the Kanul dynasty as so omnipresent and politically powerful.[21]

Kanul's aggressive stance toward Mutul culminated in April 30, 562, when Sky Witness defeated the king of Tikal, perhaps Yax Ehbxok K'inich (also known as Wak Chank'awil), the son of Chaktokich'ahk II. Only a century and a half after Tikal's ties to Teotihuacan had given way, the court of Mutul at Tikal or a faction of it found itself defeated and under the thumb of yet another foreigner, now not so distant. This stands out as one of the major political shifts in the sixth century, although many aspects of the event and its actors remain obscure.[22] And it was yet another setback for the Mutul dynasty overall, which had already been involved in a power struggle during the reign of K'ahk'uti'ch'ich'.

With all this historical back-and-forth, we can now begin to understand the so-called "hiatus" at Tikal, a noticeable gap in its monumental record that has long puzzled Maya archaeologists, going back to the 1960s. With better historical context, we can now see that Tikal's possible defeat in 562 by Kanul could have easily led to a temporary flight from or abandonment of the city. It was a new setback during a protracted downturn in fortune. Similar "silent periods" appear in the records of numerous sites, as it turns out, including Naranjo and Caracol and even in the history of the Kanul kingdom itself. Maya history is a narrative of many localized "fits and starts" within dynasties, usually instigated by a disruptive war. This, we will see, is an important issue to revisit when we discuss the role of warfare in the ninth century collapse. For now, we can simply paint a picture of an expansionistic dynasty working with its allies to influence much of the Maya lowlands, with Tikal and its allies clearly in the way. Conquest was always somewhat fleeting, however, and new wars and renewed conflicts were a constant.

We begin to see a bit more clarity in Tikal's history with the accession of its twenty-second ruler in 593, whom we refer to by the provisional name "Animal Skull." Little is known of his reign, but with him, and especially through his son and grandson, we can begin to track a sequence of detailed events involving the Mutul and Kanul rivalry. Animal Skull was probably buried in a rich tomb known to us as Burial 195, located in a large pyramid (Structure 5D-32) at the eastern side of Tikal's large necropolis, facing the site's Central Plaza. This was excavated by University of Pennsylvania archaeologists in the mid-1960s, who found the chamber filled with a thick deposit of mud, evidently the result of ancient flooding. Hollows within the mud were found to be the remains of decayed wooden artifacts, and these were carefully filled with plaster to reveal their original forms. The treasures included painted statues of the deity K'awil as well as the possible remains of Animal Skull's wooden sarcophagus, composed of richly sculpted wooded panels. These depicted seated rulers holding serpents and a text bearing the Long Count date 9.8.0.0.0 (August 23, 593), a welcome chronological anchor for his reign. This key reference gives us Animal Skull's first k'atun ending. How long he reigned is unclear. His likely successor, still poorly known, is cited only in later texts as the father of two sons who eventually took over the story, playing outsized roles in the larger Kanul-Mutul drama.[23]

KANUL AND CARACOL

Among Maya kingdoms, the internal organization of the expansionistic Kanul state was probably unusual and complex. This shouldn't come as a surprise, perhaps, given its ambitions and far-flung military campaigns. For example, by the late 500s, there are hints that the Kanul dynasty developed a dualistic arrangement of governance, which we might even describe as a system of "co-rulership." This is suggested by a curious pattern where we come across two different k'uhulajaws who use the Kanul emblem title, existing at different locales. By the late sixth century, the Kanul dynasty began to look westward and expanded its administrative footprint by adopting Calakmul (Uxte'tun), located in southern Campeche, as a "second base" of its court and dynasty. This may have occurred soon after its victory over Tikal, with the need to establish an extension of its court closer to the allies and enemies of the central Peten. At first glance, this might seem a confused political situation, but we should remember that complex and varied ruling systems were commonplace in Mesoamerica and even within the Maya region in different historical eras.[24] An alternative take on the situation, perhaps even a preferred scenario, sees the "dual capitals" of Kanul as a reflection not of internal complexity within a single polity but of a fractured court with two seats of power. We will see that the 620s and 630s were a time of considerable internal friction among rival Kanul rulers and that Dzibanche and Calakmul were the seats of that divide, with Calakmul eventually emerging as a new capital. Could this fracture have emerged earlier?

Another prominent figure of Kanul history we call "Scroll Serpent" (another provisional nickname). He seems to have assumed a position of authority at Calakmul in 579, when Sky Witness was still the ruler of the Kanul realm at Dzibanche. It is hard to know their exact political or family relationship, but eventually Scroll Serpent succeeded Sky Witness as paramount k'uhulajaw and overseer of Kanul's vassals, among them, still, Ajnumsaj of Naranjo. Scroll Serpent continued the wars of Sky Witness and was responsible for his own follow-up victory over Palenque in 611. (The previous engagement was only a dozen years earlier, indicating how fleeting some military "conquests" could be.) The purpose of Kanul's continued concern with far-off Palenque is unclear, but the long-distance nature of these operations leads me to suspect that many courts and communities of the southern Maya lowlands may have drawn into these wider conflicts in one way or another, forced to form new alliances and to break others.

The Kanul network was also pushing farther to the south. By 619, the new Kanul ruler, Yuknom Uti'chan, went to work quickly exerting his own distant political influences, and in that year he oversaw the crowning of a new ruler at Carcaol, named Tumyohl K'inich. He would turn out to have an outsized influence in the eastern region, especially in the wake of Ajnumsaj's death. Caracol had its own stories of political intrigue up to this point. As noted earlier, in 553 a king named Yajawte' K'inich was installed under the authority of Mutul's (Tikal's) king Yax Ehbxok K'inich. This lasted no more than a decade, and Yajawte' K'inich later displayed a complete turnaround in his loyalty, coming under the control of Kanul's lords. One suspects that this may have been due to the important war of 562, still only tentatively understood, when Sky Witness defeated Tikal's ruler. With that defeat, Caracol may have simply redirected its loyalty to the victor. In time, Yajawte' K'inich married a woman who seems to have had ties to Kanul, who arrived at Caracol with great fanfare in 584. A son named Tumyohl K'inich came from that union, and he would ascend to Caracol's throne in 619. Now, Caracol's ruling family was firmly in the sphere of influence of Kanul, or a faction of it.

Ajnumsaj of Naranjo died around the time of Tumyohl K'inich's ascendancy at Caracol. The timing of these two events seems related, as the demise of one important Kanul ally and the rise of another. This was a time of increased turmoil within the Kanul political system and perhaps even a crisis in Kanul's own ability to hold its expansive political ambitions in check. We can be certain that in 626 Tumyohl K'inich waged war against Naranjo's forces and emerged victorious ("the Naranjo person(s) fell"). Naranjo and (more recently) Caracol were both allies of the Kanul kingdom, so why were they now at war? Perhaps we can best understand this as a conflict between two very different sorts of vassals. Ajnumsaj had been a loyal ally for over six decades, subservient to the four successive kings who ruled at Dzibanche. His successor at Naranjo was an obscure figure named K'uxaj, who may have been his son. Tumyohl K'inich by contrast represented a much newer allegiance, a switch from what had been a Mutul-Caracol alliance. In this new role, Tumyohl K'inich appears to have had closer affiliations with the Kanul court or a faction based at Calakmul. He was their ally, in other words, not necessarily aligned with Dzibanche. As a partner of that newer Kanul faction, Tumyohl K'inich's installation as ruler in 618 was perhaps indicative of rising tensions within Kanul's system and of the continued emergence of Calakmul as an alternate seat of Kanul authority.[25]

By 631, a new Kanul ruler ascended to the throne at Calakmul. His name still eludes a full decipherment, and we refer to him only as "Yuknom Head." That year his forces attacked K'uxaj, resulting in Naranjo's defeat. The full statement of the victory was recorded on a stone block discovered at Naranjo, oddly enough (Figure 6.5; see Plate 11). It says: "On the day 7 Ak'bal the Sixteenth of Muan, Sa'al, the realm of K'uxaj Sak Chuwen, falls. It is the work of the Yuknom (Head), the Kanul Lord, along with Uxte'tuun and those of Chihknahb." The written history here

FIGURE 6.5. Text recording the Kanul-Naranjo war, originally from Caracol's Hieroglyphic Stairway. Drawing by Ian Graham.

takes pains to mention that in his attack against Naranjo, the Kanul king had mustered allies from Calakmul, not Dzibanche. And according to another inscription, the war was sanctioned by the ancestors (*mam*) of the Kanul court, lending an air of credibility to the whole messy affair.

KANUL'S INNER TURMOIL

The Kanul kingdom and court, with its "twin cities" of Dzibanche and Calakmul, now faced its own internal division, perhaps an inevitability given the system of co-rulership that it seems to have maintained for a time. Our first, vague inklings of a rift came several years ago, in 2012, with our discovery of an interesting inscription at La Corona (among the set of stones described in the preface). One stone block, a portion of a longer, incomplete text, related more on the intertwined histories of La Corona's local rulers with their Kanul allies. The narrative included a new event not seen before—that on April 10, 635, the Kanul court "began at Chihknahb," using a place name that I knew referred to Calakmul or a large sector of that site. From parallel wording elsewhere, it was clear that such statements referred to the establishment of a formal political base or center, a significant political event. This was especially intriguing because, after this, Calakmul does in fact appear to assume a role as the "main" Kanul of the Late Classic (so much so that we had long called the Kanul emblem the "Calakmul" emblem glyph).

What would have had led to this change of status, a shift in capitals away from Dzibanche? The circumstances behind this were more complicated than I realized. This came into better focus with the further study of another very important narrative from Caracol, once inscribed onto a monumental stairway dedicated by Tumyohl K'inich on December 4, 642, just a decade after the victory over rebellious Naranjo. Built onto a pyramid in one of Caracol's main plazas, this grand staircase was composed of beautifully carved hieroglyphs and sculpted skulls—probably indicating its role as a place of execution and decapitation. Its construction marked the major calendar station at the half-point of the k'atun period (9.10.10.0.0), and the point of the inscription was to chronicle the events of Tumyohl K'inich's reign over the previous twenty-five or so years, including his participation as a loyal advocate and ally within the Kanul alliance. As we have seen, its narrative prominently featured the 631 conquest of K'uxaj at Naranjo nine years earlier. Also mentioned were some important personal episodes in the life of the local king, such as the death of his mother, possibly a Kanul princess, in 638. The original inscription on the steps also included many details about the unstable goings-on in Kanul's court and an important change in its own political history.

Parts of this larger story lay hidden until 2016, when portions of the Caracol Stairway were unexpectedly discovered in excavations conducted by my colleague Jaime Awe far away at Xunantunich, located some thirty kilometers to the north. It seems that the monumental staircase at Caracol was dismantled by the Maya only a few decades after its construction, with some of its pieces eventually finding their way to Xunantunich (Figure 6.6). Many more were sent to Naranjo. This

FIGURE 6.6. Portion of Caracol's Hieroglyphic Stairway discovered at Xunantunich, Belize. Photograph by Jaime Awe, courtesy of the Institute of Archaeology, Belize.

dramatic "afterlife" for the Caracol Stairway is an interesting story, to which we will return. For now, we need only mention that these newly discovered passages provide some key missing elements to the story, as well as brand new and unexpected actors.[26]

One surprise from the newly revealed sections was a royal name never seen before, Uaxaklajun Ubahchan, identified as a k'uhulajaw of the Kanuls. His known history spans only four years, from 636 to 640. On

March 2, 636, Waxaklajun Ubahchan was defeated in battle, an event recorded using the language typically reserved for vanquished enemies ("his knife and shield fell"). What is more, according to the new Xunantunich blocks, Waxaklajun Ubahchan died a few years later, and his death seems to have been no accident. On July 4, 640, "he died by the point of the stone," according to the newly found section of the narrative. This wording we find elsewhere, and it seems to refer to a killing, to the king's being dispatched by means of an execution or an "inside job" in terms of political rhetoric. But just who was he fighting, and what could have led to this death? Here the establishment of a new courtly base at Calakmul a little earlier in 635 must be significant. Waxaklajun Ubahchan had nothing to do with that event; rather, it was overseen by a protagonist named Yuknomch'en II, also identified as a k'uhulajaw of the Kanuls. As Simon Martin has suggested, it is very possible that the mysterious "Yuknoom Head" who defeated Naranjo in 631 is actually an alternate name for Yuknomch'en II. Whatever the case, within weeks of Waxaklajun Ubahchan's defeat, Yuknomch'en II assumed the throne at Calakmul, on April 29, 636, and he would remain there as the singular ruler throughout his long reign.

Piecing this all together, it appears that there were once two Kanul rulers who fell into conflict. The Calakmul faction led by Yuknomch'en asserted its primacy in 635 and fought the other Kanul bloc led by Waxaklajun Ubahchan, defeating him a year later. Yuknomch'en II was crowned as a head of the Kanuls and in a few years saw to the murder of his former rival, perhaps in captivity. In another section of the newly revealed text, the scribe described the new political order in direct terms:

Machaj k'awil tahn ch'en kanul
Patal k'awil uxte'tuun
Authority was removed at the town of Kanul,
Authority is established at Uxte'tun.

When first reading this passage, soon after receiving field photos from my colleague Jaime Awe, I was thrilled by its verbal clarity and implications. The word for "authority" or "power" here is *k'awil*, common in so many royal names and also known as an animate force associated with lightning—the axe of the rain god Chahk. Here then was a succinct statement of a turning point in geopolitical history, putting the transfer of rule from Dzibanche to Calakmul into raw political terms: Power was lost at one place and gained in another.

A decade or so of Kanul infighting had led to the founding of Calakmul as the formal new capital in 635, with Yuknomch'en II as the decisive figure. This great ruler would go on to reign at Calakmul for about fifty years, during which he solidified a new, wide-ranging network of vassal kingdoms and courts, building on the previous efforts of Tunkabhix, Scroll Serpent, Sky Witness, and his other ancestors. All of these rulers did their part in the protracted war with the Mutul dynasty, giving us a common thread with which to understand the detailed history during this long span from 500 to 650 CE. Looking at the bigger picture beyond Tikal, we see that there was no "hiatus" for the Maya as a whole, but a long period of political intrigue and of realignment on local and regional scales, as Tikal was confronted by new enemies and new challenges. Yuknomch'en II's new court at Calakmul provided a new springboard to push things further, setting the stage for rich, even more detailed stories that would play out over the next couple of centuries. These narratives are of several new rises and falls, fleshing out the Classic period even further and accentuating the unstable and fleeting nature of Maya politics.

PART III

Chante'chan

THE FOUR HEAVENS

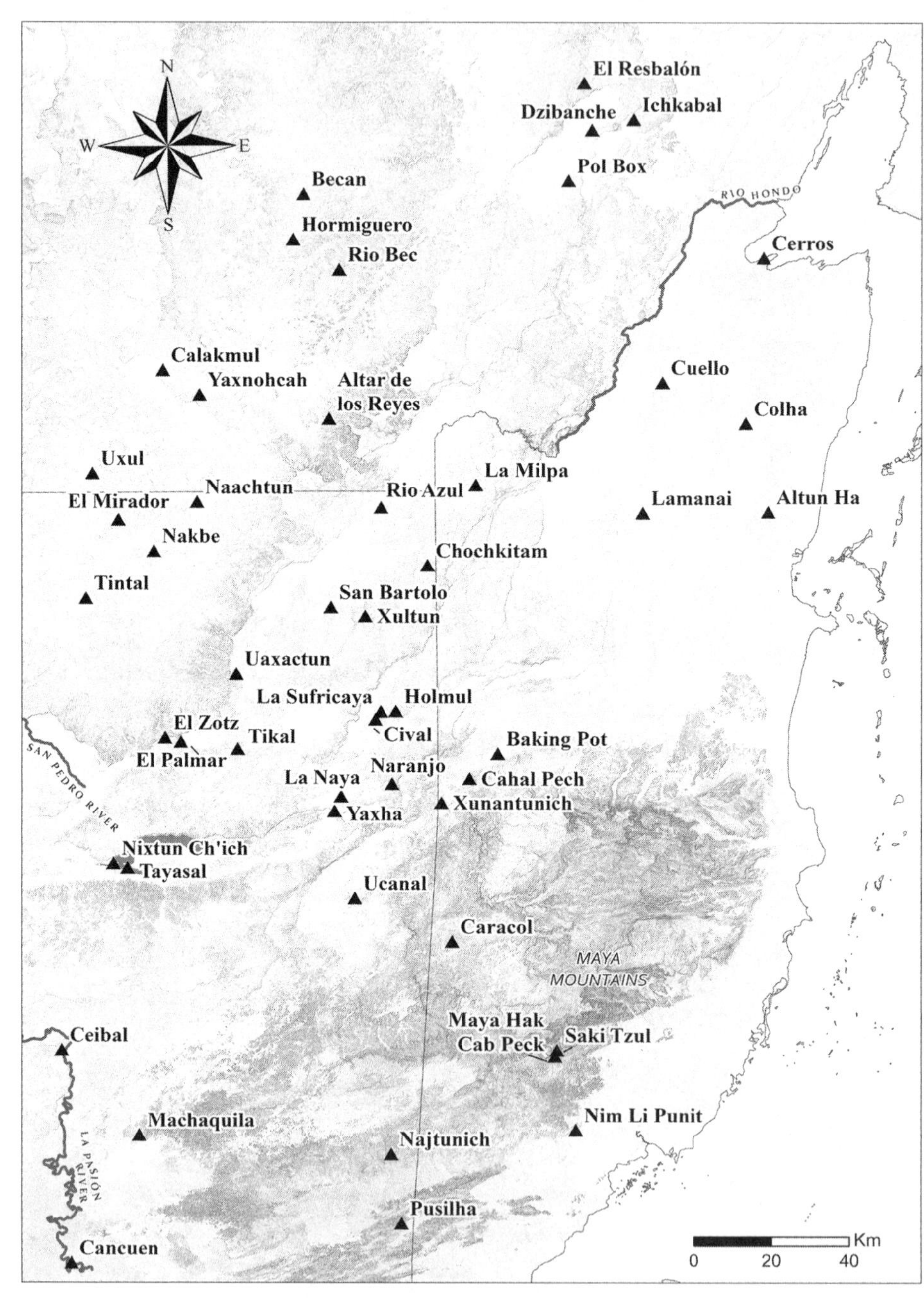

MAP 3. The eastern region.

CHAPTER 7

East

FOR RULERS SUCH as Yuknomch'en II (hereafter just Yuknomch'en), authority was defined not only by political maneuvering and military ambition but also, on a more abstract level, by their individual place in the grand cosmological scheme of things. A k'uhulajaw was tasked with maintaining the regular cadences of time, with sustaining myriad deities and ancestors through ritual action, always reliant on the preexisting, well-ordered structure of the universe to fulfill their proper duties. That cosmos was in essence a four-part system, reflecting the fundamental symmetries of everything large and small: the human body with its four limbs, the four stations or "paths" of the sun over the course of the year (the solstice points), and the four quadrants to the sky, or what we consider as the four cardinal directions. At the time of the Spanish invasion, Maya towns in Yucatán were laid out as miniature versions of this same model, with four roads reaching into the town center through four entrances. Earlier, ancient Maya rulers existed at the figurative center of this same fractal-like conception of space, as the pivot of everything: the court, the kabch'en (polity), and the idealized totality of the world. As much as we might view the latter as highly abstract and removed from the politics on the ground, there are strong indications

FIGURE 7.1. The Kalomte' title of Maya kings and queens. Drawing by the author.

that large-scale Maya political geography was envisioned as a similar quadrilateral archetype.[1]

Major kingdoms of the Classic era were probably arranged in similar spatial fashion, at least conceptually. That is, k'uhulajaws of particularly powerful kingdoms identified themselves as inhabiting and acting within a four-part spatial, directional scheme. We see this in an honorific title used by members of Kanul's ruling family in the Late Classic, *elk'in kalomte'*, "the Eastern Kalomte'." This was based on the paramount title Kalomte' we have seen used for hegemonic rulers (Figure 7.1). Thus, Kanul lords were linked to the direction of sunrise within the larger Maya world. In contrast, select rulers at Palenque and Yaxchilan were *ochk'in kalomte'*, West Kalomte'. Still other kings based at Copan and Quirigua were of the south, *nohol kalomte'*, and at least one ruler in ancient Yucatán claimed to be of the north, a *xaman kalomte'*. All these directional labels are remarkable in that they reflect what we see on the map, implying a broader, mutually agreed-on system covering the entire Maya area. Maya geopolitics was not just a patchwork of small polities, but something more coherent and cosmologically conceived. And it also reflects a possible larger hierarchy among the many kabch'ens, with an upper tier of four paramount rulers at a given time. Over the decades and centuries, articular cities and rulers changed within this arrangement, but there seem to have always been "four heavens" within the greater Maya world.[2]

The meaning of *kalomte'* is not obvious, although we know that functionally it was reserved for the very upper echelon of kings and queens—basically in reference to hegemonic kings who could rule over other k'uhulajaws. Some have seen it as a military term of some sort, probably due to the visible axe in the hieroglyph, but I think it is best understood as a religious title first and foremost. I translate the word literally as "plant-maker" or "tree-maker" (*kal* is "to create", *te'* is "plant," and *-om* is a grammatical suffix much like English "-er.").[3] This would be an apt description of what the hieroglyph shows: the storm god Chahk wielding an axe, with which he brings rain. A "West Kalomte'" is thus "the West Plant-Maker." In Maya religion, the rain deity Chahk had four iterations occupying each of the four world quarters, and these political titles are clear allusions to these forceful beings. The powerful rulers who made use of these titles were therefore assuming identities as the four directional rainmakers of the Maya cosmos—entities that still exist to this day in the traditional worldview of Maya communities. The many portraits we see of kings wielding the axe of Chahk are direct allusions to this cosmological role.

All of this begs an interesting question: If one king was the "East Kalomte'," another the "South Kalomte'," and so on, would this not imply a spatial center point, a vantage point where one holds the "compass"? It is interesting that the conceptual center of such a system falls geographically close to what we today call the "central" Peten, the homeland of Preclassic El Mirador, and the precocious Early Classic centers of Tikal and Uaxactun. Perhaps it is no coincidence that it is at Tikal where the title Kalomte' first appears in our records, in reference to a ruler who reigned before 317 CE, in the Early Classic.[4] It was also used for later figures who wielded power at Tikal, including Sihyajk'ahk' and Spearthrower Owl, of the west. It continued to be featured there without any directional specificity, throughout the Late Classic period, as the status to which all Mutul kings were seated upon their inauguration. This scenario deserves further study, but I am prepared to see Tikal and its importance in Maya history as related to its possibly unique place in the cosmology of Maya politics as a truly central place. Later, during the Late Classic, Kalomte' increasingly lost some of its exclusivity, and various claimants came to use it, even at small centers. In the next several chapters, we will focus on several of these prominent Kalomte' rulers of Maya history, shifting our narrative through the directions as we consider the rulers of the "four heavens." We begin by picking up on the story of those who were called the "East Kalomte'," rulers and nobles of Kanul dynasty, and of their relations in the eastern regions. They occupied the principal "side" or quadrant of Maya cosmology, where the sun and various time cycles began.[5]

• • •

The movement of the court from Dzibanche to Calakmul was a fresh start for the Kanul and their greater ambitions. Yuknomch'en may have sought to keep himself at a good distance from Dzibanche, the old seat of his rival that had recently been enmeshed in political tensions and infighting. Occupying the "twin capital" of his kingdom would put him and his forces closer to the central Peten, as he strategized to form new and more distant alliance networks against Kanul's old rival.

Not long after he formally established the court at Calakmul in 635, Yuknomch'en oversaw the construction of the city's large marketplace, in an open plaza located just to the north of the city's old E Group. At its center, amid the market stalls, was constructed a small, beautifully painted pyramid with staircases facing out toward each of the four world directions, the same four heavens of cosmos and politics. In so doing, he established the market and its pyramid structures as a central place, much like an E Group of the Middle Preclassic period. At Calakmul, the cosmological structure probably symbolized the city's new role as a true "center," a magnet for commerce and trade within the Kanul realm. The paintings on the outer walls of the pyramid, revealed in excavations in the early 2000s, are unlike anything ever seen in ancient Maya art or archaeology, with scene after scene of commercial activity with people eating, drinking, selling, buying, and conversing (Plate 10). Different vignettes show different commodities: corn drinks, tamales, salt, ceramic wares, incense, and more. Clearly the pyramid's colorfully decorated sides, like mirrors, reflected the activities once taking place around it. Some of the traders and commodities depicted in the paintings came from a considerable distance. (Salt, for example, could only come from far away, from the coast or a few inland sources.) One person shows up in several of the scenes, a high-ranking woman dressed elegantly in blue who may be overseeing many of the market's activities. Her identity is unclear, but I wonder if she was a Kanul queen, the wife of Yuknomch'en himself. The historical records speak little about the economic interests that were underlying the incessant politicking and conflict, but in the Calakmul murals, we have a small window into how important the market economy was to the strategies of alliance-making and geopolitical maneuvering. Calakmul was a "new Kanul" reflective of Yuknomch'en's regional ambitions, looking outward toward distant political interests and commercial resources across the Maya world.[6]

THE WAYWARD MUTUL KINGS

Historical records from the mid- to late 600s are more numerous than in previous eras and more detailed in their narrative content. Other kingdoms and actors begin to enter the larger geopolitical story of the Classic Maya, and the storylines of various dynasties become more intertwined with one another. For the scribes of this era, there was clearly a need to document the complex tensions of the time, writing the detailed accounts in official, public inscriptions. The resulting history begins to resemble a "game of thrones" that, rather than a patchwork of rulers and places, is in essence a single larger story of politics, alliance betrayal, and intrigue.

As we will recall, the Mutul lords had suffered a series of setbacks and misfortunes over the sixth century. Many factors were against them, the most obvious being Kanul's persistent alliance-building to Tikal's east, like storm clouds on the horizon. These efforts seem to have culminated in Mutul's defeat in 562 by the lord of Kanul, perhaps Sky Witness. In the ensuing decades and during the time of Kanul's own internal frictions, we know very little of Tikal's own history, save for "Animal Skull," who probably reigned at 593. We begin to get more resolution through stories told in the inscriptions of Dos Pilas, a small but significant area located about one hundred kilometers to Tikal's southwest. It was there where I did fieldwork as a graduate student, at a time when we were beginning to work out some of the essential elements of the story, even with the help of some texts we discovered in our excavations. These tell a detailed story of place-making, war, and shifting alliances involving Mutul's kings in the early seventh century, reviving the story of that dynasty (or a faction of it) after a long period of silence.

Dos Pilas was formally established around 632 as a southern outpost for the Mutuls, perhaps similar to how Calakmul had served as a "sister city" to Dzibanche, though on a far smaller scale. The timing of its establishment is fascinating, coming just one year after Kanul's victory against Naranjo, which had helped set in motion Kanul's own political resurgence a few years later. It is hard not to think that the founding of Dos Pilas was directly related to those distant events, setting up a courtly center for the Mutul dynasty, removed from the turmoil that was brewing to Tikal's north and east. Naranjo's defeat may have put Mutul's rulers on notice, motivating the need to seek out a more distant backup seat of power. And we must remember that this came only three years before Yuknomch'en's move to Calakmul, as he encroached ever farther into the central region. The 630s were an especially intense time of shifting courts and countermoves.

Why would a distant place like Dos Pilas be established as an outpost for a young Mutul prince? The southwest region was important for its access to trade networks that reached farther into the north and west with its two key rivers, the Pasión and the Usumacinta. Dos Pilas was also in a particular region known as the Petexbatun, near two very ancient and well-established kingdoms based at the sites we know today as Ceibal and Tamarindito. These once powerful places had shed much of their old political power and influence in the Classic period, making Dos Pilas somewhat of a "startup" amid old establishments. I see one small clue about Dos Pilas's founding by looking at the deeper history of Tamarindito, whose records tells of a dynastic founder we will call "Macaw Star." He evidently ruled in the very beginning of the Classic period, probably in the first or second century CE, and like other such obscure figures, he came to be semi-mythologized over time. Significantly, he was claimed by Mutul rulers as their own heroic ancestor, too. Several stelae from Tikal show its rulers dressed in the guise of Macaw Star, reenacting his rituals, and clearly pointing to the importance of this legacy. We cannot say for certain where the historical connection lies, but Tikal's hearkening back to a Tamarindito ruler as one of its own "founding fathers" is revealing, leading me to think that the founding of Dos Pilas in the 630s, in what amounted to Tamarindito's territory, represented a return to what was considered an old ancestral homeland of sorts, where Macaw Star once ruled.[7]

A central actor in this new place-making was a young prince named Bajlaj Chank'awil, who had been born only a few years earlier in 625 (Figure 7.2). He was the son of an obscure Tikal king (probably a successor of "Animal Skull"), and his detailed biography is told in an extraordinary text inscribed on the steps on Dos Pilas's main temple, where we read of his relations with both Tikal and Calakmul (Figure 7.3). Bajlaj Chank'awil arrived at Dos Pilas as a young boy in 632, only six years old (no doubt in the company of many other Mutul nobles, of course). Once again we are reminded of other youthful kings in our history, including Yaxnunayin, Ajnumsaj, and K'inich Janabpakal, all of whom were placed in their roles in times of great change and instability.[8] His father also had a son named Nunujolchahk, who carried the same royal title, the "k'uhulajaw of Mutul." He first appears on the scene as an adult in 657, and we are unsure if he was the older or younger brother of Bajlaj Chank'awil. What is clear is that the siblings, while allies for a time, eventually developed a fraught relationship. Eventually, as we will see, they became outright enemies, engaged in protracted war with one another throughout the middle years of the seventh century. Their story, recounted in extraordinary detail in the inscribed stairway of Dos Pilas, is very reminiscent of the conflict that confronted Kanul's rivals a few decades earlier.

In adulthood, Bajlaj Chank'awil became a successful warrior, and it is at this time that we begin to see the evidence of a fissure within the Mutuls. When twenty-three years old, in 648, he claimed victory in a war against a person named Lamnah K'awil, named also as a "lord of Mutul." We have no idea of his identity. Was he a Tikal ruler, even an older brother? Clearly the readers of the Dos Pilas narrative were assumed to know such details of the backstory. One intriguing possibility to consider is that a rival faction of the Mutuls, perhaps led by Lamnah K'awil, had already entered into an alliance with the Kanul court and Yuknomch'en (maybe hinting at the urgency of Dos Pilas's founding in the first place). This is suggested by an event that comes two years later, also included in Bajlaj Chank'awil's biography: In 650, Yuknomch'en waged a war directly upon Dos Pilas, extending farther southward than any previous Kanul campaign we know of. The war resulted in Dos Pilas's

FIGURE 7.2. Bajlaj Chank'awil, the Mutul king of Dos Pilas. Photograph by the author.

FIGURE 7.3. The Hieroglyphic Stairway 2 of Dos Pilas. Photograph by Ian Graham.

defeat, and Bajlaj Chank'awil forced him to flee to a nearby stronghold named K'inich Pa'witz, an ancient fortress we know today as the ruins at Aguateca, located high atop a defensive position on the escarpment overlooking Lake Petexbatun and near Tamarandito. Yuknomch'en probably sensed a weakness and internal division within the Mutuls and sought to exploit it.

With Bajlaj Chank'awil exiled from Dos Pilas, Nunujolchahk, for now still an ally, was also targeted by the Kanuls. In 657, he was also defeated by Yuknomch'en's forces. Exactly where this battle took place we cannot say, but we know he was not captured. The Dos Pilas Stairway suggests that both brothers may have even met at some unknown location, each having been targeted and defeated by the relentless Kanuls in the span of seven years. They would also come to spend some time together at the site of Yaxha, in mutual exile. Some of these details are murky due to damaged portions of the written narrative on the stairway, but it seems safe to conclude that Tikal itself was off-limits for both brothers. Each was adrift amid a new wave of Kanul wars and pursuits.

In defeat, Nunujolchahk may have moved westward, establishing himself at a place we know today as Santa Elena, located on the San Pedro River in Mexico. If so, it was his sanctuary by 659 and for a lengthy time thereafter, long enough to acquire a new title as *ajaw* of Santa Elena (its emblem sign remains undeciphered).[9] We then seem to pick up his story in the historical records of Palenque, located still farther west and away from the fray of the central Peten. There, an important foreigner bearing the very same name, Nunujolchahk, is featured prominently in histories from the reign of the great king Kinich Janabpakal. It is very likely to be the same person, given the timing. Nunujolchahk's reason for being at Palenque is difficult to understand in many ways, but we know he "arrived" there on August 14, apparently with great fanfare. As context, we need only recall how Palenque was a long-term enemy of the Kanul kingdom, having suffered its own conquests decades earlier at the hands Scroll Serpent and Sky Witness. In 659, Pakal was engaged in its own ambitious military campaign against Kanul's allies, and on August 8—just days before Nunujolchahk's arrival—he captured a number of nobles from Kanul's allied provinces to the east. It seems that Nunujolchahk was a friend to Palenque in these campaigns, arriving to Pakal's court as a victorious ally. To further complicate matters, Yaxchilan (Pa'chan) was part of this complex, far-ranging war as well, according to a statement found in Pakal's palace. The exact nature of this event in 659, remains cloudy, but I suspect that if nothing else, it must have been a grand encounter, even the forging of new political and military alliances involving the Mutul ruler.[10]

Now isolated from one another, the brothers came to a dramatic falling-out soon after the Palenque visit or perhaps because of it. However we interpret some of these events, the years between 660 and 670 represent a real turning point in their relationship and, I think, for much of Maya politics. During this short span, Bajlaj Chank'awil "went rogue," turning fully against his brother. Adding insult to injury, the biographical account on the Dos Pilas Stairway is explicit in documenting his emergence as a key ally of Yuknomch'en of the Kanul dynasty. It was the greatest political reversal we know in all Maya history.

By 672, if not earlier, sibling rivalry turned to civil war. Nunujolchahk was on the move again and attacked and burned Dos Pilas that same year, forcing his brother to flee once again, two decades after the first exile. Now Bajlaj Chank'awil moved to a safer spot called Chahknaah, a place we cannot yet correlate with any archaeological site. (Evidently the fortress at Aguateca was unavailable or too risky.) Within six months Nunujolchahk was in pursuit yet again, attacking Chahknaah and forcing his brother to move northward, to a kingdom called Hixwitz (Jaguar Hill), another strong ally of the Kanuls and of Yuknomch'en. This is today identifiable in the ruins of Zapote Bobal.[11] Bajlaj Chank'awil was now a turncoat, and a constant target. In constant pursuit, Nunujolchahk was highly mobile, perhaps maintaining Mutul's royal court along the way, at several different places. The great city of Tikal was perhaps still too venerable to attack after its defeat back in 657, requiring the king to maintain his distance. One of these temporary spots for Nunujolchahk was a place called Pulil, although its modern location remains a mystery.[12] Even more than his estranged brother, most of Nunujolchahk's reign, if we can call it that, was spent on the move and away from Tikal, a capital still perhaps without any resident king.

As if the narrative of conflict was not complex enough, Nunujolchahk soon was a target of an even greater force. Yuknomch'en and his Kanul allies went after the Mutul ruler, attacking and defeating Pulil in 677, forcing Nunujolchahk to run away once again. There is suggestive evidence that he sought refuge at Yaxchilan, on the Usumacinta River, perhaps eager to enlist the aid of allies to the west. Shortly afterward, Bajlaj Chank'awil emerged in a stronger position, and with his brother on the run he had a triumphant return to Dos Pilas after his five years of exile. He was now in the alliance network of the Kanuls and, with an upper hand, determined to exact his own revenge on his brother.

The final attack by Kanul's forces came on May 1, 679, when "the shield and weapons of Nunujolchahk fell." After so many years and repeated exiles, Bajlaj Chank'awil at last attained true victory, with violent and decisive results. According to the epic narrative of these battles on the Dos Pilas Stairway, "their blood was made into lakes, and the skulls were made into mountains," the same poetic description of mass execution of an enemy force that we encountered in the violent history of Naranjo. Nunujolchahk may have survived this horrific defeat—we do not know—but his years on the throne of Mutul were over in any case. He had a son, Jasaw Chank'awil, who would assume Tikal's throne in 682, and his story would in turn see a dramatic turn in Tikal's fortunes.[13]

• • •

Kanul's victory over Nunujolchahk was a pinnacle achievement. And it happened as part of a larger, coordinated strategy undertaken by Yuknomch'en to bolster his own alliance network. On the very same day of the victory—May 1, 679—the princess named Lady Tz'ihb-winkil, another daughter of Yuknomch'en, arrived to Saknikte' (La Corona) to marry its local ruler, solidifying their long-lasting family ties. And this day, curiously, was exactly one twenty-year k'atun to the day after the key visit Nunujolchahk had paid to Palenque back in 659. It could all be a coincidence, but I believe the Maya historians and strategists were very much aware of such symmetries, anniversaries, and parallels. It is not a stretch to believe that Kanul's military victory against the Mutul king in 679 was precisely timed to occur on the anniversary of his enemy's great meeting with K'inich Janabpakal, himself a Kanul enemy.

Kanul's newly strengthened alliance during the 670s is also shown in the case of "Lady Kabel," a queen of El Peru-Waka' who was probably the daughter of Yuknomch'en. She married the local ruler there sometime around 675, and her portrait was carved upon a beautiful relief sculpture shortly thereafter (Figure 7.4). She is shown standing in her ceremonial regalia, an evocation of the Maya moon and water goddess,

FIGURE 7.4. The Cleveland Stela, with its portrait of Lady Kabel, princess of Kanuls. Photograph courtesy of the Cleveland Art Museum.

holding a ceremonial banner and war shield. Her husband was the local ruler K'inich Bahlam, whose own stela was placed nearby, facing his queen. But her portrait is the more imposing and impressive of the two, and one gets the clear sense that she is the prominent political figure of the time, solidifying El Peru-Waka's place in the larger network. Within a few short years another Kanul princess would be married off to the kingdom of Saknikte' (Le Corona), and soon, too, the daughter of Bajlaj Chank'awil would play a similar role, serving the political needs of the greater Kanul network.[14]

Nunujolchahk's exact fate is unclear, but he may have been killed in 679 as part of the mass executions. An alternative scenario is that he was captured and taken to Calakmul. On May 4, 682, his son became the new ruler and set up his base of operations at Tikal. His name was Jasaw Chank'awil, and he was ready to pick up the conflict. Just four days later, Bajlaj Chank'awil and Yuknomch'en met at Calakmul to celebrate their great victories and their fruitful alliance, and they surely were aware of the newly crowned Mutul king, the nephew of Bajlaj Chank'awil. The festive occasion marked the period ending of 682 (9.12.10.0.0), which included a ceremonial dance before the elderly Yuknomch'en, now eighty-two. This is the last known event in the life of the great Kanul ruler who over the course of his eventful reign had established Calakmul as the most powerful center in the central Maya region and who had consolidated power among numerous vassal centers, among them Naranjo, Dos Pilas, La Corona, Hixwitz (Zapote Bobal), El Peru-Waka', and Cancuen. He perhaps lived only a few more years, to the age of eighty-six.

Bajlaj Chank'awil would visit Calakmul again in 686 in order to attend the coronation of a new Kanul ruler, Yuknom Yich'ahkk'ahk'. And in the wake of that visit, Bajlaj Chank'awil had his scribes and masons design the stairway with its long biographical inscription. It is fascinating to see its design and layout in three different sections, each corresponding to a k'atun (twenty-year period) of the king's life. The first section covers his childhood, including his birth and arrival at Dos Pilas. Years later after the death of Yuknomch'en, he updated the narrative through the addition of his fuller story. A second section was added on his second k'atun of life, chronicling his years as a victim of the Kanul king's expansions. Finally, the third section highlights the campaign against Nunujolchahk and his ultimate defeat. It is a detailed remembrance and chronicling of his long, tortured history with Yuknomch'en, his enemy and patron, who had only recently passed. Bajlaj Chank'awil emerges from this storyline as one of our best-known figures of Maya history, certainly on the larger geopolitical stage of the seventh century. He occupies an unusual place as a vital "connector," joining several other narratives involving cities and kingdoms beyond those already described. Indeed, his offspring and successors shaped a great deal of Maya politics in the next decades, in the southern Peten and well beyond. Foremost among them was his daughter, arguably the most powerful woman we know from Maya history. She would soon transform the fortunes of another actor of our larger story at the great court of Naranjo.

WARRIOR QUEEN, WARRIOR PRINCE

As part of their meeting at Calakmul in 682, Bajlaj Chank'awil and Yuknomch'en probably devised strategies to keep the new Mutul king in check. What emerged was an ambitious plan to build on their recent successes, consolidating their political influence in the region and, in the process, resurrecting an old ally and client state. This strategy entailed a new character in our story, the daughter of Bajlaj Chank'awil named Lady Wakjalam Chanlem (Figure 7.5). Like other princes and princesses of Kanul's allies, she may have lived at Calakmul for an extended portion of her youth, and she may have accompanied her father on his visit there. These family connections made her uniquely powerful in the complex politics of the time, as a Mutul princess with the Kanul king as her patron, embodying the two great dynasties of Maya history. With this singular symbolic role, she was chosen to marry into the Sa'al dynasty of Naranjo, the great Kanul ally of the previous century. That old alliance needed a new boost, especially at a time when Yuknomch'en's attention was turning to the east of Tikal, in an effort to encroach upon Jasaw Chank'awil from multiple directions.

On August 28, 682, Lady Wakjalam Chanlem entered Naranjo, arriving from Dos Pilas, or possibly after a stopover with the Kanul lords at Calakmul. Others came with her, as one inscription makes

FIGURE 7.5. Lady Wakjalam Chanlem, on Naranjo, Stela 24. Drawing by Ian Graham.

clear. We can imagine a large entourage and an entrance into the city accompanied by great excitement and fanfare. That her new presence signaled a turning point for the local dynasty is emphasized throughout Naranjo's later inscriptions. Up to this point, Naranjo had been through its own "hiatus," in the wake of its reconquest five decades earlier, in 631, and its history had also been silent for a time before that, after the death of Ajnumsaj. Lady Wakjalam Chanlem's arrival, marrying the existing king of Naranjo, was designed to resurrect the long, loyal relationship that the Kanul rulers once had with Naranjo and Ajnumsaj. The k'uhulajaw she married was named K'ahk' Ubalaw Chanchahk, probably a son or grandson of Ajnumsaj. (If a son, he would have been quite advanced in years.) Their union thus represented a fusion of two key allies of the Kanul hegemony, one new and another quite ancient. Her identity as a member of the Mutul dynasty was emphasized throughout Naranjo's histories, where she was described always as *k'uhul mutul ajaw*, "the Holy Mutul Lord," making clear she was of the highest authority. Significantly, her father, ruler of far-off Dos Pilas, is described in the same sources as a "west Kalomte'," reflecting not only his geographical position to the west of Naranjo but also his new authoritative role in the increasingly complex, nested hierarchy of Maya rulers.

The larger geopolitical significance of the princess's arrival was symbolized in a less direct way by an unusual and striking monument placed in Naranjo's city center. This is the stone staircase of Caracol, portions of which were brought to Naranjo and added to the city's old E Group complex, perhaps as war trophies (Plate 11). We will recall that this stairway had been originally set before a large plaza at Caracol by Tumyohl K'inich in 642 to register his own connections with Calakmul and to commemorate his possible role in the Kanul victory over Naranjo in 631. Throughout the sixth century, Caracol and Naranjo seem to have vied for position as Kanul's eastern allies, and they were also perhaps caught at certain moments on opposite sides of Kanul's own internal conflicts, as we have seen. Just how and why would so many stones from this monument end up at Naranjo, over forty kilometers away? The circumstances are murky, as is often the case, but we do know that prior to the princess's arrival, an earlier Naranjo ruler had attacked Caracol in 680 CE, probably with the sanction of Yuknomch'en at Calakmul. The stones were probably brought to Naranjo around this time, just prior to the princess's arrival. Other blocks somehow made their way to Xunantunich, not too far to the east, for partial reassembly and display there. Another stone was found loose and discarded at Ucanal, twenty kilometers along the route from Caracol to Naranjo. The stones that made it to Naranjo were carefully reset in a new monumental staircase. However, they were intentionally positioned out of sequence, making the once-legible Caracol inscription scrambled and incoherent. What was the point? As we can best understand, the blocks were purposefully reset to create a "broken" display of recent history, not only nullifying the narrative of Naranjo's old defeat but also signaling its return as Kanul's main ally in the east, replacing Caracol's claims. Kanul's defeat of Naranjo back in 631 was an event of the old order, from the time Naranjo had gone against Calakmul. Now, with Naranjo reestablished under Kanul's sphere through marriage, that old arrangement and Caracol's place in it could be represented as something "out of order," in a very literal way.[15]

In 688, six years into her reign as Naranjo's queen, Lady Wakjalam Chanlem bore an heir, a boy named K'ahk'tiliw Chanchahk. He was the Naranjo heir and was crowned as a young king at only five years old, in 693. This occurred under the direct supervision of Kanul's new ruler, Yuknom Yich'ahkk'ahk'. Lady Wakjalam Chanlem served as regent, and as the boy grew older, the mother and son operated like corulers of the kingdom, at least until he came of age. The birth of Kahk'tiliw was clearly a momentous event in terms of the extended family histories we've touched on so far—he was the grandson of Bajlaj Chank'awil of Dos Pilas and the great nephew of Nunujolchahk and therefore a cousin of the recently installed king of Tikal, Jasaw Chank'awil. Through the line of his father, K'ahk'tiliw was also the grandson (or great-grandson) of Ajnumsaj of Naranjo. His very impressive family pedigree placed him at the intersection of several royal family trees, and illustrates the close, personal dimension of Maya geopolitics during this era. The detailed history we read at Naranjo and elsewhere soon came to resemble an internal family drama, encompassing many related royal courts and individuals. Together, the son K'ahk'tiliw and his mother, Lady Wakjalam Chanlem, were a formidable and ambitious duo, and they quickly reestablished the kingdom of Sa'al as a powerhouse of the East.

In several portraits, Lady Wakjalam Chanlem appears as a regal figure and actor, often trampling bound prisoners under her feet, like so many warrior-kings we have seen. Her monuments single her out as the principal power, at least for a time, and as her son grew in age, they often performed rituals and other royal duties as a pair. One stela narrates the scope of their military ambitions in the years after the boy-king's accession to the throne, when K'ahk'tiliw was still a boy. One inscription records his birth on January 4, 688, and then enters a tally of eight victorious wars waged in 701, shortly before the monument was erected. The conflicts came quickly, within only a few months, indicating a new campaign of conquest against enemies to the east and south. We must imagine that the Kanul lords were behind the queen's new effort to exert control in the region. This outbreak c3ulminated in the burning of the city named K'anwitznal, today known as the ruins of Ucanal, located to the south of Naranjo. Its king was captured and brought to Naranjo, where he was presented to K'ahk'tiliw, who was by this time only a teenager of fourteen years of age (Figure 7.6). The inscription on the monument commemorating the victory makes clear that the young Kahk'tiliw was the one who oversaw the victory. Although no mention is made of his mother, she was clearly involved.[16]

TIKAL'S RESURGENCE

Tikal's fortunes appear to have revived with the crowning of Jasaw Chank'awil in 682, reversing decades of setbacks and inner conflict. This was despite the disruption that occurred with his father's final defeat and ultimate death. Yuknomch'en's own demise a few years later, in 686, must have been seen as an opportunity for the new Mutul king, maybe even a bit of a breather that would allow him to revivify his

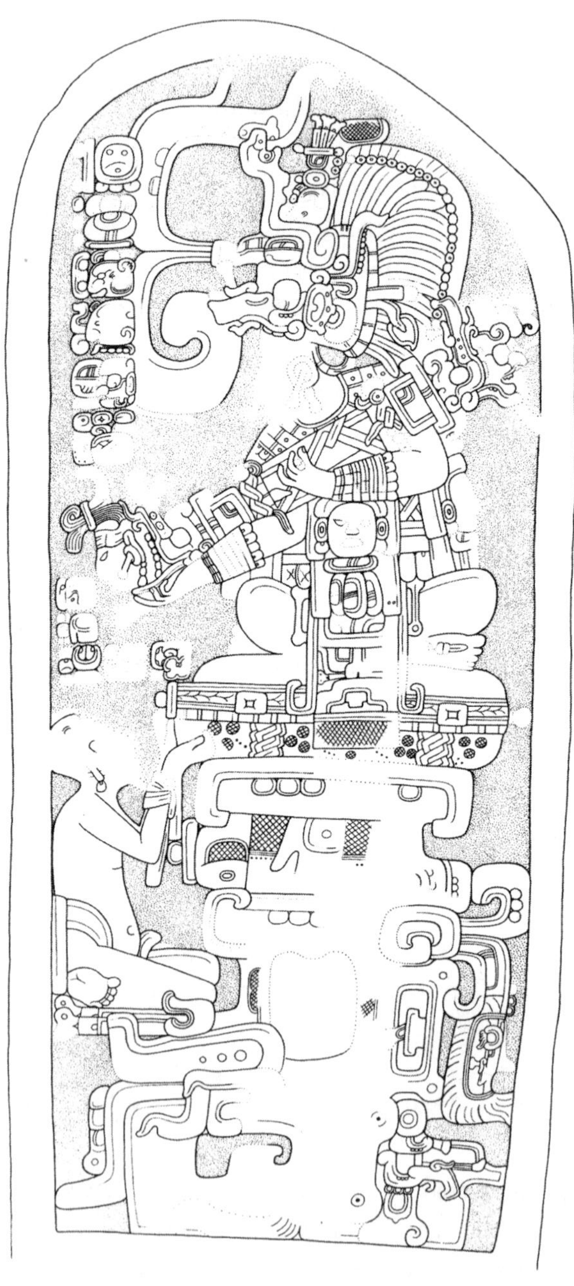

FIGURE 7.6. K'ahk'tiliw Chanyopat, boy-king of Naranjo, with his Ucanal prisoner. Naranjo, Stela 22. Drawing by Ian Graham,

city and court. A sense of this renewed optimism and stability at the old center of Tikal can be seen in Jasaw Chank'awil's construction programs there, including a new temple complex to commemorate the k'atun ending of March 16, 692, on the 9.13.0.0.0. This day was of special significance, with thirteen being a sacred, cosmological number. The temple designed for this occasion was innovative for its time and a new take on the old idea of the E Group, with its east–west axial alignment and focus on the calendar ritual. It is still visible at the ruins today, a modestly sized pair of mounds in the northern sector known as "Complex M," originally accompanied by a small stela with Jasaw Chank'awil's portrait and an altar with the large 8 Ahau glyph, to mark the new period ending. The construction of this ceremonial precinct was a true renewal project for the Mutul court, after the persistent attacks and machinations of Yuknomch'en and the Kanuls. It is interesting that his enemy (and uncle), Bajlaj Chank'awil, celebrated the k'atun as well, performing a ceremonial dance when he was sixty-six—the last firm date we have for him. Having experienced decades of war, the Maya world was now commemorated through this momentous and universally recognized day, erecting monuments and temples to the ever-stable mechanisms of the cosmos.[17]

The new Kanul ruler in these years, Yuknom Yich'ahkk'ahk' ("Claw of Fire"), was enthroned at Calakmul in 686, with the loyal Bajlaj Chank'awil there in attendance. Born in 649 and presumably Yuknomch'en's son, he had come of age during the height of the Mutul-Kanul conflict. There is evidence that he spent a considerable part of his pre-accession years on the move, stationed at various locations as part of Kanul's military campaigns against Nunujolchahk. He forged and strengthened old alliances, and his crowning just a few years after the accession of Tikal's Jasaw Chank'awil set the stage for a new chapter in the old conflict, shaped by two younger and equally ambitious men.

Five years into his reign, Yich'ahkk'ahk' oversaw the inauguration of the young K'ahk'tiliw in 691, who possibly traveled to Calakmul for the occasion. The Naranjo boy-king and his mother continued to push hard against their Mutul relatives, waging several wars over the ensuing years. Naranjo was successful in the burning of one outpost and the capture

FIGURE 7.7. Tikal, Temple 1. War memorial and burial place of Jasaw Chank'awil. Photograph by the author.

of a prominent Mutul lord named Sihyaj K'awil on January 30, 695. This episode may have roused Tikal once and for all. Later that same year, on August 6, a major battle took place, and, using the very same language we saw before in the defeat of Nunujolchahk, "the knife and shield of Yich'ahkk'ahk', Holy Lord of the Kanul, fell." Jasaw Chank'awil at last could celebrate a major victory over Kanul's forces, exacting some degree of revenge for his father's defeat sixteen years before.

It was indeed a transformational event, commemorated in Tikal with the lofty Temple I, with its beautifully carved and inscribed wooden door lintels (Figure 7.7). The scene on the best-preserved of the lintels depicts a triumphant Jasaw Chank'awil, seated within an elaborate palanquin that assumes the form of a massive upright jaguar looming behind him. The celebration of the victory over the Kanuls was timed to coincide with the 13 k'atun (260 year) anniversary of Spearthrower Owl's death, linking his own military prowess with the old hegemony of Teotihuacan. The effigy of the standing jaguar represented one of Kanul's own patron deities, evidently captured in battle and appropriated by the victorious Jasaw Chank'awil. It is possible that this sacred image was housed in the small room atop Temple I, where it would have been seen from the plaza below, a powerful symbol of Kanul's defeat. Yich'ahkk'ahk' himself did not die in the 695 war, but he did pass away two years later after a fairly short reign, a humiliated figure whose military plans had gone awry.[18]

Tikal's victory in 695 seems to have weakened Kanul networks, and apart from Naranjo's constant activity, its sphere of influence may have contracted in the ensuing years. There were other disruptions coming at the close of the century, including the death of Bajlaj Chank'awil, who was by this time was seventy years old, after an eventful and dramatic life. The circumstances of his death are unclear, but we can surmise that it came at some point not long before March 25, 698, when his son assumed the throne at Dos Pilas. Significantly, the Kanul ruler Yich'ahkk'ahk' himself died at about the same time, in late December 697, at forty-eight years old. That two military allies would perish within such a short window suggests a connection, perhaps even a follow-up war with Tikal when both rulers saw the end of the spear. Whatever the specific events, it is possible that Jasaw Chank'awil was ultimately successful in overturning the long era of Kanul domination, having defeated the son of the great ruler who had defeated his father.

Jasaw Chank'awil held the throne for many more years, until 734, during which he continued to build and transform Tikal. Temple I was built to commemorate the defeat of the Kanul. It was here that Jasaw Chank'awil chose to be buried nearly four decades after his glorious achievement. Located on the east side of the site's central plaza, the tomb may reflect the idea of the king's solar rebirth and resurrection, themes we see repeated elsewhere in the designs and iconography of Maya tombs. When the crypt was discovered in 1962, archaeologists noted a large stone that capped the vault and bore a painted red circle on its underside, most likely a depiction of the sun at zenith, "shining" down upon the king's richly clad body. He wore a collar of 114 large jade beads, all still in place, and was placed atop layers of several jaguar pelts. Twenty ceramic vessels with elaborate decoration were placed within the chamber, as was also a lidded cacao vase in the form of the Maize God, whose outer surface was covered with numerous jade tiles. These symbols of resurrection echoed the political fortunes of Tikal in these years as well, for it was once again a major player on the political stage.[19]

A TALE OF TWO PYRAMIDS

On April 3, 698, a new Kanul king assumed power at Calakmul. His full name remains difficult to read, so we refer to him provisionally as Tok' K'awil. Dos Pilas's new ruler Kokaj K'awil had assumed the throne there only days before, on March 25, suggesting that this was a time of broader change and adjustment within Kanul's alliances. Naranjo's queen and boy-king were still actively engaged in their wars in the east, but, for now, Tikal seemed the more stable center of power in the central lowlands. Tok' K'awil may have been reluctant to confront the resurgent Tikal in a direct way, so the history of the early eighth century is again largely one of proxy wars and the targeting of local allies. Over the course of more than three decades on the throne, Tok' K'awil strengthened his connections to El Peru-Waka' and to La Corona, both in the west. His thirty-eight-year reign culminated with a major new construction project at Calakmul to renovate the massive pyramid known as Structure 1. This stands today as one of the largest buildings in the Maya region. The many inscribed stelae placed before the pyramid refer to it as a sacred mountain, built to celebrate the k'atun ending of 731, on 9.15.0.0.0. This period ending was of special significance, for it was a recurrence of the date 4 Ahau, the same day on which creation itself had occurred at the start of the current Long Count. Three large circular stones placed in a triangular arrangement in the same plaza indicate that the pyramid was the conceptual and ritual center of Uxte'tun, meaning "Three Stones." The pyramid and its sculptures were especially elaborate and ambitious in scale, more than we ever really see with other k'atun celebrations at Calakmul or elsewhere. Amid the records of performance and ritual, there is no mention of the Kanul wars against the Mutul rivals or of Tok' K'awil's own efforts in that protracted conflict. It was a "quiet" but religiously active time, at least from the Kanul perspective.

Things were different for the Tikal ruler who succeeded Jasaw Chank'awil. His son, named Yik'in Chank'awil, assumed the Mutul throne in 734, just three years after the turn of the k'atun and the dedication of Tok' K'awil's signature mountain-pyramid. His reign represents the high point of Tikal in the Late Classic period, and the apogee of its own military and political power in the central lowlands. His first stela was dedicated in 736, in front of an isolated ancestral shrine at Tikal known as Temple VI. While damaged, the stela and its altar show enough detail to reconstruct its date as well as a curious and important detail on its disc-shaped altar placed in front. Elaborately carved in deep relief, it shows a bound captive prone on his belly with a hieroglyphic caption above his body. Such altars were sometimes used for the ritual execution of prisoners, and here the lifelike carving was probably meant to convey that very purpose. When viewing the stela-altar pair from the front, one would see the ruler (the stela) standing behind the prone captive (the altar). Just enough of the hieroglyphic label is preserved to read "holy lord of Kanul" in the last glyph, and what is preserved of the prisoner's name shows elements that may well correspond to the name of Tok' K'awil. If so, we have a remarkable documentation of Yik'in Chank'awil's physical capture of the king of the Kanul dynasty sometime before 736. His father's war in 695 ended in Kanul's defeat, but not in the capture of the enemy ruler; here the son may have surpassed that victory with his own stunning success, just a few short years into his reign.[20]

Having dealt so decisively with the Kanuls, Yik'in Chank'awil forged ahead with more plans of conquest and revenge. His targets were due east, at Naranjo, Yaxha, and Holmul, all enemy allies or vassals who had become far weaker in the wake of Calakmul's defeat. In fact, after about 730, the history of Naranjo becomes very obscure, and there are good indications that K'ahk'tiliw and his mother were considerably undermined by the defeat of Tok' K'awil. Naranjo's inscriptions become far fewer in number, with no information about the Naranjo king's fate, but we do see a new ruler in power by 746. Lady Wakjalam Chanlem, once such a pivotal figure in the Kanul alliance network, died in 741, as recorded in an inscription excavated at her home site of Dos Pilas. As a Mutul princess under the sway of the Kanuls, her death must have resonated far and wide, and for many it may have symbolized the passing of an old political order.

Sensing weakness, Yik'in Chank'awil began his series of eastern campaigns, attacking Yaxha in 743. This large city, built on the high bluff above beautiful Lake Yaxha, once had strong historical connections to Tikal. Naranjo had conquered it in 710, sending its ruler, a Tikal ally, into exile and absorbing Yaxha into the Kanul sphere. By the 740s Yaxha was ruled from the Kanul outpost at El Peru-Waka', another telling indication of Naranjo's (and Kanul's) waning spheres of influence. The record of Tikal's attack against Yaxha' describes it as "the eastern Waka'," presumably meaning it was the eastern seat of that dynasty. Yik'in Chank'awil was successful, and in victory he captured the sacred image of El Peru-Waka's patron deity. The following year, in 744, he turned his attention to Naranjo and was again victorious, taking prisoner a member of its royal family, Yaxmayuy Chanchahk, as well as its sacred palanquin. These eastern campaigns were strategic in clearing out old elements of Kanul's encircling alliance, accentuating Tikal's political and military resurgence.

To commemorate these victories, Yik'in Chank'awil built his own massive structure in 746, the spectacular Temple IV, the tallest pyramid at Tikal and one of the largest buildings in all ancient Mesoamerica by volume. It stands on the western edge of Tikal's center, its upper shrine looking eastward high over the tree canopy and dwarfing the other great pyramids of his predecessors, including Temple I, visible in the distance. In facing eastward, Temple IV looked toward an old landscape of enemies newly defeated. As with Temple I, the purpose of the temple was perhaps to house the sacred images of captured enemies, all spelled out in the inscriptions within. The dedication ceremony occurred in the summer of 746, accompanied by dances and performances, according to the inscription on one of the spectacular wooden door lintels placed within the shrine. Its powerful portrait of Yik'in Chank'awil projects his newfound authority (Figure 7.8). In the accompanying narration, Yik'in was careful to mention his father Jasaw Chank'awil, viewing his achievements as a continuation of his father's success fifty years before. It is tempting to see Temple IV's size and majesty as a response to the Tok' K'awil's "mountain" at Calakmul, dedicated fifteen years earlier.

I sense that the Kanul rulers at Calakmul, once the most powerful in Maya history, never quite recovered from Tikal's steady countermoves of 736 to 746, when Yik'in Chank'awil captured Tok' K'awil and engaged in relentless campaigns against the Kanul network. Stelae continued to be erected at Calakmul, but not quite so many, and the records of its kings fall off dramatically. The balance of power now changed from what had existed a century earlier, with the dismantling of the old alliance networks of Yuknomch'en and his predecessors. It represented a firm takedown of Tikal's ancient enemy, countering a foreign force that had been active against the Mutul dynasty for two centuries, at least. Again, however, we must remember how these wars were permeated by an intimate family dynamic as well. For example, in capturing Yax Mayuy Chanchahk of Naranjo, Yik'in Chank'awil had captured the probable half-brother of Kahk'tiliw, who, as the son of Lady Wakjalam Chanlem, was his cousin once removed. Jasaw Chank'awil's victory over Kanul

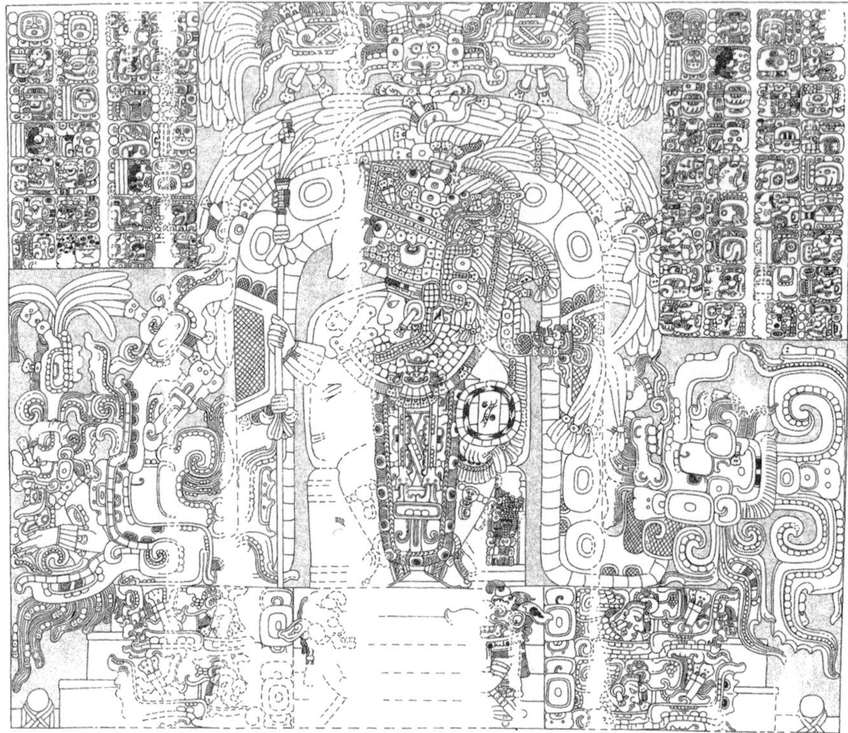

FIGURE 7.8. Sculpted lintel from Tikal, Temple IV, depicting the victorious Yik'in Chank'awil. Drawing by William R. Coe.

also channeled the legacy of his distant ancestor, who was the ruler of Teotihuacan. Earlier, Bajlaj Chank'awil battled his own brother, Jasaw's father, who had been a onetime ally in fighting the Kanuls. And so on and so on. The shifts, twists, and turns often are difficult to follow, yet we see here how so much of Late Classic Maya history is a drama that played out not just among a litany of kings and courts but among only a handful of extended families and royal lineages.[21]

After 750, lowland Maya history is no longer couched so explicitly in terms of this binary rivalry between the Mutuls and Kanuls and with the handful of related dynasties that were enmeshed in their fates. As we will explore in the following chapters, new players beyond the central and eastern regions appeared on the scene, vying for influence among the older, more established kingdoms, and power spread among several stakeholders. The dispersion of influence and of ruling factions is a theme we will see over the ensuing decades, and to anticipate where this all leads, the lowland Maya would eventually face a systemic political collapse in the span of only a few generations. In the meantime, the tangled history of alliances and wars would spread out in the other directions.

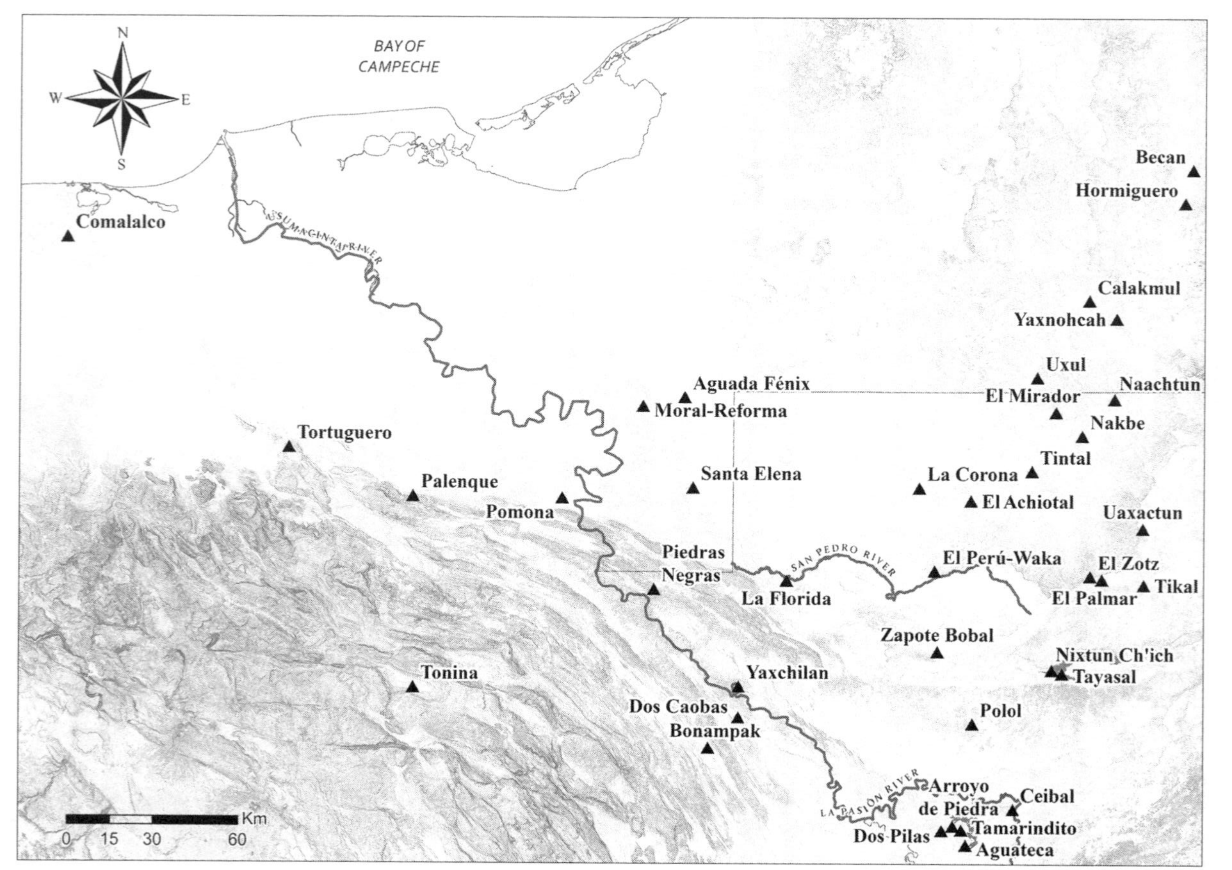

MAP 4. The western region.

CHAPTER 8

West

FEW ANCIENT CITIES can claim to be as beautiful as Palenque, located in the western Maya region, in what is today Chiapas, Mexico. Since the beginnings of Maya exploration and archaeology, as we have seen, its ruins have been a prime destination for explorers and visitors. Palenque's setting has much to do with its allure, sitting astride a high limestone ridge, looking out for miles over the rolling terrain to the north. Many of its temples and terraces were constructed directly against mountain slopes, integrated into the natural rocks and springs, making them appear as extensions of the natural landscape. Coursing through the center of Palenque's site center is a clear, cascading stream that was channeled by the ancient Maya to run close to the palace and elite residences of the city. These beautiful falls gave Palenque its ancient name, which I deciphered several years ago as *Lakamha'*, "Wide Waters." It was here that the court associated with the dynasty named Bakel settled in 490 CE, having moved from an original home located elsewhere, still unknown.

Palenque's importance to Maya archaeology persisted long after Stephens's visit in 1839, as we have seen. Alberto Ruz's and Juan Chable's

FIGURE 8.1. Portrait of K'inich Janabpakal, ruler of Palenque. Detail from the Temple XXI bench. Drawing by the author.

discovery of the great royal tomb beneath the Temple of the Inscriptions in 1952 set the stage for the eventual revelation of ancient Maya history, highlighting the existence of celebrated individuals and ancestors. Two decades after the tomb's opening, the identity of the tomb's occupant was revealed to be one of the great kings of the seventh century, K'inich Janabpakal (or Pakal, as we will call him) (Figure 8.1). One of Pakal's singular honorific titles was "West Kalomte'," hearkening back to the days of Teotihuacan's influence over Maya politics in the fourth and fifth centuries. Pakal's western affiliation oriented him within the greater Maya world, on par with the "Eastern" rulers of the Kanul and as part of the larger four-directional scheme of regional authorities, as the grandeur of his tomb perhaps reflected. Not surprisingly, therefore, he was also enmeshed in the larger political drama we have described so far, especially as the Kanul and Mutul rivalry touched the western Maya region. For example, as we have seen, Pakal seems to have hosted Nunujolchahk during the latter's long exile from Tikal. And Palenque had a longer-term significance in Maya history as well. One inscription from Pakal's palace hints that Palenque's court was once a stopover for Sihyajk'ahk' (an earlier West Kalomte') during his journey into the Maya heartland from Teotihuacan in 378.[1]

The interwoven nature of events in Maya history is well illustrated also by Pakal's early years. He came to power as a boy of twelve years old in 615. Only three years earlier, Palenque had been defeated by the forces of the Kanul king named Scroll Serpent. And still earlier, in 599, Sky Witness had conquered it too. These were unusual long-distance conflicts, with Palenque located 250 kilometers from Calakmul, and even further from Dzibanche. We do not know the reason behind Kanul's persistent aggression, but it shows Palenque's participation in larger geopolitical struggles of the time.[2] And the timing of Pakal's crowning remains suspicious, for both the boy-king's age and its proximity to Palenque's defeat by Kanul. Was he enthroned as a youthful Kanul vassal after the 611 conquest, like a few other local rulers? We cannot be sure, but the evidence would point to his early ascendance being one result of Kanul's disruptive wars in the west.

EARLY LORDS OF THE RIVER CITIES

To understand Palenque's place in all of this and the roles of its varied neighbors, we should step back and examine the history during centuries that led up to Kanul's foray into the western region. As far back as the fifth century, other royal courts had been swept up in the fraught politicking between the Kanul and Mutul dynasties. One of the earliest of these is the important Maya kingdom named Yokib, at the site we know today as Piedras Negras, located on the Usumacinta River and roughly between Palenque and Tikal. (This was where Tatiana Proskouriakoff did fieldwork in the 1930s, formulating ideas that would lead to her breakthrough in recognizing the existence of Maya history itself, decades later.) The dates of the early sources at Yokib are not as old as we find at Uaxactun and Tikal, reaching back only into the fifth century. Still, they offer us key lines of evidence for understanding a complex political landscape, and they may even fill in some gaps we have from the "middle years" of the Peten sites.

By the sixth century, we see the beginnings of detailed history emerge at kingdoms in the west, first at Piedras Negras, where we see indications that Teotihuacan was still actively meddling in Maya affairs. Piedras Negras may have been, at least for a short time, an important nexus for a revived effort by Teotihuacan or its local agents to influence affairs and control economic resources, almost eighty years after the death of Spearthrower Owl. In 510, when we pick up the story, Piedras Negras's ruler was a man named Yatahk, depicted on a beautiful sculpture known as Panel 2 (Figure 8.2). The king appears as a richly clad warrior with his young son standing beside him in similar Teotihuacan-style regalia. The stone was sculpted much later, in 667, to recount the key moment in Yatahk's reign when he "took the helmet" in the presence of a superior named Tajom Uk'abtun. He was said to be another "West Kalomte'" and a "Lord of the Winte'nah," using titles that Sihyajk'ahk' had used a century earlier after his arrival to Tikal. On the Piedras Negras sculpture, Yatahk is shown dressed in his new finery, presiding over a line of kneeling warriors, all of whom are likewise shown in Teotihuacan armor and dress.[3] They are all named as being from other kingdoms and sites to the south and west of Piedras Negras, including Yaxchilan (Pa'chan), Bonampak, and Lacanja—all places we will return to later in this chapter. On a contemporaneous sculpture from Piedras Negras, dedicated in 514, we see the local ruler, probably Yatahk once more, with several bound prisoners identified as being from neighboring kingdoms, again all to the south.[4]

Piedras Negras was the western regional power of the time, conquering or ruling over many of its neighbors, and in an era when Tikal was on the decline. And Yatahk's conquests and hegemony were surprisingly far-reaching, covering much of the western Maya area. Still, according to the narratives, the enigmatic Tajom Uk'abtun held even higher political rank and importance, somehow a representative of Teotihuacan interests. In this way, his role might echo that of Sihyajk'ahk' at Tikal, a century earlier. Whether he was based at Piedras Negras remains unclear, for we have no record of any disruptive "arrival" echoing the Entrada of 378.

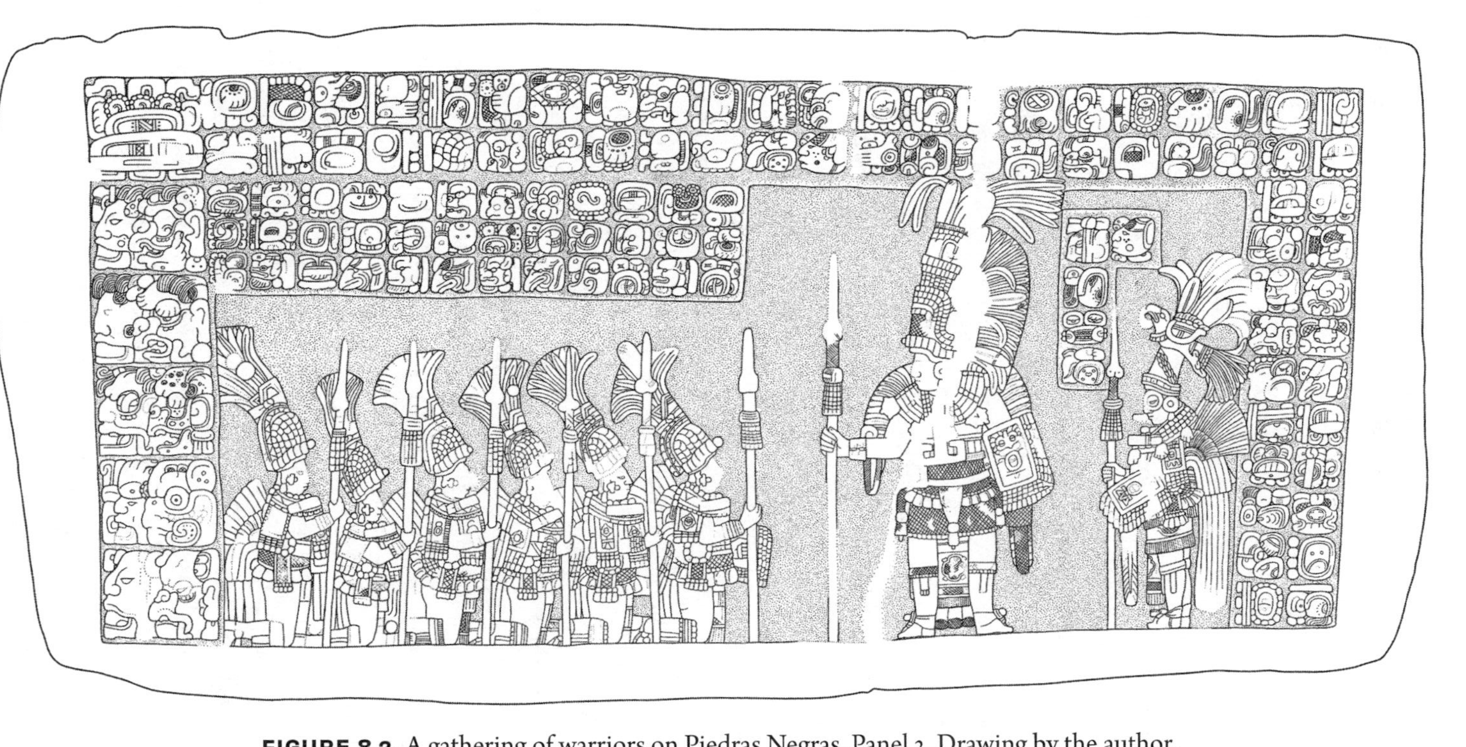

FIGURE 8.2. A gathering of warriors on Piedras Negras, Panel 2. Drawing by the author.

Nonetheless, the Piedras Negras evidence shows us how Teotihuacan was still active and involved in Maya politics well into the sixth century. The timing is interesting from an archaeological perspective, for the historical dates 510 and 514 fall shortly before Teotihuacan's own sudden demise, which we now believe took place as early as 550 CE. The end of the greatest city in Mesoamerica was a quick and violent one, as indicated by evidence of widespread burning and rapid abandonment—a collapse that, like those of the Maya, remains a profound mystery. Hints of Teotihuacan's historical involvement in the Maya world in the decades leading up to this change are tantalizing, if still poorly understood.

Yaxchilan, located upstream from Piedras Negras on the Usumacinta River, was the center of the Pa'chan court since at least the mid-fourth century. It had been founded as an offshoot or branch of a much older lineage that had roots in the central Peten, at a place we know today as El Zotz, located to the west of Tikal. As we have seen, Yaxchilan's beginnings as a dynastic seat can be traced to a man who may have come from there named Yopat Bahlam, who became king in 358. The timing of his ascendance suggests that the move of the Pa'chan dynasty or a part of it was related to the political tensions between Tikal and Uaxactun at around that same time.[5] Its founding on the Usumacinta River may have posed a threat to the older, more established dynasty of Yokib located at Piedras Negras, which had deeper historical roots going back to at least the third century.

As neighbors, the Pa'chan (Yaxchilan) and Yokib (Piedras Negras) royal houses have histories that were closely linked, and they were often at war. As early as 514 we see the ninth ruler of Pa'chan, "Knot-Eye Jaguar," depicted at Piedras Negras as a bound prisoner kneeling before Yatahk. In later centuries, Yaxchilan had the upper hand in their ongoing conflict. The wars between these river cities were perhaps connected to the larger tensions of this era and to the rise of the Kanuls. We get a small window into these larger connections with the tenth ruler of Yaxchilan, K'inich Tatab Jol, who established a diplomatic connection with Tunk'abhix, the very same Kanul king who oversaw the accession of Ajnumsaj at Naranjo. The Kanul association played out even more in the seventh and eighth centuries, deepening the latter's sphere of influence that would eventually spur Yaxchilan's own regional ambitions.

Also in the west, farther up in the highlands, lies the important site of Tonina, the capital of a court and kingdom called *Po'* or *Popo'* in Classic times. Located in the picturesque mountains of Chiapas, directly south of Palenque, it stood in a more isolated position from its neighboring kingdoms and perhaps protected from some of the bellicose events that defined much of Classic period of history. Its visible history also begins in earnest around 514, when its ruler marks the same important k'atun ending (9.4.0.0.0) we find highlighted at Piedras Negras, Yaxchilan, and Palenque—another indication of some sort of regional coherence or common historical arc. Later, in the late seventh and early eighth centuries, Tonina would become embroiled in a series of military conflicts with Palenque, during a time when it was very clearly allied with Kanul lords at Calakmul. We will return to this relationship shortly, for that dynamic helps us understand Palenque's own shifting connections in later decades.

PAKAL'S RISE

The history of the Bakel court clarifies during the eventful fifth century. Its dynastic founder was named K'uk'bahlam (Quetzal Jaguar), who acceded in 431 just short of his thirty-fourth birthday.[6] The timing of this initial accession, in the last years of the reign of Spearthrower Owl, echoes similar royal seatings and foundations of dynasties elsewhere. We have no contemporary records from K'uk'bahlam's time, and what we do know only comes from the histories recounted in later inscriptions, from Pakal's era and after. Reconstructing details of Bakel's early history therefore presents some challenges. One thing we do know is that K'uk'bahlam and his close successor ruled at a location different from the place we today call Palenque (ancient Lakamha'). Inscriptions tell us that they were based instead at a locale called Toktahn, the location of which still remains a mystery. It may refer to a sector of the greater archaeological site of Palenque, located farther to the west. K'uk'bahlam lasted less than five years on the throne, but he was venerated as the dynastic founder in later centuries. His successor came to power in 435 and seems to have reigned for a long span, up to about 487. Unfortunately, we still cannot decipher his name hieroglyph, so we refer to him simply as "Ruler 2."

With the death of Ruler 2, the Bakel kingdom approached a major change. Two brothers, perhaps sons of Ruler 2, emerged as leaders, the elder assuming the throne in 487. His name was Butz'aj Sakchihk, and his younger brother bore the name Ahkul Mo'nahb. Within a few short years, they both were responsible for the move of the Bakel court to Lakamha', the place we know today as Palenque, where it would remain for the next three centuries. So important was this new "founding" that it was celebrated in a much later temple at Palenque dating some two centuries later. There, in a building known as Temple XVII, a beautifully carved tablet depicts a warrior with a prisoner, linking the foundation of the city to an important war in the same year. The image is that of a later king, K'inich Kanbahlam, as a reenactor of that earlier, formative event (Plate 12). What stands out from this image is that the warrior wears battle regalia in the style of Teotihuacan, another indication of that city's influence and power during the Early Classic.

Several rulers reigned at Palenque over the next century, each helping establish it as a regional capital. Again, the historical details are sketchy. The significance of the site has much to do with its location, at the foot of the high mountain range, looking out over the rolling plains that served as a key communication route between the Maya area and the rest of Mesoamerica. During these early years, Palenque's elite ceramics were highly distinctive and very unlike those we find in the central areas of Tikal or Dzibanche. They are comparatively simple in form, lacking the colorful painting or imagery seen elsewhere. This leads us to believe that for much of this period, into the sixth century or so, Palenque's royal court may have operated in relative isolation from the central parts of the Maya world, perhaps a bit outside the tight network of cities and courts in the northern Peten. Palenque nevertheless grew, and it would not be long before it caught the attention of the greater powers to the east, especially the Kanuls.

Palenque's middle years are obscure, again known only from later retrospective accounts. The city quickly grew in importance throughout the rest of the fifth and sixth centuries, still small compared to its later grandeur.

In both 599 and 611, under two successive kings, Kanul's forces conquered Palenque, inflicting a memorable blow. It is difficult to explain the motivations behind this conflict, but it left lasting historical repercussions. The asymmetry between these kingdoms in those years was profound, and it may well be that Palenque was embroiled in some far larger regional campaign brought on by the Kanuls and its allies. We simply don't know the bigger picture. At the time of its first defeat in 599, Palenque had been ruled for several years by a queen named Lady Yohlik'nal. She was enthroned in 583 and later oversaw the commemoration of the k'atun period ending (9.8.0.0.0) in 593. We know little about her, but she must have brought some important changes to Palenque's court despite the setback of 599. For example, it was during her reign that we see a curious change in the title Palenque's rulers assumed upon their accessions: She and her predecessors were "seated with the headband," but after her reign, all kings were "seated in the kingship," implying some important uptick in status. Lady Yohliknal's portrait is included among the illustrious warrior-ancestors on the walls of the famous tomb in Palenque's Temple of the Inscriptions, dating to a century after her reign. The conquest of Palenque did not result in her death; she died five years later, in 604, apparently still in authority but perhaps still under the watchful eye of the Kanuls and their regional allies.

Palenque was an uncooperative vassal in these years. A new ruler named Ajen Yohlmat appeared early in 605 and was ruling when Kanul felt it had to strike once again, in 611. This had a negative effect; one historical account notes that in 613, at the turning of the k'atun period, "the gods were lost, the lords were lost." This poetic turn of phrase may describe the temporary abandonment of the city by its rulers and its patron deities. Ajen Yohlmat and another prominent nobleman or coruler named Janabpakal each perished in 612, which may be a clue to their violent end. Exactly what the circumstances were and how long they lasted we cannot know, but the stirrings of a remarkable change were already in place, involving a new group within Palenque's royal family.

Between the two Kanul wars, on March 24, 603, a woman named Lady Sakk'uk' (White Quetzal) gave birth to a son later known as K'inich Janabpakal (or Pakal). He assumed the throne on July 27, 615, when only twelve years of age. His family connections to the earlier rulers of Palenque's history are hard to ascertain, probably due to the instabilities brought on by the Kanul wars, but the new king's name points to an intentional connection with the earlier Janabpakal, who had died in 612. The installment of a new child-king under such circumstances probably reflects the instability of the Bakel court at the time, when the recent conquest by the Kanul ruler was still resonating.

Given the timing, it is possible, in fact, that Pakal was installed as a young vassal of Scroll Serpent, who is named as Palenque's conqueror. If so, Pakal's mother, Lady Sakk'uk', would have played an important role as the regent and true power behind the throne. We find them both depicted on the limestone tablet that still adorns Pakal's room, in the miraculously preserved palace that he built over the course of his long reign (Figure 8.3). Lady Sakk'uk' is shown presenting her son with the ceremonial headdress of a warrior. She was the real power in Palenque's court to the time of her death in 640, and she even takes the title "Holy Bakel Lord" on one occasion. It is a situation highly reminiscent of Lady Wakjalam Chanlem at Naranjo a few decades later, and I cannot help but wonder if, like the Naranjo queen, Lady Sakk'uk' had her own family connections to the Kanul court, marrying into the local Bakel dynasty in the wake of Palenque's defeats. It was she, not Pakal, who oversaw the katun celebrations of 633 (9.10.0.0.0), when her son was already thirty years old. It may be that Kanul was still exerting a strong influence on Palenque's local affairs, given the expansions of its own power at the very same time (its conquest of Naranjo was less than two years earlier) and the shift of its court to Calamkul in 635. In any event, her death in 640, as well as the birth of an heir in 635, seems to have presented Pakal with a new ability to set his own course and formulate his own strategies and goals as a local leader at long last.

FIGURE 8.3. The Oval Palace Tablet of Palenque, showing K'inich Janabpakal and his mother, Lady Sakk'uk'. Drawing by Linda Schele.

It was around this time that we see that Pakal took his revealing title as a "West Kalomte'," a sure indication of his newfound power and regional influence. (As we have seen, Kalomte' was reserved for the very highest level of Maya kings.) Up to now, we have seen it only used in reference to the powerful lords at Dzibanche and Lamanai in the east, the kings at Tikal, and the Teotihuacan invaders of the fourth century. By 654 Pakal took it on as well, the first Palenque king to ever do so. Soon he began a series of his own military campaigns toward Palenque's east while also initiating an ambitious program to expand the Palenque's palace into an imposing complex, repurposing some of its courtyards and buildings for the artistic display of his new conquests. His early successes are indicated by several plaster sculptures of the palace that depict him as a warrior standing above seated prisoners. His most significant victory came in August 659, when he captured several nobles from the kingdom of Pipa', located to the east near the ruins we know today as Pomona. Elegant portraits of these six captives, all shown kneeling in supplication and carefully labeled by name, were displayed in the inner courtyard of the palace, where they can still be seen today. In the accompanying text, we read of their capture and humiliation, juxtaposed with Palenque's much earlier defeat in 599 at the hands of Sky Witness of the Kanul. It seems that Pakal's victories in 659 represented a war of revenge *against* the Kanuls.

Now the story of Pakal and the western regions intersects directly with the complex narratives of the Mutul-Kanul conflict, as presented in the previous chapter. In the immediate wake of Pakal's victory, a man named Nunujolchahk arrived at Palenque with great fanfare, in the company of several other lords and bearing the god effigies of his own court. Historical texts from Palenque highlight the great visitation as one of the principal events of Pakal's reign, even more than the victorious war itself. I have long debated the question of whether this is the same Nunujolchahk of the Mutul dynasty, the brother or half-brother of Bajlaj Chank'awil, but I now believe they are likely the same person. He bears no Mutul emblem with his name and is instead identified as a lord of Santa Elena, a site located to the east on the San Pedro River. But we must remember that this is precisely the time of Nunujolchahk's exile and "wandering years," after his defeat by Yuknomch'en's forces in 657. It remains difficult to understand the visitation of 659, but I interpret it as a meeting of powers old and new, with Nunujolchahk as an ally in Pakal's wars of revenge against the Kanuls and Calakmul.[7]

By 648 Pakal's spouse, Lady Tz'akab Ajaw, had given birth to three sons whose lives would eventually shape most of the rest of Palenque's history in one way or another. The first son would be Pakal's eventual successor, K'inich Kanbahlam, born in 635. The second son, K'inich Kan Joy Kitam, was born in 644, and he would later rule as well. The third son, Tiwohl Chanmat, offers a poignant story, however, for he passed away at a young age in 680, when Pakal was in his very last years of life.

The elderly father oversaw Tiwohl Chanmat's burial in a pyramid known as Temple XVIII, and his son would later modify this building as an ancestral shrine and oracle. Lady Tz'akab Ajaw had died in 672, and so she did not live to see the death of her youngest child. She was interred in a small funerary temple aside Pakal's own famous pyramid, the Temple of the Inscriptions. When her tomb was discovered in 1994, archaeologists saw her well-preserved skeleton covered in red cinnabar, the skull still wearing the jade headband she wore when she was interred. In death, she came to be known as *La Reina Roja*, the "Red Queen."[8]

A fascinating moment in Palenque's political history occurred in 679, when Pakal gathered his three sons to discuss his plans for their succession. A scene of this meeting, sculpted in stucco, once graced the rear wall of Tiwohl Chanmat's funerary shrine, and it is most remarkable for having quotations—spoken words—written near the captioned figures. Much of the sculpted scene is lost today, but we can see that Pakal was seated in the center, with his three adult sons behind him. Three nobles appear before Pakal, and a snippet of their conversation with the king is preserved: "... my lord, the Matwil lords are set in order, (and) your heart is satisfied." The decision here was evidently to have the three brothers in line to succeed their father—an arrangement that went against the more typical father-to-son inheritance of power. Kanbahlam and K'anjoykitam seem to have had no spouses or offspring, perhaps forcing the need for an important decision within the Bakel court. However we eventually come to understand the complex details of the succession, it is astounding that we have here the elements of a speech delivered in an ancient Maya palace, preserved for history. Other orations are known from Palenque and other sites.

Pakal's death came soon after in 683, when he was interred within his great tomb, deep within the Temple of the Inscriptions. He had ruled for a remarkable sixty-eight years, transforming Palenque into a regional power and becoming a cultural hero in the process. In the spacious shrine atop his pyramid, three tablets presented a continuous text recounting the political and religious history leading up to and including his long reign. The lavish tomb inside the temple is itself a carefully designed artwork, with iconography that places Pakal within

FIGURE 8.4. Sarcophagus lid of K'inich Janabpakal, showing him deified and rising from the earth. Drawing by Merle Greene Robertson, courtesy of The Mesoamerica Center, The University of Texas at Austin.

the celestial and earthly realms of his deceased ancestors (Figure 8.4). In the afterlife, he arose with the sun and entered the earth, where his parents and others resided. His apotheosis is depicted on a sculpted lid of the sarcophagus, recognized today as one of the most famous—and misunderstood—of Maya carvings. In the complex scene, we see Pakal in the center, reclining within a bowl or dish designed for sacrificial instruments. This vessel is animated, as indicated by a front-facing skull at the base of the image, representing an animate seed. From this dish, behind Pakal, rises a sacred tree of jade. In essence, the deceased king is shown as an infant who is sacrificed and "planted" within the earth to emerge into the sky as the eastern sun. In this way, in death, Pakal joins his ancestors on the sacred path of the sun, in its infinite cycles of movement. The scene is a depiction of "entering the path," the euphemism for death in the inscriptions around the sarcophagus. The sides of his coffin, below this celestial scene, show his ancestors emerging out of the earth as fruiting trees—an earthly metaphor of rebirth and resurrection (see Figure 2.4). As a poetic artwork, Pakal's sarcophagus gives us a compelling window into Classic Maya religion and the place of dynasties within the symmetries of the cosmos.

SHIELD JAGUAR

During Pakal's long rule at Palenque, Yaxchilan continued to increase its profile as the seat of the Pa'chan dynasty, heading its own regional state, or kabch'en. Its ruler during most of this time was Yaxun Bahlam III ("Cotinga Jaguar"), who we know mostly through retrospective accounts. He was an active warrior, conquering numerous enemies in the region, including the kingdom of Hixwitz, in the direction of the central Peten, but it remains difficult to know how Yaxun Bahlam III fit within the wider regional conflicts brewing at the time. It is likely that Palenque and Yaxchilan had sour relations throughout much of this era, given what we know of the connections between Pa'chan and Kanul in both earlier and later years. Yaxun Bahlam III reigned for over fifty years, from 629 to about 681, leaving the scene just after the Pakal's death. Few of Yaxun Bahlam III's own monuments have survived, which is perhaps an interesting indication of some friction at the end of his rule.[9] Whatever the case, important political changes were afoot just when these two long-lived western rulers passed away. Their deaths came very soon after the defeat of Nunujolchahk in 679, which had established Kanul's victory over the Mutuls in the central region, at least for the time being.

A major new ruler of Yaxchilan came on the scene in 681, a man we know as "Shield Jaguar" (his true name may have been Kokaj Bahlam, but we are still unsure) (Figure 8.5). I cannot help but see the timing of his accession as related to these larger geopolitical developments, and it may be confirmed by one key detail in Yaxchilan's family tree: One of Shield Jaguar's wives, a woman named Lady Uhchanlem, was a princes of Kanul, probably another daughter of Yuknomch'en. The significance of this family connection is hard to overstate, for it likens Yaxchilan's relationship with the Kanul family to that enjoyed by El Peru-Waka' with "Lady K'abel" and the princess who married into the family of La Corona. Shield Jaguar's accession might be understood as part of Yuknomch'en's wider efforts to forge alliances to the west of the central area. Here the prior splintering of the Pa'chan dynasty from its Peten origin spot at El Zotz, near Tikal, is perhaps relevant. As with the fractured house of Mutul, the two political identities that called themselves Pa'chan may have offered Yuknomch'en an enticing opportunity at wider alliance-building, working even further against Tikal's interests. Whatever the case, Shield Jaguar's accession represented a newfound status for Yaxchilan and the Pa'chan court, as indicated by his being the first local ruler to ever take the title "West Kalomte'," a title he may have appropriated from Pakal after the latter's death the previous year.

Like other kings of the era, Shield Jaguar celebrated many military campaigns and conquests during his long period on the throne. Several stelae and sculpted door lintels (a preferred medium at Yaxchilan for relating historical events) depict him in action, standing with weapons over defeated captives from neighboring city-states. No previous Yaxchilan ruler had ever been shown so directly engaged in active warfare, and it must have been a novel sort of representation for its time. Given his ties to the Kanul dynasty through marriage, Shield Jaguar's accession and frequent wars might be seen as extensions on Yuknomch'en's geopolitical ambitions in the west.

FIGURE 8.5. Shield Jaguar, warrior-king of Yaxchilan. Detail from Dos Caobas, Stela 1. Photograph by the author.

Another prominent woman was celebrated during Shield Jaguar's reign, Lady K'abalxok, who was portrayed on several spectacular sculptures alongside the king (Plate 13). In one scene she performs a bloodletting ceremony, passing a thorny rope though her tongue, as she kneels before Shield Jaguar, who holds a "fiery spear" (Figure 8.6). In another, she presents Shield Jaguar with his jaguar war helmet in preparation for battle. We are unsure of Lady K'abalxok's place of origin, but she was probably the first wife of Shield Jaguar, with him at the day of his accession in 681. Our first indication of Lady Uhchanlem's presence comes later in 709, after her arrival from Calakmul, when she gave birth to her son, the eventual heir. The two women coexisted at the court of Pa'chan, and both survived Shield Jaguar by several years. Their prominence was also reflected in their residences at the site, well-built structures that were small palaces, used for formal occasions and to conduct their own affairs. Lady K'abalxok's house, known as Structure 23, was dedicated in 723, and she was buried under the building forty years later.[10]

Shield Jaguar's death in in 742, at age ninety-six, seems to have brought about an internal crisis of succession. The event is followed by a glaring ten-year interruption before the crowning of the next ruler, at least as recorded in the extant records. A new Yaxun Bahlam, the fourth with this name, took the crown in 752. We lack many of the background details of this glaring gap in the site's history, but one likely scenario is that the two wives each eventually gave birth to a rival heir. Lady K'abalxok, as Shield Jaguar's initial wife, may have had a son who would have naturally claimed the inheritance after his father's death. Yaxun Bahlam IV, the son born to Lady Uhchanlem of Kanul, was very likely the grandson or great-grandson of Yuknomch'en, and he may have put a stop to these plans or engaged in a protracted conflict with his half-brother (a familiar pattern by now).

A telling clue for this comes from Yaxchilan's neighbor and sometime rival, Piedras Negras. There, in 749, the local king named Itzamk'anahk celebrated his first k'atun (twenty years) on the throne of Yokib. The happy occasion was recorded for posterity on a beautifully carved tablet and involved diplomacy, dancing, and the drinking of cacao. In attendance was a "Holy Lord of Pa'chan" named Yopat Bahlam, *not* Yaxun Bahlam IV. It is a unique reference, and it seems likely that this was a ruler of Yaxchilan who ruled for a time after Shield Jaguar's death, taking the name of the Pa'chan earlier founder. We cannot be sure he was the son of Lady K'abalxok, but that to me seems a workable scenario to consider.

FIGURE 8.6. Yaxchilan, Lintel 24, showing the bloodletting rite of Lady K'abalxok. Drawing by Ian Graham.

Yaxun Bahlam IV spent a good deal of years maneuvering to take the throne in 752, soon after the passing of his mother, the former Kanul princess. If any monuments ever mentioned that Yopat Bahlam existed at Yaxchilan, they were erased from history. Yaxun Bahlam was careful in presenting his close connection to his father, especially in his early monuments. Immediately he emphasized one of his most famous titles, "He of twenty prisoners," to demonstrate his warlike history and success (see Figure 11.2). In addition, he claimed his father's most illustrious title as the "West Kalomte." The Yaxchilan interregnum is yet another complex story of an internal rift within a royal court, perhaps with Kanul's meddling, with a bellicose warrior-king emerging as the winner.

THE GODS' SHRINES

Upon Pakal's death at Palenque, his eldest son, K'inich Kanbahlam, assumed the throne on January 8, 684, and quickly planned several ambitious architectural projects, including the final details on his father's shrine in the Temple of the Inscriptions. Another focus was on a new design for a set of three temples in honor of the patron gods of the dynasty, known as the Palenque Triad (individually as GI, GII, and GIII). These temples still stand today as some of the most elegant examples of Maya religious architecture, and many of their sculptures strive to legitimate Kanbahlam, who, at forty-eight, was at last able to rule after his father's long and eventful reign. They were big shoes to fill.

Kanbahlam and his priests crafted a complex message that carefully mixed mythology, cosmology, and politics. The three temples today stand as the most accessible window into the ways the ancient Maya wove these strands together into a powerful ideology, albeit one that would only last a couple of more centuries. The physical backdrop of the three shrines was a prominent hill overlooking Palenque's site center.[11] One shrine was built directly at its base, known today by the poetic name the Temple of the Foliated Cross. Atop a limestone rise at the left was the tallest of the three shrines, the Temple of the Cross, facing south toward the sacred spring or *ch'en* named Lakamha', giving the city its ancient name. Facing the mountain and forming a direct alignment with Pakal's tomb and the Foliated Cross was the Temple of the Sun, the smallest of the shrines. Each building was the "house" of an individual member of the Triad, and, like the gods, each had its own special symbolism and cosmological meaning. The Temple of the Cross was the sky, home of the deity GI, named as Junyehwinik, "One-Toothed Person." He was associated with the rising sun and ancestral resurrection. The Temple of the Sun was dedicated to sacred war and represented the earth, housing the second-born deity GIII, who was also an aspect of the sun god. The Foliated Cross and its looming mountain were the focal point of the entire complex, and the temple housed Unen K'awil ("Infant K'awil"), the last-born of the three sibling deities (Figure 8.7). This patron god symbolized the power of regeneration and growth, symbolized by the bejeweled maize tree that is the central image of the temple's great tablet. It is no accident that Kanbahlam's father, Pakal, was shown on his sarcophagus as Unen K'awil, being reborn and rising into the sky. The new temple to this important deity directly faced the father's funerary pyramid, a short distance away.

The temporal backdrop of the three temples is also important. Pakal had passed away in 683, less than nine years before the coming of the great k'atun celebration of 9.13.0.0.0, on March 16, 692. The anticipation of this turning point was great, for thirteen k'atuns represented a sacred number of creation, a hugely important and even cosmic event. The patron gods had to be rehoused for the new era, and so construction began, with work completed two months before the k'atun, on January 9, 692—the exact eight-year anniversary of the king's accession. In conceiving of the three themes—royal ancestry, sacred warfare, and maize agriculture—the temples worked together to crystalize the "holy trinity" of Classic Maya religion and political ideology. The point was to celebrate the gods and the new k'atun but also to put Kanbahlam squarely amid those themes and ideas, as protector and procreator. I suspect, too, that the idea of three sibling deities finding a new purpose resonated with Kanbahlam, the eldest of three brothers who were designated to succeed their father on the throne. His brother, the youngest of the three sons, died shortly

FIGURE 8.7. K'inich Kanbahlam (adult and child) venerating sacred maize. Tablet of the Foliated Cross from Palenque. Drawing by the author.

before Pakal himself passed away, yet I must wonder if the three shrines held some personal symbolism for Kanbahlam too. One detail of the narrative in the Temple of Cross may even confirm this—the Maize God who engendered the Triad gods in primordial time was born on the day 8 Ahau, the same day on which Pakal was born. The k'atun ending on 9.13.0.0.0 also was an 8 Ahau. As my colleague Floyd Lounsbury long ago demonstrated, several numerological and astronomical patterns were factors used to link the primordial birth to that of Pakal, the father. In a not-so-subtle way, the three sons of Pakal, living and deceased, *were* the three newly housed gods, all representatives of cosmic power and of time.

Early in his rule, and before the dedication of the three Triad temples, Kanbahlam had serious geopolitical problems to confront. One was a war that flared up with the kingdom of Po' at Tonina, in the high mountains to the south. There are scant historical records of a conflict between these cities before Kanbahlam's reign, but it would seem to have been an old rivalry, and we do know that both kingdoms were great enemies in later generations. Kanbahlam won his war in 687 and Tonina's ruler was deposed, an event celebrated in the narrative of Palenque's war shrine in the Temple of the Sun. As part of the Triadic complex of new temples, Kanbahlam also inserted a small shrine for a god who was specifically identified as a "Kanul being," which is difficult to interpret—was it a reflection of Palenque's diplomatic connection to the Kanuls, or was it a captured deity? It is hard to say, but we do know that Tonina was allied with the Kanul rulers not long after this, in the reign of Tok' K'awil, suggesting that Kanbahlam was proudly housing a captured image of a foreign deity as part of his ambitious and highly symbolic temple complex. A new Tonina king, K'inich Baknal Chahk, took up the conflict soon after his crowning in 688. These two new kings continued the war, which played out over several years and even decades. Shortly after the turn of the thirteenth k'atun, in 693, Baknal Chahk took a number of Palenque captives, many of whom are prominently displayed in Tonina's sculptures, bound with ropes, which he dedicated in 699.

Kanbahlam would reign until his death in 702. He perhaps was buried in the small shrine near his mother and father, known today as the Temple of the Skull. His younger brother K'anjoykitam took the throne a few months later. He is most famous for his portrait discovered at Tonina, as a bound prisoner wearing his crowned jewels. He was captured in 711 and displayed in humiliation, a further act of revenge that must have been particularly satisfying. And here we come to a curious pattern in the written history: According to a handful of Palenque texts, K'anjoykitam continued to rule, even overseeing the construction of a new wing and tribute hall within the palace despite the rough patch. The simplest explanation is that he was somehow reinstalled as Palenque's king as a vassal to Tonina, a place with a long history of its own as a regional power. It is worth remembering here that the 690s were the time of Kanul's dramatic defeat by Jasaw Chank'awil of Mutul, which initiated Tikal's dramatic resurgence in the eighth century, taken up by Yik'in Chank'awil. It is possible, if not likely, that the protracted Palenque-Tonina wars were somehow a part of that larger geopolitical clash.[12]

Palenque regained its footing with the crowning of K'inich Ahkul Mo'nahb in 721. He was the son of Tiwohl Chanmat, Pakal's third son who had died before he could himself rule. Ahkul Mo'nahb's role as heir, through his uncles, was therefore somewhat unusual. He took pains to document his family connections not only to his father but to his grandfather, Pakal. For the time being, the wars with Tonina had calmed and Ahkul Mo'nahb's reign enjoyed an era of relative quiet for Palenque, if not resurgence. He set about on new conquests, revived the old spaces of his grandfather's palace, and left his own mark on Palenque's cityscape of shrines, dedicating two new temples for the Triad deities, known today as Temples XIX and XXI. These were excavated in the late 1990s and early 2000s, revealing a trove of new inscriptions and artworks. One highlight among the discoveries was an intricately carved bench or platform in Temple XIX, built within a temple constructed before the sacred spring. It shows an intimate scene of Ahkul Mo'nahb's crowning ceremony, attended by his maternal uncle and several other court members seated around him. Ahkul Mo'nahb sits on a cushion throne and leans forward to receive the paper headband of rulership (Figure 8.8). The new king wears the emblems of the deity GI of the Palenque Triad, and he clearly is shown as the embodiment of that god, reenacting a scene of mythology. As we saw with his uncle Kanbahlam,

FIGURE 8.8. K'inich Ahkulmo'nahb receives the royal headband. Temple XIX bench. Drawing by the author.

there was evidently a strong need for Classic Maya rulers to identify themselves with certain heroic figures of primordial time.[13]

One important member of Ahkul Mo'nahb's court and inner circle was a military leader named Chaksutz' who, in his mid-fifties, assumed a new role as a *Yajawk'ahk'*, a "Lord of Fire." This title we find at Palenque and a few other sites in reference to warriors who hold a special connection to the cult of sacred warfare associated with Teotihuacan. It rose in importance in western Maya kingdoms especially in the years following the collapse of Teotihuacan, almost as if they were "keepers of the flame" of that ancient city and its legacy. Chaksutz' therefore had a religious charter behind his military role. From 725 to 729, he oversaw several military engagements on behalf his king, involving enemies more to the east than south, toward the Usumacinta River. In those years, a new uneasiness was percolating in the river cities of Piedras Negras and Yaxchilan, with the imminent death of Shield Jaguar and the discord between his two sons.

• • •

At Yaxchilan, Yaxun Bahlam IV consolidated his rule after taking the throne in 752, and he spent the ensuing three decades projecting Yaxchilan's authority north and south along the river. He attacked the kingdom of Lakamtun, like his predecessors, and he continued his incessant hostilities toward Piedras Negras. Late in his reign, in 783, a loyal lieutenant named Tilom captured a member of the royal house of Piedras Negras named T'ulchihk, perhaps the principal heir to the Yokib throne. (The captive, as a boy, had long before attended the anniversary party attended by Yaxun Bahlam's half-brother, Yopat Bahlam.) In a painful scene on the sculpture that commemorates the event, Tilom presents T'ulchihk to his king, who looks down upon the miserable, pleading captive.[14] Yaxun Bahlam was not too concerned with Palenque or Tonina, apparently, which may have been a bit too distant to the west to present a threat. Were they allies, even? It is around this time that we start to lose a firm sense of just who was aligned with whom, and I wonder if this reflects the political realities on the ground.

In the west, as elsewhere, Kanul's influence began to weaken, and Calakmul was no longer the great center of alliance-making that it once was. A couple of generations had passed after Yuknomch'en's long, influential rule, and by 750 the fates of city-states such as Palenque, Yaxchilan, and others became more inward-looking, the landscape even more balkanized. A period of new instability and violent conflict was taking hold throughout the lowlands, to the south and the north as well. Soon, the troubled years of the late eighth century would lead to a final political implosion that would sweep across the entire Maya world.

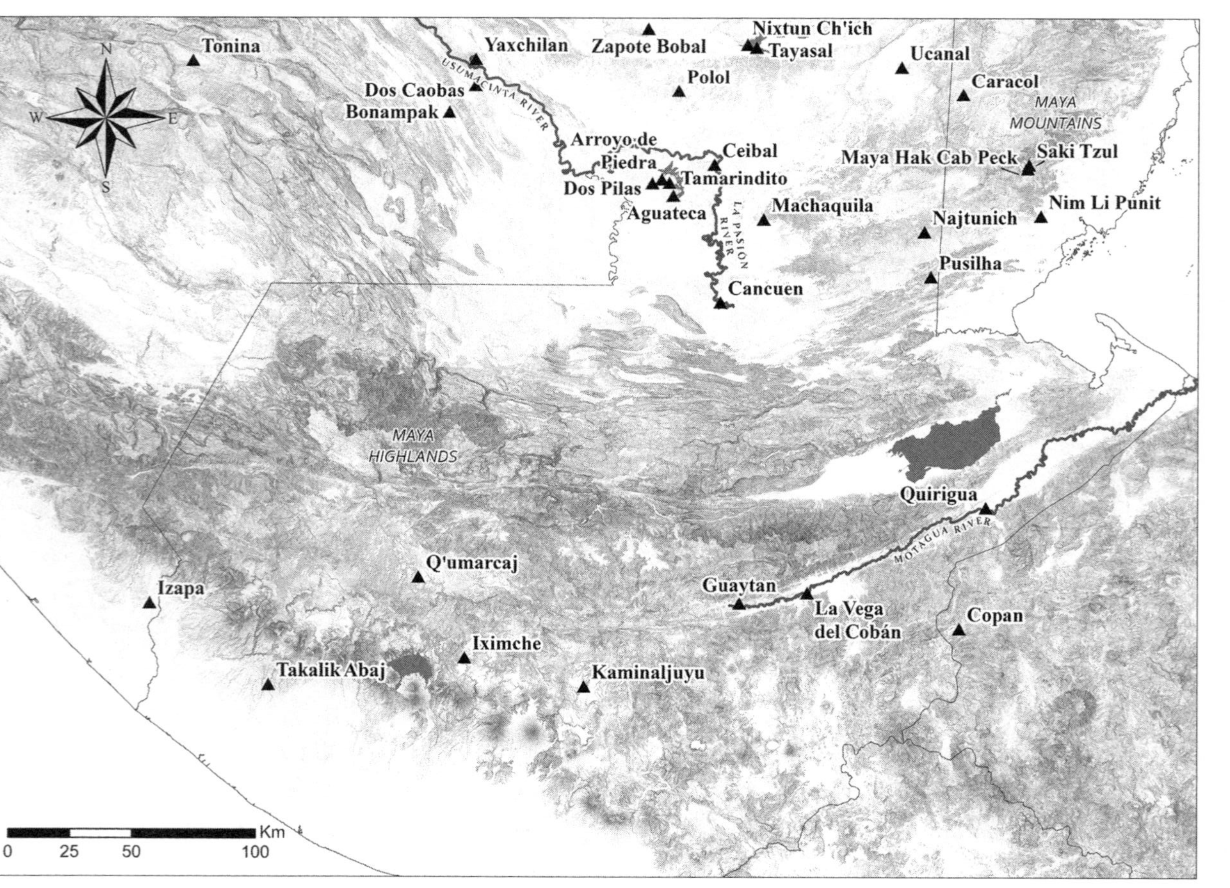

MAP 5. The southern region.

CHAPTER 9

South

ON THE SOUTHEASTERN edge of the Maya region, far from the more closely knit network of city-states in the west and central lowlands, two important cities blossomed over the course of the Classic period. Copan and Quirigua were each founded in the Early Classic as cultural and political "outposts" of Maya dynastic culture, off in a distant and mountainous frontier. A close reading of the histories of these places shows that they were nevertheless also participants in the wider political and family tensions of the Classic period and were drawn into them in surprising ways. History suggests that Copan and Quirigua may have been geographical and cultural offshoots of the dynasties that developed in the Peten and the central area, developing their own strong identities and regional styles over the centuries, striving to present their true "Maya-ness" within a diverse landscape, where local populations may not have Maya at all. Just how and why they were founded in the southern borderlands is unclear, and it raises several questions. Trade networks in the Maya highlands and reaching into Honduras and El Salvador were certainly important motivations. (Cacao and quetzal feathers were abundant in these regions.) Over the past five decades, archaeological excavations and epigraphic work at both sites have recovered a large part of their complex, interwoven story.

Today, Copan's temples and plazas sit within a beautiful archaeological park nestled in a small mountain valley of western Honduras, near the border with Guatemala. Its large acropolis dominates the flat valley floor, built up over several centuries into a dense assembly of grouped pyramids, courtyards, and plazas. It was the first Maya ruin that Stephens and Catherwood ever encountered, in 1839, and they were startled and intrigued by what they saw. Most of the stelae that they came across and sketched remain standing, carved in the round with portraits of kings and bearing long inscriptions. This area was Copan's main religious precinct, a place of ancestral shrines and other ceremonial spaces. A short distance away lies an elevated area where I suspect many of its elite population lived, now built over by the modern town of Copan Ruinas. In ancient times, the place we call Copan was named Uxwitik (at least when the Maya occupied it), and it had been home to a small center for many generations, dating back to Olmec times.[1]

Quirigua is a smaller site than Copan, located forty-five kilometers north as the macaw flies, in the great Motagua River valley. This was a major conduit for communication and trade, much as it is today, and it was here in the high mountains above the river that early Mesoamericans discovered boulders of precious jadeite, which they began to exploit as an important resource. The elite Olmec of the Middle Preclassic were especially well known for their fondness for jade, and its trade spread far and wide as an important expression of status. The Motagua Valley remains the only confirmed source of jadeite in all of Mesoamerica, and this may well account for the widespread interest in this southeast region by the Classic Maya, as well as other Mesoamerican civilizations both before and after. Trade networks and connections farther south into Central America, beyond the confines of Mesoamerica itself, also played a role in the economic lives of both Quirigua and Copan.

The royal courts at Copan and Quirigua seem to have been founded in coordinated fashion in the early fifth century, so it is not surprising that their histories are more closely linked than most other city-states. Stepping back a bit and taking a broader look, we see that Copan and its neighbor were geographical anomalies—centers of elite Maya dynastic culture located on a cultural frontier. They were old places to be sure, long settled since the Formative period, but unlike many cities of the central lowlands, these courtly centers did not develop from the fabric of Late Preclassic Maya culture and the rapid political, social, and artistic developments that led up to it. Instead, Copan and Quirigua were relative latecomers in their own locales, established rapidly as cultural and political "outposts" of the Classic Maya world. It may be that some Maya elites from the central area had become adventurous and expansionistic, inspired or directed by their powerful Teotihuacan authorities of the time. It may also be that local non-Maya elites of the southeast region were themselves eager to participate in the new political and ideological changes taking place near the beginning of the Classic era, "buying in" to Maya ways and linking themselves to the new dynastic culture that had emerged out of the Preclassic.

K'INICH YAXK'UK'MO'

In 426, still in what we call the Early Classic era, a Maya lord traveled a great distance to Teotihuacan to acquire the official and proper sanction to rule. The long-lived Spearthrower Owl was still on the throne, fifty-two years into his reign, with the conquest of Tikal already decades in the past. The Teotihuacan ruler still held considerable power and influence of Maya politics, having overseen the installations of Maya rulers at many courts and kingdoms. The newly arrived lord was K'uk'mo' Ajaw (Quetzal-Macaw Lord), and he would come to establish one of the most important dynasties in Maya history, at Copan, in today's western Honduras. The ritual may have taken place at the massive structure we today know as the Ciudadela, facing west and looking over the great Avenue of the Dead.

Upon his accession, the "Quetzal Macaw Lord" took the royal name K'inich Yaxk'uk'mo', "the Radiant Quetzal-Macaw," referring to a hybrid form of a great mythic bird with long tail feathers, embodying the sun in its movement across the sky. He arrived at Copan after an arduous three-month trip, crossing over seven hundred miles. And it was at this point that the first main buildings of the central Copan site were constructed, on the flat bottomland of the valley, adjacent to the river. Today the remnants of these modest buildings lie deep beneath the acropolis of Copan, but many were investigated by an ambitious excavation in the early 1990s, tunneling into the earliest layers of construction beneath. These revealed a layer cake of four centuries of construction, beginning with the modest structures built for or by K'inich Yaxk'uk'mo'. Small houses and platforms were of river cobbles and covered with adobe, in many respects echoing the style of Teotihuacan itself, as if to replicate a very small version of the great Mexican city. In fact, the main west-facing shrine at the core of the acropolis would grow over the centuries with the buildings around it and come to be called the W'inte'nah, probably a conceptual copy of Teotihuacan's architecture.

Our knowledge of Yaxk'uk'mo's journey and his role as Copan's founder comes from what local scribes had to say in the later years. They celebrated him as an illustrious ancestor who brought power and pedigree to the elites of the Copan Valley. Most revealing is a large, cube-shaped stone known as "Altar Q" that rested atop the acropolis in front of the unusual pyramid knows as Temple 16, the last iteration of the shrine bult over the founder's tomb (Figure 9.1). Exposed to the elements for thirteen centuries, the carved details on the altar have remained in remarkably good condition. (The volcanic tuff with which Copan's sculptors worked suffers erosion far less in the rain than limestone.) A long inscription is on the altar's top, and the sides depict sixteen seated and nearly identical figures. John Lloyd Stephens took special interest in the stone when he gazed upon it in 1839. The individuals on the sides (four on each) sit on a hieroglyph, he noted, "which probably designates his name and office."[2] Stephens was correct—each "cushion" glyph is indeed the name of the king, as was confirmed in the 1970s. The names

FIGURE 9.1. Altar Q of Copan, with portraits of the local dynasty's sixteen rulers. Photograph by the author.

match those for the various rulers mentioned throughout Copan's other monuments, giving us an unusually complete picture of a Maya dynasty. As a visual king list of the entire dynasty, Altar Q's design evokes the name the ancient Maya had for "dynasty": *bolon tz'akab ajaw*, the "many totaled lords." The sequence begins on the west side, with a scene of the first and last king, each facing one another with a date glyph in between. This was the day of the inauguration of the sixteenth ruler who erected the altar in 776 CE and whose story we will come to shortly. In the scene, the final king converses over the generations with K'inich Yaxk'uk'mo', receiving from the founder a dart with an obsidian point, an emblem of the sacred militarism of Teotihuacan. It is a powerful political image of continuity and cosmological symmetry, with its sixteen (four by four) portraits. The inscription atop the altar recounts Yaxk'uk'mo's "taking of the k'awil" at the sacred structure, the Winte'nah, in 426, and of his arrival to Copan ("he rested his legs") on February 9, 427. The sacred office Yaxk'uk'mo' assumed at distant Teotihuacan allowed the honor of being a "West Kalomte'," which he was called in numerous inscriptions. Like Sihyajk'ahk', that connection established his credentials as a representative of authority in central Mexico in the Early Classic. We should be careful to contrast this sense of "west" in Copan from how it was used as a directional and cosmological title by Pakal, Shield Jaguar, and Yaxun Bahlam IV in the western regions. Importantly, it was only Yaxk'uk'mo' who ever took the "west" title; his successors in office were consistently "south" lords, as we would expect.

Yaxk'uk'mo' was already Copan's ruler before his pilgrimage to Teotihuacan to receive the necessary credentials as a new and even more powerful political authority—to "take the *k'awil,*" as Altar Q puts it. Two text fragments from Copan show that he was ruling in 416, more than ten years before his trip to central Mexico. When he went to Teotihuacan, it was therefore as a Maya ruler, perhaps joining other important early *ajaws* and dynasts who were required to make the same journey. (We should remember that Teotihuacan housed a large population of Maya elites during the fourth century.) Through his example, especially, we see the scope of Teotihuacan's geographical influence in these early years of Maya dynastic history. Whereas Tikal was clearly the "hub" of much of that activity, I see Copan as a smaller, more local iteration of the same idea, coming several decades later. It also raises the possibility that there were other regional "sub-centers" like Copan in the greater Teotihuacan arrangement of things, but it is difficult to say, given the lack of comparable good sources in other regions.

Although Yaxk'uk'mo' was a Maya nobleman and had spent time at Copan, he was still a foreigner. Sometime before 416 he arrived from the central Maya region, possibly with the aim of establishing a new Maya political identity in the fledging kingdom. Our main clue for this comes from the analysis of his likely skeleton, found buried deep within Copan's acropolis by archaeologist Robert Sharer and his colleagues. The signatures of strontium isotopes preserved in ancient teeth allow us to know in a general way the regions and environments where individuals spent their youth and the diet they consumed. Yaxk'uk'mo's teeth revealed that he was not from Copan but had grown up in the Peten or some nearby region.[3] This scientific evidence was highly confusing to me back in the early 1990s, when my colleagues and I were still sorting out the details of Copan's dynastic history. The founder now was associated with three places, not just one or two. In time, it turned out that the historical record agreed with the strontium analysis. The clue came from Stela 63, a tall, pillar-like stone that we discovered in excavations in 1988, set into the back wall of a buried chamber that served as a shrine to the dynastic founder. It is covered with beautifully carved hieroglyphs and bears the date of the bak'tun ending 9.0.0.0.0 (December 11, 435), perhaps contemporaneous with its carving. I recall the excitement at seeing the fragments of the stela in the excavation tunnel shortly after their discovery, for few Early Classic monuments had ever been recovered at Copan. Those that we knew were only in small fragments, but Stela 63 was complete or nearly so. In ancient times, it had been burned by the ritual fires placed before it, so that several details of its carving were spalled off and missing. Just visible in the burnt section are the name glyph of Yaxk'uk'mo' and a distinctive title naming him as the "Lord of the Three-Mountain Waters." This specific name appears elsewhere in Maya records as the place name for Caracol, Belize. Evidently, Copan's dynastic founder was from there, a region adjacent to the Peten.

Why Caracol? It is difficult to say, but the sites did have a long-lasting connection. A later king of Copan is mentioned in a Caracol inscription in 534. Caracol had played a pivotal role in the fraught politics and alliance networks of the sixth century onward, mostly as an ally of various Kanul kings. And it was also a significant Preclassic and Early Classic site, with a dynasty that we can trace as early as the second-century CE and to even earlier constructions covering a wide territory including several E Groups and Triadic complexes typical of the Late Preclassic.[4] We see little evidence of Caracol's direct involvement in the complexities of Teotihuacan-Maya relations in the fourth and fifth centuries, but perhaps the adventures of Yaxk'uk'mo', if he was from Caracol originally, offer a hint of a wider involvement in the geopolitics of the time. At any rate, Copan and Caracol appear to have maintained a close association over the centuries, traceable to a family connection that was established in the Early Classic.[5]

Another interesting revelation from Stela 63 was a statement inscribed on its side, referring to Yopat K'inich, the second ruler of Copan, as well as K'inich Yaxk'uk'mo'. On first inspection, soon after its discovery, I remember thinking how odd it was that both rulers were named. But between their glyphs was the term *yune*, "is the child of," establishing that they were in fact father and son. So, from this evidence, there was little doubt that by 435 Yopat K'inich was ruling at Copan. The founder, who came to the throne only ten years earlier, is also often mentioned in connection with this all-important date, so it is possible that he was alive at the time and that father and son were corulers, both celebrating the beginning of a new era.

Amid these developments came a natural disaster on an epic scale: the eruption of the Ilopango volcano in present-day El Salvador. It was one of the largest volcanic eruptions of the past 10,000 years anywhere on Earth, ejecting thirty cubic kilometers of magma and an ash plume nearly fifty kilometers (160,000 feet) high. The pyroclastic flows were ten times the volume of those ejected by Mount Vesuvius over Herculaneum and Pompeii. The resulting caldera is today a large and beautiful lake, just east of the capital San Salvador. Working with a variety of data across the globe, geologists and paleoclimatologists have only recently refined the date for the eruption to around 431, give or take a couple of years.[6] The explosion was cataclysmic, devastating everything in a forty-kilometer radius, and its affects would have been seen and felt much farther, with falling clouds of ash throughout for thousands of square miles. We can only imagine what the inhabitants of Copan saw and felt, living only 130 kilometers north of Ilopango itself. The newly refined date is extremely interesting, as it comes so close to the time when Copan was officially founded as a dynastic center, after K'inich Yaxk'uk'mo' arrival there in 427. The eruption happened only a few years before the coming of the new bak'tun in 435. It is tempting to think that the initial years of recovery in the region included a concerted effort to establish Copan as a political and religious center, jump-started by the start date of the bak'tun cycle.

Maya history makes no direct mention of Ilopango's impact, so we can't be sure exactly how the people of the southern Maya regions experienced it or how it displaced populations around the southern Maya region. Some have claimed that it must have had a profound effect on the course of history, forcing large groups of people to move northward from El Salvador and into the Maya lowlands. We have no direct evidence of such migrations, but we can suppose that Copan and its lush valley were attractive places for those displaced, just outside the area of intense environmental destruction, and a newly established center of trade and high culture.

THE SOUTH KALOMTE'

After the second ruler and for the next two centuries, Copan's historical record becomes much more fragmented and difficult to piece together. We have the king list from Copan's Altar Q and names cited in a few other places, but coherent history is still elusive for this "middle period" between the Early and Late Classic, a span covering 500 to 600, more or less. In a way this fits the larger pattern we see in the Peten, where the late fifth century and sixth century are replete with gaps in the records, with spotty history as a result. All we have is assurance that Copan's rulers came and went with great rapidity, indicating an unstable period. The situation is a bit like that for Tikal and its troubling Hiatus, where both the archaeology and the historical data are broken and scarce. Even so, a couple of important names stand out, who were responsible for additions to the ever-growing Copan acropolis and who dedicated several monuments. One important character was the fourth ruler named Tunk'abhix, using the same name of the Kanul ruler who ruled at Dzibanche in the early sixth century. (The Copan king is earlier in time by a few decades, but the shared name is highly suggestive of some family connection.) Another important king who came later was K'ahk'uti'chan ("Fire Is the Mouth of the Snake"), who was seated as ruler in 578. He ruled for nearly fifty years, no doubt helping reestablish Copan as a major region after a protracted period of difficulty.

The greatest ruler of the later Copan dynasty was its twelfth king, the son of his K'ahk'uti'chan, named K'ahk'uti'witz' K'awil,[7] who came to the throne in 628. He was probably a young man of twenty-four at the time, if I am correct in interpreting a date featured in later records as his birth date, in 604. His claim to fame was his widening interests well beyond the Copan region, expanding its influence far from the confines of the Copan valley and nearby areas, exerting his control as far as Quirigua, in the Motagua Valley to the north, and down into present-day El Salvador. He dominated much of the southeast Maya area, as the "South Kalomte'," the first Copan ruler ever to use the directional title. The timing of the title's appearance in the mid-600s is striking, for K'ahk'uti'witz' K'awil arrived on the scene and ruled at almost the same time as Pakal of Palenque, who ruled from 615 to 682 and who was the first in the Late Classic era to adopt his own regional label as "West Kalomte'." The two were contemporaries, expanding their respective city-states as regional powers, and so the stories of their reigns hold some interesting similarities.

Copan's transformation into a major political center did not come immediately. Few inscriptions were dedicated (or survived) during the first twenty years of K'ahk'uti'witz' K'awil's reign, after he acceded to the throne in 628. It is not until 647 that we find the first contemporaneous records, when he began a program of monument dedications in and around the Copan valley. Over the course of a few years, the twelfth ruler dedicated several inscribed stelae on the hillsides and mountaintops around Copan, not in the plazas of the site's center. While these pillars were ritual markers celebrating the movements of the sun and the ceremonies devoted to the kingdom's mountain ancestors, they were also political statements by a king who was now asserting his power in the greater landscape. It is no accident that the altar bearing K'ahk'uti'witz' K'awil's portrait at faraway Quirigua was also from this time, dedicated in 652. Copan's influence and power were expanding twenty years into his reign, and the mountain monuments designed for him probably symbolized these expanding horizons. The archaeology of the mid-seventh century also backs up these hints from written history, as indicated by a substantial and rather sudden appearance of a distinctive type of pottery known as Copador, which was manufactured well to the south of Copan in the El Salvador area. It probably developed as a conscious imitation of elite Maya polychromes.

K'ahk'uti'witz' K'awil, the South Kalomte', was about ninety years old when he died around 695, after a reign of 67 years. His life bears a remarkable parallel to that of his contemporary, K'inich Janabpakal of

Palenque. Both were long-lived rulers who put their respective kingdoms "on the map" as major regional powers of the Late Classic. The early years of their respective reigns were also largely quiet until about 650, when both started ambitious construction programs and expansive military campaigns. I suspect that these trajectories of a "West Kalomte'" and a "South Kalomte'" are in fact related. Their timing came on the heels of the Kanul's formal move to Calakmul in the 630s and the ensuing wars that followed throughout much of the Peten. Were these kings, both on the "peripheries" of the Maya world, somehow embroiled in that larger drama? The records of K'ahk'utiwitz K'awil's reign make no mention of those distant tensions, but there is one intriguing, isolated mention of a Kanul ruler in a Copan inscription from a subsequent reign. In some way, the fates of these two kings were tied into that larger story, and I suspect that their novel statuses as "directional lords" relate to these larger geopolitical dynamics. For whatever reason, they both were keen to mark themselves as major religious and political actors on the Maya stage.

THE SPEAKING STEPS

When K'ahk'uti'witz' K'awil died, his son Waxaklajun Ubahk'awil ("Eighteen Are the Bodies of K'awil") took the throne, on July 7, 695. The date is significant, for it was only a month before the great victory Tikal celebrated over Yuknom Yich'ahkk'ahk' of the Kanul dynasty. I suspect that Copan's royal court was very aware of the conflict raging in the Peten, but it is impossible to draw any direct connection between the great changes that came to the Maya world that eventful summer. In any event, Waxaklajunubah K'awil quickly went into action to design and construct the funerary temple of his father and to assert his own mark on Copan's history. The situation is much like that of Pakal's son at Palenque, Kanbahlam, who also had to confront the challenge of assuming rulership after a father's very long reign of more than sixty years. The k'atun ending of 9.13.0.0.0 had recently passed, and a sense of change and of a new era must have been in the air.

FIGURE 9.2. The Hieroglyphic Stairway of Copan. Photograph by the author.

His main goal was to transform Copan's main plaza into a new ritual space, envisioning a set of new stelae, rebuilding the ballcourt, and adorning the shrine and pyramid above his father's recent tomb. For this last effort, Waxaklajun Ubahk'awil and his architects conceived of a large, sculpted stairway that would be erected directly over the tomb, each riser with an elaborate inscription (Figure 9.2; see Figure 2.9). As we have seen, hieroglyphic stairways appear with some frequency elsewhere in the Maya world, usually as constructions sanctioned by allies of the Kanul dynasty. But nothing of this scale and narrative complexity had ever been built before. The stairway inscription presented a detailed account of Copan's royal seatings, deaths, and burials, beginning in myth and continuing with Yaxk'uk'mo' leading up to his father's own demise and entombment. The monument was dedicated in 710, composed of hundreds of hieroglyphs, interspersed with sculpted portraits of various Copan kings of the past, seated on the steps as if on thrones. One is probably a portrait of Yaxk'uk'mo' himself, as a Teotihuacan warrior-king.

Waxaklajun Ubahk'awil began his ambitious rebuilding program in the center of Copan's great plaza. Between 702 and 736, every five or ten years, he erected an elaborate stela—a portrait of himself—to mark a period ending in the Long Count calendar (Figure 9.3). When Stephens first laid his eyes on these standing monuments in 1839, on his first day exploring Copan, he remarked that "the beauty of the sculpture, the solemn stillness of the woods, disturbed only by the scrambling of monkeys and the chattering of parrots, the desolation of the city, and the mystery that hung over it, all created an interest higher, if possible, than I had ever felt among the ruins of the Old World." Waxaklujunubah K'awil's stelae in the great plaza are indeed among the most beautiful of Maya

FIGURE 9.3. Waxaklajun Ubahk'awil on Stela A, in the Great Plaza at Copan. Photograph by the author.

artworks. Each is an imaginative, three-dimensional image of Copan's king in the guise of a deity, engaged in rituals to conjure the spirits of his predecessors and to renew time.

Having inherited his father's domain, including the northern satellite of Quirigua, Waxaklajun Ubahk'awil oversaw the installment of a new ruler there in 724, named K'ahk'tiliw Chanyopat.[8] Over the centuries, Copan had become the far more powerful of the two southeastern "twin cities," and K'ahk'tiliw Chanyopat may have been placed on Quirigua's throne as a way of asserting control over the region, maintaining Copan's recently acquired influence. But the subservient ruler was about to make his presence felt, too, resulting in a dramatic turn of events and Copan's sudden downturn as the regional authority. Hints of what led up to this were revealed by a recent discovery not at Copan but far away at the ruins of El Palmar, in the heart of the lowlands in what is today southern Campeche, not far from Calakmul. This was found in 2009, when archaeologist Kenichiro Tsukamoto was surveying a cluster of structures north of El Palmar's center. His team noticed that the largest of the mounds showed the remains of a stone staircase, made of 164 blocks with carved hieroglyphs. Excavations then revealed a lengthy text dedicated by a local nobleman named Ajpach'wal. The remarkable text revealed a surprise, for it commemorated Ajpach'wal's visit to Waxaklajun Ubahk'awil of Copan on June 26, 726, shortly before the period ending that fell on September 14, 726 (9.14.15.0.0). The text is direct: "He ascended up to Uxwitik (that is, Copan), to the Xukpi Lord, to Waxaklajun Ubahk'awil." Such a long-distance journey is very rare to see in written Maya history, so why would Ajpach'wal travel 350 kilometers distant? As it happens, a prominent clue stands out in the El Palmar stairway narrative, in the mention of K'awil Tok', the Kanul ruler who had assumed the throne in 698, shortly after the war with Tikal. Evidently, he helped oversee the dedication of the El Palmar steps in 726, and Ajpach'wal was one of his allies, if not representatives. Ajpach'wal's specific role is given by his special title, *lakam*, which we believe may refer to a class of warrior or to some sort of diplomat or ambassador. It was in this capacity that he paid his visit.[9] Clearly Copan was already involved in the wider political affairs of the era, and it is likely that its efforts to establish a client in the Motagua Valley should be seen in that wider context. Did Copan's efforts to reinforce its hegemony over Quirigua spur larger geopolitical problems? I wonder if it attracted the attention of the Kanuls, who become more directly involved in affairs of the southeast around this time. Was the visit to Copan designed negotiate a conflict or to possibly represent Kanul's interests in the southeast?

A short time later, the reign of Copan's king came to a dramatic and violent end. Waxaklajun Ubahk'awil completed his second refurbishment of the great ballcourt in January 738, directly adjacent to the Hieroglyphic Stairway. A few months later, on April 24, we read of a ceremonial fire-drilling at Quirigua, apparently on behalf of the patron gods of the Copan king. I interpret this as the beginning of a military campaign, a "stoking of a fire" linked to the creation of the brand-new ballcourt, a place of sacrifice and military execution.[10] Then, within days, on April 30 of 738, Copan's centuries of dominance in the southeastern Maya region were over. Waxaklajun Ubahk'awil was captured and ritually killed by its ruler, K'ahk'tiliw Chanyopat. We find records of this momentous event in the inscriptions of both cities, giving us an unusual double perspective on the conflict from the viewpoints of both victim and victor. At Quirigua we read in several texts that on April 30 "his head was cut," in reference to the violent demise of the defeated Copan king. This was couched as a religious ceremony, reenacting an event of mythic sacrifice of a vanquished foe. And while it is clear enough that the Copan ruler had been taken prisoner, the circumstances that led to his being held are never mentioned. Was he captured days or months before? Inscriptions at Copan record the defeat within the complex narrative offered on the Hieroglyphic Stairway, as part of the text that was composed for its refurbishment around 755. There we read of Waxaklajun Ubah K'awil's death "by the weapons" of Quirigua's ruler, perhaps at a place called "Turtle Mountain" (Kokwitz). Most interestingly, the Copan scribes went on to describe the consequences, a place of "no city, no pyramids, no altars." The once powerful capital of the Maya on the southwest frontier was no longer the center of the action, and Quirigua and the Motagua River valley assumed the role for many years to come.

A later monument from Quirigua, dating to 800, looked back on Quirigua's victory, eager to relish in the old glory of K'ahk'tiliw Chanyopat's reign. Clearly Copan's defeat was a transformative event for the local dynasty. There we read a key detail that helps us frame the Copan-Quirigua war within the larger context of Maya geopolitics and even within the story we have woven so far. According to the retrospective narrative of Stela I, K'ahk'tiliw Chanyopat had once dedicated a new monument in the year 736, less than two years before the war (a stela that has never been found). This was done in collaboration with one Wamaw K'awil, the Kanul king who succeeded Tok' K'awil in on the throne, confirming the suspicions that Kanul's hydra-like network of influences reached as far as southeast Maya region, well into the Motagua Valley. At the very least, Quirigua was allied with Wamaw K'awil in the time just leading up to the Copan war. So it is tempting to see Quirigua's defeat of Copan as part of the wider, much older conflict between our familiar powers of the Classic period, the Kanul and Mutul dynasties. Here we need only remember that both Copan and Quirigua were founded during the Early Classic as "outposts" of the central Peten Maya, at a time when Teotihuacan had exerted great control over select sites, and long-distance "dynasty building" seems to have been a frequent aspect of Mesoamerican politics.

K'ahk'tiliw Chanyopat was the usurper, overturning Copan's long hegemony and asserting Quirigua's new role as the region's most powerful leader. He assumed the title of "South Kalomte'," which had been used by the earlier Copan ruler, Kahk'uti'witz' K'awil. He even claimed to be the direct successor of the Copan ruler, the "fourteenth in the sequence." (Waxaklajun Ubahk'awil was the thirteenth in the line of Copan's founder, Yaxk'uk'mo'.) But his foothold on power may have taken some time, as indicated by the span of fifteen years before he erected the first of his major monuments, dating to 751 The interval may indicate that the political dust needed to settle after Copan's defeat, as well as protracted struggles with other unknown power players in the region. K'ahk'tiliw Chanyopat soon began a new and ambitious program of construction and artistic expression at Quirigua, clearly modeling his new court after Copan's urban plan and working with artisans to sculpt some of most imposing stone monuments ever created in Mesoamerica (Figure 9.4).

FIGURE 9.4. View of Quirigua, Stela F, in 1892. Photograph by Alfred Maudslay. © Trustees of the British Museum.

These included not only the tallest stelae ever made but also several elaborately carved boulders, representing the effigies of cosmological beings. They are among the most beautiful and baroque examples of Maya art.

Copan's situation was now highly unstable. A new Copan ruler took office within days of Waxaklajun Ubahk'awil's capture, named K'ahk'hoplaj Chank'awil. We have no securely dated monuments from his short reign, and I suspect he was placed on Copan's throne under Quirigua's watchful eye.

Just as Quirigua's ruler set out to erect his own great monuments in Quirigua's plaza, Copan was reinvigorated politically and economically, possibly independent once more, after fifteen or so years. This came with the inauguration in 749 of K'ahk'yipyaj Chank'awil ("Fire Is the Strength of the Sky K'awil"), the fifteenth ruler of the dynasty. He quickly went to work to rebuild parts of the city's central acropolis, focusing his attention on the great pyramid with the Hieroglyphic Stairway, which was now reconceived with a new message. This grand staircase, fully inscribed with history and mythology, was first designed as a funerary monument for the long-reigning Kahk'uti'witz' K'awil, who had died in 695. It had been imbued with the war iconography alluding to Teotihuacan, no doubt as a symbol of the father's power as well as the cultural pedigree of the dynasty. In essence, the original inscribed stairway was designed as a massive tally of ancestral rulers, covering the royal tomb of a beloved father and king. Now, after the Quirigua war and Copan's recovery, K'ahk'yipyaj made a bold decision to expand its thematic scope and political messaging beyond a predecessor's funerary temple. It was now conceived as a shrine devoted to sacred war and ancestry. Architects removed the older steps and reset them into a taller pyramid, with many new chapters of history to tell. The new stairway couched the old dynastic history within a "new chapter" of events, a much-needed update to the story of Copan's dynasty. The rebuilt pyramid and stairway were dedicated on May 5, 755, with a temple shrine on top dedicated a year later, all covered in symbols of Teotihuacan and sacred warfare.

The new, revised history acknowledged Quirigua's victory over Copan seventeen years earlier, using direct and evocative language. It described a place that was stripped of identity or authority, with *mih kab mih ch'en*—that is, "no territory." Then the updated history tells of new kings, new temple dedications, and other events signaling Copan's renewal after the accession of K'ahk'yipyaj in 744. One other fascinating detail of the new stairway was its sculpted balustrades, designed as images of hooked obsidian blades, perhaps adorned with figurative representations of the personal name of Spearthrower Owl, the old ruler and culture hero of Teotihuacan. This hearkens back to Copan's founding under that ancient Mexican city, lending necessary pedigree to a revived city-state under K'ahk'yipyaj.

His update of the pyramid transformed a funerary temple and ancestral shrine into a new and compelling symbol of political and military prowess while still evoking the ancient ideology of Teotihuacan and the legacy of its ruler. We see this most clearly in the pyramid's upper temple, with a remarkable and ornate text that was carved into its back wall. This inscription was composed of two concurrent and parallel texts, one composed in standard Maya form, the other in a "Mexican" or Teotihuacan style. The other text is still very much in Maya writing, but with what might be called a different "font" that evokes another culture and perhaps even another time. At this point in Mesoamerican history, Teotihuacan had collapsed yet was apparently remembered and celebrated for years afterward. The text in the Copan temple may even be somehow evoking the "old country" by lending the structure an old and sophisticated feel (Figure 9.5). When we understand that the Hieroglyphic Stairway on this temple was principally a dynastic record of the kings of Copan—a sort of text version of what we see on Altar Q—this may come as little surprise. Like the founder's shrine, the final version of the Hieroglyphic Stairway and its temple were consciously recalling this historical origin of the Copan dynastic line.[11]

DAWN BEFORE THE DARK

K'ahk'yipyaj Chank'awil died after thirteen years on the throne, around the year 762. His tomb, yet unexcavated, most likely lies within the upper portions of Temple 11, the largest of Copan's pyramids.[12] The subsequent king, Yaxpasaj Chanyopat ("Newly Dawned Sky Yopat"), set about modifying the city's architecture and monuments soon after his accession that same year. Most ambitious of all was the design of the immense new shrine that was built over his predecessor's tomb and that was conceived as a visual replication of the four-sided cosmos. Then, in 775, he directed his attention to another funerary space, constructing a new shrine over the old dynastic founder K'inich Yaxk'uk'mo'. Appropriately, this building was covered in neo-Teotihuacan iconography, evoking the founder's close associations with the great foreign city and

FIGURE 9.5. Full figure hieroglyphs from the Temple Inscription, above Copan's Hieroglyphic Stairway. Drawing by the author.

power. In front of the shrine, Yaxpasaj dedicated a cube-shaped Altar Q, with its important representation of all sixteen kings. Yaxpasaj was shown there facing the founder, the culmination of that long numerical sequence that began in the fifth century, and as the figure that "closed the circle," it is interesting that we soon come to Copan's final decades, before the collapse after 800.

Yaxpasaj stands out as an unusual figure within Copan history. His parentage is obscure, and he may have been quite young when he assumed the rulership. And with his inauguration came a new political arrangement. This was revealed by a number of enigmatic texts that emerged in the late 1980s, when workers repairing a street in the modern town unearthed several inscribed stone fragments, once associated with an ancient building now lost. (Nearly all the impressive ancient architectural remains that were once located on the site where the town now lies were dismantled for building materials.) I vividly recall seeing these stones the very day they were unearthed, resting on the tile floor of the Copan archaeological lab, still covered in dark soil but with visible remains of glyphs. It was immediately clear that they were the carved lids of ornate stone vessels, of a type known in Copan as containers for ritual incense burners. At least three bore the familiar inscribed date of the inauguration of Yaxpasaj in 763, along with the verb "he sat." However, the people named as seated on that very day were three other individuals. Another stone that was discovered bore a later date from the year 780, when yet another man named Yaxk'amlay "was seated." Some of the names were familiar from Copan history, mentioned here and there in some inscriptions of the same period, when Yaxpasaj was the ruler of Copan.

The roles of these other individuals remained uncertain for several years. Who were they? After many years thinking on the question, I'm confident that they were prominent men who served in the court, perhaps even as "corulers." Two of these individuals bore the title k'uhulajaw, "holy lord," suggesting a religious and political rank equal, or nearly so, to that of the sixteenth king. The situation presents an interesting conundrum for reconstructing some aspects of Copan's political structure at the time, for these men look like rulers, even when Yaxpasaj appears to be “the” singular king. I now suspect that it all points to some structure of joint rule or a shared system of authority at Copan in the late eighth century, when Yaxpasaj may have been the first among equals. A sculpted bench from the largest temple of the time shows the inauguration of 763, with Yaxpasaj as one of twenty seated individuals whose identities are unclear (Figure 9.6). Could this be a scene of a “group seating” of a ruling council, Yaxpasaj chief among them? Nothing like this joint system appears in the records of earlier Copan dynasts, and the evidence would at least appear to point to a novel structure of governance. And it may be an experimental arrangement that resonated beyond Copan at the end of the Classic period, with vaguely similar structures perhaps emerging in Yucatán and the northern kingdoms at about the same time.

This was not his only break with long precedent. Yaxpasaj never dedicated a stela to commemorate the cycles of the calendar that he oversaw. While he celebrated such rituals, their records are always on altars or in architectural texts. His “surname” Chanyopat was different, too, and conforms to the names of rulers at Quirigua. Was there a connection to the old enemy? Relations between these kingdoms after about 750 are difficult to track, but we should remember that his accession came only thirty years after Copan’s defeat. Perhaps he was installed as part of the long-term political fallout from that key event and reflecting the deeper shared history between these sites. Whatever the case, the families associated with the Copan and Quirigua royal courts had close associations going back centuries.[13]

In the last years of Yaxpasaj, approaching the abandonment of the city, the record of Copan’s late history becomes scattered and fragmented, with only a date here or a name there. One exception is a building at Copan known as Temple 18, built in 801 above the royal residences on the southern end of the acropolis. Its sculpted jambs depict Yaxpasaj Chanyopat as a dancing warrior in four different supernatural guises. At this point, he had been on the throne for nearly forty years. While not an imposing structure, Temple 18 represents a final flourishing of Copan architecture, beautifully and innovatively designed (Figure 9.7). A large, empty tomb within the building can be seen today, accessible by carefully hewn stone steps. Was this the king’s intended burial place? Perhaps.

FIGURE 9.6. The inauguration of Yaxpasaj Chanyopat with gathered nobles. Drawing of the interior bench of Temple 11, Copan. Drawing by Linda Schele, courtesy of LACMA.

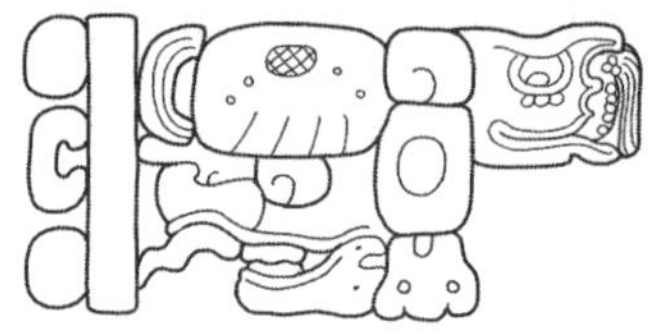

FIGURE 9.7. Facade detail, Temple 18, Copan. The glyph for Ukha'nal (Seven Waters Place) was originally below a statue of the dancing Maize God. Photograph by the author.

It was looted in antiquity, forcing us to speculate identification of its intended occupant. Temple 18 was an elegant structure in its day, its outer walls sculpted with the forms of long, flowing quetzal feathers. Statue-like images of dancing maize gods adorned its outer corners and inner walls. These surely relate to the intended funerary role of the structure, for the maize gods are specifically identified as dancing in the waters of the underworld, shortly before their rebirth and resurrection as maize plants. These mythic sacred waters were called Ukha'nal ('Seven Waters Place'), and its glyph still adorns the outer corners of the temple. Yaxpasaj may have conceived of the building as his own tomb and place of resurrection, channeling the same cosmological themes of death and rebirth we have associated with other great Maya kings, such as Pakal of Palenque. Temple 18 was the last temple of Yaxpasaj and stands as a poignant monument not only to his own death but also to Copan's own looming demise in the early ninth century. On its interior wall was carved one of the very last dates we have anywhere in the city, falling in 801. The last firm date we know from his reign comes only a few years later, on July 21, 805. One stone monument left unfinished bears the date 822, after which all is quiet.[14]

With some irony, the end of Copan's royal history takes us back to Quirigua, the once-subordinate kingdom that developed in the eighth century as a rival and, eventually, its own dominant power in the southeast. The last known building at Quirigua was dedicated on the k'atun ending of 810 (9.19.0.0.0), and the inscription within records its celebration by its rather obscure king at the time named Kahk'holow Chanyopat. He marked the occasion with an incense-burning ceremony, and the inscription goes on to mention the participation as well of Yaxpasaj Chanyopat, the lord of Copan. If not physically present at Quirigua, the Copan king co-sponsored this last k'atun at the end of the great bak'tun period. Their paired mention at the end of their respective stories reflects, as we have seen, an unusually intimate connection between the two courts that developed in the wake of the war of 738, playing out over many decades. I suspect they had close family connections. The two kingdoms at the south represent an unusual and long-lasting presence of elite Maya identity in a region of ethnic and linguistic complexity, near the edge of the Maya world. For four centuries, Copan and Quirigua had thrived, even in conflict, as elite cultural outposts in a volatile landscape.

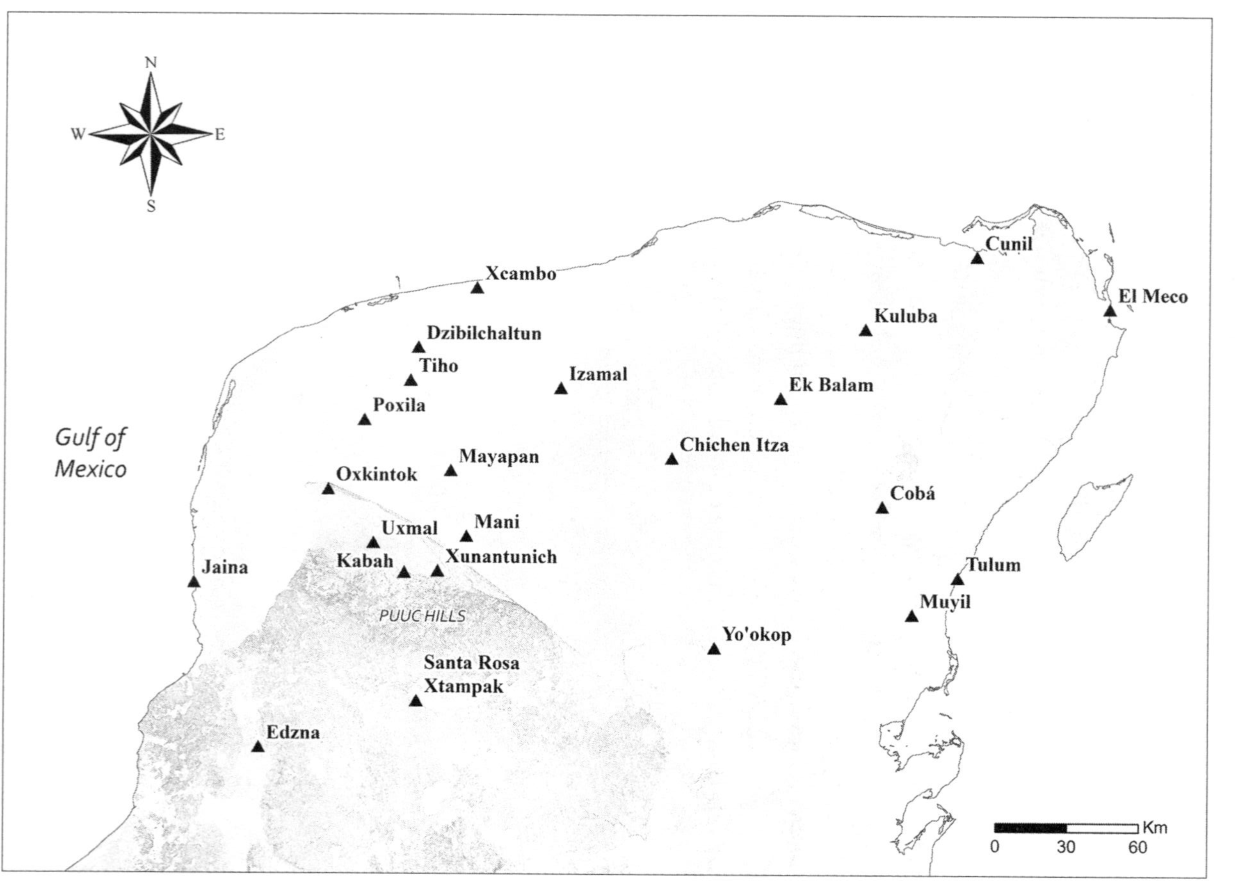

MAP 6. The northern region.

CHAPTER 10

North

THERE IS AN unintended poignancy in the mythological symbolism of Copan's last known building, the elegant Temple 18, with its focus on the bejeweled and dancing Maize God. Jun Ixim, "One Maize Kernel," had deep roots, as one of the oldest icons we find in Maya and Olmec art. At Copan, on the final temple, small statues showed him bejeweled and dancing, at the moment of his resurrection out of the primordial waters of the earth. For Yaxpasaj the message was personal, for Jun Ixim's mythic rise symbolized his own resurrection as sacred maize, as reenactor of the archetypical myth of cyclical existence and regeneration. The king and the brilliant designers who conceived of Temple 18 probably were not aware that a couple of decades later, the temple would be abandoned, its sculpted stones reused in the construction of modest houses.

As noted earlier, Jun Ixim's watery locale, from where maize was perpetually reborn, was called Ukha'nal, "Place of the Seven Waters." As depicted on numerous Maya vases, Jun Ixim symbolized the primordial seed wading in water, where he was met by young women who dressed and adorned him with jade jewels, right before his reemergence as the first maize plant, resplendent and green. The primordial waters of this epic story have an animate form in many scenes, as the undulating, dragon-like Water Serpent. It was animate fresh water of the earth's interior, the stuff of life. The myth of Jun Ixim's watery rebirth plays an important role in the history of the northern Maya, the last in our four-part consideration of directional kingdoms during the Classic period. Remarkably, the name Ukha'nal survived in the much later historical chronicles of Yucatán, in the *Books of Chilam Balam*, amid their scattered elements of history, prophecy, and esoteric knowledge. The very same name was also the ancient designation given the famous *cenote* or "well of sacrifice" at Chichen Itza, one of the great landmarks and sacred sites in all the ancient world. This connection provides us with a rare and precious link between the Classic Maya and the colonial history as we will explore later. And it may also offer a useful inroad for understanding some of the religious and political changes that the Maya were encountering in the ninth century, as more foreigners were arriving on the scene and when the old dynastic system was quickly fading away. A new form of Maya culture was about to be reborn, like Jun Ixim, in the northern lowlands.

• • •

So far, our historical accounts have skewed heavily toward the central and southern areas, highlighting the kingdoms whose textual records provide the most detail, covering the longest span of time. The north participated in those narratives in ways we are still trying to assess and understand. The Maya of northern Campeche and Yucatán were always active players in the broader cultural developments of the entire region, going back to the Middle and Late Preclassic. It was in this era that we see the rapid rise of powerful centers such as Edzna, Santa Rosa Xtampak, and Izamal, to cite just some examples. The problem we quickly encounter in looking at the history of the Classic period, however, is a relative lack of readable texts. By contrast, the archaeological remains of Yucatán are breathtaking in their richness, variety, and cultural complexity. In material culture, ceramics, architecture, iconography, and writing, Yucatán consistently had its own flavors and innovations. To weave these into our grander narrative is not an easy task, yet there is still a good deal of history to tease out, especially in the great cities of Coba, Uxmal, Ek Balam, and Chichen Itza. Here, at different times and in different ways, powerful Maya elites participated in the wider political and ideological movements that pervaded the Maya area. And in these northern narratives we see strong evidence of long-term connections, influences, and the movements of peoples, especially as the Classic period was ending abruptly.

Like other regional terms (Peten, Chiapas, and so on), the word "Yucatán" does not always conform to political borders we see today, but rather to geographic and demographic regions that existed at the time of the Spanish invasion. The *Provincía de Yucatán* in the colonial era had loose edges and frontiers as well. For our purposes, we will consider Yucatán as this northern region, the land of Yucatec speakers, mainly, and the lands generally lying to the north of the ancient Kanul capitals of Dzibanche and Calakmul. We will recall that the name of Dzibanche in ancient times, Kanul, "Place of Snakes," is a Yucatec Mayan word in origin. Their ties to the north therefore may have been especially strong, and their military forays into the south and west may have been an intrusion of one Maya group into another.

The question of language affiliation raises some important questions about how Maya art and writing began. Their appearance in Yucatán is early, during the end of the Late Preclassic. Literate culture existed in Yucatán before about 200 CE based on the inscription we see at Loltun Cave, for example, and on inscribed jade fragments recovered in the cenote of Chichen Itza. The latter bear early glyphs, some probably Late Preclassic in date, but it is difficult to know if these come from the Yucatán or were brought from a great distance. As we have seen, the writing system itself probably developed farther south in the Ch'olan regions during the Middle Preclassic. When writing and visual culture spread northward, into areas where Yucatec was widely spoken, it was part of a wider adoption of "high culture." Early on in Yucatán and throughout the Classic period, writing would have communicated a non-local prestige language, used within royal courts for their official inscriptions, part of a system that helped define elite status and pedigree.[1]

FIGURE 10.1. The "Iglesia" pyramid at Coba, with Stela 11. Photograph by the author.

COBA AND THE EARLY CITIES

The political landscape of the north region comes into focus soon after the Early Classic period. Major power centers, presumably the seats of royal courts, can be identified at several locales, among them Oxkintok, Dzibilchaltun, Yaxunah, and Coba. Among these places, Coba, in the eastern region was the largest, a vast site covering some seventy-two square kilometers and built around a string of five lakes (Figure 10.1).

Starting in the sixth century, Coba's ancient inhabitants built many large architectural complexes, including a main collection of palaces and temples adjacent to two of the largest lakes, known as the Coba Group. In the sixth century, Coba was probably the most dominant political center north of Dzibanche, at least on the eastern side of the peninsula. It has only been partially excavated.

The sheer number of Coba's monuments and the lengths of its inscriptions stand out among northern cities. Most are very poorly preserved, unfortunately. One inscription from the ballcourt of Coba records the city's establishment as a dynastic center shortly before 500 CE, under a ruler with the formidable name Junpiktok' ("Eight Thousand Knives"). This name is remarkable to see in so ancient a text, for it corresponds to one we know from the later historical record of Yucatán as the name of a major pyramid at Izamal as well as an obscure historical figure attributed to that city, cited in Fray Bernardo de Lizana's 1633 treatise on the conquest of Yucatán.[2] As we will see, the very same name is also cited in the texts of Chichen Itza in the late ninth century in reference to yet another person. Coba's Junpiktok' is said to have built a ballcourt there in 505, at the place identified as **ko-ba-a**—"Coba" spelled out in phonetic signs.[3] This is one of only a handful of cases where a modern place-name makes an appearance in ancient texts.

In addition to its vast size, Coba stands out among Maya sites for its large network of ancient roadways, known as *sacbes* ("white roads," or "artificial paths") (Figure 10.2). We have seen similar regional road systems in the Late Preclassic, in the Mirador region, and Coba's example is similar, its map resembling spokes radiating out from the center, connecting outlying architectural complexes—one lies eight kilometers to the south, another twenty kilometers to the southeast. The longest road is a monumental construction of its own, linking Coba to the site of Yaxunah one hundred kilometers to the west. Today it is hard to understand the significance of these myriad sacbes radiating around Coba—more than seventy have been found—but they seem to speak to the city's regional reach in the northeast part of the Maya region.

Representations of bound prisoners appear throughout Coba's sculpture, suggesting that it was the center of a network of regional conquests

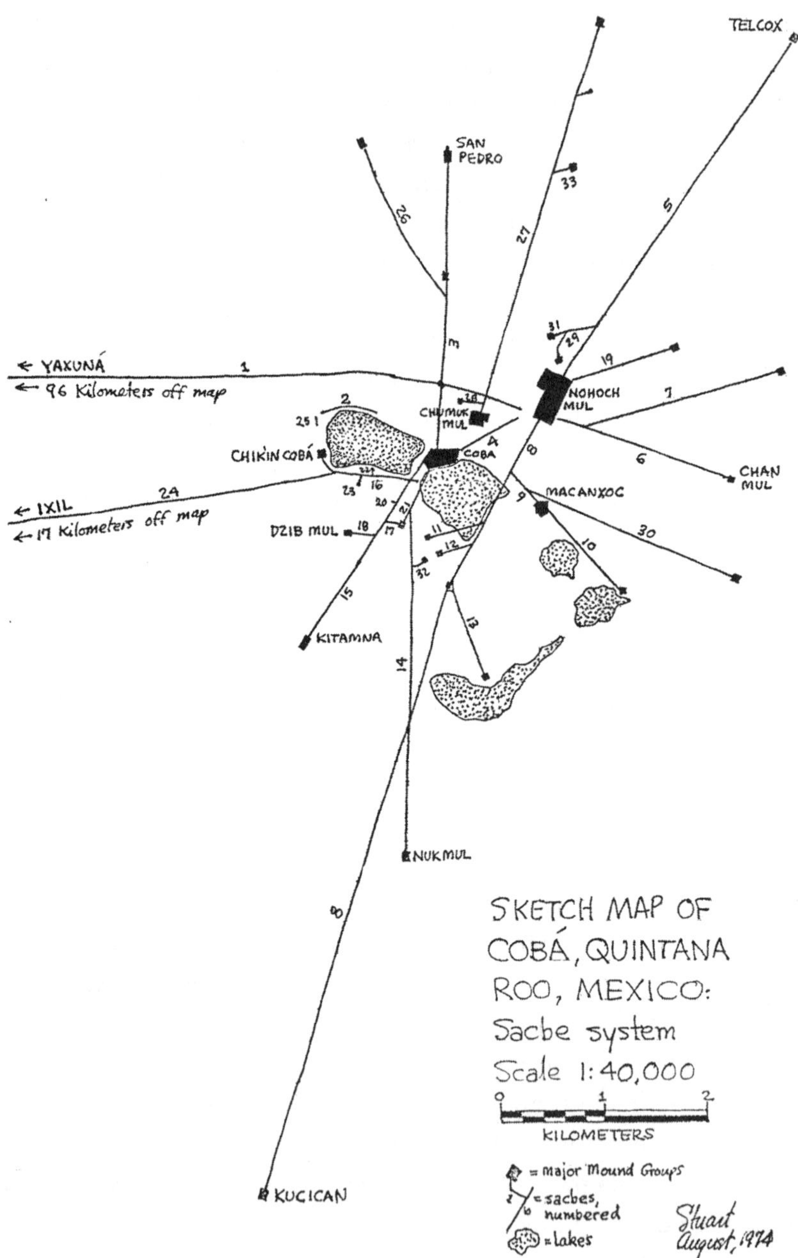

FIGURE 10.2. Sketch map of the road network at Coba, Mexico. Map by George E. Stuart, National Geographic Society survey, 1974.

over several generations. One stela dating to 623 shows a bound captive with an Oxkintok place glyph, indicating that one of Coba's significant military excursions may have been against a city far to the west. Located south of the modern city of Mérida, Oxkintok emerged as an important center in western Yucatán in the sixth century, in some ways on a parallel track with Coba, and we may imagine a significant east–west rivalry between these two major early kingdoms, at least in the seventh century.[4]

Several of Coba's rulers who came after Hunpiktok' took the Kalomte' title, the honorific religious term reserved for major rulers who had hegemonic control over their respective regions. They are among the earliest historical figures to consistently use this title in the northern area, pointing to the dynasty's power among northern polities in the sixth and seventh centuries. The first ruler who bore the Kalomte' title was a formidable queen we will call Lady Ch'akch'en, whose name stands out as especially important in Coba's early years. We became aware of her existence only very recently, in 2024, with the discovery of a remarkable inscription near another imposing group of buildings known as the Nohoch Mul Group ("Big Mound," named after the site's largest pyramid). The hieroglyphic text of 103 individual glyph blocks was carefully hewn into the exposed bedrock at an ancient reservoir, clearly a sacred pool. Although poorly preserved in places, we can tell that the inscription relates the beginning of Coba as a major political power, in 569. The city already had a long history leading up to this time, as we know from the story of Junpiktok' and other sources, but this was the year of the city's formal political renewal, introducing Lady Ch'akch'en as the initial Kalomte'.

The timing of this event is highly suggestive. We will remember that just a few years before, around 561, a new Kanul ruler we call Sky Witness assumed the Kanul throne at Dzibanche and perhaps also at Calakmul. He continued the political conquests of his predecessors, especially to the south and west. Was Coba part of this rapid Kanul expansion as well, now reaching the northern lowlands? I suspect that this is the case, based on a telling piece of evidence from a site located between Coba and Dzibanche called Yo'okop. There, three fragments of a still-hidden hieroglyphic stairway show a revealing connection—the name glyphs of both Sky Witness and Ix Ch'akch'en, possibly on the k'atun station in 573. This association, and the timing of her start at Coba as a Kalomte', hints that the new queen may have been established as part of Kanul's wider expansionistic strategy in the sixth century. Coba's history notes that she rededicated the large ballcourt in central Coba in 574, where a stone monument portrays her in the regalia of a scribal deity, inkpot and paintbrush in hand (Figure 10.3).[5]

In 633, another Coba ruler came to power, bearing the title *xaman k'awil*, "the northern authority," providing an important window into the large-scale conception of Maya geopolitical organization. Another ruler, possibly another queen, assumed the throne on August 28, 682, and while we cannot be sure of her name, the date of her crowning provides a clue of wider connections in Mayan history. That was very same day that saw the arrival of Lady Wakjalam Chanlem to Naranjo—a turning point in the history of the Peten, clearly coordinated by the Kanul king Yuknomch'en at the end of his life and reign. The timing here could be a coincidence, but I doubt it. This single date saw the arrival and inauguration of two powerful queens and would imply some sort of coordination with the Kanul lords, who reigned 230 kilometers to Coba's south. Coba continued as a major dynastic center and militaristic power through the Classic period, and its final stela was dedicated in 780. Populations lived around the lakes after it collapsed

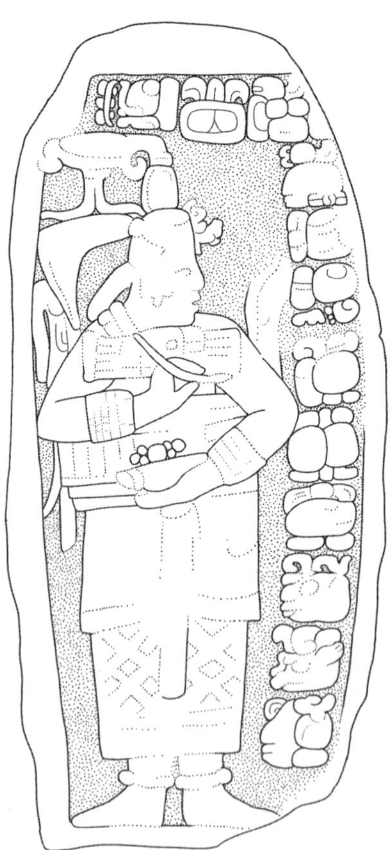

FIGURE 10.3. Coba's queen, Lady Ch'akch'en. Coba, Stela 26. Drawing by the author.

as a dynastic center, and eventually, after several centuries, there were a resurgence and reoccupation in the Late Postclassic, probably in the fifteenth century. At this time, many of Coba's ancient stelae were reset in new shrines, as late Maya venerated the images of ancient rulers.

Coba's possible rival in the north, Oxkintok, was one of at least two powerful centers that emerged in the Early Classic in the western part of Yucatán, at the end of the range of hills known as the Puuc. Oxkintok had a long-lasting dynasty, with several rulers with the Kalomte' title. One of its Late Classic rulers is called the "twenty-seventh king," giving an important clue of Oxkintok's longevity as a dynastic center, reaching back to the beginnings of the Classic period.[6] Another major center in western Yucatán is Dzibilchaltun, just to the north of the modern city of Mérida. It too emerged as a regional power sometime after 600 CE, possibly in the wake of Coba's victory over Oxkintok in 623. It was spread over a wide area, and it clearly grew out of older communities with deep roots in the Preclassic era. Several Late Classic texts from Dzibilchaltun refer to an important ruler and Kalomte' named Uk'uw Chanchahk, who ruled around 790. Most significant, to my mind, is another title we find with Uk'uw Chanchahk: *tijo' ajaw*, the "Lord of Tiho'." This can only be an ancient citation of the name Tiho', the Maya name for Merida used before the sixteenth century and even up to the present day.[7]

EK BALAM

The late years of the Classic period, especially the ninth century, saw remarkable cultural and political changes in the Maya region. We will examine these in greater detail in the next chapter, but it is important to note here that some inscriptions in Yucatán lay out a part of that story and some details of what may have happened. The site of Ek Balam, located in central Yucatán, plays an interesting role in that narrative of the "Classic end" and changes that ensued. Excavations at El Balam's majestic Acropolis (Structure 1) revealed almost perfectly preserved temple facades, numerous hieroglyphic texts, most of which cite the name of a historical ruler named Ukitkanlek (Plate 14). His luxurious tomb was also discovered within the structure, revealing massive numbers of shell adornments, jade, and inscribed ceramics. Ukitkanlek acceded to the throne in 770, seemingly under the authority of yet another powerful foreign ruler named Chakjutuw Kanek'. (Kanek', or "Sky Star," is a distinctive name we find associated with the later Itza lineage.) According to one lengthy painted text uncovered in the acropolis, Chakjutuw Kanek' arrived at Ek Balam April 8, 770, leading up to the Kitkatla's accession a short time later, on May 27. The relationship of these two individuals is difficult to know, but it seems that Chakjutuw Kanek' was of higher rank, bearing the title *xaman kalomte'*, "the North Kalomte'." This implies the broad regional nature of his power, but we must remain tentative on this point, given that Chakjutuw Kanek' is otherwise unknown in Maya history. And where was his base of power, if not Ek Balam? He bears an emblem glyph court title representing a possum's head that is otherwise unknown, but I suspect it will eventually be linked to a well-known Classic center in the region, perhaps one already well known and discussed in this text. Curiously, emblem glyphs are very rare in the inscriptions of Yucatán, never cited in the many extant texts of Coba or Oxkintok. Yet we have two mentioned at Ek Balam. In addition to the "possum" of the foreign ruler, the emblem glyph of Ek Balam itself is cited throughout the inscriptions of the site.[8]

Ukitkanlek ruled at Ek Balam for several decades, and many parts of the famous, well-preserved facade of the Acropolis can be ascribed to his time in office. The very last date we can associate with him is 802, on a painted capstone from the Acropolis. His successor, probably a son, is only named in a few scattered locations and seems to have reigned over Ek Balam's in 830, at the bak'tun ending at 10.0.0.0.0. The stela erected at that time is one of the very last in Yucatán that conforms to the old standards of Classic Maya iconography, with its frontal portrait of the local ruler dancing and holding a k'awil scepter, with his father shown above as the sun, an illustrious ancestor and warrior. These are motifs we will not see used for long anywhere in the Maya region.

A major political change came to Ek Balam in the ninth century, when large architectural programs and carved monuments ceased. The timing recalls the collapses we see among Classic-era dynastic centers to the south. The final historical mention of Ek Balam and its rulers comes from a stone monument found near Chichen Itza, which cites someone called K'inich Junpiktok', a name we have already seen in the early history of Coba. According to that inscription, on March 30, 870, he oversaw a ceremony known as the "conjuring of fire," and the rite is perhaps depicted in the accompanying figural scene.[9] There the main figure is accompanied by two men dressed as Chahks, or rain deities. Their presence suggests to me that "fire-conjuring" may have been a ceremony associated with the agricultural year. Its timing here is suggestive, corresponding with the traditional season of burning the corn fields in northern Yucatán. In any event, Kinich Junpiktok' was apparently an important noble in the history of Chichen Itza in the ninth century, just as that city was growing in importance and soon to dominate the region of northern Yucatán. His identification there as a lord of Ek Balam strongly suggests that the dynasty of that city played a role in Chichen Itza's development as an important political and ritual center. That history, as we will soon see, becomes very complex.

THE HILL CITIES

When we consider the history of the northern realms, it is helpful to revisit the late evidence we have for the later Kanul kingdom. When we left its rulers, they were based at Calakmul, responsible for a relatively late spurt of activity there before about 750. This was especially visible during the reign of K'awil Tok', who converted Structure 1 into a sacred mountain to mark the great k'atun ending on 9.15.0.0.0, in 731. But after 750 or so, Calakmul seems a quieter place, with fewer major monuments or constructions. The archaeology of the region instead reveals an interesting movement away from Calakmul and other major site centers. Between 750 and 800, we see a great increase in the number of new, smaller sites just to Calakmul's north, in the region of southern Campeche. Many are small, nonurban centers with distinctive architectural monuments, including richly decorated, multi-room structures and patio groups whose function is not particularly clear. Clusters of

FIGURE 10.4. A Chenes style shrine at Hormiguero, Mexico. Photograph by the author.

these structures probably represent elite residences spread throughout the landscape and not so geographically attached to major cities. Rio Bec, Xpuhil, and Hormiguero are sites that typify this sort of more isolated and dispersed pattern of settlement. Their major structures very seldom include lofty pyramids but instead emphasize low buildings with elaborate stone mosaic decorations, including serpent masks associated with facades and doorways (Figure 10.4). An especially elegant type of building shows a central door or set of doors leading to interior rooms, and lateral "towers" that are playfully represented as false pyramids, with stairways no one can ascend. Recent archaeological work in this region, centered on the site of Rio Bec, has clarified the time frame of these architectural styles known as "Rio Bec architecture." They evolved out of more modest construction in the seventh century, but after 750 they burgeoned in the region, just as populations grew very rapidly and as the centralized political influences of Calakmul and Dzibanche were not so powerful as they once were.

One way to interpret the spread of these elaborate "country estates" is to see them as a proliferation and dispersal of the nobility, a spreading out of elites over the countryside, possibly with the intent of overseeing and coordinating agricultural production. The cellular design of the numerous rectangular rooms within these structures suggests that they were used for the storage of key commodities such as maize and cacao—a function perhaps directly indicated by epigraphic clues in the similar multi-roomed buildings we find later in northern Campeche. There is little historical context for these sites in the late eighth century, but I am intrigued that so many in southern and central Campeche have buildings that emphasize serpents in their facade decoration. Some of the so-called Chenes style, overlapping temporally with Rio Bec, exhibit central doorways that are the form of an open serpent mouth, where one enters through the open maw of a snake. The development of these serpent buildings in a region between Dzibanche and Calakmul, the major political seats of the Kanul, suggests a connection to that storied dynasty.

The Rio Bec and Chenes styles spread rapidly to sites in the north and the west, into the rich agricultural lands of central Campeche. Ever since the Preclassic era, these had been fertile "breadbaskets" for local populations, and we see a dramatic population increase around them during the late 700s and into the 800s. New centers spread among much older ritual and regal centers that already had deep historical presences in the region, such as Edzna and Santa Rosa Xtampak. Edzna was a particular old and important center dating back to the Late Preclassic, and it developed into a dynastic seat of considerable size and importance. Its inscriptions show a series of kings and queens from the Late Classic period who oversaw a significant regional power, including a man named Janabyok K'inich, who ruled in 682, and his father, Sihyaj Chank'awil, who used a name we know from Tikal's early history. One monument also hints at a possible conflict with Coba, whose place-name accompanies the portrait of a vanquished prisoner.[10]

Later in the Classic period and farther north, Santa Rosa Xtampak rose to new prominence as well, occupying a center that had once been among the largest Late Preclassic sites in the north. Its major palace complex, dating to the late 700s, is an intriguing, multistory construction with a central staircase leading to a serpent-mouth door, where visitors and supplicants possibly entered a throne room. The most intriguing aspect of the building is its many cell-like chambers. Several such chambers from this building and others surrounding it once had painted "capstones" in their upper vaults—small, rectangular images of deities that looked down from above. Many of these have elegant paintings of the deity K'awil, shown with large bundles of cacao beans or maize kernels (Figure 10.5). It seems likely that these provide a clue to the function of these rooms as storage areas, possibly the tribute or deliveries brought into the palace from the surrounding agricultural lands.

The rapid growth of these sites during the Late Classic reflects a wider population boom that is visible in the settlement data from throughout most of the Maya lowlands. Variation in regions and ecologies resulted in different local trends, but there is no question that after 700 or so, the number of people and their densities grew very rapidly. The growth is perhaps most noticeable in the so-called Puuc region, encompassing northern Campeche and western Yucatán state. "Puuc" derives from the Maya name of a range of low limestone hills that runs diagonally through this region, and the name has been given to the architectural style we find in nearby sites especially to the south, near to Oxkintok and where the soils were particularly fertile. Here many sites took on new importance and experienced nearly exponential growth in numbers. The timing of the boom in the Puuc region after 800 CE may also reflect movements of large numbers of people resettling from the south, as Classic period centers there underwent their own demographic downturns and abandonments after 800. As we will explore later when we consider the ninth-century collapse of the Classic Maya, people were on the move in many areas, and it is difficult to be certain just how and why this was taking place. While we can see long-term continuities in the Puuc region (Oxkintok was an important precursor), we must understand it especially as a new and energetic political and social movement, a new iteration of the old Classic Maya elite system just as it was undergoing strong changes and outside pressures.

FIGURE 10.5. K'awil, deity of power and sustenance, with a basket of maize. From a vault capstone at Santa Rosa Xtampak, Mexico. Drawing by Octavio Esparza Olguin.

The greatest city of the Puuc region was Uxmal, a majestic site nestled in the rolling green hills of western Yucatán (Figure 10.6). Not far away are other large centers, such as Nohpat and Kabah, all linked by a long sacbe or causeway. Stephens was enamored by Uxmal's ruins when he first came upon them in 1839, and he noted how different its buildings seemed from both Palenque and Copan. He was left speechless on first seeing them: "In attempting a description of these ruins, so vast a work rises before me that I am at a loss where to begin." Many of its major architectural monuments are still standing,

FIGURE 10.6. Palatial buildings of the Nunnery Quadrangle, Uxmal, Mexico. Photograph by the author.

well preserved and displaying unequaled mosaic stonework and detailed decoration on their facades. These are hallmarks of the Puuc architectural style, which grew out of simpler geometric patterns in use in the region during the previous two centuries. The elaborate Chenes style found to the south was clear inspiration, too. After 800 CE, the Puuc style was widespread in the western Yucatán, appearing in both large, monumental constructions and in much more modest elite houses. Other important centers in the Puuc area include Sayil and Kiuic, but Puuc elements are also found at more distant sites, including Dzibilchaltun to the north and Chichen Itza and Kulubá in central Yucatán.

The intricate stonework of Puuc facades formed elegant geometric patterns, both simple and complex. On many of the larger structures, we also see front-facing serpent masks, usually over doorways or "stacked" on the corners of buildings. The resulting designs are often stunning and among the most beautiful architectural adornments from anywhere in the ancient world. Their geometry and linework exerted a strong and conscious influence on American architectural design in the early twentieth century, especially in the early works of Frank Lloyd Wright and in the development of the Art Deco style.

Repeating "masks" give many Puuc buildings their distinctive look, but we should also bear in mind that they are a part of a long history of "messaging" on Maya architectural facades, reaching far back to the Late Preclassic. Their mosaic stonework reflects a relatively late technique, at sites such as Uxmal and Kabah, but earlier examples can be found at many Maya centers. Their direct antecedents are the many serpent masks we find in the Chenes and Rio Bec region near Calakmul and Dzibanche. And those, in turn, have clear precedents in some of the representations of serpents we find in Classic and even Late Preclassic iconography. Many have interpreted the Puuc masks as the rain deity Chahk, whereas others emphasize that they may be the faces of mountains. My own view is that most of these animate faces are representations of the "Water Serpent," a dragon-like character whose forehead was adorned with a waterlily pad and flower. Vestiges of these diagnostic features appear with regularity, enough to show a strong connection to earlier, more obvious forms. These formal public buildings and temples were marked with the Water Serpent because, simply put, the Maya of Yucatán and the northern peninsula were rightly obsessed with water and its procurement. Water may well have been one of the bases of royal power among the late north Maya, building on a very old ideology we can track a thousand years earlier.

The major Puuc centers all have inscribed dates that fall within a remarkably short time span of about sixty years, between about 850 and 910. It was during this time that Uxmal emerged as the most imposing city of all, and shortly after 900 its major architectural monuments were refurbished and constructed in close coordination, including the so-called Nunnery Quadrangle, the Ballcourt, and the final phase of the House of the Governor. The first two buildings have inscriptions that span a very short period from 905 to 907, and all mention a man named K'ahk'bablaj Chanchahk. This formal name, invoking an aspect of the storm deity Chahk, is a type we have seen many times before the history of the southern lowlands, from earlier generations. I sense that this major ruler, probably Uxmal's greatest king, was still looking to the Classic past for his "vocabulary" of divinely sanctioned power. His reign may represent a short period of political consolidation around western Yucatán and northern Campeche when Uxmal was a central seat of authority, at least for a short time.[11]

Given the critical era when they rapidly came on the scene, Uxmal and its Puuc neighbors could easily be considered within our later discussion of the Maya collapse in the ninth century. After all, Uxmal reached its apogee at the time when most of the great Classic period kingdoms were already being abandoned, among them Palenque, Copan, and Coba. However, I place the Puuc sites here in our discussion of the Classic period because of the clear ways the artists of the time sought to channel the old ideologies of the Classic period, even if in new and innovative ways. For example, the stelae of Uxmal show portraits of local kings such as K'ahk'bablaj Chanchahk still in the "old mode," impersonating Chahk, wielding K'awil axe-scepters, and standing with war captives, all marking the passage of the tuns and k'atuns through ritual performance. These are features we never really see after about 900.

The angular, geometric forms of Puuc mosaic facades are often seen in contrast to the flowing, rounded aesthetic of Classic Maya art, but the underlying iconography fits very comfortably in the traditional Maya world, as we have seen. Mosaic masks representing long-nosed deities are derived from the very similar masks we see in earlier Chenes and Rio Bec architecture, which were in turn developed out of earlier representations of the Water Serpent. (Figure 10.7). The rich decorations on its buildings and on the nearby House of the Governor also exhibit symbolism from the Maya past. The central image of its facade is that of a ruler with a large quetzal-feather headdress, seated within a solar disc and surrounded by sky bands. In essence, it is the same as the roof-comb sculpture we see on the Temple of the Sun at Palenque. The Puuc architectural style was at once innovative and rooted in ancient designs and iconographic messages.

Uxmal's great Nunnery Quadrangle was a massive architectural complex that resembles some royal reception spaces from the Classic era, although with many more adjacent rooms and auxiliary spaces. Its size suggests new directions and innovations, or a more complex court structure than what we see in the earlier Classic period, accommodating

FIGURE 10.7. Serpent masks in Puuc-style architecture, from Kabah, Yucatán. Photograph by the author.

multiple administrative roles and councilors. The expansion of the court administration reflects the rapid growth of the elite governing class at the end of the Classic period, a pattern that we have seen elsewhere.

Still, at Uxmal, we see the introduction of new symbols to the old mix. Alongside the growth in the scale and complexity of administrative courtly spaces, we see new ways of representing royal authority. The most important of these is the feathered serpent, prominently displayed on the facades of the Nunnery Quadrangle and in the adjacent ballcourt. These symbols have a close affinity not so much to Maya serpents but to designs from Early Classic Teotihuacan, in particular the great serpents we see there on the terraces of the Feathered Serpent Pyramid. At Teotihuacan, the serpents are clearly associated with water, surrounded by shells and aquatic creatures. It is clearly ancestral to the Quetzalcoatl ("Feathered Snake") of Postclassic central Mexico and to the K'uk'ulkan ("Feathered Snake") of later Chichen Itza. The late Maya rulers of Uxmal were clearly tapping into an old and powerful symbol that resonated throughout central Mexico. This was innovative for its time, but we should remember that the Classic Maya had always made good use of "foreign" elements in the display of power and authority, ever since the days of the Tikal Entrada. My colleague William Ringle believes that these "Mexican" or "Toltec" symbols at Uxmal and Chichen Itza represent a new twist on rulership for the northern Maya area, when a new ideological movement was spreading throughout much of Mesoamerica. As we will explore in more detail in the next chapter, I suggest that this appearance of the feathered serpent at Uxmal and elsewhere, while innovative in its day, around 900, was a resurrection of an old symbol of rulership, a watery, feathered snake that had deep roots throughout early Mesoamerica. For the Puuc area, this new symbolism was a powerful one to add onto the old tropes of kingly art, perhaps due to the increasing lack of water and environmental change.

The rapid growth of Uxmal and nearby Puuc cities was an energetic attempt to restructure the region's elite culture and politics, adapting to the radical political and social changes happening across the Maya world at the time. The presence of a circular fortification around the center of Uxmal (perhaps later in date) is a good hint of the violent, unpredictable landscape of the northern region during and after the Terminal Classic. The late "boom" in the Puuc region was related to other innovations and changes affecting the political landscape of Yucatán, especially at Chichen Itza, in the center of the peninsula.

CHICHEN ITZA

With its visibility and iconic role in popular culture, Chichen Itza appears to many of its visitors as the quintessential Maya archaeological site (Plate 16). However, the place it holds in the world's imagination obscures the ironic truth: We know precious little about it. Chichen is at once "Maya" and "something else," a unique place in Mesoamerica, and its special mix of styles and cultures has led to endless debates among archaeologists and historians over the last century. We will discuss some of Chichen here but return to this special site when we consider the collapse and what came after. In many ways, the site represents the transition of the northern Maya world at a time of crisis, from a place rooted in the Late Classic to an innovative and cosmopolitan city that was altogether new.

Chichen Itza emerged as the most important regional center of Yucatán beginning around 800 and lasting up to 1200. Its early years were contemporaneous therefore with Uxmal and the later Puuc capitals. As a reflection of its importance and singular place in history, Chichen Itza's memory was maintained even after the conquest, mentioned throughout the chronicles written by the Maya in the *Books of Chilam Balam* and in other early sources of the sixteenth century. It was already in ruins by the time the Spanish arrived, a place of legend and ghostly history. Diego de Landa visited its overgrown buildings in the mid-1500s, shortly after the Spanish conquered the area and after Spanish soldiers used and abused the main pyramid as a lookout and fortress (hence its first name, El Castillo). Landa wrote of the local Maya beliefs about its origin, including its founding in the remote past by "three brothers who came to that land from the west," a statement that rings true with the many "Mexican" characteristics of its later art, although still ambiguous in many ways.[12] The name Chichen Itza means "the Edge of the Well of the Itzas," referring to the great circular cenote near the city's center, "where they threw living men and other precious things of sacrifice," as Landa put it. *Itza* was the name of an important lineage from Yucatán's later history, and, as we will explore more later, I suspect that the name was probably given to the site during the Postclassic period, when the Itza lineage claimed the cenote as its own.[13]

Chichen Itza is not a particularly "deep" in terms of its architecture and settlement, but the great cenote, or natural sinkhole, was a major attraction from very early times. Investigations there over the years, including a rough dredging of its bottom from 1904 to 1909, revealed numerous rich offerings and human remains, confirming the statements by Landa and others that it was used as a place of sacrifice. Jades were especially numerous, many from the Early Classic and Late Classic eras, well before any substantial architectural remains were built nearby. Several of the jades were from a long distance away, found to be inscribed with the names familiar from our earlier history—one was owned by a ruler from the Yokib kingdom of Piedras Negras and another by K'inich Kanbahlam of Palenque. Other objects included wood carvings, bowls, disc-shaped sheets of gold, incense burners, and, of course, a great deal of human remains, many of children.[14] The cenote had a long life as an important pilgrimage center, even before the major architectural monuments developed around it. This is confirmed by a statement written in 1601 by the Spanish historian Antonio de Herrera, who noted that the Indians "venerated most the temples of the island of Cozumel and the well of Chichen (Itza), which were as Rome and Jerusalem among us, where they went on pilgrimage, and those who had been there were considered sanctified, and those who did not go sent their offerings."[15] And here we should remember that according to the later Maya chronicles, the cenote's ancient name was Ukha'nal or Ukhabnal, "Place of the Seven Waters," the same name we find often used in Maya mythology for the primordial waters where the bejeweled Maize God, Jun Ixim, entered and was reborn from the earth. I suspect that this bestowed a particularly sacred essence on the place, long before its religious purpose was reimagined after the Classic period.

Chichen Itza's internal chronology has been notoriously difficult to sort out, and the timing of its different layers have long presented a puzzle for archaeologists. At first, it was thought that there was a sharp divide between "Old Chichen," with its more Maya, Puuc-style buildings, and later "Mexican" or "Toltec" monuments exemplified by the great Temple of K'uk'ulkan, the Great Ballcourt, the Osario, and other major buildings nearby, close to the cenote. Later it became clear that the divide was not so pronounced, and that parts of the site might well overlap in time, representing a varied, coeval urban landscape integrating both Maya and outside elements. These points are still debated, in fact. What is clear is that all these monuments represent constructions that were compressed within a relative short amount of time (for Maya history), spanning 800 to 1200 at most. Within this span, I believe we can seriate styles and construction projects, beginning with those buildings that we can date easily through hieroglyphic texts from the ninth century. These appear mostly on carved architectural elements, commemorating their ritual dedications of "houses" and some key information about the people involved. With one exception, they all date to a short, thirty-year span between 860 and 890, from the Puuc-style structures such as Las Monjas and the Casa Colorada. This would place them at almost the same time as the texts we know from centers in the Puuc region such as Labna and Kabah (dates at Uxmal fall later). The texts are all very repetitive and record the times when important nobles dedicated buildings or rooms, sometimes to house gods or lineage ancestors. The buildings are similar to what we see elsewhere in Yucatán in the late eighth or early ninth century, exemplifying the Puuc style with their elaborate mosaic facades and geometric forms. But the most famous buildings at Chichen are those exhibiting "Mexican" or foreign styles, featuring warriors with spear throwers and other weaponry, which seem to be only a bit later in date. This short time frame accounts for the confusion we often face in interpreting Chichen Itza's place in cultural history. It was a quickly transforming place in its heyday. If nothing else, Chichen highlights a shifting dynamic we will examine further, that the Maya after 800 were forging new political connections with their Mesoamerican neighbors to the west, either by choice or by the point of the spear thrower's dart.

As noted earlier, one important individual cited in Chichen Itza's texts from the ninth century is a ruler named K'inich Junpiktok', identified as an *ajaw* of Ek Balam. This is an interesting connection. Ek Balam, located not far to the east, was now silent as a political center, and its demise was probably linked in some way to Chichen Itza's rapid rise. Several other different individuals are also featured in the Chichen inscriptions, but one name stands out as more prominent than the others: K'ahk'upakal K'inich, meaning "Fire Is the Shield of the Sun God." (K'inich Junpiktok' of Ek Balam was one of his associates.) He appears to have been a paramount noble or even a ruler of Chichen Itza, responsible for building shrines and making offerings to various divine ancestors. A few texts at Chichen Itza commemorate how K'ahk'upakal conjured deities and ancestral spirits through the use of ritual fire (we are not told just how, unfortunately). There is also a frequent mention of religious officials called Yajawk'ahk', "Lord of Fire." We know "Lord of Fire." We have seen this title from Palenque, Pomona, and other sites that lie in the western region of Tabasco during the Late Classic, where they refer to a special office of warrior or priest (Figure 10.8). When depicted in the art, they are always shown with Teotihuacan-inspired insignia, and I suspect that they were in the late Classic considered the ritual "keepers" of that legacy, charged with maintaining the ceremonies associated with sacred war and that old ideology. The appearance of the Yajawk'ahk' officials at Chichen points to a real connection to Tabasco and to the Gulf Coast region in general.

In the late ninth century, Chichen seems to have been established anew as a place for ancestor veneration, where these individuals worked with K'ak'upakal to maintain fire rituals at a series of important shrines. Their presence at Chichen Itza, and of the shrines they maintained, was surely connected in some way to the great cenote and to its then long-established role as a pilgrimage center. The great well was, after all, the place of the Maize God's death and resurrection, an appropriate locale for a series of ritual structures devoted to illustrious ancestors. And this "new use" of Chichen Itza by the late Maya appears to have attracted the

FIGURE 10.8. The glyph for the priestly title Yajawk'ahk' (left) and its torch-wielding bearer, a noble named Iximbahlam. Detail of an alabaster vase, Museo Popol Vuh. Drawing by the author.

attention of others from afar during a time of intense disruption and instability that some have called, all too simplistically, the "Maya Collapse." As we will discuss in chapter 12, it would not take long for this religious site to assume an even more prominent role as the focal point of a new cult centered on the Feathered Serpent, K'uk'ulkan, or, as the Nahua-speaking peoples of Mexico would know him, Quetzalcoatl. This deity, so famous from Mesoamerican myth, was a distant relative of the old Maya Water Serpent, the feathery snake who had long inhabited the green, earthly waters of Ukha'nal. In this way, the religious significance of Chichen Itza, while novel, would involve the resurrection of an old idea.

• • •

The northern realms of the Classic period offer us a complex narrative of rival cities and new experiments. The people of Yucatán, speakers of a distinct language who lived in a terrain with no rivers, surrounded by sea on three sides, had a special history and identity of their own. Their geographical placement and distinct environment may also have left them somewhat immune to the pressures that had greatly affected the central region, where the major dynasties were in their own constant flux, always negotiating and renegotiating alliances and conflicts. The northern kingdoms certainly took part in those dynamics, to the extent that the major cities and dynastic centers of Yucatán were abandoned as well. But there was also something very different happening in the years leading up to the end of the Classic period. After 800 CE, the Maya of Yucatán, or at least some factions of them, began to forge something new and different while still maintaining roots within the ideas and strategies of the past. Some of these new political and religious experiments—maybe we can call them strategic adaptations—even turned out to be successful, allowing some centers of power to last centuries after those that had fallen in the south. In time, they would succumb to a similar fate, nevertheless, reaching their ends. Perhaps this is not so surprising, for they were born out of the same way of life where impermanence, cycles of rises and falls, and the anticipation of something new coming along were ever present.

PART IV

Lok'oy

THE LEAVING

CHAPTER 11

Abandonments

FOR THE ROYAL families and members of their courts, the final decades of the Classic period were a time of existential crisis. The written history we have leading to the late 700s makes clear just how severe the strains had been for those navigating the social and political world of the dynastic courts amid an elite society at war with itself. Here and there, over the centuries of Classic history, there had already been periodic gaps, hiatuses, and even abandonments of individual royal centers. Now something more systemic and seismic was at play. By this point in our story, we see that the frenzied conflicts of the Late Classic period spanned the entire southern Maya lowlands from the Usumacinta region to what is now Belize. It is reasonable to suppose that a landscape of warfare would go far toward explaining the transformative changes that were to come—what we routinely call "the Maya collapse." But was it a cause or a symptom? The situation becomes exceedingly complex when we realize that other factors were at work, too, exerting pressures on what by 800 was an old system of politics, economics, and social relations. Beyond royal history and warfare, we can see that the Maya lowlands experienced exponential population growth during the Late Classic, just as these narratives of conflict increased in frequency. As we will see, access to water was not as reliable as before, putting powerful new pressures and constraints on food sustainability. By the late eighth century, a bad mix of factors and pressures was brewing.

The word "collapse" comes from the Latin *collāpsus*, meaning a "falling in" of a building or structure. Its origin is *con-lāpsus*, with *lāpsus* a "slip" or "error." The idea is of a physical collapse that follows from some built-in mistake or flaw. And it suggests a quick, unintentional end. Can we apply this sense to the last years of the Classic period? At first glance, it would seem natural to do so. After all, the demise of the Classic dynasties and their power centers did come rapidly, within a few generations at most. Cities ceased to function as they once had, as elites and many others left and went elsewhere. By 900 CE many cities had no people to maintain them, their temples and palaces soon taken over by the encroaching forest vegetation. Here and there, including Tikal, Copan, and Palenque, squatters lived in and around the decaying palaces, but eventually they too looked for better options, moving on to other places. Tracking these population movements through archaeology is very difficult, and the written history is silent. Still, the patterns of widespread abandonment are clear, pointing to a "great leaving." Maya cities large and small went dark, as did many of the political structures and networks that supported them. In this sense, the end of the Classic period saw a demographic and social collapse.

The ruins of these cities still convey an uneasy sense of absence and abandonment. Whenever I visit one of the remote, massive ruins the Maya left behind—say, at Naranjo or Nakum—I find myself pondering the very same question that nagged at John Lloyd Stephens and other explorers in the nineteenth century: *What happened?* It is a question that drives an impressive amount of modern archaeology to this day, looking at many different factors and variables, including the interrelated aspects of demography and settlement, subsistence, disease, and paleoclimates. These all seek to explain why so many ancient settlements and individual kabch'ens were rapidly abandoned. One example that stands out is Aguateca, the fortified seat of the breakaway Mutul dynasty, where excavations revealed very clear and poignant evidence of a rapid end. At several elite residences, archeologists found numerous ceramic vessels, grinding stones, jade ornaments, and musical instruments left on floors and surfaces. The elite houses were burned, and no one ever returned. People picked up what they could and ran, clearly reacting to a grave threat. Here we are reminded of the historical accounts of fleeing kings we see in the inscriptions, sometimes marked by the glyph that reads *ani*, "he ran," depicting a human body in flight (Figure 11.1).[1] For me, "running off" stands out as an important part of how we understand the Classic collapse overall, backed by both archaeological and historical evidence.

FIGURE 11.1. The hieroglyph for "to flee, run away" (*ani*). Drawing by the author.

For many, the supposed "disappearance" of the Classic Maya makes them stand out among ancient cultures as the quintessential example of societal breakdown, as a people who somehow "didn't make it."[2] This is an unfair characterization. On the contrary, other formulations of Maya civilization continued and even thrived after 900. In the early sixteenth century, early Spanish invaders encountered densely populated towns in Yucatán, Tabasco, and the Guatemalan highlands. Even today close to five million people speak Mayan languages. To trace where the mistaken idea of disappearance arose, we only need to look back at the romanticized ideas of "lost cities" from the earliest days of Maya archaeology and the disconnect those early explorers sensed between the ruins and the Indigenous peoples around them. That set the stage for a genuine aura of mystery and the misconceptions that persist to this day.

The idea of a widespread "disappearance" is therefore a false construct, a myth, even if the abandonment of cities was a real phenomenon. What happened in the ninth century can be more correctly characterized as the collapse of the social and political world, of the royal courts that had emerged centuries earlier, at the end of the Preclassic. The commoner populations who resided among those realms were also affected by the tensions affecting the larger political order, and they may have had much more flexibility in adjusting to new circumstances or in making decisions to simply move on. In a world of warfare and raiding, they may have even initiated these population movements and abandonments, forcing elites to follow suit. The larger picture before us is nevertheless of a rapid and pervasive "end game" where the nature and timing of abandonment varied a bit from place to place. No matter how we characterize that termination of an elite society, we can still be certain that Maya people in general persevered in different ways, forging new political and economic arrangements out of the old.

Another mistake would be to see this complex phenomenon of the ninth and tenth centuries as something unique to the Maya, or unprecedented in ancient history. In fact, the changes that we see occurring after 800 were also affecting much of Mesoamerica more broadly. Teotihuacan's political and demographic fall was around 600 CE, and its cause remains a mystery. In Oaxaca, the great capital of Monte Alban suffered its own collapse around 800, concurrent with the upheavals we see among the Maya. In Central Mexico, the palace complex of Cacaxtla, with its distinctive Maya-style mural paintings and scenes of violent combat, lasted no later than 900. Not far away, the urban center of Xochicalco lasted until around 900 and was violently burned and abandoned. Whatever befell the ancient Maya may have been exacerbated by cultural and climatic factors, but it was also a region-wide upheaval affecting territories and cultures throughout Mesoamerica. Explanations of the Maya collapse fall short, I think, if they fail to consider this bigger picture of a pervasive and violent turn of events, spanning a fairly short time span.

• • •

As we have seen in many examples, communities of all sizes rose and fell many times before the ninth century. A previous episode of abandonment took place seven centuries earlier at the end of the Late Preclassic era, around 100 CE, when cities in the northern Peten such as El Mirador and Nakbe were depopulated, only to be reoccupied in the Late Classic. What collapsed back around 100 sowed the seeds of the Classic Maya, which lasted for centuries until undergoing its own cultural and political breakdown. The Classic Maya collapse, in turn, set the stage for the reimagined Maya cultures of the Postclassic. The finite nature of place and community in the Classic era seems a recurring aspect of Maya demography and even the culture's sense of place, reflected in the constant movement and adaptability we see over the centuries. It seems to be a constant element in Maya history and in the relationships of people to their local environments, that populations would pick up and move as a response to crises. It is possible that the abandonment of many sites in the ninth century represents a particularly intense and widespread example of this same dynamic.

Yet another caveat touches on the ways that we, as archaeologists, tend to perceive the "collapse" as a singular, momentary phenomenon, even channeling some of the common misconceptions touched on here. By this I mean that researchers still struggle to define exactly what calamities befell the Preclassic or Classic Maya or how rapidly these took place. Even with our detailed knowledge of ancient communities, where people lived their lives for generations, it is easy to look upon their ruined remains with an exaggerated sense of disaster. Put another way, we easily see the end result of collapse but less easily the process of abandonment or what factors really played roles leading up to it. This is certainly true of written history as well, for we would not expect a Maya dynasty of the ninth century to erect any inscribed monuments describing, much less explaining, its own ending. Still, we can tease out important historical clues about what integrated into narratives that reflect the internal political and social instabilities of the time. The particulars of how elite Maya communities behaved and interacted with one another leading up to the eighth century—at least what was written down—allow us to frame the collapse in new ways that may hold great explanatory power. The best answer to the old question of the collapse, I have long felt, lies in the wider dynamics of societal change in the eighth century and in what led up to the Maya *decision* to abandon their elite centers at the end of the Classic era.

TIMING AND PLACE

Maya stone monuments tend to have written dates, and looking at their patterns of dedication has long provided clues about the fates of individual kingdoms. Tracking the last dates is also one quick means of gauging the pace of abandonment. Among the western kingdoms, Piedras Negras has a final date of 795, Palenque of 799, and Yaxchilan of 808. Tonina, in its relatively isolated valley, was a noticeable holdout, with its final inscription dated to 909. In the central lowlands, we see last dates at Tikal in 869, with a final stand of a Mutul king nearby, at the site of Jimbal, at 889. Copan's final firm date is 805, with Quirigua a few years later in 810. In the north, Coba's last date is 780, and at Ek Balam we have nothing after 830. In just over a century, the major Classic kingdoms all stopped in their tracks, at least when it came to producing the records of royal commemorations of period endings. The tight clustering of these many end dates from across the Maya region, most falling within less than a century, speaks to the systemic nature of the social and political collapse.

This is not the whole story. As archaeological investigations expanded at many sites, different temporal patterns emerged, often adding new layers of complexity beyond what the monuments indicate. One revelation was the evidence that people often stayed for many years after the last pyramids were built and the last stelae erected. At Tikal, for example, archaeologists encountered clear evidence of generations of people living in the Central Acropolis—the ancient palace of the Mutul lords—well after the last inscribed monument at Tikal in 869. Perhaps they were squatters living in the old royal quarters, but such evidence has also been taken to contradict older characterizations that Maya elites suffered through an "unforeseen disaster" that was "catastrophically sudden," as Proskouriakoff had put it in the 1940s.[3]

Copan provides another example. The last inscribed monument we have at Copan probably dates to 822, commemorating the "seating" of a new ruler or nobleman. The major structures of the acropolis are at this point no longer modified or expanded, after a four-hundred-year era of constant growth. Copan ceased its role as a Classic dynastic center, and elite ceramics quickly stopped being produced or used. Yet after about 850 or so, we still see a substantial settlement around the main acropolis and the old royal residence, immediately adjacent to the river. Tellingly, some of the modest houses and other late buildings of the ninth and tenth centuries were constructed using the stone blocks robbed from

Copan's most elaborate temples. One house platform dating to the Early Postclassic was made of fallen stones taken from Temple 18, built in 801 and maybe housing the tomb of Yaxpasaj Chanyopat. The late occupants had no qualms about using pieces ripped from elaborate temples built at most a few generations before.

These patterns help establish a couple of important parts of the collapse narrative. One is that *overall* populations did not abandon large communities quite as rapidly as we might suppose. Abandonment, in other words, could be a more protracted phenomenon than we find reflected in the history of monuments. Do archaeology and epigraphy offer contradictory lines of evidence, then? I don't think so. My own view of the evidence, at least as we current understand it, is that the major elite courts of Copan, Tikal, and most other Maya centers disintegrated rapidly between 800 and 850, all within a few decades of one another. This represented the collapse of the Classic Maya dynastic system, a traumatic event in the world of elite society. Some people continued to occupy these same centers after elite abandonment took place, no doubt attracted to good housing in the breezy heights where elites tended to settle. There is truth in these different characterizations of pace, therefore: The end of the Classic period was catastrophically sudden for very visible, elite segments of society who were invested in the network of connections we have outlined in detail. The end of governing institutions and their associated dynastic ideology was sudden and, this time around, for good. With adjacent non-elite populations, the transformation could often be gradual and slow-going. Many lived among the "new" ruins (and even contributed to the ruination) simply because the old permanent structures were comfortable places to live or good places from which to draw construction material. In this scenario, collapse (political and among elites) and abandonment (demographic and among commoners) may be viewed as separate things, two parts of a complex process that played itself out in different ways at different locales.

One of the best places we can see this two-stage process of collapse and abandonment is Dos Pilas, the old seat of Bajlaj Chank'awil of the Mutul dynasty. Dos Pilas had maintained its role as a seat of power for several generations, up until the end of the reign of his great-grandson, K'awil Chank'inich, in or slightly after 761.[4] At this point, the dynastic seat moved to the nearby defensive location at Aguateca, high on the escarpment overlooking Lake Petexbatun. We will recall that Aguateca, or K'inich Pa'witz as it once was called, had served as a refuge for embattled nobles of Dos Pilas in the last half of the eighth century. Now it assumed a new role as the kingdom's capital, reflecting the increasing tensions of the era. After 760, the former center at Dos Pilas appears to have been minimally active, and it may have even been briefly abandoned in subsequent decades. A new, modest population settled, taking advantage of the beautiful springs nearby, building simple thatched houses in the regal plaza of the site, among the broken stelae and the hieroglyphic stairway recording the epic story of Dos Pilas's king, Bajlaj Chank'awil. The latecomers dismantled the outer stones from the surrounding pyramids, using the stones to build concentric walls around their small settlement. One rustic, defensive wall ran over one inscribed stairway, covering its hieroglyphs. The dating of these late houses and the dismantling of the Classic city is difficult to establish, but I suspect they are after 800, well after the court of Dos Pilas had moved on. Whoever they were, the people who formed this small, modest settlement were desperate to build walls around themselves, paying no regard to the great sculptures and pyramids around them. Their efforts of self-protection and dismantling were short-lived, and the complete abandonment of Dos Pilas came not long after.[5]

The collapse of the major dynasties and kabch'ens came quickly and systematically in a broad region across of the southern lowlands, running from the Gulf of Mexico, in Tabasco, through the Peten region, and down to what are now Belize and Honduras. I find it interesting that this corresponds very closely to the area where we can historically map the distribution of Ch'olan. The speakers of this subgroup were the originators of Classic Maya culture in the Early and Middle Preclassic. This included the hieroglyphic script, which originated as an expression of Ch'olan language, a courtly lingua franca also adopted among elite Yucatec Mayan speakers to the north. The rough overlap between the region of dynastic origins after the

Preclassic, the area of speakers of Ch'olan language, and areas that experienced the most intensive and numerous dynastic collapses once again emphasizes how the institutions that experienced rapid and early collapse were closely tied to the old political and religious order. From this perspective, it may not be surprising that the pace and timing of change outside this central and southern lowlands region show more varied patterns.

There were important holdouts, too, at places like Nakum and Xultun in the central Peten. One might even say these emerged as vibrant centers in the late ninth century, existing in a landscape that had already radically transformed and with the old Classic order by then largely gone. Tonina, in Chiapas, was another locale where the dynastic order was relatively slow to expire, with a final date on a stela corresponding to 909 CE. These southern kabch'ens were contemporaneous with Uxmal and its neighboring great cities of the Puuc region, in Yucatán. All of them, while very different from one another, might be seen as attempts to maintain and revive the old Maya system in the face of profound social and political stress. This is a point we will explore further, but these Classic-oriented courts would also eventually fall or radically transform in the tenth century, signaling the real end of the old dynastic ideology.

BREAKDOWN

Let's step back and look at the beginnings of the end, slow in some areas, fast in others. The history we read from across the southern lowlands shows a world that was socially, culturally, and economically integrated to a surprising degree, yet it was also politically fractured. The written records are more concerned with war than ever before and present regions of persistent conflict with rhetoric that was particularly intense and direct. There were other centers that maintained a firm grip on the way monuments and ceremonies were always commemorated, beginning centuries earlier, but after 750 or so we see a profound change. It is an image of a world being torn apart, of old family alliances disrupted, and of personal animosities brought center stage. The rhetoric of Maya

FIGURE 11.2. Glyphic titles of war: "He of Sixteen Prisoners" and "He of Twenty Prisoners." Drawings by the author.

history changed subtly but in a real way, where the celebration of dynastic prowess and ceremonialism was supplemented by detailed records of violent interaction. One particular honorific title for kings and nobles that emerges around 740 is a count of captives, reading "He of Sixteen Prisoners" or "He of Twenty Prisoners" (Figure 11.2). Never used by anyone before that time, it is perhaps one small indicator of a change toward endemic warfare.

One holder of the title was the ruler named Yajaw Chanmuwan, the k'uhulajaw of a place we know today as Bonampak, to the west of the Usumacinta River. He came to the throne there in 776, under the auspices of its more dominant neighbor Yaxchilan (Pa'chan) and its king Chelew Chank'inich. But the connections between these two cities were not always constant or friendly. We know that Yajaw Chanmuwan's father and grandfather had been allied to another influential kingdom named Saktz'i' (White Dog), located to the north and a longtime regional rival of Yaxchilan.[6] Yajaw Chanmuwan was a prime actor in realigning Bonampak with Yaxchilan, and he solidified this new alliance by marrying a woman from there in 789. Yajaw Chanmuwan's lasting, most famous monument was a small building that still stands today, holding in its three chambers one of the great masterpieces of world art, the famous Bonampak murals, dedicated in 801. The inner walls were brilliantly painted in blue, orange, red, and green with scenes of pomp and celebration, dancing, and musicians (Plate 14). But the initial room shows a strikingly violent scene of a chaotic battle in the forest, with tangled warriors and dying victims. Another room of the murals shows a judgment of several captives taken in the war, presented before the standing Yajaw Chanmuwan, his wife, and his mother (Plate 15). Several naked prisoners sit tortured and bleeding, and one lies dead, slumped on the steps before the ruler. Why were the war and victory being commemorated in such a staged and violent way? Sculptures associated with these mural chambers strongly point to a conflict with Saktz'i'. The convergence of historical detail suggests that the murals commemorated Bonampak's newfound role as a subordinate court under the sway of Pa'chan, depicting its violent battle against its previous overlord. The subjects of the Bonampak murals—a viscous war coupled with pageantry and courtly politics—are different from any paintings or sculptures seen before. The war and the torture are brutal, far more explicit than the customary static images of kneeling or prone captives.[7]

At nearby Yaxchilan, the Pa'chan capital, we see a similar trend. Its late history, after 750 or so, is of little else but war. I see this especially in a particularly bellicose inscription on a stairway dedicated by its king Chelew Chank'inich, only a few years after the Bonampak murals were painted. What survives of the inscription is a list of captures (*chuhkaj*, "he was bound up"), all involving foreign nobles and falling between 796 and 800. There are eleven wars in total. Once again it is a unique record of intensive war, far different from the isolated records of captures we have in earlier Yaxchilan history. The scribes are recording a world where no peace is to be found.

Yaxchilan's history after 750 also emphasizes a certain class of subservient lords with the title reading *Saajal*, many of whom had direct roles in these conflicts (Figure 11.3). These were probably military captains who at times also ruled over smaller satellite centers. (Chaksutz' was another Saajal at Palenque, as we have seen.) Many of these officials appear in Yaxchilan's art together with Yaxun Bahlam or his son, Chelew Chank'inich, and they seem to be the coordinators of battles, taking prisoners who they later present as formal gifts to their kings. These were powerful nobles in their own right, and one must wonder if over time their increasing authority and visibility weakened the bonds of alliance, making them a threat to the centralized power in the larger court. As we have seen at Copan and elsewhere, this would fit a persistent pattern in Maya archaeology and history of subservient nobles rising in prominence and expressing their status much as a k'uhulajaw would.[8]

And only a few years later, it was all gone. The final, momentous event in the history of Yaxchilan came in 808, when its last known king, K'inich Tatbujol, captured the ruler of its persistent rival Piedras Negras (Yokib),

FIGURE 11.3. The presentation of bound captives by a lord, Ajchakmax, to his king, Chelew Chank'inich of Yaxchilan, in 783 CE. Lintel from La Pasadita, Guatemala. Drawing by Marc Zender.

K'inich Yatahk. The new royal prisoner had been an active warrior in his own right, "He of Ten Prisoners," battling not only Yaxchilan to its south but also the kingdom of Pakbul to its north. The last words of the last known inscription at Yaxchilan states that "K'inich Yat Ahk is the prisoner of the Captor of Akulmo', of the Holy Lord of Pa'chan." It is a telling last statement of local history, for most records of capture in Maya history are of junior nobles or warriors, not kings. From 808 onward, the history of Yaxchilan goes quiet, and few people seem to have lived there in the ensuing years.[9]

Another region where we see clear evidence of increased warfare and a new emphasis on militaristic themes is the eastern Peten. Here, as we have seen, Naranjo had long been a principal operator, playing an active role in the region's history since the sixth century. Aj Numsaaj, who ruled from 546 to 615, was one of the great alliance builders of his day, working closely within the expansionistic Kanul network of that time. Later, and still under Kanul's domination, Naranjo was chosen as the seat for Bajlaj Chank'awil's daughter, Lady Wakjalam Chanlem, and her own son, K'ahk'tiliw Chanchahk. Their joint reign had been an especially active one in terms of conquest and area-wide disruption, foreshadowing the expanding rhetoric of war several decades later. Two of their consistent enemies were Yaxha and Ucanal, located to Naranjo's south. At those two centers we find interesting accounts involving two unfortunate figures of the time, one named Xubchahk, the ruler of a site we know today as Ucanal, and a neighboring ruler named K'inichlakamtun, the *ajaw* of the great city of Yaxha. Like many of their contemporaries, both men lived difficult lives at the end of the eighth century. The known parts of their story begin the 796 (the same year when Yaxchilan's intensive wars began) with a stela erected at Yaxha, depicting K'inichlakamtun in the act of capturing Xubchahk. The event is visually couched in elaborate mythological imagery, conveying a message of war as a reenactment of a mythic episode among gods. The story of victor and vanquished might have ended there with a singular reference, but we know from other sources that Yaxha's king experienced his own travails in the ensuing years. Only three years after his victory, Yaxha was attacked and defeated by Naranjo's king, Kokajk'awil, on July 16, 799, forcing the Yaxha ruler to flee.[10] A lengthy account we have been able to reconstruct tells of a further series of attacks against K'inichlakamtun throughout the summer of that year, and eventually, he was captured.

Xubchahk's story was far from over, however. We might think that the defeat of his conqueror would have led to his emancipation and a happy return to Ucanal's throne, but no. A sculpture at yet another city, Caracol, dedicated in 800, shows two bound prisoners, one of whom is clearly named as Xubchahk, with an Ucanal attribution. Naranjo's defeat of Yaxha a year earlier somehow led to Xubchahk's being kept as a prisoner, and this probably occurred when K'inichlakamtun had to leave him behind as he fled his own capital of Yaxha. He may have been shuffled around the region as a valuable prisoner, it is hard to say, but we do know for certain that he arrived at the court of Caracol after a short period. There he was "owned" as a prisoner or slave of the local ruler Tumyohl K'inich, who died soon after in the later months of 799. To my knowledge, Xubchahk is the first attested example of one captive being portrayed as a prisoner at two sites, under two masters.

One dramatic example of the violence and trauma that befell Maya elites at this time is the massacre of royals at Cancuen, located on the upper reaches of the Río Pasión in the southern Peten. The royal center had been established under Yuknomch'en II during the seventh century, as a long-distance ally and outpost of the Kanul regime. Its location near the foot of the volcanic highlands made it an ideal trading port, dealing with jade and other precious commodities from the southern Maya world. Its palace housed the lords of a dynasty named Yahkk'in, and the surrounding community expanded over time, especially in the reign of a local king named Taj Chanahk; by 790 Cancuen was one of the most powerful kingdoms of the southern Maya world. Within a few short years, however, all of this changed with a violent overthrow of the ruling family. Direct evidence of this emerged several years ago during archaeological investigations at Cancuen. Numerous human bones were found at the bottom of an ancient stone-lined pool or cistern adjacent to the palace, representing at least thirty-one individuals—adult men and women as well as children. Preserved adornments of their clothing pointed strongly to their elite status, and it is natural to suppose they were residents of the royal house, including the close descendants of Taj Chanahk. Most individuals showed evidence of blunt-force trauma, and one person was decapitated. All victims were deposited in a single, violent episode, around 800 CE. The palace itself was "terminated" at about the same time, with two other royal skeletons found buried not in tombs but simply in the architectural fill used to cover the palace's entrance—an intentional act of cancelation. The evidence found points to a military conquest and a massacre of the local nobility. It is hard not to see this episode as linked to the cascading wave of violence that was overtaking the region, visible in the west, central area, and east.[11]

A couple of things stand out from these different narratives, ranging across the Maya lowlands. One is their condensed time frame. All the events occurred in these different kingdoms in the span of only a few years, pointing to a time when the whole southern Maya lowlands seem to be overcome by intensive war on a scale we have not seen before, with courts and armies on the run. In Maya terms, it fell within the twenty-year k'atun that began on 9.18.0.0.0 (790) and ended on 9.19.0.0.0 (810). These years strike me as a particularly important and transformative time in Late Classic Maya history, a window into a systemic collapse that was playing itself out and a culmination of pressures and instabilities that had been building for decades, if not centuries. After 790, we can look in retrospect on the society as quickly approaching its breaking point.

Militarism was nothing new. Going back centuries to the Early Classic, we see ample evidence of war, even in the first historical records at Tikal and Uaxactun, with their clear visual allusions to a conflict around 350 CE. And we can also point to the formative event of the Early Classic that came a short time later—the Entrada of 378—a conquest that would resonate for centuries among Maya kings and queens, a foundation of a new militaristic ideology. That said, our readings of Classic history point to a significant uptick after 790 in the frequency of war as a topic of official histories, especially in the Peten and Usumacinta regions, where texts are so numerous. The shift is subtle yet significant, suggesting a change in intensity or a way that conflict began to take over elite Maya affairs at the end of the eighth century. For me, this is an essential part of how we account for the collapse of the southern kingdoms. And it is likely that the endemic warfare of that era, at least in the eastern Peten, had its political origins in old rivalries and conflicts going back centuries. On present evidence, we can approach the collapse of the Peten kingdoms as a culmination of deep-seated historical tensions we are now able to document in detail. Still, this begs a question: Was the culture of elite warfare and competition enough to take down the Classic Maya world from within, even without the external pressures of changing climate and the delicate balance of sustainability?

Put another way, what was at the root of these ongoing conflicts and their steady rise throughout the eighth century? Here is where we are on somewhat shaky ground. The historical records are never too explicit about motives or causes. They emphasize instead the episodic nature of the acts involved—the captures, the taking of jade treasures, the burnings, and the fleeing. They are stories of royal houses against neighboring royal houses, not major armies attacking one another. The narrative arc we examined earlier, focused on the ambitions of the Kanul kingdom and its alliances from sixth century onward, offer an interesting contrast to this later era. The Kanul alliances in the central lowlands were large in their scale and ambition, but such far-reaching narratives drop off about 750. War is more local as well as more pervasive in its character. This leads me to wonder if those ambitious political networks had suppressed regional tensions and instabilities that soon emerged anew and at a more frantic pace. However we choose to couch the motivations of war at the end of the Late Classic, it is clear that by the end of the eighth century, the Maya world had more than its fair share of tipping points.

THE CLIMATE OF COLLAPSE

Historical details help us flesh out the nature and intensity of warfare and elite society at the end of the eighth century, but they have their limitations in any grand theorizing about underlying causes. For the most part, Maya history gives us a list of symptoms. While warfare was perhaps the most acute indicator of elite society being wrenched apart of the Classic period, other elements were at play, some perhaps causing these pervasive tensions.

One is population. The later years of the Late Classic were a time of stunning demographic growth across the lowlands, as reflected in nearly all settlement surveys done in the region over the past six decades, even at centers with very different histories. A long-term program of research by Arlen and Diane Chase at Caracol, Belize, revealed a major shift in the sixth century: Before 550 or so, the estimated population was conservatively 30,000 people; by 700, Caracol had expanded as an urban area, incorporating a population of more than 100,000. It was a radical transformation and probably tied directly to Caracol's own military successes at the beginning of the Late Classic, especially in its wars against both Tikal and Naranjo.[12] But nearly all major centers of the Classic period show a similar trajectory of rapid, even exponential growth. The high density of populations in the central Peten after 700 stands in stunning contrast to the paucity of people in the same area just two or three centuries later, after most cities were abandoned.

As elite populations grew, the numbers of potential claimants to the ranks of the nobility must have become unwieldy. Beginning in the seventh century, courts and royal households that were once small and restricted burgeoned in number and in their makeup. New roles for members of the royal families emerged at this time, along with an increase in those who could claim inheritance to high status and access to the resources that defined being an *ajaw*. The new official positions included the roles of *Saajal*, a type of military leader; the *Ajk'uhun*, a court officer and administrator; and the *Ti'sakhun*, possible court messenger or "speaker." It is interesting that these roles seem to emerge first in the western Maya kingdoms of the Late Classic, in texts from sites such as Tonina, Palenque, Piedras Negras, and Yaxchilan, before we see them anywhere else. These were far from just bureaucrats. They were members of the inner circle to the royal families and probably, in many cases, members of the royal families. As a group, they could have easily been riven by inherent conflicts and contradictions. With time, numerous individuals could begin to claim access to luxury goods and services associated with palace economies—exotics such as jade, featherwork, and other adornments (the royal "cargoes")—as well as vie for the long-standing roles in palace society. This would naturally undercut the presumptions of privilege and the exclusivity that goes along with it. An expanding elite class that grows rapidly over only a few generations creates a self-contradictory conundrum, where the meaning of "elite" begins to lose its very significance. This would seem a vital factor leading up to the eventual breakdown.

In times of steep population growth, the sustainability (or lack thereof) of communities emerges as an obvious factor determining economic, political, and social change. In fact, strategies of sustainability are now a vibrant area of research within Maya archaeology, looking at systems of intensive agriculture and how they changed over the long course of the Preclassic and Classic periods.[13] For a time, the Maya were able to feed their growing numbers, but it seems probable that, in some areas, growth outstripped capacity, influencing a desire to seek food and resources elsewhere. The historical sources are silent on the topic, always emphasizing the personal nature of conflict among elites. In no inscription do we ever read of conquest for territory or for the appropriation of agricultural goods. If anything, the histories mentioned how war sometimes involved the sacking of palaces and the capture of royal goods, the exotic materials associated with courts and elite households. When K'inich Lakamtun of Yaxha was attacked by Naranjo in 799, for example, one text states that his *ikatz,* "cargo," was captured, using a term that we know refers to bundles of jade and courtly treasure. If the procurement of agricultural resources was ever a goal of Maya warfare, the texts say nothing about it. This may not be too significant, and we can probably surmise that the need for food and resources, especially exotics such as cacao, was concerning to all elites near the end of the Late Classic. Whether it was a factor behind warfare on such a pervasive scale remains unclear.

Related to these conditions are the changes we can discern in local climate, in particular the profound effects of drought. Water was already a precarious resource in many lowland regions, as in Yucatán, where cenotes and caves were always the sole access point for water. Early Spanish chroniclers mentioned famine and drought as a common topic of the older indigenous histories, and the annals of the colonial era took special note of particularly strong droughts and their social and economic effects. Further south, in the central lowlands, there is good evidence that many perennial wetlands dried up at the end of the Preclassic, producing the low-lying *bajos* we see today. Tellingly, these former lakes and marshes are often surrounded by the ruins of early urban settlements, such as El Mirador and Tintal, which were only sparsely populated for centuries after their abandonment.[14]

For growing numbers of urban elites, the quality of life deteriorated noticeably toward the end of the Classic period. Basic access to water became a challenge at Tikal, for example, as it surely did elsewhere. For centuries, the large artificial reservoirs in the center of the city had collected the runoff of the wet seasons to provide a secure, year-round source of water for the urban population, including the members of the Mutul royal family who lived in the great palace (Central Acropolis). Recent studies have shown that two of Tikal's largest sources of perennial water were highly contaminated by the ninth century, on the cusp of the city's abandonment. The standing waters within the so-called Temple and Palace Reservoirs contained toxic stews contaminated with very high levels of mercury, phosphate (a proxy indicator of organic pollution), and cyanobacteria. Rainwater washing over Tikal's plazas and temples would have deposited cinnabar, a mercury compound used in architectural paint, directly into the pools. And decades of dumping food waste into the same reservoirs contributed to the mix. What was once clean and reliable was now filthy, at times undrinkable. The detrimental effects would have been obvious to any who used these reservoirs, especially in a region such as Tikal where alternative sources of good water were few. And in a period of extended drought, the problems of Tikal's reservoirs would compound further. One might wonder if those not so reliant on these central reservoirs—the non-elite populations surrounding Tikal—were more able to adapt, not so wedded to the failing palace infrastructure. They perhaps had some options to move to places with better resources, whereas many elites could not. If nothing else, this new evidence points to a breakdown of elite sustainability due to several factors—periods of dryness, overconstruction, lack of maintenance, and overpopulation. The problems of the time created their own toxic stew.[15]

Our understanding of shifting climate conditions in the ancient Maya world relies on ample scientific data, of course, but we also have a single, tantalizing reference in the written history that illustrates how dire conditions were in at least one region. This comes from a short text inscribed on a small stingray spine (barb) unearthed at Comalcalco, on the far western frontier of the Maya world in present-day Tabasco, Mexico (Figure 11.4). This is where the Bakel dynasty or a branch of it seems

FIGURE 11.4 Inscribed stingray spine from Comalcalco, Tabasco, recording a drought and famine in 783 CE. Courtesy of Marc Zender and the Proyecto Arqueológico Comalcalco.

to have established itself after the 780s, moving from its long-standing capital at Palenque. The sharp spine, a common type of ritual bloodletter, was used in various ceremonies by priests and rulers. It was discovered along with numerous other inscribed artifacts within a burial urn, probably accompanying the remains of a local Comalcalco priest named Ajpakaltahn. Most texts are highly repetitive, recounting a series of rituals he performed as a member of Comalcalco's royal court. But the inscribed spine stands out among the rest, jarringly different in its tone. In direct, simple language, it notes that in the year 783, "there was drought (and) there was famine." These words were written on an implement used for piercing the flesh and offering one's blood, and there's little doubt that Ajpakaltahn himself performed the act to appease the ancestors and gods. Several of the deities mentioned in Ajpakaltahn's ritual texts are aspects of the storm god, Chahk—another indication of the concern for rain during his time as priest. However we look at the context, the inscribed spine is unique; no other text from the Classic period refers to the famine and conditions of life in such a direct and unflinching way. The times were changing.[16]

The year 783, evidently a stressful time in the western region, is also one of the last historical dates we know from nearby Palenque. There and then the beautiful Tablet of the 96 Glyphs was carved, celebrating the twenty-year anniversary on the throne of K'inich K'uk'bahlam, the great-grandson of the great K'inich Janabpakal. Afterward, Palenque falls silent. Could there be a connection, given that both Comalcalco and Palenque shared roles as seats of the Bakel dynasty? The disruption of royal activities at Palenque after 783 seems abrupt and early when compared to other kingdoms. Did a region-wide "drought and famine" entice a faction of the royal family to move westward to Comalcalco, establishing the latter as an alternate capital? If nothing else, there are indications that the western lowlands, and the area of present-day Tabasco in particular, were a place of instability and even human suffering as the eighth century ended.

We've already touched on the significance of climate in accounting for the demographic and political stresses of earlier centuries, long before the drought and famine of Comalcalco. In the Late Preclassic, we saw a great drying of the wetlands that had once sustained El Mirador and other early centers in the central lowlands. Reduced rainfall and the overexploitation of the fresh water threw off a delicate balance of sustainability. Not surprisingly, people were a part of the problem, much as they had been for centuries. Even before the Middle Preclassic, prior to the advent of agriculture and permanent settlements, the ancestors of the Maya worked at ways to dramatically change their own local ecologies.[17] Looking over the long term, it appears that every few centuries the delicate balancing act could be thrown off, sometimes with dramatic consequences. Although data related to long-term climate change is still being collected and analyzed, it seems clear that areas of the Maya lowlands again experienced protracted periods of drought between 800 and 1000, just in the era where we see major political and social change between the Classic and Postclassic eras. The crisis that saw the eventual collapse of so many Classic period kingdoms should be seen in the light of these larger patterns of ever-shifting environments, even if it was unprecedented in terms of scale and human consequences.[18]

Was climate, in the end, the singular cause of the Classic period abandonments? Here we are on uncertain ground. Noting the role for climate is one thing, but promoting it as *the* cause or trigger of the collapse may be too simplistic. For one, it is difficult to escape the pattern that historical accounts of intensive Maya warfare predate the apparent onset of extreme drought. At least, the most extreme conditions did not lead directly to the conflicts we see already existing on the ground. Perhaps we can entertain a more subtle dynamic of cause and effect, where limited or localized droughts could have tipped the scales, leading people to make drastic decisions to move or to engage in new conflict. The military raiding we read about in the histories, with its specific targeting of elite-controlled goods and resources, may provide a hint of the stresses of those times. And given what we know of varied ecologies within the Maya lowlands, it is likely that the effects of several back-to-back droughts were more pronounced in some areas than in others. The kingdoms of the central Peten, near where the great Preclassic cities once ruled, would have been especially vulnerable once more, especially in regions that had long worked at developing systems of intensive agriculture, channeling and managing water in highly sophisticated ways. Other cities located near rivers, lakes, and cenotes probably had more stable and perennial access to water, even in very dry times.[19] But still, without steady rain from the sky, the agricultural infrastructure of these kingdoms would have been susceptible to lasting damage, if not collapse.

My personal sense of these dynamics comes from my experiences many years ago as a child, living with my family at Coba, in what was then a small Maya village surrounded by the ruined city. In the summer of 1975, the area suffered an intense drought, and my memory of its effects remains vivid fifty years later. A desiccated, wilting forest surrounded our thatched house, and all was brown, dusty, and searing hot. The lakes were the only places within miles where standing water was visible or could be collected, but their welcome existence could not help the dying crops in the surrounding milpas or household gardens. Rain was the only answer. The people of Coba therefore arranged to have a ceremony to conjure the rain, a *ch'a'cháak* or "summon rain" ritual. This was held in the plaza of the vast ancient ruins adjacent to the village, just in front of a large, towering pyramid that the locals called La Iglesia, "The Church." A *ch'a'cháak* was a communal prayer for rain, practiced by countless generations across the Maya world in one form or another. The Cháak of modern Yucatán is the Chahk of the ancient Classic period, the deity of storms, thunder, and rain who wields his machete to break upon the clouds, a direct survivor of the ancient Chahk who used his flint axe to do the same. As I look back on the 1975 crisis at Coba, I can see how the villagers' determination to conjure rain was a demonstration of their own adaptability, a striving for cosmic balance and order. That dismal summer, the people relied on alternate foodways, hunting, or trade with distant neighbors. The rain ceremony was the most important strategy of all, a communal effort necessary to make things right and to persevere. Eventually, later in the summer, the rains did return, and Cháak lived up to his side of the bargain, machete in hand to strike the dark clouds.

Of course, things did not always end so well in deeper history. Having lived through the stresses of one drought at Coba, I can easily envision how several seasons of little rain could break any community. The notable "drought and famine" of 783 would have seen many priests and farmers practicing their desperate rites to invoke rain, including Ajpakaltahn with his handy stingray-spine bloodletter. He and his ruler had beckoned Chahk, probably on multiple occasions, but received no quick answer. A protracted few years of aridity in specific areas would have easily placed unbearable stress on an already-fragile social and political system wracked by warfare and a culture of elite conflict. As resilient as the Maya have always been, the environment they knew so well could be, in certain moments, unreliable, unforgiving, with life unsustainable. The question we must ask is what role the droughts may have played in the wider dynamic of the Maya collapse, as populations grew and wars raged. No one element was the cause of the collapse, but their complex interplay almost certainly was.

KINGSHIP TRANSFORMED

The one political institution we often use to define the Classic period was divine kingship, the concepts of sacred authority that were crystalized in the widespread title K'uhulajaw, or "holy lord." This title, along with its variants (*k'uhulwinik*, "holy man"), was used by the numerous kings or queens we have brought to light in this book, all of whom claimed their status and authority through lineage and dynastic pedigree. It was their ability to perform as various gods that became the basis of their own "divinity," a concept that may not have been so constant and visible on a day-to-day basis. As I prefer to see it, this divine quality, rather than a constant attribute of royals throughout their daily lives, was a recognition of their specialized roles as occasional "living images" of deities under highly specialized circumstances. K'uhulajaw was a political title by virtue of who held it, but in its essence, it was a religious moniker, giving its holders the authority to represent and embody their respective dynasties and the myriad ancestors and gods that that role entailed.

From what we know of Classic ideology, the main religious and political responsibility of rulers was to maintain and engender the world, including its cycles of time and growth. A burgeoning population of elites inside an already tight court society would have undercut their own sense of exclusivity, challenging the ideological system predicated on the maintenance of the cosmos or of sustaining the animate structures that bolstered the essential order of things. In a very public way, royal rituals were meant to sustain time itself, through constant efforts of replanting and renewal. A political ideology that hinged on ceremonial duties of "temporal agriculture"—the harvesting and regeneration of time itself—would have been severely undermined in a world where food procurement and distribution systems were at a breaking point. The agricultural metaphors at the heart of royal ritual—the "replanting" of time and the "casting of drops" to engender it—would have had little meaning in a world where the rains themselves were less than reliable. The underlying meanings of these old ceremonies were what gave Maya rulership its religious charter, yet they were becoming increasingly undercut by a social and natural environment in flux. Another key part of this ideological system was elite competition and the maintenance of sacred warfare (*tok' pakal,* the "knife-and-shield") as mentioned in several royal inscriptions.[20] The endemic wars I have described after 790 point to a time when warfare had gone off the rails, seemingly "unmaintained." The duty of sacred warfare was more important than ever and emphasized constantly, but it began to spill out of its old social and political boundaries, discarding much of its old decorum. These ideological aspects of war in the years before the abandonment of the Classic system seem important and as yet underappreciated.

The k'uhulajaw title, so emblematic of rulership in the Classic period, can be tracked through the early ninth century, but no later. Some have interpreted this as indicating a cessation of divine rulership at the time of the collapse, implying that it took on more "secular" attributes in the later Postclassic times. While rulership obviously changed and the dynastic system mostly died out, I am hesitant to follow any religious vs. secular line of thinking. The k'uhulajaw title became less visible to us simply because royal texts were no longer made or displayed. In fact, I think "holy lords" existed in some way throughout the ensuing centuries, as indicated by the use of the very same title into the twentieth century, among the Tzotzil Maya of Chiapas. In the town of Chenhalo', the anthropologist Calixta Guiteras-Holmes noted that local religious officials were called *ch'ul ojow,* which she translated as "Holy Lord." This is the same title, only pronounced slightly differently. I suspect in Classic times that K'uhulajaw had similar religious importance, alongside a heightened political role as well. Whatever the case, not all k'uhulajaws died out at the end of the Classic period, even if their political roles changed radically.[21]

The measurement of time may also have been a factor in the fall of the dynasties. Can it be a coincidence that the bak'tun that began in 435, after the Entrada, ended in 830, just as the Classic period was experiencing its crisis? In other words, did "temporal destiny" have a role in how history played out? This idea may not be as odd as it may seem. The historical chronicles of the *Books of Chilam Balam* are predicated on the symmetries of the k'atun periods, each of which saw the establishments and abandonments of towns, often in repeated cycles or "folds" of time. In the Classic period, we see how the start and end of the bak'tun period provides a remarkably accurate "bracket" to the sources we have for the Classic period and to the era of dynasties we know of historically. The "crisis" of the ninth century may well have been, in part, an acknowledgment of a new era that had turned and the recognition of a new order of business as a result.

Copan's dynasty and the symmetry of Altar Q provide a remarkable vision of this idea of history as symmetry and as periodic. The first ruler, K'inich Yaxk'uk'mo', celebrated the bak'tun ending on 9.0.0.0.0 in 435. The last ruler depicted, Yaxpasaj Chanyopat, was the sixteenth of the dynasty, the last of a cosmological set (four by four) whose very last recorded date was 9.19.0.0.0, twenty years before the bak'tun period turned again. It is difficult to see this as a fortuitous pattern.

How do we reconcile this ideological view of history with the real external factors we have described, such as climate change or overpopulation? I am not sure, nor am I certain that we are confronted by an either-or sort of explanation. Copan's royal court may have had plans to move on and reestablish itself elsewhere, under a new structure, and maybe they even did, along with other elites across the Maya world. This is where the sources fall silent, becoming of little help in explaining an era of great change. A changing climate and increased populations may have exacerbated a preexisting acknowledgment among Maya rulers and elites (and others) that their way of doing things was somehow finite or bound for an adjustment when the time was right. In a way, I wonder if this built-in recognition of beginning points and endpoints grew out of the very old sensibility, hard-won by the Maya over previous millennia, that the world operates in nested cycles, natural, cosmical, social, and political.

COHESION, CONFLICT, AND FLIGHT

If we were to single out the one prominent institution that did end dramatically, it is what we might loosely call the "dynastic system." After 900 there are few if any historical vestiges of the Classic-era royal houses and the tightly connected network built between them. It is hardly a sophisticated analytical term, but to me it nicely encapsulates the lattice-like arrangement of courts and royal families who had coexisted for centuries, many closely intermarried and forging a common elite culture. These were integrated not only by family ties but, when on good terms, also by the flow of market economics, tribute goods, and gifts. They were united in a common recognition of a cosmology where the supreme rulers, the k'uhulajaws, were the active agents of world renewal. Warfare, competition, and even "ethnic" conflict were part of the system, too, which suggests that the seeds of ultimate destruction were already in place centuries before the collapse. These features of the dynastic system were parts of an integrated whole that, by the middle of the ninth century, was no longer up to the task of self-maintenance and survival.

The historical records are consistent in their portrayal of a tangled web of family connections, political alliances, and interfamily conflict. They show a Classic Maya social landscape consisting of mutually reliant allies *and* rivals, never too centralized politically or economically but always existing within a tight system, forged by centuries of family ties and close networking. What emerges from this evidence is a curious situation that might at first seem contradictory—a landscape of conflict and warfare that masks a strong cultural cohesion among the elites, where communication, mutual awareness, and even mutual reliance kept a certain sense of social order together, even amid the cycles of conquest and insurrection. Maya dynasties were always glued to one another socially and culturally, if not politically. This interconnected world of elites represented a dynastic system that I see as particularly important for our study of the collapse. Warfare and other stresses were not necessarily presenting existential challenges from the outside; they were chipping away *within* a tight social and political network consisting of, in the end, a handful of interrelated lineages. While it may go against some of our assumptions about how societies fall apart, I see the interwoven threads of Maya dynasties and politics as the real and fateful vulnerability.[22]

The frantic narratives of Bajlaj Chank'awil, Nunujolchahk, or Xubchahk offer good illustrations of this singular, networked system during times of extreme stress. In Classic Maya history, people were constantly on the move, shifting their bases of operation and violently striking local rivals who were often relatives. One gets the strong sense that instability grew out of the predilection of dynasties and lineages not to exist on their own but to seek out political alliances and to join in with (or break with) hierarchical structures. These were never permanent or even meant to be so, for they were built into the larger political culture of the time as a means of control and reliance (depending on one's place). As noted previously, the impermanence of things was an element of the greater system's political and religious worldview. It was its own strategy in a way, allowing adaptation in difficult times, but it brought along an inherent instability as well, especially within a political culture where things were so interconnected. War, in the short term, gave the elite network of the Classic Maya a strong sense of purpose and identity and was ultimately, perhaps, at the root of its own downfall.

Many localized episodes of what looks to be "collapse" might instead be better couched as withdrawals or exit strategies in the face of intolerable, unlivable situations. This may seem like a weak distinction, but it involves more agency on the part of the Maya than we might otherwise envision or assume. The large elite households we see on the landscape—small palaces with temples, courtyards, and so on—often arose suddenly and were abandoned just as quickly after only a few generations. These places reflect the process of impermanence and change that I see as an essential assumption of Maya life and culture, reflected in resource procurement, history, and cosmology, perhaps from the very beginning. Over the course of two millennia, we find countless examples of communities and regal courts that reset themselves through such moves. Sometimes this was voluntary, and sometimes it was forced, but I see the overall pattern as an old adaptation, a reflection of a semi-sedentary lifeway that was well in place centuries before the grandeur of the Classic period. The mobility of Maya courts gave them a good deal of flexibility and an ability to forge networks on a larger geopolitical canvas.

But mobility also may have had its negative consequences, as the system was breaking down. In the face of attacks and hostilities, rulers and courts were very much "on the run," as we have seen in the varied cases of Dos Pilas, Yaxha, and Naranjo. What was once a sensible, anticipated custom of picking up and shifting places after several generations seems to have morphed at the end of the Classic period into a more frantic, unpredictable, and unsustainable pattern. With their near-constant movements, rulers, elites, and whatever support structures they maintained would have had a difficult time maintaining any sense of political or economic stability, stripped of having any choice in their movement.

From my perspective, this "flee factor" has its own powerful, explanatory role in understanding what we call the collapse. By 800 the central

Maya lowlands were a landscape of perennial war, and with threats on many sides, rulers and the royal families of the old established courts could never be comfortable. Two important historical accounts from this time make this abundantly clear. One is the Komkom Vase excavated at Baking Pot, Belize, with its long historical text narrating a story of flight and court destruction (see Figure 2.8). At its center are the Yaxha ruler K'inich Lakamtun and his constant running around as Yaxha and its nearby refuges are raided and burned, a target of a lord from Naranjo who was his neighbor and likely relative. K'inich Lakamtun's story overlaps considerably with other accounts that tell of his captive Xubchahk, once a lord of Ucanal who eventually ended up a prisoner of Caracol. These dizzying shifts in place and in fortune open a window on a late elite world fighting against itself, in constant motion and instability.[23]

MORE NEWCOMERS

The social network of elites that had defined much of Classic Maya civilization in the southern lowlands was in deep existential crisis after 830 or so, and neighboring peoples to the west may have taken advantage of the deteriorating situation. Many old power centers were by now abandoned, a few persisted, and new ruling structures and centers of authority emerged. Much as we have described for Chichen Itza, it was representative of a quickly changing political world, a dramatic reshuffling of political culture and the underlying social system that had long defined it. Most tellingly, we see a wave of new, foreign elites appearing on the scene in the central Peten, near the turn of the bak'tun. Their presence is clear in sculptural representations, in ceramics styles, and in the historical details that talk of outsiders from the west, who seem to be the new power brokers in the changing Maya world.

For many years, archaeologists recognized the archaeological and artistic changes of this time, pointing to a sudden, increased presence of foreigners in the Maya lowlands. But who were they? Teotihuacan was a distant historical memory, having been abandoned in the sixth century. What other powerful forces were at work? Based on a variety of lines of evidence, most scholars have looked still to the west, but not quite so far afield as central Mexico. Rather, it seems these newcomers were from the borderlands of the Maya region, in what are now the Gulf Coast regions of Tabasco and Veracruz. Some of the ceramics used by lowland elites in this so-called Terminal Classic era (after 830 or so) come from this region, exhibiting very different styles and decor, with styles sometimes describes as more "Mexican" than Maya. Several major sites in the southern lowlands show this new influx, including Ceibal, Nakum, Ucanal, and even sites in the region of Tikal. The closing decades of the Classic period play out in a concentrated fashion at these and a few other kingdoms, showing a clear tension between a maintenance of a traditional Maya dynastic ideology and a radically new system of power from elsewhere.

My colleague Simon Martin has studied this complex period in detail, looking at the historical details surrounding this rapid cultural transformation. He notes how a handful of new authority figures emerged at this time in the central lowlands, named in the inscriptions and wielding a significant degree of regional influence. They do not simply "arrive" or "conquer" according to the sparse narratives we have at our disposal, yet they were still disruptive of the old order. Their mentions appear in historical records up to about 870 or so, and they seem to have been important power brokers at the very end of the Classic period, interacting extremely closely with the old, traditional dynasties of the central lowlands.

One name that stands out in the inscriptions of the time is Papmalil, who was a ruler of Ucanal, located in the eastern part of the Peten, to the south of Naranjo. In ancient times, this was the kingdom named K'anwitznal. Papmalil ruled around the year 820, and for decades his political influence seems to have extended to some the old, traditional powers of the Classic period, including Tikal, Naranjo, and Caracol (Figure 11.5). He used the familiar title "West Kalomte'," which in this late era was quite rare and a clear hearkening back to the time of the Entrada and its legacy of foreign intrusion. As Simon Martin has suggested, the very name *Papmalil* stands out as odd-sounding for a prominent figure of Maya history. It may be non-Mayan, or it may reflect a linguistic connection to ruler names we know from Chontal, a variety of Ch'olan

FIGURE 11.5. Caracol, Altar 13, showing the foreigner Papmalil and a local Caracol lord. Drawing by Simon Martin.

Mayan spoken in the coastal region of Tabasco in much later years, in the early colonial period. Curiously, one inscription also calls him a "North Kalomte'," which may wellassociate him with the important cultural transformations brewing in Yucatán, in the Puuc area, and at Chichen Itza. Whatever the case, it seems Papmalil has far-flung connections.

Slightly later in Peten history, we encounter another important player in our story, a curious figure named Olom (only part of his name; the second part is missing or eroded in the examples we have). Again, his name is rather strange-sounding. He makes an appearance as a ruler in an inscription at Uaxactun in 830, when he witnesses or oversees the ceremonies marking the change of the bak'tun period of the Long Count calendar, a hugely important time in Maya cosmology. He is named again in connection with the year 840, on a badly broken stela from the nearby ruins of Nakum, a massive center of the Terminal Classic period that had been built atop the impressive remains of a Late Preclassic center. Olom seems to have been a key regional leader in the central Peten in this transformative time, and I wonder if the sheer scale of Nakum's palace makes it a good candidate for his base of operations in the region, ruling over much of the surrounding political landscape. Most significantly, Olom's honorific title was once again "West Kalomte'," a term we have come across many times so far, especially in connection to the Entrada and the Teotihuacan-affiliated lords. The "west" reference does not tell us exactly where Olom was from, but it provides good evidence that he was a regional outsider to the Peten region, perhaps from the western edges of the Maya world. Both Papmalil and Olom appear to have played similar roles as outsiders and influencers in the central Maya region between 820 and 840, a couple of decades that saw intensive political change.

Largely absent from these narratives is Tikal, the great Mutul seat of power. Our records of Mutul's very late history is extremely patchy and—tellingly, I think—scattered among many different sites in the area. In 810, one ruler had undertaken an ambitious plan to add a new pyramid to Tikal's soaring architectural monuments, a towering structure we know today as Temple III. Erected in front was Stela 29 and its altar, dating to the katun ending on 9.19.0.0.0 (June 25, 810). As Martin notes, Stela 29 did not last very long and was targeted for violent destruction within only a few years, intentionally bashed into many fragments. Tikal may have fallen victim to a violent overthrow just after 810, and it is difficult not to think that a new political order, as indicated by these likely foreigners at nearby Ucanal and Nakum, had something to do with it. The most important of the late Mutul sites are on large lakes south of Tikal, where water was plentiful, at ruins known today as Ixlu and Sacpeten. These late political centers most likely represent a further fragmentation of the Mutul dynasty into different factions, and here it is interesting to see that one of the lords cited at Sacpeten was named Bajlajchank'awil, reusing the name of an important historical "turncoat" from the seventh century. And, significantly, a text from nearby

Ixlu dating to 859 names Papmalil as the overseer of the local Mutul king's ceremony. There he is called a "North Kalomte'."

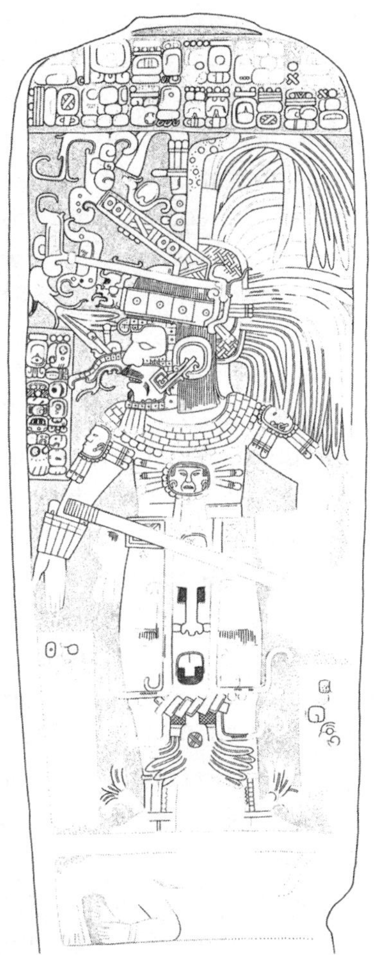

FIGURE 11.6. Ceibal, Stela 11. Drawing by Ian Graham.

Another foreigner who plays an important role in Maya affairs was named Wat'ulk'atel. By 849 he governed at Ceibal, the center of an old Maya kingdom located southwest of the central Peten and, as we have seen, one of the earliest sites we know of in the Maya lowlands. Four of Ceibal's monuments were erected around a radial pyramid there, each facing one of the cardinal points and showing portraits of Wat'ulk'atel in traditional Maya regalia, celebrating the first k'atun ending that came after the new bak'tun on 10.1.0.0.0 (Figure 11.6). The main east-facing monument of the set, Stela 11, gives a bit of background to this occasion, telling us that the ruler had arrived at Ceibal on March 12, 829, precisely 365 days before the turn of the bak'tun period. This was under the authority of a lord or group of lords from Ucanal. There is little doubt that Wat'ulk'atel was installed as king with the looming bak'tun in mind, and the mention of Ucanal's oversight again highlights its unusual importance in this era. The Ceibal monuments were erected in 849 to celebrate the passing of the k'atun that came twenty years later, and they each cite the participation by five different kings from the north: a ruler of Kanul named Kanpet, one of Mutul named Junixim K'awil, and a king of the Ik'a' kingdom named Kanek'. Taking part as well was a lord from the west, from the kingdom of Lakamtun, and a ruler from the south, hailing from some center we cannot yet identify. This extraordinary assemblage of rulers at Ceibal is unique, representing Ceibal's special place as the singular "node" of politics and ceremonialism in the mid-ninth century and in a new era of Maya history. It does so by reasserting a traditional ideology, maybe as an effort to restart a system that was clearly waning and broken. Now, however, it seems to have been under the very watchful eye of a new foreign authority from the west. I suspect that the choice of Ceibal as the center of this new effort at political consolidation has something to do with the city's great antiquity, even in the historical memory of the Classic period.[24]

The situation that played out in the central lowlands over these two or three generations was the last gasp of the Classic Maya, and it shows a few fascinating parallels to the history of three centuries earlier. Once again, we have the rather sudden appearance of foreign-looking individuals with a strange look marrying into local royal houses and even carrying the evocative directional titles, citing the west and the north. The end of the Classic period was another flash point in the long history of interaction with foreigners, either Maya or non-Maya peoples. The west was the direction of constant interaction and awareness, a place which in turn seems to have been constantly aware of the Maya and their long, deep history. As touched on earlier, it is possible that early urbanism in highland central Mexico was inspired to some degree by the precocious monuments built by the lowland Maya. In the Early Classic, Teotihuacan was so tightly integrated in the elite Maya society that the conflicts we read about in the fourth century amounted to an interfamily struggle. Here in the Terminal Classic, I sense that we have a new iteration of an old pattern of awareness and outside influence.

The influx of foreign authorities from the west and north represented yet another new political arrangement, an even more disruptive and violent flashpoint than had occurred centuries before during the Entrada and its aftermath. The earlier event of 378 was a "conquest," the overthrow of a king, but we also see a certain steadiness of place and of participants in the decades that followed. Tikal was always the seat of the Mutuls. In contrast, the overthrow of Tikal in the ninth century seems more consequential and disruptive, involving significant displacement. Even though late kings of the Mutul dynasty established several new courtly centers over the next two generations, they were never comfortable in their attempts to create a lasting place, an old-style kabch'en, for their venerable dynasty.

The stelae and altars at these late Mutul enclaves are very conservative in their design, attempting to replicate the look of Tikal's monuments from generations earlier. In this they stand out from other late monuments of the same era, such as those we find at Ceibal, Ucanal, or Nakum, with their channeling of foreign stylistic elements. Another site where we see an even longer persistence of Classic Maya art and ideology is nearby Xultun, an old city founded deep in the Early Classic period, perhaps as early as the first or second century BCE. Today it is a vast, tree-covered ruin, distant from any major settlement and still being actively explored and excavated. It probably was the local successor to nearby San Bartolo, famous for its Late Preclassic murals. Xultun was one of the oldest dynasties we know, its origins probably going back in the Late Preclassic period. In the Early Classic, it had emerged as a major kingdom, ruled by several powerful kings and at least one warrior queen. Its last stela is the latest dated monument known from anywhere in the Maya lowlands (see Figure 1.1). It was erected in 899, a century after the wars that we have discussed and even after most of the inscriptions we know from Uxmal, Chichen Itza, and others in the Puuc region. The monument shows a local lord grasping his two patron deities, replicating a formal scene of presentation that goes back to the beginnings of the Classic period. We do not know his name, but he was arguably one of the last Maya rulers of the Classic era, a desperate holdout in an area where neighbors were already gone or radically changed.

All these profound changes after 830 are related to the mysterious phenomenon of Chichen Itza far to the north, still unique in its overt expression of a foreign presence and of a new, militaristic ideology, as we will explore more in the next chapter. Just how Papmalil (a Kalomte'), Olom, and their contemporaries fit into our understanding of that cultural mix in the north remains to be seen. All we can say is that these rapidly breaking waves of western influence into the northern and southern lowlands begin at roughly the same time in the ninth century. Chichen Itza should be seen, I think, as a "crescendo" within this broader trend of interaction, probably as a singular "foreign place" in the Maya landscape after 900 CE. Chichen Itza persisted for a couple of centuries still, well after the major kingdoms of the southern lowlands could no longer sustain themselves, even with an influx of new political actors.

The very last stela we can firmly date from the Classic period is from Tonina, erected on the k'atun ending 10.4.0.0.0, in 909 CE. The location of Tonina far to the southwest in the Chiapas highlands may have shielded it from the disruptions of the central lowlands, but it too underwent a violent overthrow shortly after this time. Most of its beautiful sculptures were intentionally shattered around this time, in the 10th century. The final stela, broken in two, shows the last portrait we have of a king from the Classic period, perhaps the last of his dynasty. Just who he was and the circumstances under which his "last" dynasty fell remain mysteries.

• • •

Many things played a part in the collapse of the dynasties. It was an era of climate stress, foreign elites encroaching from the west (again), and internal population pressures. All these elements will continue to be studied and refined as important factors in multicausal models. For me, another compelling way to account for what happened rests on a human scale, seeing how the Maya themselves represented their own world at this time of radical change and transition. And one factor appears repeatedly in the historical record, perhaps even rising above all the others: internal conflict. If we were to interpret the situation at the end of the Classic period through the lens of historical events of most concern to scribes of the time, war comes out as the paramount issue, dominating so many written and artistic narratives in the decades leading up to the end. So many persistent conflicts among related lineages and their courts no doubt exposed some key vulnerabilities in economic structures, settlement patterns, and a sense of community cohesion.

The ideology of rule that had long couched itself in terms of agriculture and production may have been undercut by the real-world economic disruptions of the time.

My sense is that the top-heavy nature of elite Maya society also played a major role in the larger existential crisis. Kings, queens, and other rulers were by their nature cosmic actors, whether the manifestations of divine warriors or the planters and harvesters of time. But there were too many of them. Severe drought placed its own stresses on this delicate system that was predicated on the idea of royals as agents of sustainability, indicating to all that the cosmos was not cooperating quite as before. The premise of kingship was severely undercut by numbers and by circumstances. It had long been rooted in previous centuries of religious belief and ideology, but it could not sustain its inherent belief in the singular importance of action by a single individual, nor, in a time of endemic war, could it sustain its core belief in a cosmos that was constant and repetitious in its character. It was a double conundrum that set the stage for the breakdown of an elite society.

Here it is significant to think back on how Maya communities have long been mobile and "cyclical" from very early on, rooted in a well-established adaptation to life in the neotropics. The ability and even predilection to move formed a strategy of life that existed at many scales, whether it is the farmer who practices swidden agriculture, making a milpa, using it for several years, and then going on to plant another; a small village around 1500 BCE that is experimenting with horticulture and exploiting the forests and lagoons, moving with the seasons; or in the methods of naming and recording time that reflected these same cadences and cycles of nature.[25] It is a way of existence that is very unfamiliar to us today, with our assumptions that communities ought to be permanent, ever-growing. This may be at the root of our misunderstandings of the "collapse" as something so final and decisive. For the Maya, change was a natural thing, long a part of the ebbs and flows of existence, giving people opportunities to be proactive in making a necessary change when the time was right. Sometimes it was flight; sometimes it was in making a reasoned choice to find a better life elsewhere and not so dependent on an old, weakening system. The influx of new elites from the edges of the Maya world after 800 represented the end of an old political system, allowing new choices and options for many, even for the old dynastic royalty. Out of those troubled times emerged innovative places and individuals with new ideas, still as ever building on the legacies of deeper past.

CHAPTER 12

Revivals

THE DYNASTIC WORLD was mostly gone by the end of the ninth century, with just a few holdouts here and there. Tonina, Xultun (Baxwitz), and Nakum were among the handful of political centers that attempted to carry on much as before, each in a rapidly transforming political landscape. They would be able to do so for only a short time before they succumbed too. Tonina, in the highlands of Chiapas, offers an interesting case study of a holdover that lasted longer than many of its neighbors, its old enemy Palenque among them. Since the Early Classic Tonina was very much a "lowland" Maya city, with art, ceramics, and other material culture that reflected strong ties to the lowlands. It also erected the last known Maya stela at the k'atun ending in 909 CE. Afterward, the monuments ceased, and there came a radical change in the site's material culture, including a very different ceramic tradition with affinities to the south and to other regions of the highlands. Unlike many cities of the Peten and the central region, people continued to live at Tonina and in its lush valley, but they were no longer insisting on the "Classic Maya" culture. The changes were a drastic turn, a rejection of what existed before. A systematic destruction of sculpture at Tonina—myriad portraits of kings and captives—probably took place around these years of transition. I take the year 909 to be close to the "last breath" of the Classic period, occurring just at the time a major change was happening far to the north.[1]

RESURGENCE IN YUCATÁN

At the same time, in the ninth and tenth centuries, the northern regions experienced a significant boom in political and religious significance, perhaps with the help of populations moving in from the south. We have seen how Uxmal emerged as the dominant center in the Puuc region around this time, the focal point of authority in western Yucatán, and how Chichen Itza began as an important center farther to the east. Both sites can be seen as attempting to inject a new life and energy into the old system. By the mid-800s, Uxmal was the center of a large regional polity with a dynastic ruler yet with art and architecture that channeled a new "international" awareness, alongside practical innovations in politics, economy, and ideology. Chichen Itza had seen its own quick development at the same time, alongside the demise of the nearby Classic dynastic centers of Ek Balam and Coba. But Chichen Itza was different from Uxmal in many respects, smaller in size (at the beginning, at least) and with shrines devoted to a cult of divine ancestors and warriors, as we have seen. For centuries, its primary role was as a religious site and pilgrimage center focused on its great cenote (Figure 12.1). Then, after 800, it became a regional political center, probably spurred on by the new religious and political movements we see at the end of the Classic period, as the old dynasties weakened.

Soon Chichen Itza transformed itself even further, becoming the singular focus for a new movement that channeled foreign interests and ideas. Massive new constructions of temples, plazas, and gathering spaces were added, particularly to the north of the Maya buildings that were only slightly earlier by a few decades. Some of these buildings were covered with imagery of foreign militarism, with warriors bearing spear throwers (atlatls) and wearing distinctive foreign regalia (Figure 12.2). Their representations dominate the Great Ballcourt and the so-called

FIGURE 12.1. The great cenote of Chichen Itza, called *Ukha'nal* or *Ukhabnal*. Photograph by Nelda Issa Marengo.

Temple of the Warriors—two monumental buildings without precedent in the Maya world. In some places, the warriors are individually named with hieroglyphic labels, but in a script that is not Maya and rather uses a writing system like that of the later Aztecs of the Late Postclassic era. It is possible that this script, like the new iconography we see, had its roots in central Mexico or among cultures on the Gulf Coast. Their individual identities must have been important, resonating with the history of that era. Many of the buildings are also covered in the powerful images of feathered serpents. We see this most in the "Castillo" of Chichen Itza, still known in Landa's time as the Temple of K'uk'ulkan ("Feathered Snake"). The balustrades of its northern stairway, as well as the columns of its upper temple, are carved as descending feathered serpents. Taken together, these new architectural elements evoke a decidedly non-Maya, or nonlocal, flavor. But it wasn't a complete overlay of new over old, for in many places we still see the mosaic masks of Puuc style integrated

FIGURE 12.2. Foreign warriors and deities portrayed in the Temple of the Warriors, Chichén Itzá. Drawing by Linda Schele, courtesy of LACMA.

with this new imagery or even familiar elements of Maya iconography. There is an imposition of a new ideology and art over what was before, but it is not a wholesale replacement of the Maya by foreigners. It is this mix that makes Chichen Itza so compelling—and so complex for us archaeologists.

As noted earlier, a persistent problem is understanding Chichen Itza's chronology, seeing just when these changes and cultural patterns occur amid the overall mixture of Maya and external "Mexican" features. In the early years of research, it was thought there was a simply a before-and-after sequence to the Maya and "Mexican" elements, what is sometimes called "Old Chichen" and "New Chichen." One represented the Late Classic Maya, followed by the "invasion" of outsiders, possibly identifiable as "Toltecs." This also resonated with local histories that emphasized the arrival of outsiders to Yucatán, sometimes called the Itza. The great Mayanist Alfred Tozzer was an advocate for this view in the mid-twentieth century, and it emerged for a time as the standard model. Ceramic changes seemed to support this view, too. In Yucatán, a collection of pottery wares known as Cehpech was commonly found at Puuc sites, and a much more localized Sotuta type was found mostly at Chichen Itza. Long ago these were considered sequential ceramic phases, one following the other. More recent studies and refined chronologies make it clear, however, that these ceramic types overlap a great deal, at least for much of their history. In other words, if we imagine Uxmal at its height between 850 and 950, we might entertain that the first iterations of "Toltec Chichen" date to the same time. Within Chichen itself, it turns out that many aspects of "old" and "new" represent "the same Chichen." The ceramics from the Initial Series Group, located to the south of Las Monjas and the Caracol, in "Old Chichen," suggest little chronological distinction from the major architectural monuments on the Great Terrace and its Temple of K'uk'ulkan. While not exactly contemporaneous in construction, these and other areas of the site were occupied and used concurrently between about 900 and 1100.[2]

But not everything at Chichen overlaps. The early Maya structures in the Puuc style, including the ancestral shrines at the Monjas and other buildings, have hieroglyphic inscriptions that we can date precisely between 850 and 890. Other architectural monuments appear to be later, including the major monuments once ascribed to "New Chichen," such as the Temple of the Warriors, the Great Ballcourt, and the Temple of K'uk'ulkan. Other structures may be even later still, including some showing Maya elements. The overall picture is one of cosmopolitanism, a city with a complex internal history involving a coexistence and give-and-take among different peoples and maybe even different governors. The chronology of all of this at Chichen is still remarkably compressed.

Almost all of what we see on the surface was built in a 250-year span, before 1100. A Maya center from 800 to 890, it was like other "Puuc" cities in some respects, transforming into a new and much bigger hybrid community that incorporated foreign elements alongside overlapping Maya styles and iconography.[3]

It took an outside force to have these trends coalesce into something innovative. They were elites and warriors from the west, fellow Mesoamericans yet difficult to identify. I would hesitate to call them "Toltec," as some have, for this term is highly specific in its cultural connection to the ruins at Tula, in the distant highlands of Hidalgo, Mexico. Tula was long thought to be the origin place for the newcomers to Yucatán, based on the clear cultural and artistic connections between the two cities. But, as some have suggested, some of the so-called "Toltec" art and architecture at Chichen Itza might predate what we see in Tula. In other words, the site of Tula in highland Mexico may have been inspired by religious developments in the Maya region, in a scenario that "flips" the traditional model. The timing of it all presents a difficult question to resolve.[4]

The outsiders who established a new system of political and military dominance at Chichen Itza in the late ninth century may somehow relate to the curious individuals who stand out within very late history of the Peten, mentioned at Nakum, Uaxactun, and Ucanal, after about 830. These include Papamalil, Wat'ulk'atel, and Olom, along with many others whose names we have lost. They too have an obscure origin, but they need not be from a place as distant as Tula. As Simon Martin suggests, it is equally plausible that these historical characters came from areas more adjacent to the Maya region, just to the west, in the coastal regions of what are today Tabasco and Veracruz. The "foreigners" may be from the edges of the Maya world, in other words, and therefore not quite so removed from the dynamics of Maya culture and history as we might at first think. Eric Thompson and other early scholars proposed to call these people the "Putun Maya," perhaps equivalent to the historical populations who speak a Mayan language called Chontal. Both archaeology and historical records from the colonial period suggest that they were coastal traders and merchants who, by the end of the Classic period, had developed close connections throughout Mesoamerica. Their increasing presence in the Maya political world may foretell their eventual roles as power brokers at Chichen and elsewhere once the old Classic system had collapsed for good.[5]

We can interpret their influence in light of events and trends occurring in this same region. Tabasco and the coast of the Gulf of Mexico are where we see some of the first disruptions and instabilities among kingdoms of the Classic period, including Palenque. These may have been among the earliest courtly centers to fall, just as wars were spreading and expanding toward the east. It was here, too, at Comalcalco where we encountered the singular written account of severe drought and famine, taking place in the 780s. That may have spurred the displacement of many people and the political instabilities of the following decades. The emergence of newly powerful figures from this same western region, on the edge of the Maya world, would seem to be connected to these historical patterns.

The new kind of art arose at Chichen Itza after 900, emphasizing war and militarism even more explicitly than we see even at the end of the Classic era. The sculptures of the Great Ballcourt and Temple of the Warriors are the most imposing displays of military might from anywhere in the Maya world. Adjacent to the former, perhaps integral to it, is a large platform decorated with carved images of human skulls attached to poles. This was probably the foundation for an actual construction of this sort, for the display of row upon row of skulls of executed prisoners—a *tzompantli,* as the later Aztecs would call such constructions. The great Ballcourt, with its arena, long sidewalls, and paired stone rings, may look like other ballcourts we see elsewhere, but it is truly vast in its scale and design, the largest of any such court in all of Mesoamerica. I suspect this architectural wonder was a "symbolic ballcourt" more than an actual one, a venue for gladiatorial performance and for executions (hence the nearby skull-racks). Chichen Itza's entire central ceremonial area, adjacent to the great cenote, crystalized myth, and cosmos, and a new ideology of miliary power in ways the Classic Maya would have been familiar with, yet on a vastly different scale. It stands as a reflection of the violent political environment out of which this all was forged in the final decades of the "old order." Chichen Itza presents itself as an imperial capital, a centralized conquest state that reached across much of Yucatán, with warriors and captives everywhere.

Added to the mix at Chichen Itza were new and powerful cosmological symbols, no longer concerned with the passage of the k'atuns and other cycles. One featured motif was the feathered serpent, a clear reference to K'uk'ulkan, whom the Aztecs would later call Quetzalcoatl. By the Late Postclassic images of this fantastic creature were used as symbols of rulership and authority, channeling an old icon that has its roots many centuries earlier at Teotihuacan, where it was featured prominently in its architectural decoration and in mural paintings. Early Maya art also shows feathered serpents, as embodying the sea as well as earthly waters. The appearance of K'uk'ulkan as a religious and political symbol in Yucatán and elsewhere after 900 represents a new ideology, reasserting an old, powerful icon under a new military regime. The great cenote of Chichen Itza played a role in this, I believe, for it was always the city's religious focal point, the pilgrimage site called Ukha'nal. We will recall that, in Classic Maya art, this was the place where the Maize God was resurrected after death, associated with a being known as Water Serpent, sometimes depicted as a feathery snake.

Chichen Itza's unique and imposing cenote, a wide hole into the watery "otherworld," had always been a profoundly sacred place. Now, its role was renewed and repurposed in the wake of the old Classic order, as it came to be appropriated by a group of powerful outsiders as the epicenter in a new ideological, political, and commercial system. I suspect the great cenote was the main attraction all along, a powerful draw for elites even as the political and cultural world was rapidly changing. Chichen's ambitious design might have even been a conscious effort to re-create a new cultural center—a "new Teotihuacan"—in the wake of all the collapses, a much-needed place of religious and political authority in the Maya world. It is perhaps no accident that the official role we find emphasized in Chichen Itza's texts—Yajawk'ahk', "Lord of Fire"—was in the Classic Maya world as closely linked to Teotihuacan as its symbolism. In this way, Chichen may not have been quite so radically different, new, or out of place but rather a re-creation of an older legacy of militarism and of certain religious ideas.

The larger history of Mesoamerica is, after all, full of cycles and revisitations to the past. During the tenth and eleventh centuries, Chichen Itza was the dominant political center of the region, but it was also a radical experiment, built to express a newly forged ideology of warfare, sacrifice, and sacred water. It represented an idea that later Mesoamerican histories cite using the concept of a *Tollan*, the Nahuatl name meaning "Place of Bulrushes," referring to an idealized place of origin and political authority. Tollan was cited often by the Aztecs and by later Maya groups as the origin place for Postclassic lineages and ruling families. From that name we get the word *Toltec*, "a person of Tollan," which in the late histories of Mexico referred to a learned person, an artist, or any civilized person who channeled the aesthetics of the past.[6] The Aztecs may have considered Teotihuacan as the "original" Tollan, and Tula itself took on this role. (*Tula* is a shortened form of *Tollan.*) So was Cholula, near modern Puebla, Mexico, also a very ancient city with a pyramid dedicated to Quetzalcoatl. As several scholars have proposed, Chichen Itza was also probably conceived as a "Tollan" in its day, serving much the same role as Teotihuacan did in the more ancient past. This is when the Early Postclassic era truly began, and the Classic system of Maya courts was no more.

The cultural synergy expressed at Chichen Itza and Tula forged new ideologies and images that came to be emulated by later Postclassic Mesoamerican rulers. The later art incorporated elements of Classic Maya iconography, such as the solar disc and the celestial band, which were soon adopted into central Mexican iconography in following centuries. The Aztecs, the self-proclaimed inheritors of the Toltec legacy, ended up channeling much of this visual culture as well, and it is interesting to see how symbols originally from the Classic Maya were often reenvisioned in Aztec symbolism. One good example is the famous Sun Stone or Calendar Stone of Tenochtitlan, a solar disc that ultimately owes its form to representations found at Chichen Itza, which can be traced to even earlier Maya precedents. We are still teasing apart the ways that Late

Postclassic cultures in highland Mexico recycled many elements of Maya art, much like the Maya reutilized visual forms from Teotihuacan. Ideas and images moved back and forth across Mesoamerica for centuries.

THE MAYAPAN CONFEDERACY

Chichen Itza's later history is lost to us, adding yet another layer to the Great Rupture in the historical memory of the Classic period. The old place figures prominently in the later Maya histories of the sixteenth century and in Landa's *Relación*, but the accounts are notoriously garbled and inconsistent. Some say the ancient city had been "founded by three brothers" who ruled jointly and later warred with one another. If true, it only highlights its structural distinctiveness from the Classic era. As for the Itza lineage, also "founders" in some sources, the Yucatán chronicles emphasize how they were foreigners "who speak our language brokenly." Many scholars took this to mean that the Itza were those "Toltec" outsiders who came from distant Mexico or from the Gulf Coast regions, but this is not necessarily the case. I believe it far more likely that the Itza of Yucatán's history were not "Toltecs" or "Mexican" but very Maya.[7] Its strongest historical connections are outside Yucatán, far to the south, to the central Peten region. This is reflected in the name of the great lake near Tikal, Lake *Peten Itza* ("Lake of the Itza"). The small island in what we know today as Flores was, at the time of the Spanish invasion, Taitza', ("At the (Place of) the Itza"), or Tayasal. There, Hernán Cortés encountered the Itza ruler named Kanek' on his march to Honduras in 1524. All of this strongly suggests that the Itza were Maya, and they may have had little to do in the end with the complex issue of identifying "Mexican" foreigners in the history of Chichen Itza. They can be historically linked to the lake area, and it seems that a faction of them traveled north into Yucatán during the Postclassic era, perhaps lending the site its name only at that time.

The name *Itza* is also contested in the history of the Classic period in this same region. One intriguing reference comes from an Early Classic vessel from the Peten, dating to about 400 CE, which notes a Maya ruler who was an *Itza' ajaw*, "an Itza lord," spelling it clearly as **i-tza-a** (Figure 12.3). While difficult to track, I have wondered if this name could be related to that of the ancient kingdom we know as Ik'a' ("Windy Waters"), which was based on Late Peten Itza during the Classic period, at the important ruins known today as Tayasal, (from "Ta-Itza'").[8] Ik'a' was likely the name of the vast lake itself, and as a royal emblem it appears in some of the oldest texts we have from the Early Classic. (By the late seventh century, a ruler of the Ik'a' kingdom named Tayel Chank'inich was subject to Jasaw Chank'awil of Tikal during its resurgence against the Kanul lords.) The surname *Itza* still exists in many towns in Yucatán and in Guatemala to this day.[9]

FIGURE 12.3. The hieroglyph for *Itza'*, ca. 400 CE, from an early Peten vase. Drawing by the author.

Chichen Itza's domination of Yucatán ended around 1100 or 1200, perhaps even earlier. The city had a short life, with its major architecture constructed only within a three-hundred-year span—far shorter than we see in other Maya ruins. The cenote continued to be a major pilgrimage site for people from great distances, much as it had been during the Classic era and earlier. In its depths archaeologists found ritual incense burners and many other artifacts from the Late Postclassic and probably from historical times too. The sacred site persisted despite the political changes and turmoil. The social and political world of Yucatán had fragmented once more, and the history of this era becomes very difficult to grapple with, for, aside from archaeology, our only sources are the chronicles in the *Books of Chilam Balam*, a series of Indigenous accounts compiled in various versions during the decades and centuries after the Spanish invasion. These give us a framework for understanding much of Postclassic Yucatán's history, but their contents are highly inconsistent, even contradictory at times. The books were also instrumental in early efforts to understand the structure of the ancient calendar, as Pío Pérez and Stephens recognized in the mid-nineteenth century. Despite what some have claimed, these records, focused on the major lineages of Postclassic Yucatán, offer scant connections to the deeper past of the

Classic period. The most important section is the *u kahlay katunoob*, or the "Remembrance of the K'atuns," where history is divided into the familiar twenty-year periods we have often seen employed in the ancient accounts of the Classic period. The cyclical nature of the k'atuns explains some of their frustrating aspects as historical records. They are not a linear sequence of periods and events that we can simply extend back in time, but more likely involve the repetitions of the same k'atuns, emphasizing the histories of different locales.[10] Time, in other words, may be more compressed than it might seem at first, reflecting the Maya sensibility of history as cyclical and repetitious.

In time, one lineage with deep roots in Yucatán, the Cocom, emerged as the most powerful. In the messy aftermath of Chichen Itza's demise, it strong-armed other noble families into establishing a new capital, sometimes called a "confederacy," at a capital it came to call Mayapan.[11] Notably, the place name is a hybrid of Maya and Nahuatl, which by this time had emerged as a lingua franca among elites in much of Mesoamerica. Meaning the "Wall of Maya," it refers to the imposing defensive wall that surrounds the city, and *Maya* was a name for the larger region of Yucatán, setting the stage for its use today. The ruins of Mayapan, located ninety-three kilometers to the west of Chichen, is a place of profound historical importance. As a collective effort among different lineages, Mayapan represented the last large-scale political movement by the later Maya in Yucatán.[12]

In its conception, Mayapan seems to be an idealized revival of Chichen Itza and its past glory, assuming a similar role as *the* central place of Yucatán, both politically and religiously. It even included a central temple with radiating staircases, replicating the great Temple of K'uk'ulkan (Figure 12.4). The Itza lineage still had ties to Chichen Itza and its cenote, giving the place the name ("Well of the Itzas") by which we know it today. Their claim of that old grandeur may have derived from their original identity as southern foreigners with deeper roots in southern Maya history. Other ruling lineages in the Mayapan confederacy also probably had distant historical connections to the great courts of the Classic period. One lineage was named Kanul, who members were also said to be old outsiders who came from the south. It is no stretch

FIGURE 12.4. The central area of Mayapan, late capital of Yucatán. Photograph by Jean-Pierre Courau.

at all to think they were descendants of the Classic-era Kanul dynasty we know all too well from the old histories of Dzibanche and Calakmul. Both the Itza and the Kanuls may have had direct ties to the old Classic period order in the southern region, having migrated northward into Yucatán after the fall of the Classic period kingdoms. Another prominent lineage that participated in the league of Mayapan was the Xiu, whose members are said to have had their own strong historical roots in Uxmal and the Puuc region. Their name is probably from Nahuatl (Xihuitl), suggesting yet another group of outsiders with ties to central Mexico. In both history and ideology, the ruling families of Mayapan were much like others throughout Maya history, relying on these outside connections, real or imagined, as a way of defining their rule and authority.[13]

These complex backstories among the elite families should sound familiar. The idea of "outsiders" who established positions of rulership in the Maya area was an old trope that we have already seen, even in the earliest historical records we have from the Classic period (the "West Kalomte'"). Such claims to the outside continued to serve a powerful political message over the course of a thousand years. But for the later Maya, some of these origin stories relied on a real sense that there existed an earlier phase to Maya civilization, to the Classic period itself. The Itza and the Kanuls were presumably very conscious of their own legacy and connections to that deeper past, more so than many later Maya groups. Landa gave a strong hit of this when he noted:

> The Indians relate that from the south there came into Yucatán many people with their lords, and it seems they came from Chiapas, although the Indians do not know this. But the author conjectures thus because many words and verbal constructions are the same in Chiapas and in Yucatán, and there is much evidence in Chiapas of sites that have been abandoned. They say that these people wandered for forty years through the uninhabited regions of Yucatán, without there being any water there except for the rains, that at the end of that time they reached the mountains that lie almost opposite the city of Mayapan, ten leagues from it, and here they began to settle and put up very fine buildings in many places.[14]

The "very fine buildings" near the mountains or hills is surely a reference to Uxmal and the nearby sites of the Puuc region. Portions of this story are apocryphal, but Landa is making an important and genuine observation here about the awareness of a southern connection of "many people and their lords," including the rulers of Mayapan. For Landa, "Chiapas" meant the region to the south of Yucatán, where there were speakers of Ch'olan and Tzeltalan, as there are today. The "much evidence" of "sites that have been abandoned" is a remarkable statement for a Spanish priest writing in the sixteenth century, showing that reports of intriguing ruins had already spread far and wide. Here he may well be referring to Palenque or Tonina. The key point in all of this is to realize that there may be some truth behind the idea that the late ruling families of Yucatán were rooted in the much older histories of the south and central lowlands. In this way, Mayapan was a culmination of many previous efforts to revive an idealized past, to keep cycling through history as before. It also pooled the diverse narratives of distant origins within a single regional capital, lending it even more stature as an expression of Maya rulership and its deep legacy.

In his *Relación,* Landa had this to say about the remote past, the calendar, and Mayapan:

> According to the reckoning of the Indians it has been 120 years since Mayapan was abandoned. In the plaza of that city are to be found seven or eight stones, each ten feet high, round on one side, well worked and containing several characters they use, so worn away by the rain as to be unreadable, although they are thought to be a record of the foundation and destruction of that city. . . . The natives, when asked what they were, replied that they were accustomed to setting one up every twenty years, which is the number by which they count their time periods.[15]

Landa is here describing a very old and traditional way of marking time with the erection of stelae—a tradition that had started in the beginnings of the Classic period. The sole Mayapan stela that has survived, Stela 1, indeed bears a scene that strongly resembles one of the "k'atun pages" from an ancient Maya book known as the *Paris Codex.* Its long text is now illegible (perhaps painted rather than carved), but below we see an enthroned god, the "lord of the k'atun," labeled by the 10 Ahau glyph in the scene. This most likely corresponds to 11.11.0.0.0 10 Ahau 3 Mac, or April 13, 1441. This would place it at the "height" of Mayapan's power and influence, yet shortly before its own demise.

The chronicles are explicit in attributing the fall of the city to internal strife among the members of the alliance, when the Xiu grew resentful of the Cocom and waged war against them, leading to the city's abandonment. Once again, we see fraught politics among ruling families at the heart of a collapse, in this case of a late capital and its political order. Members of the Mayapan confederacy retreated to their smaller home centers—the Xiu to the town of Mani, the Cocoms to Sotuta. Another major faction within the old Mayapan alliance were the Itza themselves, who left and returned to their old homeland in the Peten, to Tayasal (today known as Flores). A fractured political landscape was once again prevalent in Yucatán and in the Maya lowlands. This is what greeted the

Spanish invaders who first encountered Yucatán in the first half of the sixteenth century. Unlike central Mexico with its imperial capital at Tenochtitlan, there was no centralized place for the Spaniards to conquer, only a complex assemblage of rulers and territories, many in conflict with one another. This led to a long, protracted history of conquest in the Maya lowlands that took decades, arguably centuries, to play out.

Early archaeologists characterized the Late Postclassic era of Mayapan as "decadent," a period of steady decline leading up to the Spanish invasion of the sixteenth century. Even the very names "Classic" and "Postclassic" reflected an idea of a protracted "down gradient."[16] Most sites were indeed smaller by comparison, public buildings were less monumental in scale, and stone inscriptions ceased to be produced. Tatiana Proskouriakoff noted that the late Maya of Yucatán, leading up to the Spanish invasion, represented "a dramatic culmination of a long process of cultural decay."[17] Writing about the same time, Eric Thompson wrote that "the picture of the last six centuries of Maya history is somewhat disheartening . . . the story of a series of declines in art, architecture, and religion, due primarily to the deviation into militarism."[18] He would later say even more forcefully that the later years of the Postclassic represented "a manifestation of great cultural dislocation resulting from a shift from a hierarchic to a secular and militaristic culture."[19] Given what we have learned of Classic period history since Thompson's day, it is easy to see that Thompson was very mistaken in his characterization of the Classic as non-militaristic. And one only needs to look at the myriad incense burners and temples of Mayapan to reject any notion that the Postclassic Maya were in any way more "secular." It is difficult to gauge exactly what "decay" or "decline" meant to earlier scholars, other than a supposed absence of the old elite hallmarks of the Classic period—writing, large-scale monuments, realistic painting and sculpture, and so on. Those existed too. Today, we understand the Postclassic era in a different and far more nuanced way, as one more reformulation of Maya culture, always adapting and on the move with the circumstances and often in negotiations with persistent outsiders.

That process of course continued with the most persistent outsiders of all: the Spanish invaders of Yucatán and Guatemala. And here our history of the ancient Maya will need to find closure. One of the valuable Maya chronicles, *The Chilam Balam of Tizimin,* included a record of the arrival of Francisco de Montejo, noting that "11 Ahau was the first k'atun, the start of the k'atun count. In the first part of the k'atun, the white men arrived." This k'atun ending corresponds to 11.16.0.0.0 13 Ahau 8 Xul, or November 5, 1539. Yet another k'atun had come, and another wave of foreigners along with it, this time from the east. It reads like so many other changes that came and went throughout the course of Maya history, but this is the most transformational episode of all and one that has continued to be negotiated in the past five centuries. Many Maya communities continued for generations to keep records of their past, copying and recopying their books and chronicles. And some kept copies of the hieroglyphic books, perhaps even not knowing what the old drawings and characters meant.

THE LAST KINGDOM

Early Spanish chroniclers such as Diego de Landa were very aware of the cycles of the k'atuns and of the influences they exerted. Landa even included a circular diagram or "wheel" of the thirteen k'atun cycles in his sixteenth-century *Relación,* presented essentially as a map of the world with the periods of the k'atun grafted onto the world directions (east is at the top, represented as a cross, toward Jerusalem) (Figure 12.5). The periods of time and history were inherently cosmological and cyclical. In the center of the diagram is Landa's comment "In their language they call this count *uazlazon katun,* which means the war of the k'atuns." Landa's reading is mistaken, for the Maya phrase translates as "the turn of the k'atuns." Landa can be forgiven here, for *k'atun* was not only the name of the twenty-year period but also a word for "war" (the words have different origins.) Landa's mistake may be revealing nonetheless, suggesting that the cycles of warfare were embedded into history, much like the repeating cycles of time.

He and many other early Spanish friars in Yucatán were very interested in the ancient calendar, understanding its singular importance in

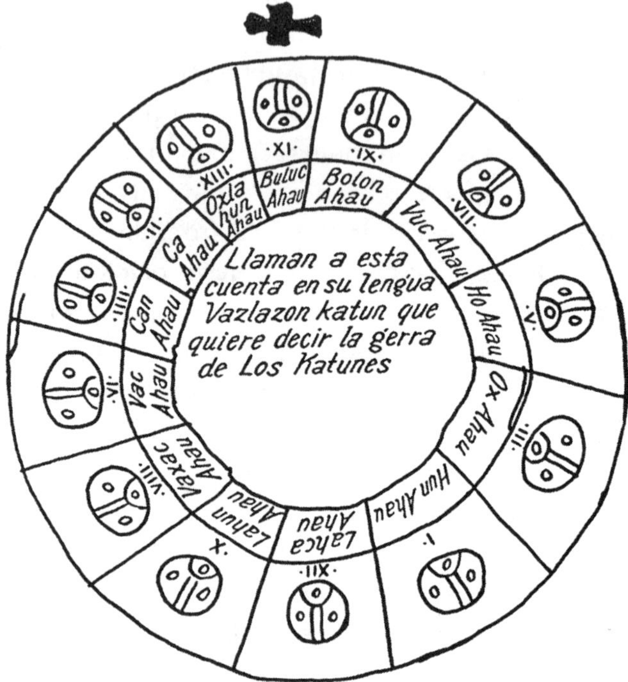

FIGURE 12.5. Maya time and space, the "Turn of the k'atuns," from the manuscript of Landa's *Relación*. The thirteen Ahau glyphs represent the twenty-year periods.

religious life. And they also looked for ways it could serve their own purposes. This became most important in the seventeenth century, when Spanish authorities were involved in repeated efforts to "reduce" or conquer the very last Maya kingdom, centered in the Itza capital of Tayasal, on Lake Peten Itza. This had been established (or reestablished) after the Itza migration from Yucatán following the fall of Mayapan. By the late 1400s, the Itza were established as rulers of the entire central Peten, maintaining a network of alliances around the lakes. The Itza kingdom was perhaps even a regional state, larger than any of the contemporary polities that formed in Yucatán. As the colonial worlds of New Spain and Yucatán took shape, the Itza of the lake district remained relatively isolated from Spanish authority, and alone they kept their independence.

Early on, in 1524, Tayasal and its ruler Kanek' had been visited by none other than Hernán Cortés, who was passing through the Peten on his audacious journey to quell a compatriot's rebellion in Honduras. A famous story told by Cortés at the time is that he had to leave behind one of his prized horses, which had become lame. Kanek' and the other Maya at Tayasal promised to care for the animal, the like of which they had never seen before. Nearly a century later, in 1617, a Franciscan priest just newly arrived from Spain, Fray Juan de Orbita, set out from Mérida for the long walk to Tayasal, hoping to convince the current Itza ruler that the time was approaching for him to submit himself to Spanish rule and to the Christian faith. Orbita apparently understood that in 1678 a new k'atun was to arrive, k'atun 3 Ahau, and with it a possible prophecy that would lead to change. He quickly immersed himself in the arcane elements of Maya timekeeping and prophecy, probably with the aid of numerous treatises and documents now lost. Whether Orbita knew it or not, k'atun 3 Ahau was also the turn of the four-hundred-year bak'tun, or 12.0.0.0.0 as an earlier Maya priest would have represented it. Orbita reached Tayasal, initiating what would turn out to be long, protracted conversations about prophecy with Canek and his council. These led to some success, and Orbita returned to Mérida with 150 converts from Tayasal, along with several nobles who served as a diplomatic delegation.

Orbita organized another trip that same year, this time in the company of another Franciscan named Bartolomé de Fuensalida, a fervent man with few social skills. Upon their arrival at Tayasal, Orbita and Fuensalida were shown a venerated stone statue representing, of all things, a horse. This was the idol of Tziminchaak ("Tapir of Thunder"), the name they had bestowed on the horse Cortés had left. The Maya of Tayasal, seeing the animal a sacred being, offered it turkey, fish, and flowers, and it soon perished for want of food. Its stone image was made, and the idol was placed in its own shrine (one way to "take care" of a horse, I suppose). Fray Orbita was reportedly so appalled at the sight of the idol that he destroyed it then and there, leading to great consternation among the Itza nobles. The situation calmed in time, and the two priests resumed their discussions with Kanek'. Central to their claims once again was that the k'atun was turning over and now was the proper time to convert. Kanek' responded, "The time had not yet arrived in which their ancient priests had prophesized that they would have to give up the worship of their gods, for the age at which they were in the present time was that which they call oxahau (3 Ahau), (which means third age) and the one that had been indicated to them was not approaching so soon."[20] That future age was evidently k'atun 8 Ahau, which would come in 1697. Soon Orbita and Fuensalida were chased out of Tayasal, lucky to escape with their lives.

This left an opportunity for another Franciscan priest, Fray Andrés de Avendaño, who came four k'atuns later. After years of stalemate and cautious back-and-forths, Avendaño made his own incursions into the Peten from far-away Mérida, and new conversations began with the Itza lords, picking up on the same points of timing and k'atun counts that Orbita and Fuensalida had initiated. The current ruler of the Itza, a new Kanek', was more receptive this time around and acknowledged the old prophecies. It is likely that this Canek was eager at any rate to make peaceful relations with the Spanish, whose armies were now making inroads throughout the Peten. And he was clearly willing to open trade routes with Yucatán, where his forebears once ruled. Opportunism worked on both sides of these negotiations. Inner conflicts and debates within the court and among old Itza allies led to a fracturing among the Maya stakeholders, and the attacks by the Spanish armies soon began. Tayasal fell in 1697, not long after the passing of the k'atun on 8 Ahau. Just four years later, an account of its conquest was published in Madrid in 1701 (Figure 12.6).[21]

The Itza polity was the last independent Maya kingdom. Taking the long view of history, there is reason to think that it had been founded, or re-founded, on the great lake named "Windy Waters" in the center of the Maya world, a place that was considered the old homeland of the Itza lineage. They had ruled in Yucatán for generations, but before that, their roots may have gone back to the Classic period, to the Ik'a' kingdom whose ruined palaces and temples are just a few hundred meters away, at the site we call Tayasal. An even more ancient part of the surrounding area was Nixtun Ch'ich', the major Middle Preclassic center only a short distance on the lake's western shore. Standing today on the shore of old

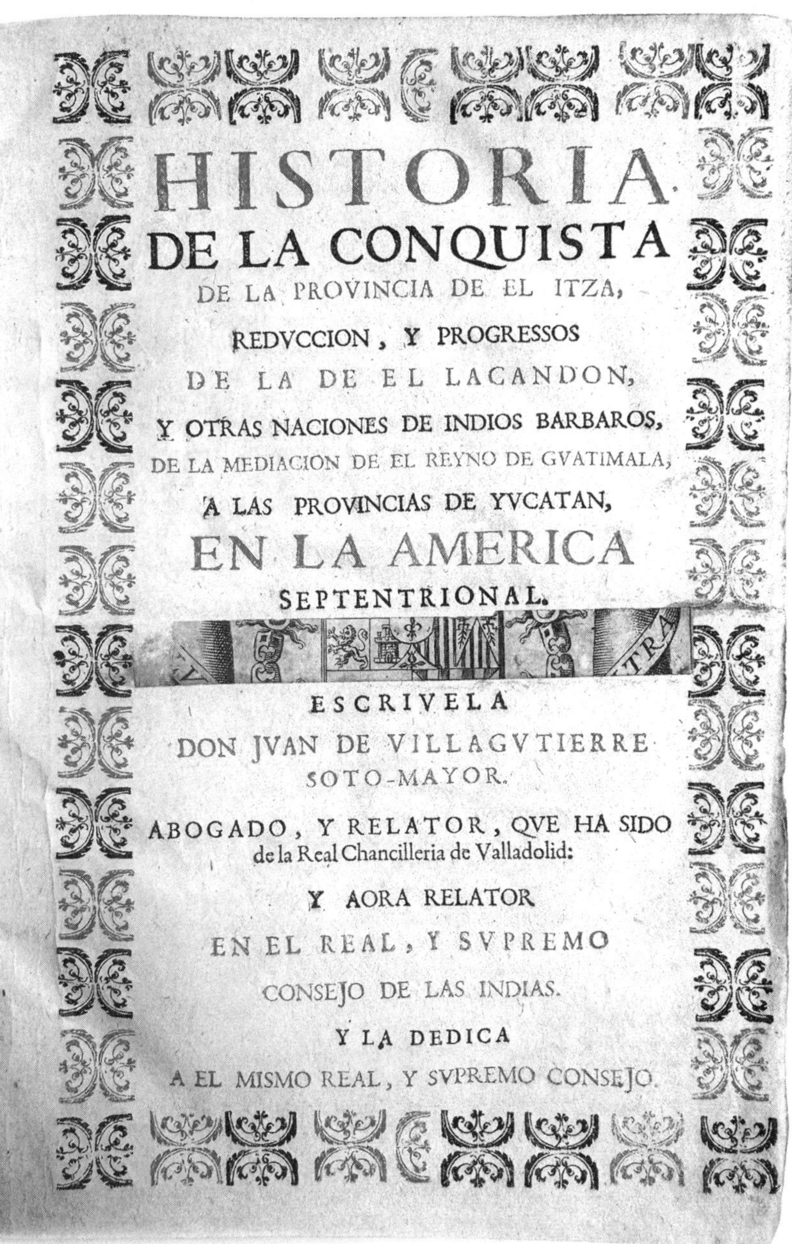

HISTORIA
DE LA CONQUISTA
DE LA PROVINCIA DE EL ITZA,
REDVCCION, Y PROGRESSOS
DE LA DE EL LACANDON,
Y OTRAS NACIONES DE INDIOS BARBAROS,
DE LA MEDIACION DE EL REYNO DE GVATIMALA,
A LAS PROVINCIAS DE YVCATAN,
EN LA AMERICA
SEPTENTRIONAL.

ESCRIVELA
DON JVAN DE VILLAGVTIERRE
SOTO-MAYOR.
ABOGADO, Y RELATOR, QVE HA SIDO
de la Real Chancilleria de Valladolid:
Y AORA RELATOR
EN EL REAL, Y SVPREMO
CONSEJO DE LAS INDIAS.
Y LA DEDICA
A EL MISMO REAL, Y SVPREMO CONSEJO.

FIGURE 12.6. Title page from Villagutierre Soto-Mayor's *Historia de la Conquista de el Itza,* 1701.

Tayasal, on the island town we know today as Flores, one can see all these places at once, taking in the wide spectrum of Maya history—different places where rulers and kings reigned and where centers of power came and went. The long comings and goings of settlements and kingdoms on this lake show us that, at least for some Maya, some places never experienced much of rupture at all.

CHAPTER 13

Rises and Falls

BY THE EIGHTEENTH century, the destructive nature of the invasion had taken its toll, and the rupture in the deep historical memory of the Maya widened into a massive rift. The first recorded explorations of Maya ruins began at Palenque only a century after the fall of the Itza kingdom. Still, all was not erased or forgotten. I am reminded of this through a revealing incident related by John Lloyd Stephens, which took place during his explorations in Yucatán in 1841. One day after documenting the great buildings of Uxmal, Stephens found himself in the nearby town of Ticul, where he also came upon many ruined mounds "of the same character." Here he was determined to find an ancient burial, something that had so far eluded him throughout his investigations and that he hoped would shed light on the questions of the antiquity of the mysterious ruins and of their builders. With the local *cura*, or priest, and a team of Maya workmen, Stephens set about excavating a small pyramid in a cornfield. Soon they came upon a buried skeleton, well preserved. Stephens took note of the reaction of the men: "The Indians were excited and conversed in low tones. The cura interpreted what they said, and the burden of it was 'They are the bones of our kinsmen' and 'What will our kinsmen say at dragging forth his bones!'"[1] Stephens had just seen Uxmal, a place shrouded in mystery. Now, as he listened to his helpers, he felt there was no question who Uxmal's builders were. They were the ancestors of these men, the *uchben maakoob'* ("ancient people"). What still eluded everyone that day, looking on the old bones, was any sense that those ancient kinsmen might have a history to someday tell. Now, nearly two centuries later, many of their words and the stories of their time have come a little bit back to life.

When embarking on my journey in Maya archaeology in the late 1970s, the idea that one might study the fabric of ancient Maya history in any detail was still unimaginable or at best some futuristic ideal. Despite a few important breakthroughs back then, the ancient Maya remained mostly "prehistoric." This was still the case through much of the 1980s, as I entered graduate school and worked on field projects at Copan and Dos Pilas. In those days, we could identify a few name glyphs and a few historical events, but reading the inscriptions presented more of a challenge. "History" still only applied to colonial documents, the texts written down after the invasion in Spanish or a Mayan language. Those that contained details of pre-Columbian people and events were compelling, as we have just seen, but as retrospective accounts, they were piecemeal, incomplete, and often contradictory. Now with the decipherment of the script, ancient Maya history has broken through the long-lasting barriers, revealing a deeper past spanning some two thousand years.

This book has presented details and narratives of this newly revealed Maya history and frames that history within a new model of long-term development, rejecting any idea that there was a single "rise and fall" of Maya civilization. The old bell-curve trajectory that spans the two thousand years from the Preclassic to the Spanish invasion gives two false impressions. For one, it simplistically depicts Maya culture as reaching its height and heading on its way out not long before the conquests of Alvarado and Montejo. The idea of a "diminished" or "decadent" Maya world perhaps even implies an inevitability to the Spanish invasion, a self-fulfilling prophecy. The same might be said for the highly romanticized notion of "lost cities," some of which are still being revealed today. Their very existence quickly conjures up interest in the so-called "collapse" of Maya civilization in the ninth and tenth centuries. Our assumptions have often missed the point, not considering a wealth of new information from written and archaeological sources.

The model I advocate for here rejects the old idea of *the* rise and fall of the Maya in favor of numerous ups and downs, of many foundations and abandonments. Maya history shows us a story of communities being founded, experiencing a period of vibrancy and importance, and then ending, with their leaders and residents deciding to move on to other places. This dynamic operated at all levels of society and on numerous scales, reflecting an important aspect of Maya cultural history that I see as a "persistent impermanence" of place. What we can glean from the detailed narratives of the Classic period presented here, during the supposed "apogee" of everything, reveals in fact a precarious existence, evident at nearly all scales: households, hamlets, communities, courts, cities, and city-states. Cities could be politically and economically stable and vital for long stretches of time, but instability and demise were seen as almost always in the cards. Few centers of authority or concentrations of population existed for more than a few centuries. And once "done," such places tended to be left and forgotten, even centuries before archaeologists would show up to consider the meanings and explanations of what led to "collapse." The patterns reveal a Maya or Mesoamerican sense of place where permanence and stationary existence never made much sense, for whatever reasons. This was a fundamental aspect of ancient Maya life that was even noticed by Fray Diego de Landa, who wrote: "There are in Yucatán many beautiful buildings, which is the most remarkable thing that has been found in the Indies.... The reasons... may be that the towns changed their location for some reason, and so wherever they settled they bult anew their temples, sanctuaries, and houses for their lords."[2]

Even in places with permanent water and good living—I think here of the beautiful Lake Peten Itza—we find a sequence of major power centers that come and go over time. People were rooted to the area, surely, but communities and polities seem somehow malleable. Why didn't Nixtun Ch'ich' grow and develop into a city over the long haul? Why was the Classic center of Tayasal largely empty and long abandoned when the Spanish friars visited the Itza rulers nearby? There were myriad factors at work in these shifts and movements, some related to climate, others related to population and food, and yet others related to conflict. Choosing among these for any one ancient settlement or city is a tall order, given the complexity of the history and of the data at our hands, ever improving and expanding. History is helpful at times, but mostly still invisible for the long-term study of these phenomena.

The "collapses" we infer from abandoned sites need not be thought of as just "failures" or breakdowns. As a long-term view shows, resettlement was a very old way of adapting to change and stressful circumstances, and one that I suspect both commoner and elite were sometimes prepared to make. Like the repeating cycles of time, movement and "resets" were a feature of lowland Maya life, a long-term strategy for environmental adaptation and subsistence. Here we should remember that only a few centuries separate the advent of intensive agriculture in the Maya area and the earliest monumental projects, as the early Maya quickly forged a delicate sense of both community and of place. It was an adaptation that arose out of an old, rhythmic cadence to life in both the long and short term, where pressures of shifting climate, of violent conflict, and of resource procurement were real and everlasting. Ideas of permanence and of constant occupation seem odd in such a world. Maybe "collapse" is an inadequate term for us to describe the complex shifts and adjustments we see in Maya history, in a natural and social environment where change, movement, and renewal were just necessary.

This is not to discount the disruptive nature of events that occurred at certain times, such as at 100 CE or 900 CE. Those were large-scale, systemic episodes of "communal death," but I think they involved the same natural and cultural processes we see operating on a smaller scale many more times over the course of Maya history. A farmer at some point may be done with his cornfield, as the soil is depleted of its nutrients; a small village of a hundred people may at some point be eager to find a new place to settle somewhere else, farther upriver, where the fishing is better; a Classic-era court of five hundred people may decide that the prospects of violent attack and conflict are too much to endure, at least for the moment, and opt to move to a neighboring allied province. And so on. The point here is that abandonment was something of a constant for the Maya, for whatever reasons. I suspect that similar cycles of existence, location, and identity hold true throughout much of the ancient world, well beyond the Maya and Mesoamerica.

The ongoing cadence of beginnings and endings at the community scale is also reflected in the structures of Maya timekeeping and in the ceremonies performed to mark their stations. Rites of dedication, place-making, and agriculture were often considered as acts of renewal, bound to the natural cycles of time. They were also proactive, in the sense that humans and forces of nature must together "enact" time and its constant recurrence. This metaphysical idea was basic to their political ideology. Maya rulers were the keepers of time in a real sense, given the task of maintaining the comings and goings of years, of twenty-year k'atuns, and of the far higher periodicities of cosmology. This was no small obligation, as seen in the constant mention of temporal ceremonies in the Classic period texts. Kings and queens "planted" time and blessed the periods with drops of ritual water and their own blood to engender time's continuance. These acts were often depicted on the physical markers (tuns, or stones) that embodied the periods themselves, merging the ruler with the abstract structures of the cosmos.

It is no accident that in the *Books of Chilam Balam* we see history structured and punctuated by ever repeating k'atuns, each a temporal "creation" that served as a framework and armature for events, including "foundations" and "abandonments." The cycles of time were instrumental in understanding of history's patterns, real or imagined. Twenty years was a convenient way to divvy up human events, for it covered enough temporal ground to encompass several important events, say from one's birth to adulthood—but still small and wieldy enough for historians to track patterns, real or imagined. We do the same thing with our decades, characterizing the "sixties" one way, the "seventies" another. For the Maya of Yucatán, the re-occurrence of specific k'atuns were poetically seen as "folds" of time and of events, meaning that time and events could fold back onto one another like the pages of a codex, merging their identities and associations. In Yucatán, for example, "k'atun 8 Ahau" was seen as especially meaningful as a time of major change and abandonment.

Mayapan was abandoned by the Itza in a k'atun 8 Ahau, so was Chichen Itza beforehand, and Chakanputun before that. These events even become conflated and "confused" in many of the narrative we have, but I suspect this was very much the point of such records. The k'atuns had personas and qualities that could influence, even merge, the course of events, much as they could help with prophecy.

I suspect the same idea was at work in ancient times, too. At Copan, there is a small, modest-looking stela with a text that opens with the statement "on 8 Ahau the *winte'nah* is brought down," referring to Temple 16, the large temple nearby, a replica of a Teotihuacan pyramid overlaying the tomb of the dynastic founder (Figure 13.1). The stela cites the old hero-king, K'inich Yaxk'uk'mo', along with the name of the last known ruler, Yaxpasaj Chanyopat, who dedicated the stone. "8 Ahau" is the date, and it has multiple meanings here. It refers to the bak'tun period that had been overseen by the founder over four centuries earlier (9.0.0.0.0) but also to the time when the stone seems to have been erected, on 9.19.10.0.0, or May 3, 820. The 8 Ahau statement is reminiscent of the destructive episodes of the later chronicles from Yucatán, and in the case of Copan, I suspect it refers to the actual physical destruction of the founder's pyramid and thus the termination of the place we know as Copan as a dynastic center. The periods named "8 Ahau" bracket its history and the dynastic line. (At this moment, Yaxpasaj Chanyopat may have been residing at Quirigua.)

The "folding" of time and history is emphasized in the great inscribed tablets above the tomb of K'inich Janabpakal at Palenque. These take pains to carefully mark the k'atuns that he celebrated over the course of his eighty years of life. "Four were his seatings of the stone," as the texts put it (a "stone seating" being the k'atun's beginning). Each arrival of a new k'atun was described as the crowning of the number that accompanied the Ahau day, so that on his first k'atun (9.10.0.0.0 1 Ahau 8 Kayab), "Jun Ixim becomes Ahau." The maize god Jun Ixim was the embodiment of the number one, so 1 Ahau was formed by his accession, as if he were a new king. Then on the next k'atun (9.11.0.0.0 12 Ahau) the number 12, a celestial deity, assumed the throne. On the next one (9.12.0.0.0 10 Ahau), the number 10, a death lord, assumed office. Appropriately for 10

FIGURE 13.1. Copan, Stela 11, a possible end-marker of Copan's dynasty. Photograph by the author.

Ahau, Pakal died not long before the arrival of the next k'atun, 9.13.0.0.0, which fell on 8 Ahau. The tablets anticipated this calendar period, and the scribe made note of the fact that Pakal himself had been born on the day 8 Ahau. For the readers of the tablets in Pakal's shrine, it was important to realize that the passing of the k'atun resonated with the deceased king's birth. His rebirth is depicted in the design of his sarcophagus for this reason. The merging and folding of time can be used to great poetic effect, making connections across lifetimes and among ancestors. What Maya history allows, therefore, are many new beginnings. Renewal was a basic aim for many a Maya ruler, resident, or farmer, expressed through both ritual action and the work of survival.

According to early histories of the highland K'iche' and Kaqchiquel Maya, origins were all about movement. It began with migration, followed by important turning points that were also defined by dramatic movements of people and communities. The epic *Popol Vuh* and other documents note that, long ago, civilized people came to the western highlands from a place of origin called Tulan Zuyua or simply Tulan. Chief among them were four lineage founders named Balam Quitze, Balam Acab, Mahucutah, and Iqui Balam, the distant ancestors of the great lords who ruled the royal houses of the K'iche' and Kaqchiquel in the decades before the Spanish invasion. These founders experienced the first dawn of Creation after carrying their patron gods through the primordial dark forests. As the *Popol Vuh* describes it, "it was there that the grandfathers and fathers were sown, when they dawned."[3] Much like the noble families of Postclassic Yucatán, their origins were very much elsewhere, and their rise to status came via arduous and long-lasting journeys. The ruling lineages of the Nahuatl-speaking cities of highland Mexico told very similar stories, of a migration from an island in a lake called Aztlan to settle at an island in a lake called Tenochtitlán. Such accounts involve long lists of places where various lineages paused, reflecting how individual seats of power could be fleeting and impermanent. Communities could be seen as more social and political than location based. We see this in Classic Maya history, as royal houses moved and took up residence in new places with surprising regularity.

The name "Tulan" mentioned in these origin narratives is by now familiar, and intriguing in this context. It comes from the Nahuatl place name *Tollan* cited in numerous histories of central Mexico, meaning "among the cattails." It seems likely that this name goes back in further in history, referring to the place that even Classic Maya elites saw as a primordial place of early civilization. In the art and inscriptions of Tikal and Copan, a cattail hieroglyph was used to refer to distant Teotihuacan, the urban center that was long viewed as the singular place of high culture and political authority. The same idea was extant among the later Aztecs, who referred to several old, established cities of the central highlands of Mexico as Tollans, including Teotihuacan, Cholula, and the archaeological site today known as Tula. As we have seen, their old, cultured inhabitants were the "Toltecs" (*toltecatl*), or the people of Tollan. The name points to a remarkable continuity in the myth of an ancient, idealized city. Most remarkable is the way that the K'iche' and Kaqchiquel historians of the sixteenth century saw Tulan, or *Tulan Zuywa,* as an ancestral city "in the east," toward the direction of sunrise. It was there that the great lineages first acquired their patron deities, amid the darkness before sunrise. Most scholars suggest that it was situated in the wetlands close to the Maya world, near the Gulf of Mexico. As the historian of Maya religion, Garry Sparks, notes, "the name (*Tulan*) is more probably a general term for an urban area, with implied reference back to the earliest cities, such as the Olmec settlements of La Venta and San Lorenzo among the marshes of present-day Tabasco."[4] The very last Maya kingdoms saw Tulan as a place of origin and of historical imagination, a mythic realm equated with the dawning in the east and the dawning if civilization itself. While it may be a romantic notion, I must wonder, like Sparks, if the highland Maya of the sixteenth century somehow had an inkling where it all came from, hearkening back to the lowland marshes where places like Aguada Fénix and many other E Groups were designed to observe the dawn, built and rebuilt again and again. Multiple sunrises of cities and eras imply the existence of multiple "sunsets," too, giving Maya history its familiar cadence. Tulan was an idea that encapsulated the same notion, in a way. Time and again, the Maya built new shrines, communities, and capitals with that eastern directional anchor in mind, always awaiting a new dawn.

• • •

History is never a static construct. It can be lost, recovered, and constantly reimagined. Our own narratives of the deep past are always imperfect compositions, and they sometimes are crafted to resonate within contemporary debates of politics, education, nationhood, community, and ethnicity. This makes archaeology and its enticing access to the "glories of the past" an especially powerful tool and one often subject to manipulation and bias. Where does Maya history exist, then, in our own shape-shifting imaginations of what came before? Because much of the history recounted here is new to the wider world, it is difficult to say how it might be perceived by different stakeholders. I often reflect on how, even in the Americas, the pre-Columbian world has little presence in education, culture, or politics or is just ignored outright. It is only an impression, but I sense that with few exceptions, schools in Mexico, Guatemala, Belize, or Honduras seldom mention the names of Yuknomch'en or Jasaw Chank'awil but might bring up Julius Caesar, Akhenaten, or Charlemagne when talking about a deeper past. Ruins of ancient Maya cities such as Chichen Itza or Palenque are visited by thousands of people every day, but usually without much explanation or context. The imbalances of knowledge and its dissemination still exist after centuries of negating Indigenous identity and its history. It is all another legacy of the Rupture in history I have described and of the unresolved tensions stemming from conquest and colonial rule. But positive change is looming. I hold out hope that the names of Maya history, of kings, queens, artists, and warriors, will take their rightful place among the significant actors of the human story and breathe life into the ancient sites still around us.

The most important change of all is that the direct historical narratives we can study and teach no longer have to come from the quills of Spanish conquistadors or friars. Many of them can now be appreciated as coming from the ancient Maya themselves. We have a new set of primary sources at hand, and their very existence—the oldest extant voices from anywhere in the Americas—is a truly remarkable gift, allowing us to fill in gaps of history that we did not even realize were knowable. The descendants of the ancient Maya are still on the move, and they have a history that they can continue to embrace, study, and ultimately refine as new parts are revealed. And above all else it is a history they can call their own.

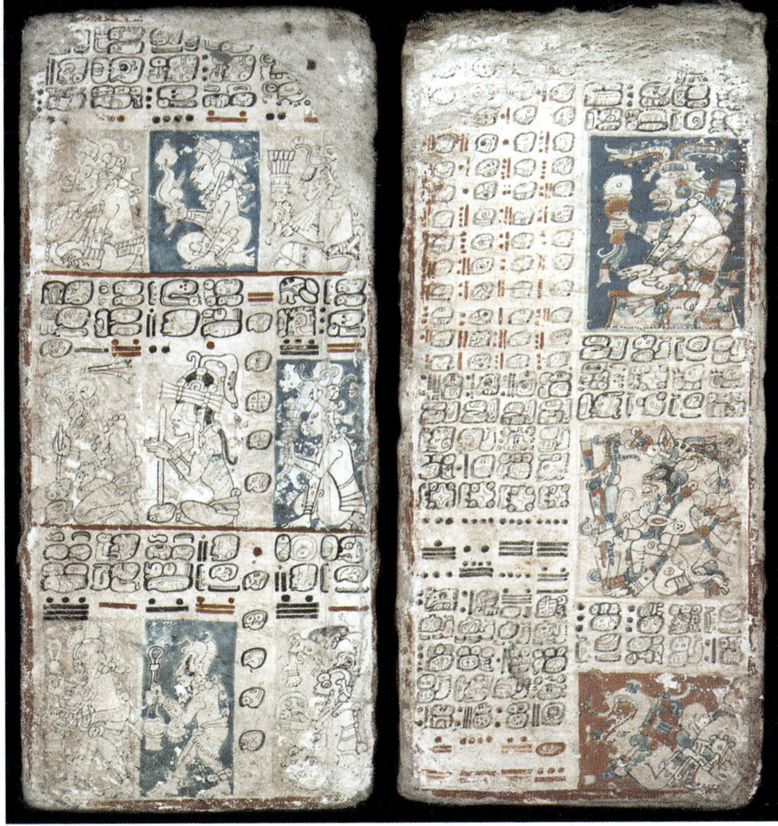

PLATE 1. (top) Sculpted blocks from La Corona, Guatemala. Photograph by the author.

PLATE 2. (bottom) Two pages of the *Dresden Codex,* a twelfth-century Maya book. Page 6 (left) includes sections of calendrical almanacs devoted to various gods; page 51 (right) is a part of a table for the cycles of Venus. Courtesy of the Staats-und Universitätsbibliothek Dresden (SLUB).

PLATE 5. (top) The Maize God and the mountain cave, north wall, San Bartolo murals. Illustration by Heather Hurst, ©2004.

PLATE 6. (bottom) Images of water and rain on the El Mirador stucco frieze. Photograph by the author.

PLATE 7. (top) Maya calligraphy on a "Dynastic Vase," Calakmul region. Photograph by Justin Kerr.

PLATE 8. (bottom) Lower part of Tikal, Stela 39, showing Chaktokich'ahk standing over his Uaxactun captive. Photograph by the author.

PLATE 9. (top) The stucco facade from Holmul, Guatemala. Image by Alexandre Tokovinine, Courtesy of the Proyecto Arqueológico Holmul.

PLATE 10. (bottom) Detail of the mural paintings at Calakmul, Chihknahb complex. Photograph by the author.

PLATE 11. (top) The inscribed stairway blocks found at Naranjo, originally from Caracol. Photo by Teobert Maler. © President and Fellows of Harvard College, Peabody Museum of Archaeology and Ethnology (PM# 2004.24.3432).

PLATE 12. (bottom) K'inich Kanbahlam as warrior-king and ancestor. Panel from Palenque, Temple XVII. Photograph by Jorge Pérez de Lara.

PLATE 13. (top) Shield Jaguar, king of Yaxchilan (Pa'chan), embodies the War Serpent. Lintel 25 of Yaxchilan. Photograph by Justin Kerr.

PLATE 14. (bottom) A royal dance performance, from the Bonampak murals, ca. 800 CE. Courtesy of Bonampak Documentation Project, illustration by Heather Hurst and Leonard Ashby.

PLATE 15. (top) Judgement of captives by Yajaw Chanmuwan, from the Bonampak murals, ca. 800 CE. Courtesy of Bonampak Documentation Project, illustration by Heather Hurst and Leonard Ashby.

PLATE 16. (bottom) The Temple of K'uk'ulkan, Chichen Itza. Photograph by the author.

APPENDIX A

Family Relations

THE CHARTS presented here give family trees from the Classic period, one centered on the Kanul dynasty of Dzibanche and Calkamul and its relations, and the other on the Mutul dynasty of Tikal. Not all individuals are discussed in the main text. These complex relations, alliances, and networks illustrate the interconnectedness among the royal families of the Classic period.

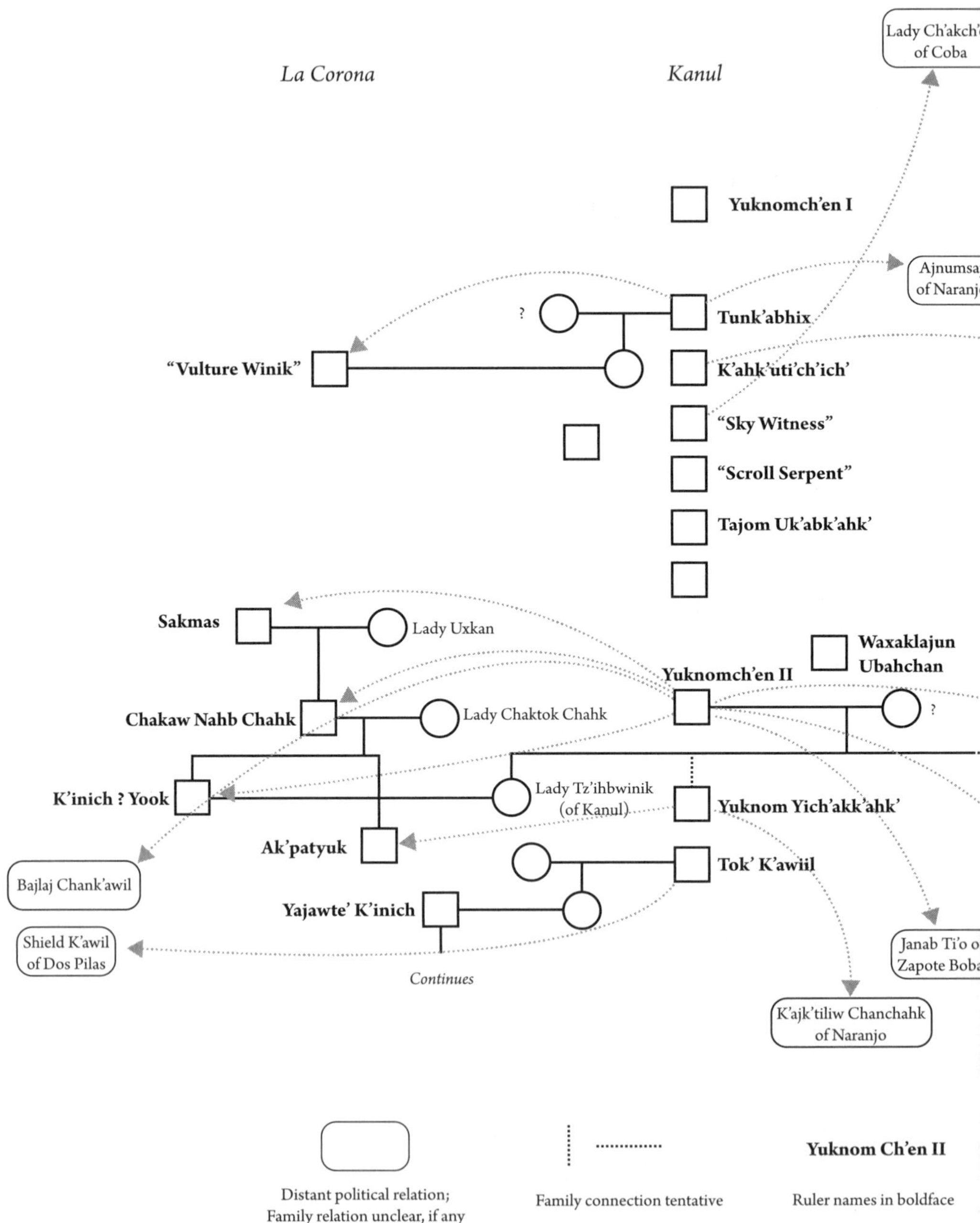

La Corona
Kanul
Lady Ch'akch'e
of Coba
Yuknomch'en I
Ajnumsaj
of Naranjo
?
Tunk'abhix
"Vulture Winik"
K'ahk'uti'ch'ich'
"Sky Witness"
"Scroll Serpent"
Tajom Uk'abk'ahk'
Sakmas
Lady Uxkan
Waxaklajun
Ubahchan
Yuknomch'en II
Chakaw Nahb Chahk
Lady Chaktok Chahk
?
K'inich ? Yook
Lady Tz'ihbwinik
(of Kanul)
Yuknom Yich'akk'ahk'
Ak'patyuk
Tok' K'awiil
Bajlaj Chank'awil
Yajawte' K'inich
Shield K'awil
of Dos Pilas
Continues
Janab Ti'o of
Zapote Bobal
K'ajk'tiliw Chanchahk
of Naranjo
Distant political relation;
Family relation unclear, if any
Family connection tentative
Yuknom Ch'en II
Ruler names in boldface

El Peru-Waka'

Yaxchilan (Pa'chan)

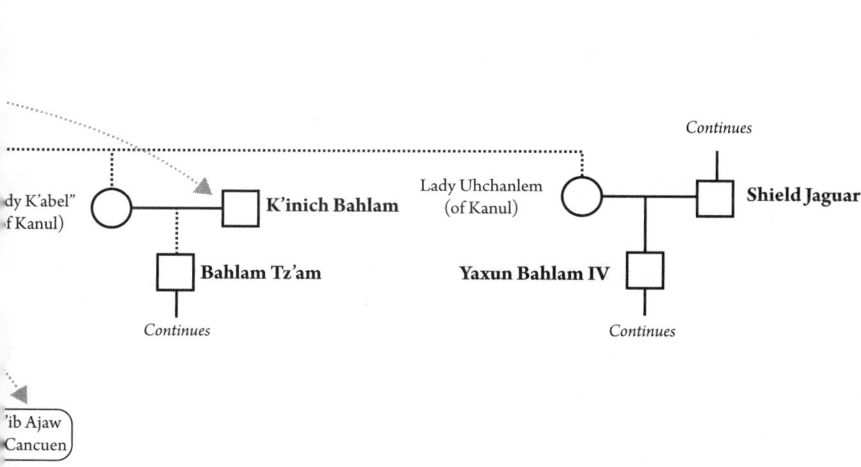

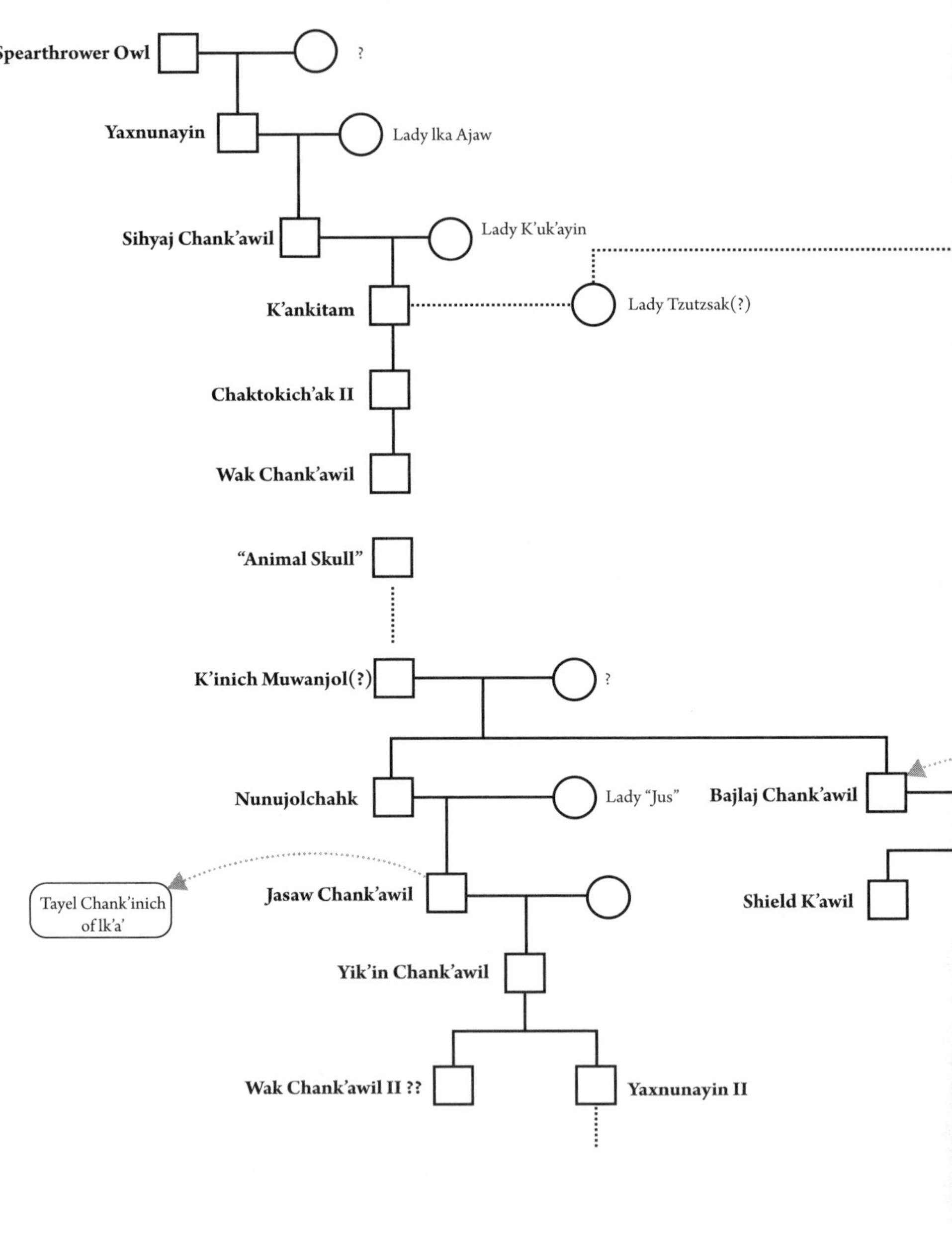

Mutul (Tikal)
Spearthrower Owl
?
Yaxnunayin
Lady Ika Ajaw
Sihyaj Chank'awil
Lady K'uk'ayin
K'ankitam
Lady Tzutzsak(?)
Chaktokich'ak II
Wak Chank'awil
"Animal Skull"
K'inich Muwanjol(?)
?
Nunujolchahk
Lady "Jus"
Bajlaj Chank'awil
Tayel Chank'inich of Ik'a'
Jasaw Chank'awil
Shield K'awil
Yik'in Chank'awil
Wak Chank'awil II ??
Yaxnunayin II
Distant political relation; Family relation unclear, if any
Family connection tentative

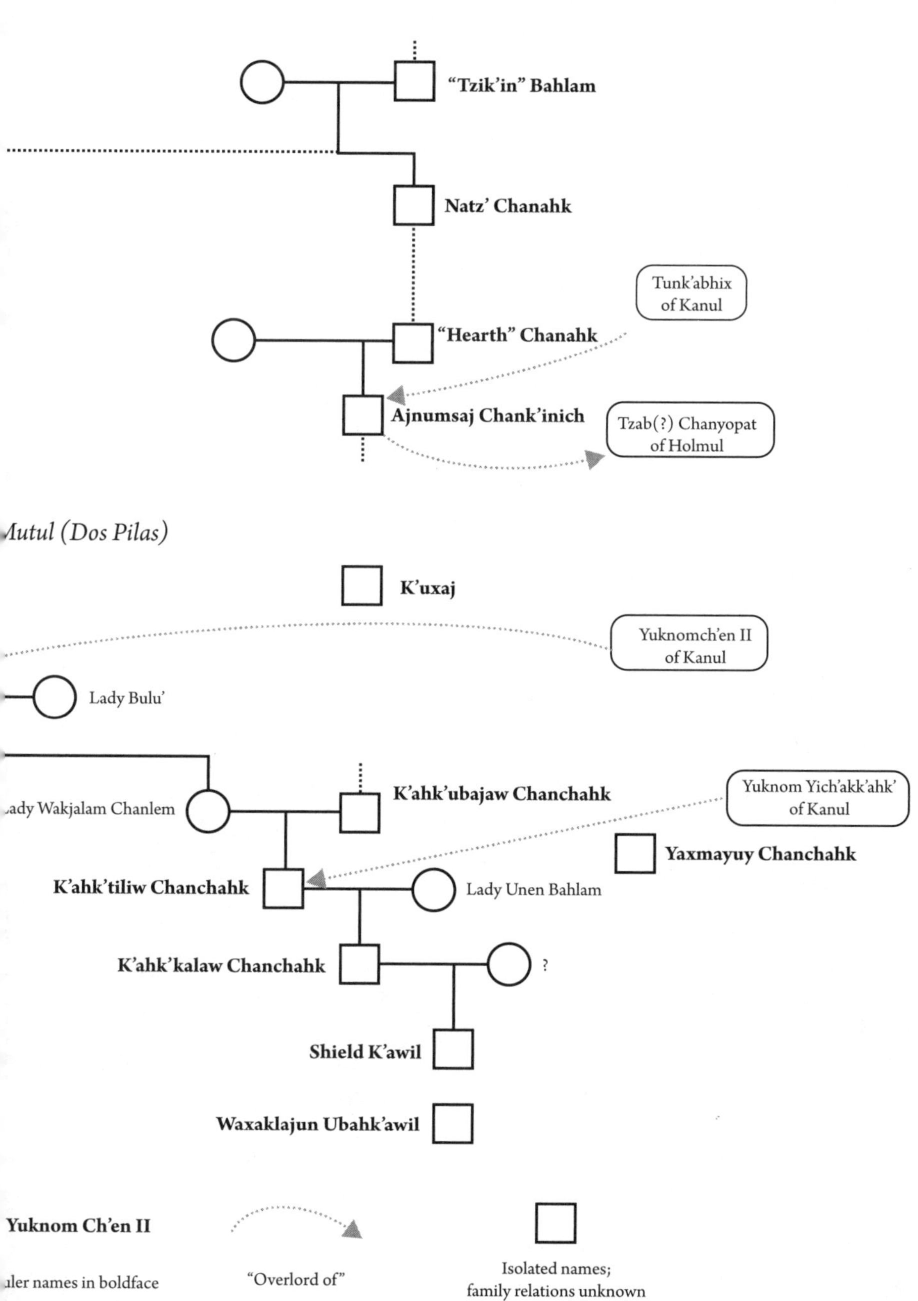

Sa'al (Naranjo)
"Tzik'in" Bahlam
Natz' Chanahk
Tunk'abhix of Kanul
"Hearth" Chanahk
Ajnumsaj Chank'inich
Tzab(?) Chanyopat of Holmul
Mutul (Dos Pilas)
K'uxaj
Yuknomch'en II of Kanul
Lady Bulu'
Lady Wakjalam Chanlem
K'ahk'ubajaw Chanchahk
Yuknom Yich'akk'ahk' of Kanul
Yaxmayuy Chanchahk
K'ahk'tiliw Chanchahk
Lady Unen Bahlam
K'ahk'kalaw Chanchahk
?
Shield K'awil
Waxaklajun Ubahk'awil
Yuknom Ch'en II
Ruler names in boldface
"Overlord of"
Isolated names; family relations unknown

APPENDIX B

Selected Timeline

THIS TABLE INCLUDES many events and people featured in the book and is not meant to be an exhaustive overview of Maya history. Many episodes are omitted. The correspondence of Maya and Christian dates uses the Martin-Skidmore correlation. Other accepted correlations are offset from that by one to three days. (Note: Approximate dates or ranges do not show a Maya day equivalent.)

YEAR	EVENT	MAYA DAY
ca. 1000–400 BCE	Middle Preclassic era	——
1142 BCE	Bak'tun ending 5.0.0.0.0; mythic date Sakhixmut of Mutul dynasty	5.0.0.0.0 12 Ahau 3 Zac
992 BCE	Birth of Ukohkan Chan of Bakel (Palenque) dynasty	5.7.11.8.4 1 Kan 2 Cumku
966 BCE	Accession of Ukohkan Chan	5.8.17.15.17 11 Caban 0 Pop
900–800 BCE	Construction of the great platform at Aguada Fénix	——
400 BCE–100 CE	Late Preclassic era	——

YEAR	EVENT	MAYA DAY
400 BCE–100 CE	Late Preclassic era	——
257 BCE	Record of possible historical ruler "Ik'mihin" at Naranjo (Sa'al)	7.4.17.0.14 13 Ix 12 Xul
252 BCE	Early Palenque ruler dedicates shrine	7.5.3.10.17 10 Caban 5 Muan
ca. 100–0 BCE	San Bartolo Murals painted	——
36 BCE	Earliest contemporaneous inscribed date at Chiapa de Corzo, Chiapas	7.16.3.2.13 6 Ben 16 Xul
ca. 100	CE Classic dynasties begin	——
141	Foundation(?) event recorded at Pol Box	8.5.0.14.4 10 Kan 12 Yax
158	Early dynastic event at Naranjo (Sa'al)	8.5.18.4.0 4 Ahau 3 Kankin
159	Katun ending 8.6.0.0.0, mentioned at several sites with "Foliated Ahau"	8.6.0.0.0 10 Ahau 8 Ch'en
180	Possible accession of "Skyraiser," early ruler of Kanul dynasty	8.7.0.15.11 7 Chuen 19 Pop?
292	Possible accession of Yaxnunayin I, early Mutul ruler, Tikal St. 29	8.12.14.8.15 13 Men 3 Zip
317	K'atun celebration by Lady Unenbahlam of Mutul	8.14.0.0.0 7 Ahau 3 Kankin
323	Early historical date at Uaxactun	8.14.5.12.16 9 Cib 14 Kankin
333	Unknown; Uaxactun Stela 9	8.14.15.12.16 8 Cib 4 Muan
357	K'atun ending 8.16.0.0.0	8.16.0.0.0 12 Ahau 3 Kankin
359	Possible Accession of Yopat Bahlam, founder of Pa'chan dynasty (Yaxchilan)	8.16.2.9.1 7 Imix 14 Zodz?
374	Spearthrower Owl, ruler of Teotihuacan, crowned	8.16.17.9.0 11 Ahau 3 Uayeb
376	K'atun ending 8.17.0.0.0	8.17.0.0.0 1 Ahau 8 Ch'en
376	Stela 39 dedicated by Chaktokich'ak of Tikal	8.17.0.0.0 1 Ahau 8 Ch'en
378	Arrival of Sihyaj K'ahk' to Tikal; death of Chaktokich'ahk	8.17.1.4.12 11 Eb 15 Mac
379	La Sufricaya palace dedicated	8.17.2.4.16 11 Cib 14 Mac

YEAR	EVENT	MAYA DAY
379	Yaxnunayin, son of Spearthrower Owl, assumes throne at Tikal	8.17.2.16.17 10 Caban 15 Yaxkin
396	K'atun ending 8.18.0.0.0	8.18.0.0.0 12 Ahau 8 Zotz
416	K'atun ending 8.19.0.0.0	8.19.0.0.0 10 Ahau 13 Kayab
426	K'inich Yaxk'uk'mo' of Copan receives power (*k'awil*) at Teotihuacan	8.19.10.10.17 5 Caban 15 Yaxkin
427	Yaxk'uk'mo' arrives back in Copan	8.19.11.0.13 5 Ben 11 Muan
431	K'uk'bahlam is crowned king of Bakel dynasty (Palenque)	8.19.15.3.4 1 Kan 2 Kayab
ca. 431	Eruption of Ilopango volcano, El Salvador	——
435	Palenque's Ruler 2 comes to power	8.19.19.11.17 2 Caban 10 Xul
436	Bak'tun ending 9.0.0.0.0, celebrated at Tikal, Copan, El Peru-Waka' etc.	9.0.0.0.0 8 Ahau 13 Ceh
439	Death of Spearthrower Owl	9.0.3.9.18 12 Edznab 11 Zip
445	Dedication of Tikal, Stela 31	9.0.10.0.0 7 Ahau 3 Yax
458	Accession of K'ankitam of Tikal	9.1.2.2.17 3 Caban 0 Yax
486	Tikal's war against	9.2.11.7.8 4 Lamat 6 Yaxkin
487	Accession of Butz'aj Sakcihk of Palenque	9.2.12.6.18 3 Edznab 11 Xul
490	"Founding" event at Palenque (Lakamha')	9.2.15.9.2 9 Ik 0 Yaxkin
495	Katun ending 9.3.0.0.0	9.3.0.0.0 2 Ahau 18 Muan
ca. 500	Coba ballcourt dedicated by ruler Junpiktok'	——
514	Katun ending 9.4.0.0.0	9.4.0.0.0 13 Ahau 18 Yax
ca. 520–550	Rule of Tunk'abhix of Kanul	——
520	Lady Nahek' of Kanul marries into dynasty of Saknikte' (La Corona)	9.4.3.6.16 12 Cib 9 Pax
526	Accession of K'inich Tatab Jol of Yaxchilan	9.5.11.8.16 2 Cib 19 Pax
534	Katun ending 9.5.0.0.0	9.5.0.0.0 11 Ahau 18 Tzec

YEAR	EVENT	MAYA DAY
546	Accession of Ajnumsaj of Naranjo (Sa'al), under Tunk'abhix of Kanul	9.5.12.0.4 6 Kan 2 Zip
553	Accession of Yakawte' K'inich of Caracol	9.5.191.2 9 Ik 5 Uo
554	Katun ending 9.6.0.0.0	9.6.0.0.0 9 Ahau 3 Uayeb
556	K'ahk'uti'ch'ich' on the Kanul throne, oversees installation of new ruler at El Peru-Waka'	9.6.2.5.10 7 Oc 18 Tzec
561	"Sky Witness" on the Kanul throne	9.6.7.3.18 7 Edznab 1 Zip
562	Sky Witness(?) defeats king of Tikal, Wakchan K'awil	9.6.8.4.2 7 Ik 0 Zip
569	Lady Ch'akch'en established at Coba	9.6.15.6.9 13 Muluc 12 Zip
573	Katun ending 9.7.0.0.0	9.7.0.0.0 7 Ahau 3 Kankin
579	Accession of Scroll Serpent, Kanul ruler, at Calakmul	9.7.5.14.17 11 Caban 10 Ch'en
583	Lady Yohliknal of Palenque enthroned	9.7.10.3.8 9 Lamat 1 Muan
593	Katun ending on 9.8.0.0.0	9.8.0.0.0 5 Ahau 3 Ch'en
596	Mass execution of prisoners by Naranjo ruler Ajnumsaj	9.8.2.14.3 7 Akbal 11 Zodz
599	Sky Witness of Kanul conquers Palenque	9.8.5.13.8 6 Lamat 1 Zip
599	Accession of Yajawte' K'inich of Caracol	9.8.5.16.12 5 Eb 5 Xul
603	Birth of K'inich Janabpakal of Palenque	9.8.9.13.0 8 Ahau 13 Pop
604	Death Lady Yohlik'nal of Palenque	9.8.11.6.12 2 Eb 0 Mac
605	Birth of K'ahk'uti'witz' K'awil of Copan	9.8.11.6.19 9 Cauac 7 Muan
605	Accession of Ajen Yohlmat of Palenque	9.8.11.9.10 8 Oc 18 Muan
611	Scroll Serpent of Kanul conquers Palenque	9.8.17.15.14 4 Ix 7 Uo
613	K'atun ending 9.9.0.0.0	9.9.0.0.0 3 Ahau 3 Zodz
615	Accession of K'inich Janabpakal of Palenque at twelve years old	9.9.2.4.8 5 Lamat 1 Mol

YEAR	EVENT	MAYA DAY
619	Accession of Tumyohl K'inich of Caracol, under Kanul	9.9.4.16.2 10 Ik 0 Pop
625	October 26. Birth of Bajlaj Chank'awil of Mutul and Dos Pilas	9.9.12.11.2 8 Ik 5 Yax
626	Defeat of Naranjo by Tumyohl K'inich of Caracol	9.9.13.8.4 11 Kan 2 Ch'en
628	K'ahk'uti'witz' K'awil accedes at Copan	9.9.14.17.5 6 Chicchan 18 Kayab
631	Defeat of Naranjo (Sa'al) by Kanul forces	9.9.18.16.3 7 Akbal 16 Muan
632	Establishment(?) of Mutul court at Dos Pilas	9.9.19.7.8 10 Lamat 16 Xul
633	K'atun ending 9.10.0.0.0	9.10.0.0.0 1 Ahau 8 Kayab
635	Yuknomch'en II establishes Kanul court at Calakmul	9.10.2.4.5 13 Chichan 18 Uo
635	K'inich Kanbahlam is born in Palenque	9.10.2.6.6 2 Cimi 19 Zodz
636	Defeat of Waxaklajun Ubahchan of Kanul	9.10.3.2.12 2 Eb 0 Pop
636	Accession of Yuknomch'en II of Kanul	9.10.3.5.10 8 Oc 18 Zip
639	Accession of Xokmo'chahk of Piedras Negras (Yokib)	9.10.6.5.9 8 Muluc 2 Zip
640	Execution of Waxaklajun Ubahchan of Kanul	9.10.7.9.17 1 Caban 5 Yaxkin
642	Dedication of Caracol Stairway by Tumyohl K'inich	9.10.10.0.0 13 Ahau 18 Kankin
644	Birth of K'inich K'anjoykitam, at Palenque	9.10.11.17.0 11 Ahau 8 Mac
647	K'ahk'uti'witz' K'awil begins a program of monuments in Copan Valley	9.10.15.0.0 6 Ahau 13 Mac
648	Bajlaj Chank'awil of Dos Pilas defeats Lamnah K'awil of Mutul	9.10.15.4.9 4 Muluc 2 Cumku
649	Birth of Yuknom Yich'ahkk'ahk' of Kanul	9.10.16.16.19 3 Cauac 2 Ceh

YEAR	EVENT	MAYA DAY
650	Yuknomch'en of Kanul defeats Dos Pilas	9.10.18.2.19 1 Cauac 17 Muan
652	K'atun ending 9.11.0.0.0	9.11.0.0.0 12 Ahau 8 Ceh
654	Dedication of throne room of K'inich Janabpakal at Palenque	9.11.2.1.11 9 Chuen 9 Mac
657	Nunujolchahk defeated by Yuknomch'en's forces	9.11.4.5.14 6 Ix 2 Kayab
659	Pakal captures nobles from Pomona region	9.11.6.16.11 7 Chuen 4 Ch'en
659	Nunujolchahk, in exile, arrives to Palenque	9.11.6.16.17 13 Caban 10 Ch'en
667	Dedication of Panel 2 and Stela 36 of Piedras Negras	9.11.15.0.0 4 Ahau 13 Mol
672	K'atun ending 9.12.0.0.0	9.12.0.0.0.0 10 Ahau 8 Yaxkin
672	Death of Lady Tz'akabajaw of Palenque (the "Red Queen")	9.12.0.6.18 5 Edznab 6 Kankin
673	Exile of Bajlaj Chank'awil to Hixwitz	9.12.1.0.3 9 Akbal 6 Yaxkin
674	Birth of Lady K'atun of Naman	9.12.2.0.16 5 Cib 14 Yaxkin
677	Sacking of Pulil(?) by Yuknomch'en	9.12.5.9.14 2 Ix 17 Muan
677	Reinstatement of Bajlaj Chank'awiil at Dos Pilas	9.12.5.10.1 9 Imix 4 Pax
679	Pakal gathers his sons to discuss succession at Palenque	9.12.6.12.0 5 Ahau 18 Kayab
679	Defeat of Nunujolchahk by Bajlaj Chank'awiil	9.12.6.16.17 11 Caban 10 Zodz
679	Arrival of Kanul princess Iz Tz'ihbwinik to Saknikte' for marriage	9.12.6.16.17 11 Caban 10 Zodz
681	Accession of Shield Jaguar of Yaxchilan (Pa'chan)	9.12.9.8.1 5 Imix 4 Mac
682	Accession of Jasaw Chank'awil of Tikal	9.12.9.17.16 5 Cib 14 Zodz
682	Royal dance at Calakmul, on half-katun	9.12.10.0.0 9 Ahau 18 Zodz
682	Lady Wakjalam Chanlem (Lady Six Sky) of Dos Pilas arrives at Naranjo	9.12.10.5.12 4 Eb 10 Yax

YEAR	EVENT	MAYA DAY
683	Death of K'inich Janabpakal at Palenque	9.12.11.5.18 6 Edznab 11 Yax
684	Accession of K'inich Kanbahlam of Palenque	9.12.11.12.10 8 Oc 3 Kayab
686	Accession of Yuknom Yich'akk'ahk of Kanul	9.12.13.17.7 6 Manik 5 Zip
687	Accession of K'inich Yo'nal Ahk of Yokib, Piedras Negras	9.12.14.13.1 7 Imix 19 Pax
687	Palenque conquers Tonina	9.12.15.7.11 10 Chuen 4 Sac
688	Birth of K'ahk'tiliw Chanchahk of Naranjo	9.12.15.13.7 9 Manik 0 Kayab
692	Dedication of Cross Group shrines by K'inich Kanbahlam of Palenque	9.12.19.14.12 5 Eb 5 Kayab
692	Katun ending 9.13.0.0.0	9.13.0.0.0 8 Ahau 8 Uo
692	Jasaw Chank'awil of Tikal dedicates K'atun shrines	9.13.0.0.0 8 Ahau 8 Uo
693	K'inich Baknal Chahk of Tonina captures Palenque nobles	9.13.0.10.3 3 Akbal 11 Ceh
693	Accession of K'ahk'tiliw Chanchahk of Naranjo	9.13.1.3.19 5 Cauac 2 Xul
695	Burial of Kahk'uti'witz' K'awil of Copan, beneath Hieroglyphic Stairway	9.13.3.6.1 13 Imix 14 Yaxkin
695	Accession of Waxakljun Ubahk'awil at Copan	9.13.3.6.8 7 Lamat 1 Mol
695	Jasaw Chank'awil defeats Yich'ahkk'ahk' of Kanul	9.13.3.7.18 11 Edznab 11 Ch'en
695	Ceremony at Temple 1 at Tikal; 13 k'atun ann. of Spearthrower Owl's death	9.13.3.9.18 12 Edznab 11 Zac
697	Death of Yich'akk'ahk' of Kanul	9.13.5.15.0 2 Ahau 3 Pax
698	Accession of Kokaj K'awil of Dos Pilas	9.13.6.2.0 11 Ahau 18 Up
698	Accession of "Tok' K'awil" of Kanul dynasty	9.13.6.2.9 7 Muluc 7 Zip

YEAR	EVENT	MAYA DAY
702	Death of Kanbahlam of Palenque	9.13.10.1.5 6 Chicchan 3 Pop
709	Birth of Yaxun Bahlam IV of Yaxchilan	9.13.17.12.10 8 Oc 13 Yax
710	Copan's Hieroglyphic Stairway (1st phase) dedicated	9.13.18.17.9 12 Muluc 7 Muan
711	Katun ending 9.14.0.0.0	9.14.0.0.0 6 Ahau 13 Muan
711	Jasaw Chank'awil dedicates stela and altar, with ancestral bones	9.14.0.0.0 6 Ahau 13 Muan
721	Arrival of Kanul woman to La Corona (Saknikte')	9.14.9.9.14 8 Ix 17 Sotz'
721	Accession of K'inich Ahkul Mo'nahb of Palenque	9.14.10.4.2 9 Ik 5 Kayab
723	Lady K'abalxok of Yaxchilan dedicates her house	9.14.11.15.1 3 Imix 14 Ch'en
724	Accession of K'ahk'tiliw Chanyopat of Quirigua	9.14.13.4.17 12 Caban 5 Kayab
726	Visit by Ajpach'wal's to Waxaklajun Ubah K'awil of Copan	9.14.14.14.0 9 Ahau 18 Yaxkin
726	K'awiil Tok' oversees dedication of El Palmar steps.	9.14.15.0.0 11 Ahau 18 Zac
731	K'atun ending 9.15.0.0.0	9.15.0.0.0 4 Ahau 13 Yax
731	Dedication of Structure 1 pyramid at Calakmul	9.15.0.0.0 4 Ahau 13 Yax
734	Accession of Yik'in Chank'awil of Tikal	9.15.3.6.8 3 Lamat 6 Pax
736	Yik'in Chank'awil of Tikal dedicates first stela at Tikal	9.15.5.0.0 10 Ahau 8 Ch'en
738	Waxaklajun Ubahk'awil builds final Copan ball court	9.15.6.8.13 10 Ben 16 Kayab
738	Waxaklajun Ubahk'awil of Copan is executed by K'ahk'tiliw Chanyopat of Quirigua	9.15.6.14.6 6 Cimi 4 Tzec
	Accession of K'ahk'yipyaj Chank'awiil at Copan	9.15.6.16.5 6 Chicchan 3 Yaxkin

YEAR	EVENT	MAYA DAY
742	Death of Shield Jaguar of Yaxchilan	9.15.10.17.14 6 Ix 12 Yaxkin
743	Yikin Chank'awil of Tikal attacks Yaxha	9.15.12.2.2 11 Ik 15 Ch'en
744	Yikin Chank'awil wages war on Naranjo	9.15.12.11.13 7 Ben 1 Pop
746	Dedication of Temple IV at Tikal, by Yik'in Chank'awil	9.15.15.2.3 13 Akbal 1 Ch'en
749	Inauguration of K'ahk'yipyaj Chank'awil at Copan	9.15.17.13.10 11 Oc 13 Pop
751	K'atun ending 9.16.0.0.0	9.16.0.0.0 2 Ahau 13 Tzec
751	K'ahk'tiliw Chanyopat dedicates his first major monument at Quiigua	9.16.0.0.0 2 Ahau 13 Tzec
752	Accession of Yaxun Bahlam IV ("Cotinga Jaguar") of Yaxchilan	9.16.1.0.0 12 Ahau 8 Tzec
755	Rebuilding of Hieroglyphic Stairway at Copan	9.16.4.1.0 6 Ahau 13 Tzec
	Capture of Piedras Negras lord by TIlom of Yaxchilan court	9.16.8.3.18 9 Etznab 11 Yaxkin
763	Accession to Yaxpasaj Chanyopat of Copan	9.16.12.5.17 6 Caban 10 Mol
764	Accession of K'inich K'uk'bahlam of Palenque	9.16.13.0.7 9 Manik 15 Uo
770	Ukit Kanlek rules at Ek Balam	9.16.19.3.12 11 Eb 10 Zodz
771	Katun ending 9.17.0.0.0	9.17.0.0.0 13 Ahau 18 Cumku
776	Dedication of Copan's Temple 16 and Altar Q	9.17.5.3.4. 5 Kan 12 Uo
776	Inauguration of Yajaw Chanmuwan at Bonampak	9.17.5.8.9 6 Muluc 17 Yaxkin
780	Yaxk'amlay is inaugurated at Copan, a possible joint ruler	9.17.9.2.12 3 Eb 0 Pop
780	Last date at Coba, Stela 20	9.17.10.0.0 12 Ahau 8 Pax
783	Dedication of Tablet of 96 Glyphs, Palenque	9.17.13.0.7 7 Manik 0 Pax

YEAR	EVENT	MAYA DAY
ca. 783	Drought and famine at Comalcalco	——
789	Marriage of Bonampak king Yajaw Chanmuwan to Yaxchilan princess	9.17.18.15.18 12 Edznab 1 Ceh
790	K'atun ending 9.18.0.0.0	9.18.0.0.0 11 Ahau 18 Mac
790	Dedication of the Bonampak murals	9.18.0.3.4 10 Kan 2 Kayab
796	Capture of Xubchahk by Yaxha ruler	9.18.5.16.14 13 Ix 2 Zac
799	Attacks against Yaxha by Naranjo	9.18.8.8.18 1 Edznab 11 Uo
800	Court jewels of Yaxha taken by Naranjo	9.18.9.9.8 7 Lamat 16 Uo
800	Caracol altar depicting bound Xub Chahk	9.18.10.0.0 10 Ahau 8 Zac
801	Dedication of Copan's Temple 18	9.18.10.17.18 4 Etznab 1 Zac
805	July 21. Last known date of Yaxpasaj Chanyopat of Copan	9.18.15.0.0 3 Ahau 3 Yax
808	K'inich Tatbujol of Yaxchilan captures K'inich Yatahk of Piedras Negras	9.18.17.13.14 9 Ix 2 Tzec
810	K'atun ending 9.19.0.0.0	9.19.0.0.0 9 Ahau 18 Mol
810	Last known building at Quirigua, by Kahk'jolow Chanyopat	9.19.0.0.0 9 Ahau 18 Mol
820	Papmalil rules from Ucanal	9.19.10.0.0 8 Ahau 8 Xul
822?	Last date at Copan, seating of Ukittok'	9.19.11.14.5 3 Chicchan 13 Uo?
829	Arrival of priests(?) to Ceibal, in anticipation of Bak'tun	9.19.18.17.15 6 Men 18 Zip
830	Bak'tun ending 10.0.0.0.0	10.0.0.0.0 7 Ahau 18 Zip
849	K'atun ending 10.1.0.0.0	10.1.0.0.0 5 Ahau 3 Kayab
859	Papmalil oversees lord at Ixlu	10.1.10.0.0 4 Ahau 13 Kankin
ca. 870	Fire-conjuring ceremony at Chichen Itza by Ek Balam lord	——
880	Dedication of Las Monjas, Chichen Itza	10.2.10.11.7 8 Manik 15 Uo
899	Last dated monument from Maya lowlands, Xultun Stela 10	10.3.10.0.0 13 Ahau 13 Zodz

YEAR	EVENT	MAYA DAY
905	Ballcourt dedicated at Uxmal	10.3.15.16.14 2 Ix 17 Pop
909	K'atun ending 10.4.0.0.0; Final Maya Long Count date	10.4.0.0.0 12 Ahau 3 Uo
998	Last date at Chichen Itza, Osario Temple	10.8.10.11.0 2 Ahau 18 Mol
ca. 1100–1200	Date of *Dresden Codex*	——
ca. 1200	Rise of Mayapan	——
1441	K'atun ending 11.11.0.0.0	11.11.0.0.0 10 Ahau 3 Mac
1441	Fall of Mayapan	——
1519	Juan de Grijalva expedition encounters Maya on coasts of Yucatán and Tabasco	——
1524	Conquest of Q'umarkaj and Iximche' in Maya highlands	——
1525	Hernán Cortés visits Tayasal, the Itza capital	——
1539	K'atun ending 11.16.0.0.0	11.16.0.0.0 13 Ahau 8 Xul
1542	Francisco de Montejo founds Mérida at Maya city of Tiho'	——
1617	Fray Juan de Orbita begins mission from Mérida to Tayasal	——
1618	K'atun 3 Ahau; Bak'tun ending 12.0.0.0.0	12.0.0.0.0 5 Ahau 13 Zodz
1697	K'atun 8 Ahau 12.1.0.0.0	12.1.0.0.0 3 Ahau 18 Kayab
1697	Tayasal falls	——

APPENDIX C

Maya Timekeeping

SEVERAL CYCLES AND time units made the Maya calendar, each with its own distinct structure and scale. It was all part of a larger Mesoamerican tradition of timekeeping, so that the Maya system shared some basic features with the Aztecs and other neighboring cultures. For a comparative look at Mesoamerican calendars, see Caso, *Los calendarios prehispánicos*. Stuart, *The Order of Days*, provides a general overview of the ancient Maya system.

The 260-day calendar is known as the *tzolk'in* (*cholq'ij*), or the "order of the days." It was used in historical times and today as a divinatory calendar, and it may have been invented for that purpose, deep in the Preclassic period. This was composed of twenty named days in a set sequence, paired with numbers from 1 to 13, such that any combination of a number and a day would repeat every 260 days (13 × 20 = 260). So, for example, a day 8 Ahau would always be followed by 9 Imix, then 10 Ik, 11 Akbal, 12 Kan, 13 Chicchan, 1 Cimi, 2 Manik, and so on. For soothsayers, the combination of number and name conveyed great significance in knowing the good or bad prognosis of a given day and for telling the fortunes associated with everyday life, especially involving childbirth and planting. The first archaeological evidence of this calendar is from

San Bartolo, Guatemala, and dates to 300 BCE. My suspicion is that the system was invented by the lowland Maya in the Middle Preclassic and that it spread to other parts of southern Mesoamerica, including Oaxaca, before the Classic period. Remarkably, the use of this same calendar persists to this day in some regions of Guatemala and Oaxaca, carefully guarded by traditional day-keepers (Tedlock, *Time and the Highland Maya*).

The 260-day cycle was integrated with a solar year count that represented a year of 365 days. This consisted of eighteen named periods ("months") of twenty days each and ending with a small liminal period of five days, the "chamber of the year" ([18 × 20] + 5 = 365). The first day of the first month represented the day of the New Year, which the Maya of ancient Yucatán would have called "1 Pop" (the names of these months, like the days, varied considerably among the different Mayan languages). The subsequent day would be "2 Pop," then "3 Pop," and so on. In this way, any given day could be designated as a combination of stations in the 260- and 365-day calendars. Note, for example, the following list of nine sequential days and how the different systems operate separately yet concurrently (Zotz and Tzec are month names).

9 Imix 14 Zotz
10 Ik 15 Zotz
11 Akbal 16 Zotz
12 Kan 17 Zotz
13 Chicchan 18 Zotz
1 Cimi 19 Zotz
2 Manik seating of Tzec
3 Lamat 1 Tzec
4 Muluc 2 Tzec

Mathematically, any given combination of day and month will repeat after fifty-two years (18,980 days, to be exact). This is what we call a calendar round, and for many Mesoamericans it represented a major way of structuring and understanding the complex dynamics of time and history. For the Aztecs, a new year that fell on the day 2 Acatl (or 2 Ben for the Maya) represented a moment of world renewal and regeneration; on the previous evening, the Aztec ruler and his priests would gather on a sacred mountain near ancient Tenochtitlán, the Aztec capital, and perform a ritual drilling of a new sacred fire that would be distributed to the temples of the city, representing a new life and power of the cosmos. The Maya had many renewal rituals of their own, as described in the historical sources of the sixteenth century, including the destruction and manufacture of sacred images and idols.

The Maya also had a far more elaborate time structure that they integrated with these smaller cycles. This we call the "Long Count" (its ancient name now long forgotten). This is different in being a more linear place-notation system for recording large numbers of accumulated days, counted from a specific starting point in the distant past. The standard form of this calendar consisted of five units or periods. The smallest was a single day (*k'in*), and twenty days made up the next higher period known as a *uinal.* Eighteen uinals made 360 days, or a unit known as a tun. Twenty of those, in turn, made a k'atun, and twenty of those composed a lengthy unit we call a bak'tun (a term coined by modern scholars). In descending order, the periods looked like this:

bak'tun	20^2 tuns	144,000 days
k'atun	20 tuns	7,200 days
tun	18 uinals	360 days
uinal	20 k'ins	20 days
k'in		1 day

In recording a day in this system, it was necessary to assign numbers to each unit, designating their multiples as counted from a standardized base date. So an important date from Maya history—the birth of the noted ruler of the kingdom of Palenque, K'inich Janabpakal—is written as 9 bak'tuns, 8 k'atuns, 9 tuns, 13 uinals, and no days. We write this as 9.8.9.13.0. In the concurrent calendar round, this corresponds to 8 Ahau 13 Pop. So this single day in the Maya calendar we would transcribe as:

9.8.9.13.0 8 Ahau 13 Pop

Stela 36 from Piedras Negras (see Figure 2.7) opens with a Long Count date in its first two columns, commemorating the accession of the local ruler Xokmo' Chahk. This is written as:

9.10.6.5.9 8 Muluc 2 Zip

If we take each unit of the Long Count and reduce its value to zero, we come to the distant base date of the system. Curiously, however, the ancient Maya did not simply write this as "0.0.0.0.0" as we might expect. Rather they chose to write it as a station where the bak'tun was set at 13, a sacred number:

13.0.0.0.0 4 Ahau 8 Cumku

According to the widely accepted correlation of the Maya calendar with our own, this beginning point of the Long Count fell on the day we would designate as August 13, 3114 BCE. Because of its remoteness in time, some two thousand years before the Olmec, this date clearly had no historical relevance for the Maya. Why it was chosen as a starting point for the Long Count remains something of a mystery. Some have suggested that August 13 held great significance as a day of solar zenith in parts of southern Mesoamerica. The bak'tun period after this was 1.0.0.0.0, followed some four hundred years later by 2.0.0.0.0, then 3.0.0.0.0, and so on. This base date held great mythological and cosmological significance and is recorded in several ancient inscriptions, as well as in the *Dresden Codex*. The Long Count is often described as a more "linear" system of time reckoning, but it too rests on a cyclical conception of time, visible only when we see its larger extent. The distinction we often hear between linear and cyclical time is hardly a meaningful one, however, since nearly all calendar systems integrate recurring, often natural cycles within a one-directional framework. The Maya calendars are no different.

The "Grand Long Count" is the full system that consists of twenty-four units, with nineteen periods above the bak'tun. The mathematics represented by this exponential system are truly astounding, for a single bak'tun is about four hundred years. The next highest unit, called a pik-tun, is twenty bak'tuns, or about eight thousand years. The next higher unit is twenty of those, and so on, and so on. In this way, a single unit of the uppermost period represented at Coba represents 20^{21} or so years. This system was reserved for mythic dates, including the supposed base we usually find written as 13.0.0.0.0 4 Ahau 8 Cumku. On a few stelae at Coba, the date is written with the higher periods all also set at 13:

13.13.13.13.13.13.13.13.13.13.13.13.13.13.13.13.13.13.13.0.0.0.0
4 Ahau 8 Cumku

We immediately see that the supposed base date of the Long Count in 3114 BCE was not its actual beginning but a station of far more vast conception of time that began eons upon eons in the past. The Coba number represents a near incomprehensible scale of time.

How would we correlate Maya dates with European ones? What is 9.10.6.5.9 8 Muluc 2 Zip in the Christian calendar? The answer was provided by an American newspaperman named Joseph T. Goodman (who, incidentally, gave Mark Twain his first writing job in 1861; the two remained lifelong friends). Goodman was fascinated by Maya culture, having absorbed some of the native histories that had been recently published at the time, including Brinton's recent translations of the *Books of Chilam Balam* and other sources, published in 1882. Other clues were provided in the *Relación* and in the native histories Pio Pérez had compiled, published by Stephens long before. Using these scattered raw materials, Goodman replicated some of Förstemann's inroads into the structure of the Long Count calendar. He also looked closely at how these dates were written on the stone monuments of the Classic period. (Förstemann, by contrast, had confined himself mostly to dates in the *Dresden Codex*.) Going beyond this, Goodman also compiled several murky statements in the colonial-era chronicles that explicitly linked Maya dates to Christian ones. The evidence was terribly complex, but one important clue centered on the recorded death of a famous nobleman named Napot Xiu that was said to have taken place on the day 9 Imix (in the 260-day calendar) and on the 17th day of Zip (in the 365-day year).

This was said to have occurred on September 11, 1545. This alone was not enough to anchor the whole calendar system to our own, however, for any combination of the 260- and 365-day cycles can repeat every fifty-two years. (Another such combination occurred in 1493 and another in 1597.) Goodman understood that a key passage mentioned that Napot Xiu's death also was said to have occurred within the sixth year after the end of a k'atun period (a twenty-year interval) that fell on a 13 Ahau. Backtracking, he reached the k'atun ending 13 Ahau 8 Xul, which he knew had to correspond to 11.16.0.0.0 when linked to all of the other known k'atun records of ancient Maya history. In that moment, Goodman could discern that ancient dates recorded at Palenque, Copan, and other sites were earlier by about two or more bak'tuns, or roughly eight hundred years, placing those dates in the eighth and ninth centuries. Since Goodman's original insights, the details of the correlation have been tweaked and refined numerous times over many decades, such that we are confident when to place Maya dates in our own historical time frame, give or take one or two days. Most recently, Maya records of lunar phases have helped us anchor the correlation with great precision to the day, in support of the Martin-Skidmore correlation (Martin and Skidmore, "Exploring the 584286 Correlation"). So our example 9.10.6.5.9 8 Muluc 2 Zip best corresponds to April 13, 639. The debate about the details of the correlation continues, however, and more refinements to our conception of ancient Maya time and its connection to our calendar no doubt lie ahead.

ACKNOWLEDGMENTS

I OWE A profound debt to those who have written before about the ancient Maya and who have teased out the parts of history and archaeology presented in these pages. The pioneer was Tatiana Proskouriakoff, the modest artist and scholar who changed our field with a single paper in 1960. Her later book *Maya History*, published posthumously, will always remain an important and insightful source. I was fortunate enough to meet Tania when I was a young, upcoming scholar, and I was always in awe of her. Linda Schele and David Freidel's *A Forest of Kings*, published in 1990, stands out as an important milestone, too. Linda was my first real mentor, and with her brilliance and infectious energy, she was always determined to tell a good story. A decade later, Simon Martin and Nikolai Grube's *Chronicle of Maya Kings and Queens* was another landmark, distilling many dynastic narratives in a standardized format for students and scholars alike. Now in its second edition, it is still a go-to source. Simon has long been at the forefront of studying Maya geopolitics and history, and I highly recommend his remarkable book *Ancient Maya Politics* for a more in-depth and scholarly treatment of what we know.

Many colleagues and friends in Mesoamerican art and archaeology have helped me and this book, and they are too many to name. Stephen Houston, Simon Martin, and Karl Taube have always been present in my mind during the writing and thinking process. I must also acknowledge the insights, encouragement, and support over the years from Bárbara Arroyo, Jaime Awe, Tomás Barrientos Quezada, Boris Beltrán, Dmitri Beliaev, Marcello Canuto, Oswaldo Chinchilla Mazariegos, Iyaxel Cojti Ren, Maria José Con, Francisco Estrada-Belli, Barbara Fash, William Fash, Thomas Garrison, Ian Graham, Norman Hammond, Merle Greene Robertson, Stanley Guenter, Christophe Helmke, Takeshi Inomata, John Justeson, Danny Law, Maxime Lamoure-St-Hilaire, Peter Mathews, Mary Miller, Alfonso Morales, Olivia Navarro-Farr, Joel Palka, Jocelyne Ponce, Astrid Runggaldier, William Saturno, Linda Schele,

Joel Skidmore, Travis Stanton, Nawa Sugiyama, Alexandre Tokovinine, Erik Velásquez Garcia, Sergei Verpetskii, and Marc Zender. Each has contributed to the greater effort of weaving a narrative of Maya history together. My former student Michel Brun helped put together a grand timeline of Maya dates, which made the analysis so much easier. Tom Garrison and Fernando José Véliz read over a draft of the manuscript and provided extremely valuable feedback. Fernando also produced the excellent maps. For their help with the illustrations, I extend gratitude to Jean Pierre Courau, Octavio Esparza Olguín, Francisco Estrada-Belli, Richard Hansen, Christophe Helmke, Heather Hurst, Harri Ketunnen, Jorge Pérez de Lara, Nelda Issa Marengo, Simon Martin, Timothy Pugh, Franco Rossi, Alexandre Tokovinine, and Marc Zender. Daniel Salazar Lama kindly gave permission to use the reconstruction view of Calakmul Structure 2. Cynthia Mackey at Harvard's Peabody Museum was of wonderful help in tracking down images and permissions of several figures.

Rob Tempio, my editor at Princeton University Press, was always patient and encouraging, and he made this book possible. And fellow archaeologist Eric Cline, editor of this series, has been an inspiration with his brilliant treatments on collapse and culture change in the worlds of the ancient Mediterranean and Near East. Chloe Coy at the Press was of great help in steering me through to the end, and Beth Nauman-Montana crafted the index. Thanks to all.

I thank the Boundary End Archaeological Research Center and its board for a yearlong scholarship to devote to this book. And great love and appreciation to my sister Ann Stuart for helping make that happen. On the home front, George and Misty Porter were a source of constant support. To their daughter and my wife, Carolyn, and to my sons Peter, Richard, and George, I extend infinite thanks and love for their patience over these past few years. And to the cats too.

NOTES

PREFACE

1 More on the complex story of "Site Q" and La Corona will be told in chapter 6. The inscribed stones from Structure 13R-10 are still in the process of analysis and publication, but a preliminary treatment of their context is in Ponce et al., "Voices and Narratives."

2 The name of this dance presumably refers to the accompaniment of a flute adorned with a feather—a rare reference to a musical instrument in the ancient texts. First published in Stuart et al., "The Nomenclature of La Corona Sculpture."

3 Chippindale et al., "The Archaeology of Maya Decipherment."

CHAPTER I. RUPTURE

1 The ruins of Xultun (ancient Baxwitz) were visited in 1920 by the Mayanist Sylvanus Griswold Morley, who described the site in his *The Inscriptions of Peten*. See also von Euw, *Corpus of Maya Hieroglyphic Inscriptions*. The well-preserved Stela 10, illustrated here, was found by Morley, then looted in the 1960s. Its whereabouts today are unknown. The original name Baxwitz was identified by Prager et al. in "A Reading for the Xultun Toponymic Title."

2 Farriss, *Maya Society Under Colonial Rule*.

3 See Farriss, *Maya Society Under Colonial Rule*, for a thorough overview of Yucatec Maya strategies to adapt and put distance between themselves and the new colonial structures imposed by the Spanish. Mass flight was a common strategy in that era of instability and disruption.

4 From Stephens, *Incidents of Travel in Yucatán*, II:308. His *Incidents of Travel in Yucatán* was the second of his two-volume works, each bestsellers in their day. The first was *Incidents of Travel in Central America, Chiapas and Yucatán*. A modern account of his and Catherwood's journeys can be found in Carlsen, *Jungle of Stone*.

5 Of course, some Maya were aware of their connection to the pre-invasion landscape. For example, the anthropologists La Farge and Byers reported visiting a small Postclassic ruin in the highlands of western Guatemala, which the local Indigenous guides identified as being built by their ancestors just a few centuries earlier. The frequent movement of Maya populations in the lowlands probably exacerbated the historical disconnect Stephens and others described. La Farge and Byers, *The Year Bearer's People*, 19.

6 Del Rio, *Description of the Ruins of an Ancient City*.

7 "American Antiquities," *The Knickerbocker*, 371.

8 "American Antiquities," *The Knickerbocker*, 371.

9 Stephens, *Incidents of Travel in Yucatán*, II:191.

10 Stephens, *Incidents of Travel in Central America, Chiapas and Yucatán*, I:158.

11 Stephens, *Incidents of Travel in Central America, Chiapas and Yucatán*, I:104.

12 Stephens, *Incidents of Travel in Central America, Chiapas and Yucatán*, I:159–60).

13 Stephens, *Incidents of Travel in Central America, Chiapas and Yucatán*, II:356–57.

14 The ancient hieroglyph that might read **MAY-HA'** is a place name cited at three distinct locales—at Río Azul, at Yaxchilan, and on an unprovenanced ceramic vessel. It does not refer to any of these specific sites, however. I suspect, very tentatively, that it corresponds to the historical geographic name *Maya'*, perhaps originally referring to the northern lowland region or what we now define as the northern Yucatán Peninsula. The relationship of the word "Maya" to the place name *Mayapan* is discussed by Restall, "Maya Ethnogenesis," and Restall and Gabbert, "Maya Ethnogenesis and Group Identity in Yucatán." I prefer to see *Maya* as an old regional toponym that existed before Spanish contact, referring at least to the lands of northwest Yucatán and nearby territories. In the sixteenth century, "Maya" quickly came to be an ethnic and linguistic term as well, giving rise to its usages historically and today. *Mayab*, which is sometimes considered the original term, may be a more modern construct.

15 Goodman, *The Archaic Maya Inscriptions*, vi. The title of his work was among the first uses of "Maya" in reference to an archaeological culture.

16 Díaz del Castillo, *The Discovery and Conquest of Mexico*, 13.

17 For an overview of the Classic Mayan language, see Law and Stuart, "Classic Mayan."

18 For a broad comparative look at Mayan languages, see Aissen et al., *The Mayan Language*, and Kaufman, *Mayan Comparative Studies*. A recent grammatical sketch of Ch'olti' Mayan, based on Morán's writings, is in Robertson et al., *Colonial Ch'olti'*.

19 Stephens, *Incidents of Travel in Yucatán*, II:117.

20 The documents copied by Juan Pío Pérez included the *Books of Chilam Balam* from Mani and Ozkutzcab, otherwise lost. His meticulous compilation of these and other sources is known collectively today as the *Codex Pérez*, several copies of which were made and distributed in the late 1800s.

21 See Shaw, *The Sea Shall Embrace Them*. Before the *Titanic*, the loss of the *S.S. Arctic*, carrying Catherwood and four hundred others from England to America, was seen as the worst maritime disaster in the North Atlantic.

22 See Brasseur de Bourbourg and Étienne, "Relation de choses de Yucatán de Diego de Landa." For English translations of Landa's *Relación*, see Tozzer, *Landa's Relación de las Cosas de Yucatán*, and Restall et al., *The Friar and the Maya*.

23 Izamal was chosen as the seat for the bishop of Yucatán because of its long-standing importance as a place of pilgrimage at the time of the conquest. Its huge pyramids were then regarded as ancestral spaces. The large monastery of Izamal was built atop a large Late Preclassic platform in the center of the town, appropriating its sacred space (see Solari, *Maya Ideologies of the Sacred* and *Idolizing Mary*).

24 The Maya who lived in this sparsely inhabited region of southern Campeche and northern Peten were known in early colonial times as the *Kejache* or *Mazatecos* (Villa Rojas "Los quejaches"). Both names can be translated as "Deer People," in Kiche' Mayan and in Nahuatl, respectively. They were refugees mostly from northern Yucatán and likely the ancestors of the Lacandon. Given their origin, it is a bit tempting to relate their label to the geographical name *Maya'* and its possible basis in the root *may*, "young deer," as shown in the hieroglyph (see note 16).

25 Quotation from Farriss, *Maya Society Under Colonial Rule*, 199. Here she rightly noted that "the well-documented colonial patterns [of population movement] may help to interpret

earlier cycles of consolidation and dissolution that are only hinted at in the archaeological record."

26 Both Sánchez de Aguilar and López Medel are quoted in Tozzer, *Landa's Relación de las Cosas de Yucatán*, 28.

27 Tozzer, *Landa's Relación de las Cosas de Yucatán*, 169.

28 Thompson, *The Rise and Fall of Maya Civilization*, 14. His book was among the first overviews of Maya archaeology and culture.

29 Early archaeologists, mostly from the United States, were eager to excavate these sites to learn more about their age. Initial efforts included expeditions to Copan (1891–1895) and Quirigua (1910–14) with an eye to retrieving sculpture or making copies for public exhibitions, including the Chicago World's Fair of 1893 or San Diego's Panama-California Exposition of 1915. It was not until the end of World War I that any museums or research institutions could muster the time and funds for serious field research and excavations. In short order, the government of Mexico and the Carnegie Institution of Washington began ambitious programs of study at Chichen Itza and then at Uaxactun, Guatemala, with its early inscribed hieroglyphic dates. It is difficult to separate many of these efforts from the United States' economic and political interests in Central America at the time during the Cold War. In addition to the Carnegie Institution, one important funding source for Guatemalan archaeology in the mid-twentieth century was the United Fruit Company.

30 Morley, "Maya Epigraphy," 148.

31 Morley, "Maya Epigraphy," 147.

32 Thompson, *The Rise and Fall of Maya Civilization*.

33 Thompson, *The Rise and Fall of Maya Civilization*, 269.

34 Thompson was knighted by Queen Elizabeth II in 1975, the year he died. Publicly he never accepted the new wave of epigraphic work just starting around that time, but conversations he had at the time reveal his awareness that great advances were being made (George Stuart, personal communication).

CHAPTER 2. READING

1 Robinson, *Lost Languages*, 14. In Robinson's account of Maya decipherment, Yurii Knorosov and Linda Schele take center stage as the primary contributors, following much of the narrative offered by Coe, *Breaking the Maya Code*. My own interpretation is different, as presented later in this chapter.

2 Pope, "The Story of Archaeological Decipherment," and Robinson, *Lost Languages*, present accounts of various decipherments and their methodologies. Recent overviews of the decipherment of Egyptian and Linear B are Adkins and Adkins, *The Keys of Egypt*, and Robinson, *Cracking the Egyptian Code*.

3 Brinton, quoted in Rau, "The Palenque Tablet," 52–53.

4 One exception to this was Thompson, who spent all of World War II in the United States, working and writing in Cambridge, Massachusetts, much to the chagrin of his colleagues. In Thompson's defense, he had already spent years as a young foot soldier in the trenches and front lines of World War I, a traumatic experience that probably contributed to his later idealized views of a "peaceful" Classic Maya civilization that declined steadily in the Postclassic through warfare

and secularism (Thompson, *The Rise and Fall of Maya Civilization*, 86, 270–73). To some extent, his experiences in the first war drove Thompson to present his beloved Maya as an antidote to his own troubled, conflicted times.

5 Here we should recall how Brinton had accurately anticipated that Maya glyphs were a mixed system of word signs and syllables in 1879. Also in the late 1800s, the American lawyer and antiquarian Cyrus Thomas deserves credit for first discerning the use of Landa's "ca" element as a CV syllable in the spelling of the word *cacao* (**ka-ka-wa**) in 1888. Thomas was wrong about most of his other ideas. No one followed up on these initial insights until Knorosov saw the wider range of patterns and connections, providing a much-needed jumpstart to the decipherment.

6 Tozzer, in his introduction to Whorf, "The Phonetic Value of Certain Characters," ix. The former's discussion of the **ma-ka** spelling for the month *Mak* was spot-on and deserves recognition in the decipherment's history (Whorf, "The Phonetic Value of Certain Characters," 23).

7 After Knorosov's initial breakthrough papers ("Drevnyaya Pis'mennost'"), he began to overextend his arguments, proposing a great many glyph readings and text translations that were incorrect, even outlandish. Later generations of U.S.-based epigraphers accepted his initial insights on syllabic writing and then took those forward in a very different direction, as exemplified in the works of Lounsbury, "The 'Ben-Ich' Prefix," Justeson and Campbell, *Phoneticism in Mayan Hieroglyphic Writing*; Mathews, "Notes on the Inscriptions"; Houston, "The Phonetic Decipherment of Mayan Glyphs"; and myself (Stuart, "Ten Phonetic Syllables"), among others. By the 1980s, these efforts stood in direct opposition to the so-called "Soviet School" of Maya epigraphy. Despite that name, this divergence was not an ideological or political conflict of the Cold War era but a very different methodology of epigraphy. The contrast with Knorosov's later off-base approach to Maya writing plays little role in Coe's popular account of the decipherment history (*Breaking the Maya Code*).

8 Stephens, *Incidents of Travel in Central America*, II:343.

9 An engaging personal account of the tomb's discovery was written by Ruz for the *Saturday Evening Post* ("Mystery of the Mayan Temple").

10 Proskouriakoff, "Historical Implications of a Pattern of Dates."

11 Thompson eventually recognized Proskouriakoff's breakthrough, acknowledging it in the 1971 edition of his book *Maya Hieroglyphic Writing: An Introduction*.

12 In print, Proskouriakoff never commented directly on Knorosov's approach. However, her careful notes on his phonetic methods reveal an eager acceptance of his work. I was fascinated to see these when examining her papers at Harvard's Peabody Museum, where I began work in 1993, occupying her old office. Proskouriakoff's desk was still there, and her papers were still all in a nearby filing cabinet.

13 Today we read **chu-ka-ja** for the Classic Mayan passive verb construction *chuhkaj*, "is/was captured."

14 It is significant that Berlin, Knorosov, and Proskouriakoff were all to varying degrees "outsiders" in the burgeoning field of Maya archaeology, an intellectual world dominated by men and based almost exclusively in the United States at institutions such as Harvard and the Carnegie Institution of Washington. (Berlin, a German war refugee and expat, earned his living as an insurance salesman in Mexico City.) This was also true of a few others who came later to the world of Maya epigraphy. An outside viewpoint can sometimes work as an advantage, unencumbered by the internal paradigms and politics of the academic world.

15 Ian Graham initiated an important project called the *Corpus of Maya Hieroglyphic Inscriptions*, publishing an initial fascicle of drawings and photographs on Naranjo in 1975. His archives contained the raw material that spurred much of the decipherment in the next two decades. Ian's remarkable story is recounted in his colorful and highly readable autobiography (Graham 2010).

16 Justin Kerr produced five volumes of his vase photographs under the titles *The Maya Vase Book*. Today many of his images can be accessed digitally through his websites, at www.mayavase.com, or via an updated database curated by the Dumbarton Oaks Library and Collection at https://www.doaks.org/research/library-archives/icfa/collections/kerr-collection.

17 Coe, *Breaking the Maya Code*, 231–58. Important examples of this new methodology of the time include Houston (1983), Mathews and Justeson (1984), and Stuart, "Ten Phonetic Syllables" and "The Decipherment of 'Directional Count Glyphs.'"

18 The Ch'olan identification was initially outlined by Campbell, "The Implications of Mayan Historical Linguistics." It has been greatly expanded in several works on the linguistic interpretation of Maya texts, including Houston et al., "The Language of Maya Inscriptions," and Law and Stuart, "Classic Mayan," and in the edited works by Macri and Ford, *The Language of Maya Hieroglyphs*, and Wichmann, *The Linguistics of Maya Writing*.

19 See Stuart et al., "An Early Maya Calendar Record," for the earliest Maya date at San Bartolo.

20 Fash et al., "The Hieroglyphic Stairway and Its Ancestors"; Fash, *The Copan Sculpture Museum*, 101–111; Stuart, "A Foreign Past."

21 In writing these last few paragraphs on the Piedras Negras stela (in May 2023), I took a moment to look more closely at the king's name and deciphered it for the first time. I do not think it had ever been properly read as Xokmo'chahk, and we have long referred to him simply as "Ruler 2." Progress in Maya history is ever ongoing and typically comes in small steps.

22 Helmke et al., *A Reading of the Komkom Vase*.

CHAPTER 3. DAWNING

1 See Morley, "Archaeology." Morley misread one of these early dates and used a correlation between calendars now long rejected by Maya scholars. He nonetheless knew that the Uaxactun dates were very early compared to other sites known at the time.

2 For insights into the idea of civilization outside the Mesoamerican context, see Wengrow, *What Makes a Civilization?*

3 Preserved physical human remains dating before 10,000 BCE are exceedingly rare. One remarkable find in the Maya region came to light recently, in 2007, when divers encountered portions of a human skeleton deep within an underwater cenote named Hoyo Negro (Black Hole) near Yucatán's east coast. These were the bones of a young woman who died some 13,000 to 12,000 years ago, probably having fallen into the cavern after she entered the cave in search of water. Archaeologists named her "Naia." DNA extracted from Naia's teeth indicate that she was not far removed from a population that had moved out of Beringia not long beforehand and that she was part of a group ancestral to modern Native Americans. See Chatters et al., "Late Pleistocene Human Skeleton"; and González et al., "The First Human Settlers on the Yucatán Peninsula."

4 Evidence for intensive fish-trapping has been recently discovered in Belize, dating to the Late Archaic. One suspects that such techniques were already well in place even by this time. See Harrison-Buck et al., "Late Archaic Large-Scale Fisheries."

5 See, for example, Kintz, *Life Under the Tropical Canopy*, 17, in her descriptions of Maya belief at the village of Coba in the 1970s.

6 These entities of water, rain, and stone all overlapped visually and conceptually. Lightning, created by the forceful axe of the storm god, created sacred stones, including flint and obsidian, sometimes today called *piedras de rayo* (see Bassie-Sweet, *Maya Gods of War*, 38–42). Anthropologist Charles Wisdom (*The Chorti Indians of Guatemala*, 396) noted that among the Ch'orti' Maya, "wherever lightning strikes, a stone axe is believed to be buried in the ground." This may account for the visual overlap between *tun*, stone, and Chahk. The Water Serpent of Maya art is the embodiment of surface water, *ha'*. Its role in the narrative of Maya creation myth is provided in an inscription recently discovered at Lacanja-Tzeltal, Chiapas.

7 Early pre-ceramic chert extraction and tool production are discussed by Hester et al., "Exploitation of Chert Resources," and Iceland, "The Preceramic Origins of the Maya."

8 Soon after writing this, I came across a detailed discussion of the importance of limestone for the Maya by Voorhies and Michaels, "The Ancient Maya and Limestone."

9 The dating of early maize in the Maya region often is subject to revision and debate, probably reflecting an inherent variability of the first practices of maize agriculture across the region. The earliest claim of maize use comes from the site of Caye Coco in northern Belize, corresponding to about 4700 BCE (Rosenswig, "Archaic Period Settlement and Subsistence"). But it may be an outlier, with 3000 BCE a more conservative and perhaps more widely accepted view, as suggested by Lohse, "Early Maize in the Maya Area," 7. The recent data from Belize rock shelters agrees with a widespread introduction of maize use around this time, in Kennet, "Early Isotopic Evidence for Maize." Before 1500 BCE, maize may have been cultivated intermittently and in selected areas, alongside foraging and the exploitation of other food resources. Most agree that after this time maize became a basic staple crop.

10 Wild maize had been first cultivated in southwestern Mesoamerica, perhaps in the Balsas River Basin of Guerrero, Mexico, sometime before 6500 BCE, and from there it quickly spread southward through Central America yet apparently bypassed the Maya lowlands. In less than two millennia, we see evidence of its use in Colombia, whence it spread farther into South America. See Piperno, "The Origins of Plant Cultivation," for an overview of maize domestication in Mexico, Central America, and northern South America.

11 Another important natural resource for the early inhabitants of Central America was the calabash gourd, the fruit of the tree *Crescentia alata*, found in the Maya area and a bit beyond. Its importance is often underestimated, for gourds served as basic containers for water and food long before ceramics or even intensive agriculture appeared on the scene. Evidence suggests that gourds were domesticated in the American tropics by at least 7000–8000 BCE, probably brought to the Americas via seeds and fruits that floated across the Atlantic from Africa. Early Mesoamericans relied on them, and it is no accident that the first ceramic bowls of the region, mostly from the Pacific coastal regions, consciously replicate the *tecomates*, or cups made from cut gourds that would have been used for thousands of years. It is possible that early Maya populations of the lowlands saw little need to adopt ceramic technology as early on as their

neighbors simply because the need for pottery was not so pressing, especially among groups that remained semi-mobile. Gourd vessels, lightweight and difficult to break, are so practical that they continue to be widely used today, even in my own kitchen.

12 For reviews of Pre-Mamom ceramics, see, among others, Castellanos and Foias, "The Earliest Maya Farmers of Peten"; Cheetham, "Cunil: A Pre-Mamom Horizon in the Southern Maya Lowlands"; Clark and Cheetham, "Mesoamerica's Tribal Foundations"; Reese-Taylor, "Becoming Maya"; and an excellent compilation of studies edited by Walker, *Pre-Mamom Pottery Variation*. Related to this, MacLellan, "Settling Down at Ceibal," provides a valuable comparative look at the emergence of inequality in different regions during the Middle Preclassic.

13 Hammond, *Cuello*.

14 The Maize God and its Preclassic antecedents have been studied extensively by Taube, "The Classic Maya Maize God" and *The Major Gods of Ancient Yucatán*. See also Chinchilla Mazariegos, *Art and Myth of the Ancient Maya*, 185–223, and Fields, "The Iconographic Heritage of the Jester God," and Houston et al., *The Memory of Bones*. For contemporary religious ideas of maize among the Maya and others in Mesoamerica, see Faust, *Mexican Rural Development*, 113–52; Girard, *Los mayas eternos*, 147–62; Sandstrom, *Corn Is Our Blood*; and Vogt, *Tortillas for the Gods*, 55–59.

15 For general treatments of Olmec archaeology and its debates, see Clark and Pye, *Olmec Art*; Cyphers, "The Early Preclassic Olmec"; Diehl (2004); and Grove, *Discovering the Olmecs*.

16 For San Lorenzo, see Cheetham and Blomster, "Materializing the San Lorenzo Olmecs"; Coe and iehl, *In the Land of the Olmec*; Cyphers et al., *Las olmecas de San Lorenzo*; and Inomata, "Olmecs and Other Western Neighbors."

17 Lidar (short for "light detection and ranging") employs airborne lasers to penetrate forest and vegetation to detect the ground surface, creating a 3D representation of terrain and, inevitably, of evidence of its long-term modification by people. While it has transformed archaeological investigations across the globe, lidar is especially revealing in the Maya area, where the jungle canopy has always made ground-based surveying extremely difficult (as I can personally attest). See Canuto et al., "Ancient Lowland Maya Complexity"; Chase et al., "Airborne LiDAR"; and Garrison et al., "Assessing the Lidar Revolution."

18 Inomata et al., "Monumental Architecture."

19 Inomata et al., "After 40 Years."

20 See Brown and Bey, *Pathways to Complexity*, for a recent overview of research involving the Middle and Late Preclassic periods in Yucatán and the northern regions. They refer to this lengthy span of seven or so centuries (1000–300 BCE) as the "most dynamic period of Maya history" (*Pathways to Complexity*, 388).

21 Cenotes appear throughout Yucatán, formed in greatest numbers in the northwest, along the edge of the ancient Chicxulub impact crater that was responsible for mass faunal extinctions of sixty-five million years ago. If one maps the cenotes, one can see that their distribution is a semicircle, part of a geological "ring" that formed in the young, porous limestone that covers the crater today. The distribution of the first Maya cities of Yucatán, and population centers historically, is thus directly related to this notable geological history—and indirectly to the demise of the dinosaurs. See also Hildebrand et al., "Size and Structure."

22 Brown and Stanton, "Public Architecture," 33. For a general discussion of E Groups in the Maya area, see Aimers and Rice, "Astronomy, Ritual and the Interpretation," and the various

articles in Freidel et al., *Maya E-Groups*. Note that these publications all appeared shortly before the discovery of Aguada Fénix and related sites in Tabasco.

23 Inomata, "The Isthmian Origins"; Inomata et al., ""Early Ceremonial Constructions" and "After 40 Years." Reese-Taylor, "Founding Landscapes," offers an insightful look at the foundational aspects of E Groups in the central lowlands. See Stanton, "The Founding of Yaxuná"; and Collins, "Selective Memory," for a specific case study of Yaxuna's E Group as an incipient monument.

24 For Cival, see Estrada-Belli, "The History, Function, and Meaning."

25 The calendrical and astronomical implications of the earliest E Groups and related structures are presented in Šprajc et al., "Origins of Mesoamerican Astronomy." As they suggest, it is likely that the 260-day calendar was a lowland Maya or Gulf Coast invention during the Middle Preclassic, which later spread to Oaxaca and then, during the Classic period, to highland Mexico.

26 Stuart et al., ""An Early Maya Calendar Record," describes this early date fragment from San Bartolo, and Saturno et al., "Early Maya Writing," discusses early examples of writing from the same excavation levels.

27 See Stanton and Freidel, "Ideological Lock-In."

28 In Yucatec Mayan, the word *kol* refers not only to a cornfield but to a space that has been sanctified and set in order (Dunning et al., "Kax and Kol," 3656). Girard, *People of the Chan*, 188 notes the significance of milpas among the Ch'orti' Maya in the 1930s, stating that they were "place(s) as sacred as a table or altar of a temple," symbolizing "the cosmic plane." This seems to me fundamental to much of Maya cosmology and must be very old, pointing to relevance in the study of Maya plazas and E Groups. See also Doyle, "A Tale of Two E-Groups."

29 The link between plazas, gatherings, and solar calendars is encapsulated in the extended meanings of the word *k'in* in Mayan languages, "sun, day, festival." The same unified ideas apply to the Nahuatl term *ilhuitl*, showing their broad importance and antiquity in Mesoamerica. For a similar interpretation of Middle Preclassic E Groups and the cultural significance of early clearing, see Freidel, "E Groups, Cosmology," and Doyle, "A Tale of Two E-Groups." The nature of the *paskab* events of Classic texts have been studied by the author and are yet to be presented in print. The history of plazas in performance and ritual are discussed by Inomata, "Plazas, Performers and Spectators," and more broadly by Wagner et al., *Ancient Origins of the Mexican Plaza*.

30 The connection of historical patterns to the turns of bak'tuns and other periods of the calendar has been discussed previously, yet the implications of such "predestined" history are far from understood. See Puleston, "An Epistemological Pathology and the Collapse"; Stuart and Stuart, *Palenque*, 238; and Stuart, "Some Working Notes," 274–82.

31 Brown and Bey, *Pathways to Complexity*, and Brown and Stanton, "Public Architecture," offer overviews of recent research on the Middle Preclassic.

32 Excavators of Nixtun Ch'ich' Prudence Rice and Timothy Pugh make the intriguing suggestion that the plan of the site replicates the back of a massive crocodile, a known representation of the earth's surface in ancient Mesoamerica (what the Postclassic Maya of Yucatán called *Itzamcabain*). See Rice and Pugh, "Water, Centering and the Beginning of Time."

33 See Rice and Pugh, "Water, Centering," for a discussion of the water hole feature within Nixtun Ch'ich' design.

34 For more than forty years, El Mirador has been the focus of archaeological investigations under the direction of Richard Hansen, devoted to survey, chronology, and architectural

excavation (see Hansen, "The First Cities"; Hansen and Suyuc L., *Mirador*). The massive scale of the site and its architecture still presents a challenge for any effort to get a coherent sense of its overall history and development.

35 An overview of the Mirador region and the impressive roadways, based on recent lidar surveys, can be found in Hansen et al. (2002). Calakmul does not seem to be a part of the network, as has sometimes been proposed.

36 The region of El Mirador is often described as a "basin," but it is in fact situated on an upland area at the center of the peninsula, where many of the early Maya sites were founded.

37 In the Late Classic, Nakbe and El Mirador were resettled by elites, some of whom were closely allied with the Kanul kingdom, as revealed by the "codex style" ceramics that were produced at those sites. This distinctive type of vase was clearly centered on Calakmul's court in the eighth century, when it was the principal seat of the Kanul dynasty. This connection brings up a cautionary tale, for some have used this evidence to suggest that the Kanul (or "Kaan") kingdom was based at those Preclassic centers. It seems far more likely that these were late elite outposts, residences of lords allied with Kanul who were descended from the ancient people of "Chatahn," Nakbe, and El Mirador—sites that were by then abandoned and many centuries old.

38 See Martin, "Caracol Altar 21 Revisited." Velásquez García and García Barrios, "Devenir hístorico y papel," offer insights on the "Chatahn" place as an early political center. The problem with the "Chatahn" reading hinges on the first of the two signs used to spell it (**?-TAHN**), which remains unclear. Reents-Budet and Bishop, "Classic Maya Painted Ceramics," have studied the paste of inscribed pottery vessels bearing the "Chatahn" glyph and associated them to several workshops in the great Mirador-Nakbe region. The presence of the title *k'uhul winik* ("holy man") in place of the more customary *k'uhulajaw* ("holy lord") may point to a different type of political status. The ancient title *k'uhulwinik*, used in the more specific honorific term *k'uhul chatahn winik*, is otherwise rare. It survived into the colonial period of Yucatán, however, and appears in colonial documents as *kul uinic*. Hanks, *Converting Words*, 307, translates it in that context as "Spaniard," and it would seem to refer to someone of high religious standing.

39 See Hutson, "Urbanism, Architecture," for a discussion of Late Preclassic and Early Classic centers in the north. Early dates of Izamal are still difficult to define without further excavation into the site's major architecture.

40 San Bartolo was discovered in 2001, when William Saturno was guided to the site and saw the remains of the paintings within a looters' tunnel. He returned to direct the excavations of the mural chamber over several seasons. For popular accounts of those initial explorations, see O'Neil, "Uncovering a Maya Mural," and Stuart, "You Go That Way."

41 The honorific solar title or pre-nomen *K'inich* is so common on royal names that it may cause some confusion here, as we try to keep track of the distinct names in Maya history. For this reason, I will use it sparingly, as in reducing the full form K'inich Yaxk'uk'mo' to just Yaxk'uk'mo'.

42 See Kováč et al., "The Legacy of an Early Maya King," for Uaxactun cache excavation and artifacts.

43 Sakhixmut is also mentioned in two inscriptions from El Peru-Waka', a Classic period rival to Tikal. This says something about Sakhixmut's early importance in the primordial myth-histories of different dynasties.

44 Stuart and Stuart, *Palenque*, 109–11, refer to Ukohkanchan as "Snake Spine." Earlier, Schele and Freidel, *A Forest of Kings*, 254, referred to him as "U-Kix-Chan." In a similar way, readings of many other ancient personal names undergo constant revision and refinement.

45 The changes of the *bajos* and their archaeological implications are described in Dunning et al., "Arising from the *Bajos*." For a discussion of the watery decorations at the Great Central Acropolis at El Mirador, see Argyle and Hansen, "The Preclassic Frieze."

CHAPTER 4. DYNASTIES

1 Evidence for an early and intensive Maya presence at Teotihuacan before the fourth century includes ceramics and other material remains, especially associated with the tunnel under the Feathered Serpent Pyramid and in burials in the Moon Pyramid. See Clayton, "Interregional Relationships"; Gómez Chávez, "Foreigners' Barrios"; López Luján and Sugiyama, "The Ritual Deposits"; and Magaloni-Kerpel et al., "The Moving Image." As Sugiyama et al., "The Maya at Teotihuacan," explore, this interaction appears to have reached apogee in the fourth century, before the pivotal historical events of 378.

2 The translation of *k'uhulajaw* as "holy lord," using the adjective derived from *k'uh*, "god," is accurate enough, but it runs the risk of conveying that Maya rulers were "living gods." I am not sure this is an accurate idea of the ideological underpinnings of Maya kingship. Kings and queens cared for their tutelary deities and kept them close, which may convey a closer idea behind the title, as a "godly lord." Deceased ancestors, as celestial beings, were also classed as *k'uh*. This living/dead dichotomy might be the key distinction here.

3 Eberl et al., "The Early Classic Genesis," discusses the history of the Petexbatun emblem (the "Foliated Scroll" sign) and its presence in the inscriptions of Tamarindito, the major site of the region founded in the Early Classic. It suggests that the deeper historical time frame cited by Classic kings of the area was contrived, used to create a "perception of antiquity." However, the ample Preclassic remains in the area point to the strong possibility of earlier ruling centers, among them Punto de Chamino, the large Late Preclassic site on the shore of Lake Petexbatun (Stephen Houston, personal communication, 2021).

4 Naranjo's deep primordial myth-history comes from the first text columns of Altar 1, and the most distant of the royal ancestors there named appears regularly in many of the site's later texts, including Stela 13, 24, 43, and 45. Martin, *Ancient Maya Politics*, 151, refers to him as "Square-nosed Serpent," a rough description of the main element of his name glyph, which remains undeciphered. The words *ik'*, "black," and *mih or mihin*, "nothing," are discernable in most spellings of his name. For more discussion of this founder, see Baron, *Patron Gods and Patron Lords*, 59–60; Martin and Grube, *Chronicle of Maya Kings*, 70; Schele, "The Founders of Lineages," 140; Stuart et al., "La recuperación de la Estela 43 de Naranjo"; and Tokovinine and Fialko, "Stela 45," 10.

5 This foundation event (*pat tun*, "stone-building") appears on Pol Box, Stela 2, on the day 8.5.0.14.4 (in 141 CE) possibly in connection with the name "Foliated Ajaw," whom I take to be Uxyophun (Esparza Olguín and Pérez Gutierrez, "Archaeological and Epigraphic Studies").

6 The place name *Chihcha'* is mentioned in connection with the name of Kanul's ruler "Scroll Serpent" and also on a stone fragment from Dzibanche, the ancient Kanul capital. I am tempted to see a possible connection to the great Preclassic ruins of Ichkabal, located a short distance to the northeast of Dzibanche, but this is only speculative.

7 According to one text at Palenque, Uxyophun was born in the remote past on the calendar day "1 Ahau" (Jun Ajaw) in the 260-day calendar, suggesting a connection to the deity who bears the same name, Jun Ajaw. This is one of the famous "hero twins" of Maya art and clearly ancestral to Hunahpu of the epic Kiche' Maya story of creation, the *Popol Vuh* (see Coe, "The Hero Twins"). In the Classic period, Jun Ajaw was a mythical hunter wearing a modest headscarf and wielding a blowgun, and he became the prototype of a Maya king. The connection of Jun Ajaw with Uxyophun is also indicated by the latter's mythological identity as the supernatural embodiment of the royal headband, *hun*, and the bark paper material used in its crafting. Jun Ajaw wears this device as one of his diagnostic markers. Furthermore, it is probably significant here that the words *hun* ("paper headband") and *jun* ("one") were near-homophones and at times even spelled interchangeably in the hieroglyphs. See Stuart, "The Name of Paper."

8 The founder's name is sometimes spelled as Ehbxok or Yax Ehbxok. As an aside, the director of the Penn excavations at Tikal in the late 1950s was the noted Maya archaeologist named Edwin (Ed) Shook. Sadly, Ed passed away before knowing the similar-sounding name of Tikal's ancient founder. He would have enjoyed that connection, I am sure.

9 Martin, "In Line of the Founder," 5, places Yax Ehbxok in the first century. In another study, Martin, "The Painted King List," 853, estimates 22.5 years as an "average reign," based on Maya data as well as English history.

10 Yax Ehbxok was first identified as Tikal's dynastic founder by Schele, The Founders of Lineages." In a widely read source, she referred to him as "Yax-Moch-Xoc" (Schele and Freidel, *A Forest of Kings*, 140).

11 See Mathews, "Maya Early Classic Monuments," for an overview of early dated monuments and their distribution.

12 Valdés and Fahsen, "The Reigning Dynasty," 202. See Laporte and Valdés, *Tikal y Uaxactun*, for a look at Preclassic archaeology at Tikal and Uaxactun, including a comprehensive description of Group E and its architectural development from the Middle Preclassic onward.

13 All of the "Dynastic Vases" lack archaeological provenience. However, they are in the "codex style," so we can link them with confidence to the area of Nakbe. One sherd of another vase in the set was found in excavations at Calakamul, the late capital of the Kanul dynasty (or "Snake dynasty"). See Martin, "The Painted King List" and "Secrets of the Painted King List."

14 Details about the reconstruction of Kanul's early kings are in Martin, "Secrets of the Painted King List."

15 The early king list of Yaxchilan appears on Lintels 11, 49, 37, 35, 48, 47, 34, and 36 (reflecting their proper reading order). All come from Structure 12, a Late Classic building in which they were reset. See Mathews, *La escultura de Yaxchilan*, 72–102; O'Neil, "Object, Memory"; and Prager and Grothe, "From Fragments to Clarity." Stuart's analysis of Lintel 11 is in Wilkerson, "The Usumacinta River," where the founder Yopat Bahlam was first identified.

16 These two numbered succession titles come from Stela 1 at Dos Caobas, a small site in the vicinity of Yaxchilan. Another similar reference is recently documented on Yaxchilan, Lintel 34, by Prager and Grothe, "From Fragments to Clarity." The second emblem remains undeciphered, but it is also found in the inscriptions of El Zotz, further cementing the connection between it and Yaxchilan. Shield Jaguar was the first king to claim this double descent, perhaps referencing

ancestry through his mother's line as well. Only he and his immediate descendants ever took the two emblem titles together (Mathews, *La escultura de Yaxchilan*, 68).

17 The altar is from the site Altar de los Reyes, discussed by Grube, "Epigraphic Analysis of Altar 3."

18 From Avendaño y Loyola, *Relation of Two Trips to Peten*, 39.

19 See Restall, *Maya Conquistador*, 20–40. It is significant that in colonial documents from Yucatán, *kah* and *kab* are at times interchangeable with the meaning of "pueblo." The pairing of *kab* and *ch'en* survives in the Books of Chilam Balam as a phrase for lands associated with named towns (Tokovinine, *Place and Identity*, 23).

20 The Aztec or Nahua *altepetl* is discussed at great length by Lockhart, *The Nahuas after the Conquest*, 14–58. See also Noguez, "Altepetl."

21 See Isendahl and Smith, "Sustainable Agrarian Urbanism."

22 Current estimates place the population of the central lowlands in the Late Classic, around 800 CE, at between seven and eleven million people. This figure is based on a statistical extrapolation from the settlements visible in lidar surveys over two thousand square kilometers in northern Guatemala. See Canuto et al., "Ancient Lowland Maya Complexity." Even higher population densities were presented to the north, in what is now southern Campeche (Auld-Thomas et al., "Running Out of Empty Space"). At the time, these regions would have encompassed two to three dozen kabch'ens over varying size and influence, each coexisting and ruled by its own k'uhulajaw. And there was a great deal of variation at any given time. A large center such as Tikal may have had a supporting population of 60,000 to 80,000 people at its height, with Palenque perhaps 20,000 to 30,000.

23 Estrada-Belli et al., "Architecture, Wealth and Status."

24 For early Maya kingship and its religious iconography, see Fields and Reents-Budet, *Lords of Creation*, and Guernsey, *Ritual and Power in Stone*.

25 This etymology of *ajaw* as "sower" was first proposed by John Justeson (see Mathews and Justeson, "Patterns of Sign Substitution," 207). Elsewhere I expressed a preference for seeing it as "one who shouts," but I believe Justeson was correct.

26 This particular k'atun ritual is recorded on Stelae 31 and 39 at Tikal.

27 See Stuart, "Stones of Kings" and "Shining Stones," for discussions of Maya stelae and some of their underlying meanings.

28 The hieroglyph for *itz'at*, "artist," depicts the scribal patron god, a hybrid being combining the features of a howler monkey and a man, often holding or writing in a codex. This deity reflects the widespread Mesoamerican associations among monkeys, crafts, and the fine arts. See Coe, "Supernatural Patrons," and Coe and Kerr, *The Art of the Maya Scribe*.

29 Marcus, *Mesoamerican Writing Systems*, 444.

30 Research programs at Copan and Dos Pilas in the 1980s and '90s exemplified this emerging "historical" or "conjunctive approach" in Maya archaeology, as discussed in Fash, *Scribes, Warriors and Kings*; Fash and Sharer, "Sociopolitical Developments," and Houston, *Hieroglyphs and History*.

CHAPTER 5. ARRIVALS

1 See Jones and Satterthwaite, *The Monuments and Inscriptions of Tikal*, 64. A brief account Stela 31's discovery is given in Shook, *Incidents in the Life of a Maya Archaeologist*, 139–40.

2 For analyses of Stela 31's inscription, see Martin, "Moral-Reforma y la contienda," and Stuart, "Some Working Notes."

3 For overviews of Teotihuacan and its archaeology, see Cowgill, *Teotihuacan*; Hirth et al., *Teotihuacan*; and Robb, *Teotihuacan*.

4 The fourth century political changes at Teotihuacan are discussed by Cowgill, *Teotihuacan*, 148, and Sugiyama, "Rulership, Warfare and Human Sacrifice."

5 For ceramics from the so-called "Maya Barrio," some specifically manufactured at Tikal, see Clayton, "Interregional Relationships." Burial 5 in the Moon Pyramid contained two sacrificed male individuals "attired at the moment of their death as figures related to Maya dynasties" (Sugiyama and López Luján, "The Ritual Deposits in the Moon Pyramid," 86, and *Sacrificios de consagracion*, 36). The timing of the burials, at the mid-fourth century, corresponds to the Entrada or shortly before.

6 For Plaza of the Columns excavations, see Sugiyama et al., "The Maya at Teotihuacan."

7 For a recent review of the evidence of Spearthrower Owl and his political legacy, see Stuart, *Spearthrower Owl*.

8 Proskouriakoff's interpretations were presented in her important posthumous work *Maya History*. The Uaxactun stela, with its portrait of a Teotihuacan warrior, probably represents a foreigner with local ties to Uaxactun at the time of the Entrada.

9 The narrative of Tikal's Marcador text is discussed in detail in Stuart, *Spearthrower Owl*, 71–89.

10 The glyph for Spearthrower Owl was first seen by Proskouriakoff, *Maya History*, 11–13; Schele, "The Tlaloc Complex,"; and others as an ethnic name or title for Teotihuacan warriors. Its identification as a historical name was first made by Jones and Satterthwaite, *Monuments and Inscriptions of Tikal*, 65, and expanded later by Stuart, "The 'Arrival of Strangers,'" "A New Child-Father Relationship Glyph," and *Spearthrower Owl*.

11 For various perspectives on the nature of Teotihuacan politics, see Carballo, "Power, Politics and Governance"; Cowgill, *Teotihuacan*; Manzanilla, "Gobierno corporativo en Teotihuacan"; Millon, "The Last Years of Teotihuacan's Dominance"; and Pasztory, *Teotihuacan*.

12 Estrada-Belli et al., "Nuevos Hallazgos de Epigrafía."

13 Stela 51 is discussed by Kelly et al., "Waka' on the International Stage."

14 See Houston et al., "A Teotihuacan Complex," for a discussion of the "Ciudadela" complex at Tikal.

15 The ruler K'ankitam also has had various names of references in the literature, including K'an Kitam, K'an Boar, and K'an Ak (Martin and Grube, *Chronicle of Maya Kings*, 37).

16 The timing of Teotihuacan's collapse has been refined in recent years. Originally thought to have occurred as late as 650 or 750, it now is placed in 550 plus or minus twenty-five years based on refined study of ^{14}C samples (Beramendi-Orosco et al., "High-Resolution Chronology"). See Millon, "The Last Years of Teotihuacan's Dominance," and Clayton, "The Collapse of Teotihuacan," for further insights about the Teotihuacan collapse and the adaptions by subsequent populations in the Basin of Mexico.

17 Stuart, "The 'Arrival of Strangers'" and *Spearthrower Owl*.

18 For an overview of early Copan history, see Stuart, "The Beginnings of the Copan Dynasty" and "A Foreign Past."

19 The role of Teotihuacan in Copan's political history and art is discussed in Stuart, "The 'Arrival of Strangers,'" "The Beginnings of the Copan Dynasty," "A Foreign Past," and *Spearthrower Owl*; Taube, "Structure 10L-16"; and a discussion of the building name Winte'nah, possibly as the Sun Pyramid at Teotihuacan (Fash et al., "The House of New Fire").

CHAPTER 6. EXPANSIONS

1 Martin, "Moral-Reforma y la contienda," discusses the history of Tikal during this time. See also Martin and Grube, *Chronicle of Maya Kings and Queens* and *Chronicle of Maya Kings and Queens*, 2nd ed.; and Harrison, *The Lords of Tikal*.

2 In his analysis of this connection, Willey, "The Classic Maya 'Hiatus,'" went so far as to refer to the Hiatus as a "little collapse."

3 Martin, "Moral-Reforma y la contienda," 18–24; Martin and Beliaev, "K'ahk' Ti' Ch'ich,'" 4.

4 Gann ("Recently Discovered Maya Temples," "Tzibanché") "discovered" Dzibanche in the sense of bringing the ruins to the attention of the wider academic world. He visited the site briefly in early 1927, led there by local Maya guides who had known the site for some time. Gann took special notice of the large pyramids and the presence of a preserved wooden door lintel bearing hieroglyphs (hence the site's name, meaning "inscribed wood"). The date inscribed on the lintel was misread by Gann and Morley, who assigned it to the mid-eighth century. In fact, it was dedicated on the k'atun ending of 554, by which time the Kanul dynasty was rapidly expanding its power. Dzibanche ruins were largely ignored until the wooden lintels were recorded by Eric von Euw and published by archaeologist Peter Harrison ("The Lintels of Tzibanche"), who was the first to investigate the site in a serious way. Excavations there began in the 1990s under Enrique Nalda and have continued since (Estrada-Belli et al., "The Rise of the Kaanu'l").

5 Marcus's suggestion that the snake emblem was connected to Calakmul was first given in her important early paper and book on the nature of Maya political organization (Marcus, *Emblem and State* and "Territorial Organization"). These ideas built on earlier suggestions by Thomas Barthel (1968), who was first to discuss the snake emblem in detail without positing its specific place. The confirmation of its Calakmul affiliation was presented in Stuart and Houston, "Classic Maya Place Names." See Martin, "In Search of the Serpent Kings," for a thorough discussion of the history of the snake emblem.

6 The "Cleveland Stela," as it came to be called, was first published by Jeffrey Miller, "Notes on a Stela Pair." Its significance as a portrait of a powerful queen and political player has been discussed recently by Navarro-Farr et al., "Expanding the Canon."

7 See Graham, "Homeless Hieroglyphs," for a brief discussion of his finds at El Peru-Waka'. The Cleveland Stela is now known as Stela 34. The brief time span when the snake emblem was thought to be El Peru-Waka' is reflected in several articles written in the 1980s, such as that by Mathews, "Classic Emblem Glyphs," 20). See also Schele and Freidel, *A Forest of Kings*, 456–57. The true El Peru-Waka' emblem glyph was first identified by Houston (personal communication, 1984) and is discussed by Martin, "Nuevos datos epigraficos," and Guenter, "On the Emblem Glyph."

8 The shared connection of the "snake emblem" (Kanul) to both Calakmul and Dzibanche was first established by Erik Velásquez ("Los Escalones Jeroglíficos," "Los posibles alcances territoriales"), based on its repeated appearance on the stairway in reference to the local Dzibanche king, Yuknomch'en I. See also Martin, "Of Snakes and Bats."

9 This appears on Stela 2 of Pol Box, dedicated much later in 583. For an interpretation of its text, see Esparza Olguín and Pérez Gutiérrez, "Archaeological and Epigraphic Studies."

10 Dzibanche's transformation into a regional power is also visible in the site's architecture. As the site's initial excavator, Enrique Nalda ("Dzibanche," 25–26) noted, there is a radical change in the number and style of major buildings throughout the city, which are built with extremely high walls and imposing roof combs. This seems to come around 500 CE.

11 Martin and Grube (*Chronicle of Maya Kings and Queens.*, 2nd ed., 104) refer to this king as "K'altuun Hix." Ambiguity rests in the reading of the hand element in the name, so this remains a possibility.

12 Gillespie and Joyce, "Gendered Goods," and Navarro-Farr et al., "Expanding the Canon."

13 A frequent name or title associated with members of Naranjo's ruling line is *Sakchuwen,* "White Artisan." A looted text mentioning Chaktokich'ahk II of Tikal notes that his grandfather or grandmother (*mam*) (presumably on his mother's side) was a Sakchuwen. There are other hints of a Naranjo-Tikal connection as well in this early time, discussed in part by Tokovinine and Fialko, "Stela 45."

14 For the Holmul façade, see Estrada-Belli and Tokovinine, "A King's Apotheosis."

15 Martin et al., "Contexto y texto de la estela 47," reports on Naranjo Stela 47, where Ajnumsaj is described in connection with these four successive Kanul kings: Tunk'abhix, Kahk'uti'ch'ich' (by alternate name), "Sky Witness," and "Scroll Serpent." These later names will soon enter our story.

16 Martin and Beliaev, "K'ahk' Ti' Ch'ich.'"

17 The long-distance connection to El Peru-Waka' is intriguing, for it highlights how it and Tikal were enemies over a long stretch of time, going back at least to the time of the Entrada of 378, when Sihyajk'ahk' stopped there on his way to defeat Tikal's king. It was a fraught relationship in later centuries, too, as we will see in the war Tikal waged against El Peru-Waka' nearly two centuries later in 743.

18 For the Chochkitam stucco facade, see Estrada-Belli and Tokovinine, "Chochkitam."

19 Martin, "Caracol Altar 21 Revisited," notes that Yax Ehbxok K'inich seems an alternate name for the ruler otherwise known as Wak Chank'awil, who in earlier sources is known by the nickname "Double Bird."

20 Martin and Beliaev, "K'ahk' Ti' Ch'ich,'" discuss the implications of this supposed vassal relationship on the Uaxactun vessel.

21 Sky Witness's probable tomb was discovered during excavations at Dzibanche in 2003, within the foundations of a large pyramid known as the Temple of the Cormorants. This is Tomb CA6, found along with others in the same structure at Dzibanche (Nalda, "Prácticas funerarias"; Estrada-Belli et al., "The Rise of the Kaanu'l Kingdom"). He was identified by a bone instrument bearing the text "the offering bone of Sky Witness," the Holy Kanul Lord."

22 Tikal's defeat is recorded on Altar 21 of Caracol, first identified by Houston, "Appendix: Caracol Altar 21," 40. For a further discussion, see Martin and Grube, *Chronicle of Maya Kings and Queens*, 89; and Martin, "Caracol Altar 21 Revisited."

23 At first "Animal Skull" was considered to be the father of two brothers we will soon encounter, Nunujolchahk and Bajlaj Chank'awil. This would entail a very long reign. Later

refinements have shown that their father, whose name is cited in two damaged texts, may be a different king who reigned as the twenty-third successor. Martin and Grube, *Chronicle of Maya Kings and Queens*, 2nd ed., 42, cites Stanley Guenter for this observation.

24 Martin and Beliaev, "K'ahk' Ti' Ch'ich.'"

25 I would like to thank Tom Garrison for our enlightening conversations on these complex historical details involving Naranjo and reading between the lines.

26 The Caracol stairway is known mostly through the many pieces that were reset out of their proper sequence by the ancient Maya at Naranjo. This is known as Naranjo, Hieroglyphic Stairway 1, first documented by Teobert Maler, *Explorations in the Department of Peten, Guatemala*, and in by drawings of Ian Graham, *Corpus of Maya Hieroglyphic Inscriptions*. In addition to the sections recently recovered at Xunantunich (Helmke and Awe, "An Analysis of Panel 3" and "Sharper Than a Serpent's Tooth"), another piece had been found earlier at Ucanal, Guatemala (Graham, *Corpus of Maya Hieroglyphic Inscriptions*). A small fragment was also discovered at Caracol in the excavations of Structure B5, where it may have been originally constructed (Helmke and Awe, "An Analysis of Panel 3"). The realization that the full stairway was a Caracol monument is now widely agreed upon and is discussed in Martin, "At the Periphery"; Helmke and Awe, "An Analysis of Panel 3"; and a recent detailed overview by Helmke and Verpretskii, "An Account of the Kings."

CHAPTER 7. EAST

1 Coe, "A Model of Ancient Community Structure," describes the four-part community model in sixteenth-century Yucatán.

2 See Martin, *Ancient Maya Politics*, for a detailed treatment of these directional titles. "Four heavens" is taken from the text on Stela A at Copan, where the term describes four k'uhulajaws (associated with the dynasties of Copan, Tikal, Calakmul and Palenque) in connection to the four world directions. This was at least the state of affairs from Copan's perspective, when Stela A was dedicated just before the k'atun ending of 731 CE (9.15.0.0.0). This was a "4 Ahau" k'atun, which also emphasized the quadripartite metaphor. The idea of a four-part arrangement to Maya geopolitics has a long history, going back to Barthel ("El complejo emblema") and Marcus (*Emblem and State in the Classic Maya Lowlands* and "Territorial Organization of the Lowland Classic Maya").

3 Meanings of *kal* as "to make" or "to create" in a religious sense appear in colonial Ch'orti'.

4 Although kalomte' had existed as a stand-alone ritual title, the directional system of kalomte' described here may have been spurred by the Teotihuacan Entrada. Spearthrower Owl and Sihyajk'ahk', both hegemonic rulers, were each called the "west kalomte," so one wonders if the Maya extrapolated their supra-regional system from that, eventually incorporating the other world quarters.

5 The eastern identity of early Kanul lords and of the kingdoms of the eastern Peten is discussed by Estrada-Belli and Tokovinine, "Chochkitam."

6 For a discussion of the Calakmul murals, see Carrasco and Cordiero Baqueiro, "The Murals of Chihk Nahb Structure Sub 1–4," and Martin, "Exploring the 584286 Correlation." The dating of the murals to the reign of Yuknomch'en II is based on style of the paintings, which seems no later than 650.

7 "Macaw Star" remains a nickname, with some components of the glyphic name still undeciphered. He is cited on the Hieroglyphic Stairway of Tamarindito as the founder of that dynasty (Houston, *Hieroglyphs and History*; Gronemayer, "The Monuments and Inscriptions"). His name is shown as a ritual costume worn by descendants in several depictions, including Stela 16 of Tikal.

8 For a discussion of the Dos Pilas stairways and the biographical narrative of Bajlaj Chank'awil, see Boot, "The Dos Pilas-Tikal Wars," and Guenter, "The Inscriptions of Dos Pilas." The outlines of this political change and hierarchy involving to the Kanuls were first worked out by Houston and Stuart in 1990, in an unpublished report of Dos Pilas, Hieroglyphic Stairway 4.

9 The possibility remains that there were two people named Nunujolchahk, living at the same time with distinct titles linked to Mutul and Santa Elena, respectively. The timing of the dates strongly suggests their equivalence, however. See Grube, "Palenque in the Maya World," and Martin and Grube, *Chronicle of Maya Kings and Queens* and *Chronicle of Maya Kings and Queens*, 2nd ed.

10 Previously, I and others had interpreted the evidence of the 659 war as Palenque's defeat of Santa Elena (Stuart and Stuart, *Palenque*, 158–59), but on review I began to question a few of my previous assumptions. Santa Elena had in fact been Palenque's strong ally for some years. The one geographical title we can identify among Palenque's prisoners is *Pipa' Ajaw*, "Lord of Pipa'," using an old name that pertains to the kingdom of Pomona, located due east of Palenque near the modern town of Tenosique. Santa Elena is over forty kilometers to the south of Pomona, and we know it was a distinct kingdom. Moreover, Kanul's antagonism against Santa Elena in 659 is indicated by a portrait of a bound prisoner from Santa Elena on Calakmul Stela 9, associated with a capture date of September 9, 659 (Martin, *Chronicle of Maya Kings and Queens*, 2nd ed.), just a month after the war recorded on Palenque Palace stairway, with Nunujolchahk as Palenque's ally and now bearing the title "lord of Santa Elena." Santa Elena might have been his base of operations while in exile, assuming that he is the same person we know from Tikal's history.

11 Zapote Bobal was one of at least three sites we can identify with Hixwitz, or "Jaguar Hill." (*Hix* is often translated as "jaguar," but it may more accurately refer to an ocelot, or a small spotted feline.) The others are El Pajaral and La Joyanca. See Breuil et al., "Primeras noticias," and Stuart, "You Go That Way."

12 Might ancient *Pulil* be the archaeological site known as Polol? Its location north of the Pasion River is suggestive, but there is no historical evidence of a link beyond the similarity of the names.

13 The poetic description of mass execution evokes a landscape (hills and lakes) immersed in war and conflict. This phrase I deciphered in the early 1990s, after recognizing the signs for "skull" (**JOL**) and "blood" (**CH'ICH'**).

14 The importance of Lady K'abel is discussed by Navarro-Farr et al., "Expanding the Canon" and "Lady K'abel and the City's Temple."

15 Background concerning the Naranjo stairway is also discussed in Helmke and Verpetskii, "An Account of the Kings of Kanu'l." For another discussion of this complex history, see also Martin and Grube, *Chronicle of Maya Kings and Queens*, 2nd ed., 72–78.

16 Stela 24 of Naranjo depicts Lady Wakjalam Chanlem standing atop a captive from the city of K'inchil, which was probably to the east, in the region of what is today Holmul. As we see

often in portraits of royal women, she holds an offering plate with the three primary instruments of bloodletting and sacrifice—a flint knife, an obsidian blade, and a stingray spine. A glyphic label is also playfully included in the bowl, reading *ochch'en*, "conquest."

17 The k'atun ending on 9.13.0.0.0 was also marked at Palenque by the dedication of the Cross Group temples, for example. Monuments bearing the date appear at Tonina, Piedras Negras, and Dos Pilas; curiously, we have no surviving records of this major event at Calakmul. Yuknom Yich'ahkk'ahk' did oversee its celebration according to an inscription at La Corona (where he was at the time is unclear).

18 See Stuart et al., "The Death of the Defeated," for a discussion of Yich'ahkk'ahk's death and the history of his reign.

19 In connection with Jasaw Chank'awil's reign and his transformative victory over Yich'ahkk'ahk', one story stands out as an unusually poignant episode. This is from Altar 5 of Tikal, a large circular stone that was dedicated as part of the celebration of the k'atun in 711 (9.14.0.0.0). The stone shows an unusual scene of two priests kneeling on the ground, a skull and stack of long bones placed between them. The inscription that surrounds the image tells the story of Lady Tunkaywak, who "fled" from Tikal thirty years before in 691. She was likely a close relative of Jasaw Chank'awil, perhaps his first wife. Her flight from the capital may have been the result of Kanul's incursions, in a time when the Mutul court remained destabilized and perhaps not yet firmly rooted at its home base. The altar's inscription notes that Lady Tunkaywak's absence from Tikal was prolonged—and that she died eleven years later. Shortly before the turn of the fourteenth k'atun, Jasaw Chank'awil made an ambitious and it seems highly personal move, ordering Lady Tunkaywak's remains to be removed from her tomb and returned to Tikal. Four emissaries arrived at Tikal only days before the k'atun date, and the altar's scene shows the placement of her bones back on home ground. In an amazing match between history and archaeology, archaeologist Christopher Jones, digging under the altar in 1963, found a skull and bones beneath, no doubt those of Lady Tunkaywak, just as depicted on the sculpture.

20 See Jones and Satterthwaite, *The Monuments and Inscriptions of Tikal*, 48, for the identification of the captive from Calakmul on Altar 9. Martin was the first to link the elements of the personal name to K'awil Tok' (personal communication, 2007). Yik'in Chank'awil's placement of this conquest monument at Temple VI, at a remote locale within Tikal, is difficult to explain. It may have served as the formal eastern entrance into the city, perhaps designed to greet visitors approaching from that fraught, conflicted region.

21 The alliances at the heart of these conflicts between Tikal and Naranjo (among others) may be referred to as "the thirteen divisions" and the "seven divisions." The first is associated with Mutul dynasts and the second especially with rulers at Naranjo. These terms remain poorly understood, but it is interesting that the numbers involved add up to twenty. See Beliaev, "Wuk Tsuk and Oxlahun Tsuk," and Tokovinine, *Place and Identity*.

CHAPTER 8. WEST

1 The name of Sihyajk'ahk' is preserved in an inscription from House D of the Palanque's Palace, dating to the reign of K'inich Janabpakal. The context is missing, but it may hint at Pakal's desire, as a Kanul enemy, to insert himself and Palenque into the old Entrada narrative of Tikal.

2 See Grube, "Palenque in the Maya World."

3 The earliest date at Piedras Negras is a retrospective period ending, 8.13.0.0.0 (December 15, 297), recorded on Altar 1.

4 The probable portrait of Yatahk is on Panel 12 of Piedras Negras, where he is shown with four bound captives from Yaxchilan, Bonampak, Santa Elena, and Lakamtun.

5 The date of Yaxchilan's founding in 359 (more accurately, the accession of its first ruler) came just two years after the k'atun ending 8.16.0.0.0 in 357. The latter date was celebrated at Uaxactun by a local ruler who would later be captured by Chaktokich'ahk of Tikal.

6 The reading of the Palenque court name as *Bakel* is based on glyphic spellings, although *Bakal* is another possible reading. As a noun, *bakel* means "skeleton." The emblem has a deep history, at least in retrospective records. One text in Palenque cites an early "Holy Lord of Bakel" who dedicated a shrine in 252 BCE.

7 The tensions of the region between Palenque and Calakmul are also revealed by the curious history of a king at a site called Moral-Reforma, who was a Kanul ally in 662 as a child but who was "recrowned" under Palenque's authority in 690 (Martin, "Moral-Reforma"). This speaks to Palenque's role as long-term Kanul antagonist.

8 For a full account of Pakal's three sons, see Stuart and Stuart, *Palenque*. The discovery and contents of the tomb of the "Red Queen" are in González Cruz, *La reina roja*.

9 Yaxun Bahlam IV restored at least two of his grandfather's broken monuments, Stelae 3 and 6. The latter had commissioned them to honor his fortieth year on the throne. An elaborately decorated throne from the grandfather's reign was also intentionally destroyed, which may be an obvious sign of a violent revolt.

10 For further insights into these important women, see Mathews, *La escultura de Yaxchilan*; Martin and Grube, *Chronicle of Maya Kings and Queens*. 2nd ed., 125–36; and Tate, "The Royal Women." Lady K'abalxok's building is Structure 23, adjacent to Yaxchilan's lower plaza.

11 The distinctive landscape of Palenque, juxtaposing mountains and springs, was clearly important to the situating of these shrines and other buildings. See my previous study of the Cross Group (Stuart, *The Palenque Mythology*) for further discussion and for translations of the Cross Group tablets. An update of that study is in preparation.

12 In an earlier study (Stuart, "Longer Live the King"), I discuss the unusual situation of K'inich K'anjoykitam and his defeat by Tonina.

13 In a previous book (Stuart, *The Inscriptions of Temple XIX*), I present a detailed interpretation of the Temple XIX sculptures.

14 The sculpture commemorating T'ulchihk's capture is a door lintel, now in the Ethnologisches Museum Berlin. It was looted from the ruins of La Pasadita, Guatemala, an ancient satellite of Yaxchilan in the Pa'chan kingdom, and the home of Tilom.

CHAPTER 9. SOUTH

1 General treatments of Copan and its archaeology are Fash, *Scribes, Warriors and Kings*; Fash, *The Copan Sculpture Museum*; and Webster et al., *Copán*.

2 Stephens, *Incidents of Travel in Central America*, I:141.

3 Buikstra et al., "Tombs from the Copan Acropolis"; Price et al., "Kings and Commoners."

4 See Chase and Chase, "The Early Classic Period." A possible Caracol dynastic founder named Te'k'ab Chahk might be linked to a record of the year 175 CE, recorded on Ballcourt

Marker 3. However, there are possible scribal errors that cast uncertainty on the date's placement. An equally if not more plausible placement is in the early fourth century (see Helmke et al., "All That Is Old Is New Again").

5 Copan's dynasty also had a close historical association with Rio Azul, another eastern Peten site with more overt Teotihuacan relations. (Sihyajk'ahk' is mentioned there as a political overlord, after the Entrada.) A newly unearthed inscription from Copan, dating to 465 CE, mentions Rio Azul and a nearby Peten site known as Uxhaab'te' (Prager et al., "Stela 64"). These long distance connections remain murky, but they were evidently strong.

6 Smith et al., "The Magnitude and Impact."

7 In earlier sources, this king is referred to by various nicknames, including "Smoke Jaguar," "Smoke Imix God K," or simply "Ruler 12." The name provided here is an accurate reading of his name in Classic Mayan, meaning "Fire Is the Mouth of the Splashing-Water K'awil-Spirit." Like many other royal names, it refers to an esoteric figure of the religious world.

8 The hierarchical relationship between these kings is clearly expressed on Stela E from Quirigua, in a retrospective account that states that the Copan ruler had supervised the Quirigua lord's taking of power. It is interesting to note the similarity here of Quirigua's king, K'ahk'tiliw Chanyopat, and that of the Naranjo king K'ahk'tiliw Chanchahk, who reigned slightly earlier. Do similar names imply some family relationship? We cannot say.

9 Tsukamoto and Esparza Olguín, "Ajpach' Waal," discusses the El Palmar steps.

10 See Grube et al., "The Date of the Dedication," and Looper, *Lightning Warrior*, 78. Looper interprets the fire-drilling episode as referencing the destruction of Copan's deities, a sign of defeat, but parallel statements from Yaxchilan and elsewhere suggest that it was the instigation of Copan's war, couched in religious and ritual terms.

11 For the Hieroglyphic Stairway and its temple, see Fash et al., "The Hieroglyphic Stairway"; Fash, *The Copan Sculpture Museum*, 101–11; and Stuart, "A Foreign Past."

12 The inscription within the building built atop Temple 11 strongly implies that it lies directly above the royal tomb.

13 It has been proposed that Yaxpahsaj's mother was from Palenque, but this is problematic based on the misidentification of Palenque's emblem in a Copan inscription.

14 This final date is on Altar L, and it is described as a "seating" of an individual named Ukit Tok'. We could take this to be a new ruler, but his status withing the Copan court is unclear. His name is most interesting, for the "Ukit" element is known otherwise only from the inscriptions of Yucatán, from the late eighth and early ninth centuries.

CHAPTER 10. NORTH

1 The first secure evidence of hieroglyphic writing in Yucatán comes from Loltun cave, as part of the large cliff carving showing the portrait of a standing ruler. The dating of this sculpture is difficult, but the style suggests around 100 CE. This would put it around the transition between the Preclassic period to the Classic period, an era of great changes happening in the Maya lowlands, including the beginnings of dynastic history. A line of glyphs appears above the portrait, opening with a calendar record. Unfortunately, the hieroglyphs are difficult to read, beyond the day sign that seems to read 3 Chuen. The other glyphs would tell us something of the occasion and the name of the ruler portrayed, but these are impossible to

make out. A more accurate recording of the sculpture using digital scanning would probably yield new insights.

2 Quoting Lizana, *Historia de Yucatán*, 72: "There was another pyramid [at Izamal] which was the house and dwelling of a great captain named Hunpictok.... The name of this captain signifies 'the captain who has an army of eight thousand lances' because the lance and arrow points with which they fought in time of war were kept there."

3 This is Ballcourt B at Coba, located to the south of the Nohoch Mul group. The sculptures and inscriptions there were excavated by Maria José Con ("El juego de pelota").

4 Martin, "A Northern War: Coba vs. Oxkintok."

5 This is Coba, Stela 26, discussed by Esparza Olguín, "Estudio de los monumentos esculpidos." Its image of the queen with the brush and inkpot, facing an inscription, may playfully suggest that she has just written it.

6 For a discussion of Oxkintok history, see García Campillo, "Comentario General sobre la epigrafia en Oxkintok," and Rivera Dorado, "Clues to the System of Power in the City of Oxkintok." The Oxkintok region was the production center of a distinctive luxury ceramic ware known as Chocholá style, named for the town near Maxcanu where it was first identified by archaeologists. These are finely carved and incised with figural designs and inscriptions and show some of the most elegant examples of Maya ceramic art. The texts on these vessels are like many others, labeling them as drinking cups (*uk'ib*) owned by various lords of the court and rulers, both men and women. I suspect this was an especially desirable ceramic ware made for elites who lived throughout western Yucatán during the eighth century.

7 I first noticed the ancient Tijo' place-name when inspecting Stela 19 of Dzibilchaltun in 1987. My father was involved in the stela's discovery in 1959, and he was there with me when I read the title as **ti-jo-AJAW**. I recall his excitement at the time, telling me that many of his Maya coworkers on the Dzibilchaltun excavations had still referred to Mérida as "T'ho.""

8 Many of the Ek Balam excavations are described in Vargas de la Peña and Castillo Borges, "Ek' Balam" and "Ek' Balam y el reino." The inscriptions of the site were studied by my late colleague Alfonso Lacadena.

9 This is the so-called Halakal Lintel from a site within the great Chichen Itza area.

10 See Pallán Gayol, "A Glimpse from Edzna's Hieroglyphics" for a discussion of Edzna and its possible historical connections.

11 This ruler was first identified by the name "Lord Chac" in the 1980s by Jeff Kowalski (*The House of the Governor*, "Lords of the Northern Maya") as part of his important studies of the art and architecture of Uxmal.

12 For Landa's description of Chichen Itza, see Restall et al., *The Friar and the Maya*, 44–45.

13 Restall et al., *The Friar and the Maya*, 45. The attribution of a well or cenote to an elite lineage also resonates with the Classic period term *kabch'en*, or simply *ch'en*, in reference to a town or community. A Classic Mayan hieroglyphic text that states, for example, *tu ch'en kanul*, "in the town of Kanul," is conceptually related to *(u) chi' ch'en Itza'*, "(at) the edge of the 'well' of the Itza.""

14 For a discussion of the offerings recovered from the cenote, see Coggins, *The Cenote of Sacrifice*, and Proskouriakoff, *Jades from the Cenote*. The dredging of the cenote was first done by Edward H. Thompson, then-owner of the Hacienda Chichen, in an uncontrolled and haphazard way. Later efforts were a bit more systematic, overseen by Roman Piña Chan,

who reported that there were still deep layers in the muck holding earlier artifact deposits from the Classic period.

15 In Tozzer, *Landa's Relación*, 219.

CHAPTER 11. ABANDONMENTS

1 Details of the Aguateca excavations can be found in Inomata and Triadan, *Burned Palaces* and *Life and Politics*.

2 The central role of the ancient Maya in modern-day collapse narratives is exemplified in the cover of Jared Diamond's best-selling book *Collapse: How Societies Choose to Fail or Succeed*, showing a stark black-and-white photograph of the main plaza at Edzna, Campeche.

3 See Webster, *The Fall of the Ancient Maya*, 212.

4 Earlier interpretations of the end of K'awil Chank'inich's (Ruler 4's) reign posit that he was killed or captured in 761 (Houston, *Hieroglyphs and History*, 117; Inomata and Triadan, *Burned Palaces*, 184). This was based on an early interpretation of an event cited on Tamarindito, Hieroglyphic Stairway 1, which now looks to be a record of a conquest of Tamarindito by K'awil Chank'inich. We can nevertheless time the shift of the royal seat from Dos Pilas to Aguateca to around 760.

5 Demarest et al., "Classic Maya Defensive Systems," discusses the rustic, concentric walls around Dos Pilas that were first noted and documented by Houston, *Hieroglyphs and History*, 45–47. Their dating is difficult, and there is no reason to link them to any historical war we know from the inscriptions. Houston (personal communication, 2020) notes that they could have been built shortly after the initial collapse of Dos Pilas as a royal center yet probably before 810, based on ceramic evidence.

6 See Anaya Hernández et al., "Sak Tz'i', a Classic Maya Center"; Biró, "Sak Tz'i' in the Classic Period"; and Golden et al., "Centering the Classic Maya Kingdom," for discussions of Sak Tz'i' history.

7 For discussions of the Bonampak murals, see Miller, *The Murals of Bonampak*, and Miller and Brittenham, "The Spectacle of the Late Maya Court."

8 See Golden and Scherer, "Territory, Trust, Growth, and Collapse."

9 These episodes of Yaxchilan's late history come from Hieroglyphic Stairway 5 and Lintel 10 and are discussed in detail by Mathews, *La escultura de Yaxchilan*, 246–65. In another study, I identified the defeat of Piedras Negras's king as recorded on Lintel 10 (Stuart, "Una guerra entre Yaxchilan y Piedras Negras?"). See Golden et al., "Piedras Negras and Yaxchilan."

10 Two historical rulers bear the name Kokaj K'awil (possibly Itzamnaj K'awil), which might create confusion. Naranjo's ruler is late and ruled from 784–814(?), whereas another of the Mutul dynasty ruled at Dos Pilas much earlier, from 698–726. In previous literature, the Dos Pilas king has been called "Ruler 2" or "Shield-God K."

11 The Cancuen massacre site is described in detail in Demarest et al., "The Collapses in the West."

12 Chase and Chase, "Caracol, Belize, and Changing Perceptions."

13 See, most recently, Lucero, *Maya Wisdom*, and Seligson, *The Maya and Climate Change*.

14 See Hansen et al., "Climate and Environmental Variability," and Dunning et al., "A Tale of Two Collapses."

15 See Lentz et al., Molecular Genetic and Geochemical Assays," for a study of the Tikal reservoirs. Further information on the poor conditions and malnutrition of other Maya elite

populations can also be found in Cerezo-Román and Tsukamoto, "The Life Course of a Standard-Bearer"; Danforth, "Late Classic Maya Health Patterns"; and Storey, "An Estimate of Mortality."

16 The Comalcalco bone texts were excavated by Ricardo Armijo and analyzed by Marc Zender, who was the first to decipher the "famine" text. For context, see Armijo Torres et al., "Urnas funerarios," and Zender, *A Study of Classic Maya Priesthood.*

17 Anderson and Wahl, "Two Holocene Paleofire Records," sees the dramatic evidence of human populations on the forests as early as 4,600 years ago (ca. 2600 BCE), when tree pollen amounts decreased substantially and various grass species increased. Intentional burning may have been a key factor at that time.

18 Studies of Maya climate are numerous in the past three decades. Influential studies include Beach et al., "Ancient Maya Impacts"; Dunning et al., "Kax and Kol"; Gill, *The Great Maya Droughts;* Iannone, *The Great Maya Droughts in Cultural Context;* Kennet et al., "Development and Disintegration of Maya Political Systems"; and Hodell et al., "Possible Role of Climate in the Collapse of Maya Civilization." An excellent overview of the issues surrounding climate and the ancient Maya is by Seligson, *The Maya and Climate Change.*

19 Douglas et al., "Impacts of Climate Change on the Collapse of Lowland Maya Civilization."

20 On the ideology of warfare, see Chinchilla Mazareigos, "The Sustenance Providers," 304, which notes how war was "conceived as an act of piety and abidance with the will of the gods that ensured the continued rise of the sun and the fertility of the earth." The agricultural metaphors of rulership are not too far removed from those of militarism.

21 Guiteras-Holmes, *Perils of the Soul,* 334.

22 This view of interdependence among Classic Maya polities resonates with other examples of social and political collapse in the ancient world. Here I am especially reminded of the role of "hyper-coherence" among polities and cultures of Late Bronze Age Mediterranean world. As Cline, *1177 B.C.,* 168, notes, "if Late Bronze Age civilizations were truly globalized and dependent upon each other for goods and services, even just to a certain extent, then change in any one of the relevant kingdoms ... would potentially affect and destabilize them all."

23 For a discussion of the history on the Komkom Vase, see Helmke et al., *A Reading of the Komkom Vase.* A closely related text is on Stela 12 of Naranjo (Helmke et al., "The Litany of Runaway Kings").

24 Long ago, in graduate school, I wrote an overly skeptical review of the "foreign invasion" model surrounding the Maya collapse (Stuart, "Historical Inscriptions and the Maya Collapse"). Clearly foreigners from the west were important in the Peten, especially at Ucanal and Ceibal (Martin, "The Long Twilight"). Recent investigations at Ucanal are exploring its important role during the Terminal Classic (Halperin et al., "Terminal Classic Residential Histories" and "Convergence Zone Politics"; Halperin and Martin, "Ucanal Stela 29"). A detailed study of the Wat'ulk'atel's monuments is in Schele and Mathews, *The Code of Kings,* 175–96. They misread the date of the "arrival" on Stela 11. It is 9.19.18.17.15 6 Men 18 Zip (March 12, 829) as originally proposed by John Graham, "Monumental Sculpture," 28.

25 Dunning et al., "Kax and Kol," presents an insightful overview of the cycles of agricultural abandonment and clearing, and of the environmental dynamics involved in the what the Yucatec Maya call *k'ax ("forest")* and *kol ("milpa, cornfield").*

CHAPTER 12. REVIVALS

1 On Tonina's territory and chronology, see Taladoire, "El terretorio de Tonina."

2 For recent assessments of Chichen Itza chronology, see Braswell and Peniche May, "In the Shadow of the Pyramid"; Ringle, "Debating Chichen Itza"; and Taube et al., *The Initial Series Group*, 13–20.

3 The last known date inscribed at Chichen Itza comes from the Osario temple, corresponding to 998, which is well into the intense period of Mexican interaction and presence. The Osario is similar in form to the massive K'uk'ulkan pyramid, but it seems somewhat later in its sculptural style, perhaps giving us a reasonable suggestion of the early tenth century (900–950) for the intensive building of "high Toltec-Maya" architecture, including the Temple of the Warriors and the Ball Court. But this is speculative. The fine-tuning of chronology at Chichen is still ongoing.

4 See Kowalski and Kristan-Graham, *Twin Tollans*. The ninth-century influences from the Gulf Coast raise an intriguing possibility that the "Toltecs" of highland Mexico were also closely associated with the same region.

5 The so-called "Putun" or "Putun Maya" were first discussed in detail by Thompson, *Maya History and Religion*, influenced by the work of Ralph Roys (Scholes and Roys, *The Maya-Chontal Indians*). The label, while today problematic, emerged as a way to explain both archaeological patterns and ethnohistorical evidence of foreign presence in the northern Maya lowlands. Martin's recent work ("Ethnicity and Identity," "The Long Twilight") with the foreign lords in the Classic history of the southern lowlands adds an important new dimension and more nuanced argument to this scenario, using ancient historical evidence.

6 Here it is easy to be confused by the varied meanings of "Toltec." As noted here, its actual meaning in Nahuatl is in reference to a learned craftsperson well connected to the past. Archaeologists in the early twentieth century began to use "Toltec" in a different way, as a cultural label for pre-Aztec cultures in central Mexico, as found at Tula.

7 Restall, *Maya Conquistador*, 20, shows how the histories recounted in the *Books of Chilam Balam* depict the Itza in local terms, and as long-term players in Yucatán's history, albeit with murky, distant origins. As I suggest here, they may have had their beginnings in the south, in the Peten, where they ultimately resettled after the fall of Mayapan.

8 Tokovinine and Zender, "Lords of Windy Water."

9 The Ik' or Ik'a' emblem is associated with the site of Motul de San José, on the north shore of Lake Peten Itzá. However, it also appears on monuments at nearby Tayasal, a far bigger and older site that I believe to be its true courtly center during the Classic period. On Stela 1 of Motul de San Jose, the two names **i-tza** and **IK'-a** are juxtaposed and may even refer to the same location. If equivalent, the **IK'** logogram was used out of long-term convention, with the phonetic combination providing the more accurate pronunciation. Boot, "Continuity and Change," offers a very detailed discussion of some of the epigraphic issues involved in identifying the antiquity of the Itza place-name.

10 See Harrison-Buck, "Reevaluating Chronology," for a review of the issues involved in the coordination of the *Chilam Balam* narratives with Yucatán archaeology and chronology. The cyclical overlaps and "folds" of the 13 k'atun cycle of those narratives make for difficult matching with archaeological evidence.

11 We see this Cocom (Kokom) name used among nobles who are cited in the ninth-century inscriptions of Chichen Itza, suggesting that their clout in the Mayapan era may have been based partially on that old pedigree.

12 The chronicles of the *Books of Chilam Balam* place Mayapan's founding in the fourteenth century, although archaeological investigations at the site suggest it may have been earlier, soon after Chichen Itza's abandonment.

13 The southern origin of elite lineages in later Yucatán remains controversial. Restall, "Maya Ethnogenesis," suggests that such claims can be viewed as efforts by the ruling Maya families to promote their own statuses in the wake of the Spanish invasion. That is no doubt true. Still, many such claims might also be historically rooted in the known movements of elites after the Classic collapse.

14 Restall et al., *The Friar and the Maya*, 49.

15 Restall et al., *The Friar and the Maya*, 52.

16 Thompson, *The Rise and Fall*, 137, characterized his single trajectory of Maya history as "a steep rise, a lengthy section of plateau, and then a down gradient with grows precipitous as the end comes in sight."

17 Proskouriakoff, "The Death of a Civilization," 86.

18 Thompson, *The Rise and Fall*, 135.

19 Thompson, *The Rise and Fall*, rev. ed., 145. His wistful view of an old "hierarchic" society replaced by a "secular" culture that had lost faith in its earlier ways may reflect a projection of his own times, in the 1950s and '60s, and the ideological conflicts of the Cold War. As Coe, *Breaking the Maya Code*, 145–66, pointed out, the political tension of the postwar era shaped Thompson's attitudes and interpretations in no small way.

20 From the account of Fuensalida and Orbita's visit to Tayasal, quoted in Means, *History of the Conquest of Yucatán and the Itzas*, 72.

21 Villagutierre Soto-Mayor, *Historia de la Conquista de la Provincia de el Itza* (1701).

CHAPTER 13. RISES AND FALLS

1 Stephens, *Incidents of Travel in Central America*, I:278.

2 Landa citation from Tozzer, *Landa's Relación*, 171.

3 Christianson, *Popol Vuh*, 228.

4 Sparks, *Rewriting Maya Religion*, 40. Many studies address the question of Tollan and Zuyua as mythic locales. See especially López Austin and López Luján, "The Myth and Reality of Zuyua," Matthew, *Memories of Conquest*, 27–38, and Sachse and Christenson, "Tulan and the other Side of the Sea."

BIBLIOGRAPHY

Adkins, Lesley, and Roy Adkins. *The Keys of Egypt: The Race to Read the Hieroglyphs.* Harper Collins, 2000.

Aimers, James J., and Prudence Rice. "Astronomy, Ritual and the Interpretation of Maya 'E Group' Assemblages." *Ancient Mesoamerica* 17, no. 1 (2000): 79–96.

Aissen, Judith, Nora England, and Roberto Zavala, eds. *The Mayan Languages.* Routledge, 2017.

Anaya Hernández, Armando, Stanley P. Guenter, and Marc U. Zender. "Sak Tz'i', a Classic Maya Center: A Locational Model Based on GIS and Epigraphy." *Latin American Antiquity* 14, no. 2 (2003): 179–91.

Anderson, Lyssana, and David Wahl. "Two Holocene Paleofire Records from Peten, Guatemala: Implications for Natural Fire Regime and Prehispanic Maya Land Use." *Global and Planetary Change* 138 (2016): 82–92.

Argyle, J. Craig, and Richard D. Hansen. "The Preclassic Frieze of the Great Central Acropolis at El Mirador." In *Mirador: Investigación y conservación en el antiguo reino Kaan,* edited by R. Hansen and E. Suyuc. Foundation for Anthropological Research and Environmental Studies (FARES), 2016.

Armijo Torres, Ricardo, Miriam Judith Gallegos Gómora, and Marc U. Zender. "Urnas funerarios, textos históricos y ofrendas en Comalcalco." In *Los Investigadores de Cultura Maya 8, Tomo II.* Universidad Autonoma de Campeche, 2000.

Auld-Thomas, Luke, Marcello Canuto, Adriana Velazquez Morlet, et al. "Running Out of Empty Space: Environmental Lidar and the Crowded Ancient Landscape of Campeche, Mexico." *Antiquity* 98, no. 401 (2024): 1340–58.

Avendaño y Loyola, Fray Andrés. *Relation of Two Trips to Peten, Made for the Conversion of the Heathen Ytzaes and Cehaches.* Edited by Frank E. Comparato. Translated by Charles P. Bowditch and Guillermo Rivera. Labrynthos, 1987.

Aveni, Anthony, William Saturno, and David Stuart. "Astronomical Implications of Maya Hieroglyphic Notations at Xultun." *Journal of the History of Astronomy* 44 (2013): 1–6.

Baron, Joann P. *Patron Gods and Patron Lords. The Semiotics of Classic Maya Cults.* University Press of Colorado, 2016.

Barthel, Thomas S. "El Complejo 'emblema.'" *Estudios de Cultura Maya* 7 (1968).

Bassie-Sweet, Karen. *Maya Gods of War.* University Press of Colorado, 2021.

Beach, Timothy P., Sheryl Luzzadder-Beach, Duncan Cook, and Nicholas Dunning. "Climate Changes and Collapses in Maya History." *Past Global Change Magazine 66–67* (2016).

Beach, Timothy, Sheryl Luzzadder-Beach, Duncan Cook, et al. "Ancient Maya Impacts on the Earth's Surface: An Early Anthropocene Analog?" *Quaternary Science Reviews* 124 (2015): 1–30.

Beliaev, Dmitri. "Wuk Tsuk and Oxlahun Tsuk: Naranjo and Tikal in the Late Classic." In *Sacred and the Profane: Architecture and Identity in the Maya Lowlands,* edited by Pierre Robert-Colas. Verlag von Flemming, 2000.

Beramendi-Orosco, Laura E., Galia González-Hernández, Jaime Urritia-Fucugauchi, et al. "High-Resolution Chronology for the Mesoamerican Urban Center of Teotihuacan, Derived from Bayesian Statistics of Radiocarbon and Archaeological Data." *Quaternary Research* 71 (2009): 99–107.

Berlin, Heinrich. "Glifos nominales en el sarcófago de Palenqué." *Humanidades* 2, no. 10 (1959): 1–8.

Berlin, Heinrich. "The Inscription of the Temple of the Cross at Palenque." *American Antiquity* 3 (1965): 330–42.

Berlin, Heinrich. *The Tablet of the 96 Glyphs at Palenque, Chiapas, Mexico*. Middle American Research Institute, Tulane University, New Orleans, 1968..

Biró, Péter. "Politics in Western Maya Region (II)—Emblem Glyphs." *Estudios de Cultura Maya* 39 (2012): 33–66. UNAM.

Biró, Péter. "Sak Tz'i' in the Classic Period Hieroglyphic Inscriptions." Mesoweb Publications, 2005. https://www.mesoweb.com/articles/biro/SakTzi.pdf.

Boot, Erik. "The Dos Pilas-Tikal Wars from the Perspective of Dos Pilas Hieroglyphic Stairway 4." *Mesoweb Publications*, 2002. http://www.mesoweb.com/features/boot/DPLHS4.html.

Boot, Erik. "Continuity and Change in Text and Image at Chichen Itzá. Yucatán, Mexico: A Study of the Inscriptions, Iconography, and Architecture at a Late Classic to Early Postclassic Maya Site." CNWS, Universiteit Leiden, 2005.

Bowditch, Charles Pickering. *Notes on the Report of Teobert Maler in Memoirs of the Peabody Museum, Vol. II, No. I*. The University Press, Harvard University, 1901.

Brasseur de Bourbourg, Abbé Charles Étienne. *Relation de choses de Yucatán de Diego de Landa*. Arthus Bertrand, 1864.

Braswell, Geoffrey E., and Nancy Peniche May. "In the Shadow of the Pyramid: Excavations of the Great Platform of Chichen Itza." In *The Ancient Maya of Mexico: Reinterpreting the Past of the Northern Maya Lowlands*, edited by Geoffrey E. Braswell. Equinox Publishing, 2012.

Breuil, Véronique, Laura Gamez, James L. Fitzsimmons, Jean-Paul Metailie, Edy Barrios, and Edwin Román. "Primeras noticias de Zapote Bobal, una ciudad maya clásica del norocidente de Peten, Guatemala." *Mayab* 17 (2004): 61–83.

Brinton, Daniel G. "The Ancient Phonetic Alphabet of Yucatán." *The American Bibliopolist* 2 (1870): 143–48.

Brown, M. Kathryn, and George Bey III, eds. *Pathways to Complexity: A View from the Maya Lowlands*. University Press of Florida, 2018.

Brown, M. Kathryn, and Travis W. Stanton. "Public Architecture and the Rise of Complexity in the Middle Preclassic." In *The Maya World*, edited by Scott R. Hutson and Traci Ardren. Routledge, 2020.

Buikstra, Jane E., T. D. Price, Lori E. Wright, and J. A. Burton. "Tombs from the Copan Acropolis: A Life History Approach." In *Understanding Early Classic Copan*, edited by Marcello Canuto and Ellen Bell. University of Texas Press, 2004.

Campbell, Lyle. "The Implications of Mayan Historical Linguistics for Glyphic Research." In *Phoneticsim in Mayan Hieroglyphic Writing*, edited by John. S. Justeson and Lyle Campbell. IMS, SUNY, 1984.

Canuto, Marcello, Francisco Estrada-Belli, Thomas Garrison, et al. "Ancient Lowland Maya Complexity as Revealed by Airborne Laser Scanning of Northern Guatemala." *Science* 361, no. 6409 (2018). https://doi.org/10.1126/science.aau0137.

Carballo, David. "Power, Politics and Governance at Teotihuacan." In *Teotihuacan: The World Beyond the City*, edited by Kenneth G. Hirth, David M. Carballo, and Barbara Arroyo. Dumbarton Oaks, 2020.

Carlsen, William. *Jungle of Stone: The Extraordinary Journey of John L. Stephens and Frederick Catherwood, and the Discovery of the Lost Civilization of the Maya*. Mariner Books, 2016.

Carrasco Vargas, Ramón, and Maria Cordiero Baqueiro. "The Murals of Chihk Nahb Structure Sub 1–4, Calakmul, Mexico." In *Maya Archaeology 2*, edited by Charles Golden, Stephen Houston, and Joel Skidmore. Precolumbia Mesoweb Press, 2012.

Caso, Alfonso. *Los calendarios prehispánicos*. UNAM, 1967.

Castellanos, Jeannette E., and Antonia E. Foias. "The Earliest Maya Farmers of Peten: New Evidence from Buenavista-Nuevo San José, Central Peten Lakes Region, Guatemala." *Journal of Anthropology* (2017). https://doi.org/10.1155/2017/8109137.

Cerezo-Román, Jessica I., and Kenichiro Tsukamoto. "The Life Course of the Standard-Bearer: A Non-Royal Elite Burial at the Maya Archaeological Site of El Palmar, Mexico. *Latin American Antiquity* 32(2) (2021): 274–91.

Chase, Arlen F., and Diane Z. Chase. "The Early Classic Period at Caracol, Belize: Transitions, Complexity, and Methodological Issues in Maya Archeology." *Research Reports in Belizean Archaeology* 2 (2005): 17–38.

Chase, Arlen F., Diane Z. Chase, Jaime Awe, et al. "Ancient Maya Regional Settlement and Inter-Site Analysis: The 2013 West-Central Belize LiDAR Survey." *Remote Sensing* 6 (2014): 8671–95.

Chase, Arlen F., Diane Z. Chase, John F, Weishampel, et al. "Airborne LiDAR, Archaeology, and the Ancient Maya Landscape at Caracol, Belize. *Journal of Archaeological Science* 38, no. 2 (2011): 387–98.

Chase, Diane Z., and Arlen F. Chase. "Caracol, Belize, and Changing Perceptions of Ancient Maya Society." *Journal of Archaeological Research* 25 (2017): 185–249.

Chatters, James C., Douglas J. Kennett, Yemane Asmerom, et al. "Late Pleistocene Human Skeleton and mtDNA Link Paleoamericans and Modern Native Americans." *Science* 344 (2014): 750. https://doi.org/10.1126/science.1252619.

Cheetham, David. "Cunil: A Pre-Mamom Horizon in the Southern Maya Lowlands." In *New Perspectives on Formative Mesoamerican Cultures*, edited by Terry G. Powis. BAR International Series, 2005.

Cheetham, David, and Jeffrey Blomster. "Materializing the San Lorenzo Olmecs." In *The Early Olmec and Mesoamerica*, edited by J. Blomster and D. Cheetham. Cambridge University Press, 2017.

Chinchilla Mazariegos, Oswaldo. *Art and Myth of the Ancient Maya*. Yale University Press, 2017.

Chinchilla Mazariegos, Oswaldo. "The Sustenance Providers: War, Sacrifice and the Origins of People in Mesoamerica." In *3,000 Years of War and Peace in the Maya Lowlands: Identity, Politics and Violence*, edited by Geoffrey E. Braswell. Routledge, 2022.

Chippindale, Christopher, Norman Hammond, and Jeremy Sabloff. "The Archaeology of Maya Decipherment." *Antiquity* 62, no. 234 (1988): 119–22.

Christenson, Allen J. *Popol Vuh: The Sacred Book of the Maya*. O Books, 2003.

Clark, John E., and David Cheetham. "Mesoamerica's Tribal Foundations." In *The Archaeology of Tribal Societies*, edited by William A. Parkinson. International Monographs in Prehistory, 2002.

Clark, John E., and Mary Pye. *Olmec Art and Archaeology in Mesoamerica*. National Gallery of Art, 2000.

Clayton, Sarah C. "The Collapse of Teotihuacan and the Regeneration of Epiclassic Societies: A Bayesian Approach." *Journal of Anthropological Archaeology* 59 (2020): 101203.

Clayton, Sarah C. "Interregional Relationships in Mesoamerica Interpreting Maya Ceramics." *Latin American Antiquity* 16, no. 4 (2005): 427–48.

Cline, Eric H. *1177 B.C.: The Year Civilization Collapsed*. Princeton University Press, 2014.

Closs, Michael P. "The Dynastic History of Naranjo: The Early Period." *Estudios de Cultura Maya* 15 (1984): 77–79.

Closs, Michael P. "The Dynastic History of Naranjo: The Late Period." In *Word and Image in Maya Culture*, edited by William F. Hanks and Don S. Rice. University of Utah Press, 1989.

Closs, Michael P. "The Dynastic History of Naranjo: The Middle Period." In *Fifth Palenque Round Table, 1983*, vol. 7, edited by Virginia M. Fields. Pre-Columbian Art Research Institute, 1985.

Coe, Michael D. *Breaking the Maya Code*. Thames and Hudson, 1992.

Coe, Michael D. "The Hero Twins: Myth and Image." In *The Maya Vase Book: A Corpus of Rollout Photographs of Maya Vases*, vol. 1. Kerr Associates, 1989.

Coe, Michael D. "A Model of Ancient Community Structure in the Maya Lowlands." *Southwestern Journal of Anthropology* 21, no. 2 (1965): 97–114.

Coe, Michael D. "Supernatural Patrons of Maya Scribes and Artists." In *Social Process in Maya Prehistory: Studies in Honour of Sir Eric Thompson*, edited by Norman Hammond. Academic Press, 1977.

Coe, Michael D., and Richard Deihl. *In the Land of the Olmec*. 2 vols. University of Texas Press, 1980.

Coe, Michael D., and Justin Kerr. *The Art of the Maya Scribe*. Henry N. Abrams, 1998.

Coggins, Clemency C. *The Cenote of Sacrifice*. Peabody Museum Press, 1992.

Collins, Ryan. "Selective Memory: Monumental Politics of the Yaxuná E Group in the First Millennium B.C." *Ancient Mesoamerica* 34, no. 1 (2023): 140–59.

Con, Maria José. "El juego de pelota en Cobá, Quintana Ro. *Arqueología* 23 (2018): 27–50.

Cowgill, George. *Teotihuacan: Early Urbanism in Central Mexico*. Cambridge University Press, 2015.

Cyphers, Ann. "The Early Preclassic Olmec: An Overview." In *The Origins of Maya States*, edited by L. Traxler and R. J. Sharer. University of Pennsylvania Museum of Archaeology and Anthropology, 2016.

Cyphers, Ann, Virginia Arieta Baizabal, and Anna Di Castro. *Las olmecas de San Lorenzo: un nuevo vistazo*. UNAM, 2024.

Danforth, Marie Elaine. "Late Classic Maya Health Patterns: Evidence from Enamel Microdefects." In *Bones of the Maya: Studies of Skeletons*, edited by Stephen Whittington and David Reed. Smithsonian Institution, 1997.

Del Rio, Antonio. *Description of the Ruins of an Ancient City Discovered near Palenque.* Henry Berthoud, 1822.

Delvendahl, Kai. *Calakmul in Sight: History and Archaeology of an Ancient Maya City.* Unas Letras, 2008.

Demarest, Arthur, Matt O'Mansky, Claudia Wolley, et al. "Classic Maya Defensive Systems and Warfare in the Petexbatun Region." *Ancient Mesoamerica* 8, no. 2 (1997): 229–53.

Demarest, Arthur, Claudia Quintanilla, and Jose Samuel Suasnavar. "The Collapses in the West and the Violent Ritual Termination of the Classic Maya Capital Center of Cancuen: Causes and Consequences." In *Ritual, Violence and the Fall of Classic Maya Kings,* edited by Gyles Iannone, Brett A. Houk, and Sonja A. Schwake. University Press of Florida, 2016.

Diamond, Jared. 2005. *Collapse: How Societies Choose to Fail or Succeed.* Viking Penguin, 2005.

Díaz del Castillo, Bernal. *The Discovery and Conquest of Mexico.* Da Capo Press, 2003.

Diehl, Richard A. *The Olmecs: America's First Civilization.* Thames and Hudson, 2004.

Douglas, Peter M. J., Arthur A. Demarest, Mark Brenner, and Marcello A. Canuto. "Impacts of Climate Change on the Collpase of Lowland Maya Civilization." *Annual Review of Earth and Planetary Sciences* 44 (2013): 613–45.

Doyle, James. "A Tale of Two E-Groups: El Palmar and Tikal, Peten, Guatemala." In *Maya E-Groups, Solar Calendars, and the Role of Astronomy in the Rise of Lowland Maya Urbanism,* edited by D. Freidel, A. F. Chase, A. S. Dowd, and J. Murdock. University Press of Florida, 2017.

Dunning, Nicholas P., Timothy Beach, Liwy Grasiozo Sierra, John G. Jones, David L. Lentz, Sheryl Luzzader-Beach, Vernon L. Scarborough, Michael P. Smyth. "A Tale of Two Collapses: Environmental Variability and Cultural Disruption in the Maya Lowlands." *Diálogo Andino* 41 (2013): 171–83.

Dunning, Nicholas P., Sheryl Luzzadder-Beach, Timothy Beach, John G. Jones, Vernon Scarborough, and T. Patrick Culbert. "Arising from the *Bajos*: The Evolution of a Neotropical Landscape and the Rise of Maya Civilization." *Annals of the Association of American Geographers* 92, no. 2 (2002): 267–83.

Dunning, Nicholas P., Timothy Beach, and Sheryl Luzzadder-Beach. "Kax and Kol: Collapse and Resilience in Lowland Maya Civilization." *PNAS* 109, no. 10 (2012): 3632–57.

Eberl, Markus, et al. "The Early Classic Genesis of the Royal Maya Capital of Tamarindito." *Latin American Antiquity* 34, no. 1 (2023): 40–58.

Eppich, Keith, Damien B. Marken, and David Freidel, eds. *El Peru-Waka': New Archaeological Perspectives on the Kingdom of the Centipede.* University Press of Florida, 2024.

Esparza Olguín, Octavio Q. "Estudio de los monumentos esculpidos de Coba, Quintana Roo, y su contexto arqueológico." Thesis, Instituto de Investigaciones Filológicas, UNAM, 2016.

Esparza Olguín, Octavio Q., and Vania E. Pérez Gutierrez. "Archaeological and Epigraphic Studies at Pol Box, Quintana Roo." *The PARI Journal* 9, no. 3 (2009): 1–16.

Estrada-Belli, Francisco. *The First Maya Civilization: Ritual and Power Before the Classic Period.* Routledge, 2011.

Estrada-Belli, Francisco. "The History, Function, and Meaning of Preclassic E Groups in the Cival Region." In *Maya E Groups: Calendars, Astronomy, and Urbanism in the Early Lowlands,* edited by D. Freidel, A. Chase, A. Dowd, and J. Murdoch. University Press of Florida, 2017.

Estrada-Belli, Francisco, Sandra Balanzario, and Erik Velásquez. "The Rise of the Kaanu'l Kingdom and the City of Dzibanche." *Ancient Mesoamerica* (2024): 1–22. https://doi.org/10.1017/S0956536122000207.

Estrada-Belli, Francisco, Laura Gilabert-Sansalvador, Marcello A. Canuto, Ivan Šprajc, and Juan-Carlos Fernandez Diaz. "Architecture, Wealth and Status in Classic Maya Urbanism Revealed by Airborne Lidar Mapping." *Journal of Archaeological Science* 157 (2023): 105835. https://doi.org/10.1016/j.jas.2023.105835.

Estrada-Belli, Francisco, and Alexandre Tokovinine. "A King's Apotheosis: Iconography, Text, and Politics from a Classic Maya Temple at Holmul." *Latin American Antiquity* 27, no. 2 (2016): 149–68.

Estrada-Belli, Francisco, and Alexandre Tokovinine. "Chochkitam: A New Classic Maya Dynasty and the Rise of the Kaanu'l (Snake) Kingdom." *Latin American Antiquity* 33, no. 4 (2022): 713–32.

Estrada-Belli, Francisco, Alexander Tokovinine, Jennifer Foley, et al. "Nuevos Hallazgos de Epigrafía y asentamiento en La Sufricaya, Holmul: Temporada 2005." In *XIX Simposio de Investigaciones Arqueológicas en Guatemala, Tomo II*. MNAE, Guatemala, 2006.

Farriss, Nancy. *Maya Society Under Colonial Rule: The Collective Enterprise of Survival*. Princeton University Press, 1984.

Fash, Barbara. *The Copan Sculpture Museum: Ancient Maya Artistry in Stucco and Stone*. Peabody Museum Press, 2011.

Fash, William L. *Scribes, Warriors and Kings. The City of Copan and the Ancient Maya*. Thames and Hudson, 1991.

Fash, William, and Robert J. Sharer. "Sociopolitical Developments and Methodological Issues at Copan, Honduras: A Conjunctive Perspective." *Latin American Antiquity* 2, no. 2 (1991): 166–87.

Fash, William, Alexandre Tokovinine, and Barbara Fash. "The House of New Fire at Teotihuacan and Its Legacy in Mesoamerica." In *The Art of Urbanism: How Mesoamerican Kingdoms Represented Themselves in Architecture and Imagery*, edited by W. Fash and L. Lopez Lujan. Dumbarton Oaks, 2009.

Fash, William, Richard V. Williamson, Carlos Rudy Larios, and Joel Palka. "The Hieroglyphic Stairway and Its Ancestors: Investigations of Copan Structure 10L-26." *Ancient Mesoamerica* 3, no. 1 (1990): 105–15.

Faust, Betty Bernice. *Mexican Rural Development and the Plumed Serpent: Technology and Maya Cosmology in the Tropical Forest of Campeche, Mexico*. Bergin and Garvey, 1998.

Fields, Virginia M. "The Iconographic Heritage of the Jester God." In *Sixth Palenque Round Table, 1986*, edited by V. M. Fields. University of Oklahoma, 1991.

Fields, Virginia M., and Dorie Reents-Budet, eds. *Lords of Creation: The Origins of Sacred Maya Kingship*. Scala Publishers, 2005.

Fox, James A., and John S. Justeson. "Polyvalence in Mayan Hieroglyphic Writing." In *Phoneticism in Mayan Hieroglyphic Writing*, edited by John. S. Justeson and Lyle Campbell. IMS, SUNY, 1984.

Freidel, David A. "E Groups, Cosmology and the Origins of Maya Rulership." In *Maya E-Groups, Solar Calendars, and the Role of Astronomy in the Rise of Lowland Maya Urbanism*, edited by D. Freidel, A. F. Chase, A. S. Dowd, and J. Murdock. University of Florida Press, 2017.

Freidel, David A., Arlen F. Chase, Anne S. Dowd, and Jerry Murdock, eds. *Maya E-Groups, Solar Calendars, and the Role of Astronomy in the Rise of Lowland Maya Urbanism.* University of Florida Press, 2017.

Freidel, Marilyn A., and David A. Freidel, eds. *Ancient Maya Political Economies.* Altamira Press, 2002.

Gann, Thomas. "Recently Discovered Maya Temples in Yucatán with Date Sculptured on Wooden Lintel." *Man* 28 (1928): 9–11.

Gann, Thomas. "Tzibanché, Quintana Roo, Mexico." *Maya Research* 2 (1935): 155–66.

García Campillo, J. Miguel. "Comentario General sobre la epigrafâ de Oxkintok." In *VII Simposio de Investigaciones Arqueologicas en Guatemala,* edited by Juan Pedro Laporte and Hector Escobedo. Asociacion Tikal, 1994.

Garrison, Thomas G., Amy E. Thompson, Samantha Krause, et al. "Assessing the Lidar Revolution in the Maya Lowlands: A Geographic Approach to Understanding Feature Classification Accuracy." *Progress in Physical Geography: Earth and Environment* 47, no. 2 (2022): 270–92.

Gill, Richardson B. *The Great Maya Droughts.* University of New Mexico Press, 2000.

Gillespie, Susan D., and Rosemary A. Joyce. "Gendered Goods: The Symbolism of Maya Hierarchical Exchange Relations." In *Women in Prehistory: North America and Mesoamerica,* edited by C. Claessen and R. A. Joyce. University of Pennsylvania Press, 1997.

Girard, Rafael. *Los mayas eternos.* Libro Mex Editores, 1962.

Girard, Rafael. *People of the Chan.* Continuum Foundation, 1995.

Golden, Charles, and Andrew K. Scherer. "Territory, Trust, Growth, and Collapse in Classic Period Maya Kingdoms." *Current Anthropology* 54, no. 4 (2013): 397–435.

Golden, Charles, Andrew K. Scherer, Stephen Houston, et al. "Centering the Classic Maya Kingdom of Sak Tz'i." *Journal of Field Archaeology* 45, no. 2 (2020): 67–85.

Golden, Charles, Andrew K. Scherer, Stephen Houston, Whittaker Schroeder, Shanti Morrell-Hart, and Socorro del Pilar Jiménez Álvarez. "Centering the Classic Maya Kingdom of Sak Tz'i." *Journal of Field Archaeology* 45, no. 2 (2019): 67–85.

Golden, Charles, Andrew K. Scherer, Rene Muñoz, and Rosaura Vásquez. "Piedras Negras and Yaxchilan: Divergent Political Trajectories in Adjacent Maya Polities." *Latin American Antiquity* 19, no. 3 (2008): 249–74.

Gómez Chávez, Sergio. "Foreigners' Barrios at Teotihuacan: Reasons for and Consequences of Migration." In *Teotihuacan: City of Water, City of Fire,* edited by Matthew H. Robb. Fine Arts Museum of San Francisco, 2017.

González Cruz, Arnoldo. *La reina roja: una tumba real.* Turner, 2011.

González, Arturo. H., Alejandro Terrazas, Wolfgang Stinnesbeck, Martha E. Benavente, Jerónimo Avilés, Carmen Rojas, José Manuel Padilla, Adriana Velásquez, Eugenio Acevez, and Eberhard Frey. "The First Human Settlers on the Yucatán Peninsula: Evidence from Drowned Caves in the State of Quintana Roo (South Mexico)." In *Paleoamerican Odyssey,* edited by Kelley E. Graf, Caroline V. Ketron and Michael R. Waters. Center for the Study of the First Americans, Texas A&M University, 2014.

Goodman, J. T. *Biologia Centrali-Americana, Archaeology. Appendix: The Archaic Maya Inscriptions.* Taylor and Francis, 1897.

Graham, Ian. *Corpus of Maya Hieroglyphic Inscriptions: Volume 2, Number 2: Naranjo*. Peabody Museum, 1978.

Graham, Ian. *The Road to Ruins*. University of New Mexico Press, 2010.

Graham, Ian. "Homeless Hieroglyphs." *Antiquity* 62 (1988): 122–26.

Graham, John A. "Monumental Sculpture and Hieroglyphic Inscriptions." In *Excavations at Seibal, Department of Peten, Guatemala. Memoirs of the Peabody Museum of Archaeology and Ethnology* 17, no. 1 (1990): 1–80.

Gronemeyer, Sven. "The Monuments and Inscriptions of Tamarindito, Peten, Guatemala." *Acta Mesoamericana* 25 (2013). Verlag Anton Saurwein.

Grove, David C. *Discovering the Olmecs: An Unconventional History.* University of Texas Press, 2014.

Grube, Nikolai. "Palenque in the Maya World." In *Eighth Palenque Round Table, 1993*, edited by Martha J. Macri and Jan McHargue. Pre-Columbian Art Research Institute, 1996.

Grube, Nikolai. "Epigraphic Analysis of Altar 3 of Altar de los Reyes." In *Archaeological Reconnaissance in Southeastern Campeche, México: 2002 Field Season Report*, edited by Ivan Šprajč. Foundation for the Advancement of Mesoamerican Studies, 2003.

Grube, Nikolai, and Linda Schele. "Tikal Altar 5." *Texas Notes on Precolumbian Art Writing and Culture* 66 (1996). Department of Art and Art History, University of Texas.

Grube, Nikolai, Linda Schele, David Stuart, and William Fash. "The Date of the Dedication of Ballcourt III at Copan." *Copan Notes* 59 (1989). Copan Mosaics Project and IHAH.

Guenter, Stanley Paul. "The Inscriptions of Dos Pilas Associated with Bajlaj Chan K'awiil." Mesoweb Publications, 2003. http://www.mesoweb.com/features/guenter/DosPilas.html.

Guenter, Stanley Paul. "On the Emblem Glyph of El Peru-Waka." *The PARI Journal* 8, no. 2 (2007): 20–23.

Guernsey, Julia. *Ritual and Power in Stone: The Performance of Rulership in Mesoamerican Izapan Style Art*. University of Texas Press, 2006.

Guiteras-Holmes, Calixta. *Perils of the Soul: The World View of a Tzotzil Indian*. Free Press, 1961.

Halperin, Christina T., Yasmine Flynn-Arajdal, Katherine A. Miller Wolf, and Carolyn Freiwald. "Terminal Classic Residential Histories, Migration, and Foreigners at the Maya Site of Ucanal, Petén, Guatemala." *Journal of Anthropological Archaeology* 64 (2021). https://doi.org/10.1016/j.jaa.2021.101337.

Halperin, Christina T., Jose Luis Garrido Lopez, Miriam Salas, and Jean-Baptiste LeMoine. "Convergence Zone Politics at the Archaeological Site of Ucanal, Peten, Guatemala." *Ancient Mesoamerica* 31, no. 3 (2020): 476–93.

Halperin, Christina T., and Simon Martin. "Ucanal Stela 29 and the Cosmopolitanism of Terminal Classic Maya Stone Monuments." *Latin American Antiquity* 31, no. 4 (2020): 817–37.

Hammond, Norman, ed. *Cuello: An Early Maya Community in Belize*. Cambridge University Press, 1991.

Hanks, William. *Converting Words: Maya in the Age of the Cross.* University of California Press, 2010.

Hansen, Richard D. "The First Cities: The Beginnings of Urbanization and State Formation in the Maya Lowlands." In *Maya: Divine Kings of the Rain Forest*, edited by N. Grube. Könemann Verlagsgesellschaft, 2001.

Hansen, Richard D., Steven Bozarth, John Jacob, David Wahl, and Thomas Schreiner. "Climate and Environmental Variability in the Rise of Maya Civilization: A Preliminary Perspective from Northern Peten." *Ancient Mesoamerica* 13, no. 2 (2002): 273–95.

Hansen, Richard D., and Edgar Suyuc L., eds. *Mirador.* FARES, 2017.

Harrison, Peter D. "The Lintels of Tzibanche, Quintana Roo." In *Proceedings of the International Congress of Americanists (40th Session, Rome and Genova)* 1 (1972): 495–501.

Harrison, Peter D. *The Lords of Tikal: Rulers of an Ancient City*. Thames and Hudson, 1999.

Harrison-Buck, Eleanor. "Reevaluating Chronology and Historical Content in the Maya Books of Chilam Balam." *Ethnohistory* 61, no. 4 (2014): 681–713.

Harrison-Buck, Eleanor, Samantha Krause, Maireka Brouwer Burg, Mark Willis, Andrea Perrotti, and Katie Bailey. "Late Archaic Large-Scale Fisheries in the Wetlands of the Pre-Columbian Maya Lowlands." *Science Advances* 10, no. 47 (2024). https://doi.org/10.1126/sciadv.adq1444.

Helmke, Christophe, and Jaime Awe. "An Analysis of Panel 3, Xunantunich, Belize." *The PARI Journal* 16, no. 4 (2016): 1–14.

Helmke, Christophe, and Jaime Awe. "Sharper Than a Serpent's Tooth: A Tale of the Snake-Head Dynasty as Recounted on Xunantunich Panel 4." *The PARI Journal* 17, no. 2 (2016): 1–22.

Helmke, Christophe, Dmitri Beliaev, and Sergei Vepretskii. "The Litany of Runaway Kings: Another Look at Stela 12 of Naranjo, Guatemala." *The PARI Journal* 21, no. 2 (2020): 1–28.

Helmke, Christophe, Cristian Bercu, Iulian Drug, et al. "All That Is Old Is New Again: Epigraphic Applications of Photogrammetry in Ancient Mesoamerica." *Digital Applications in Archaeology and Cultural Heritage* 25 (2022). https://doi.org/10.1016/j.daach.2022.e00214.

Helmke, Christophe, Julie Hogarth, and Jaime Awe. *A Reading of the Komkom Vase Discovered at Baking Pot Belize.* Monograph 3. Precolumbia Mesoweb Press, 2018.

Helmke, Christophe, and Ivan Savchenko. "El legado de la Señora Seis Cielo: Sucesiones dinásticas problemáticas en Naranjo en el siglo VIII d.c." *Estudios de Cultura Maya* 44 (2024): 11–35.

Helmke Christophe, and Sergei Vepretskii. "An Account of the Kings of Kanu'l as Recorded on the Hieroglyphic Stair of K'an II of Caracol." *Ancient Mesoamerica* (2024): 1–18. https://doi.org/10.1017/S0956536122000219.

Hester, Thomas R., and Harry J. Shafer. "Exploitation of Chert Resources by the Ancient Maya of Northern Belize, Central America." *World Archaeology* 16 (1984): 157–73.

Hildebrand, A., M. Pilkington, M. Conors, C. Ortiz-Aleman, and R. E. Chavez. "Size and Structure of the Chicxulub Crater Revealed by Horizontal Gravity Gradients and Cenotes." *Nature* 376, no. 6539 (1995): 415–17.

Hirth, Kenneth G., David M. Carballo, and Barbara Arroyo, eds. *Teotihuacan: The World Beyond the City*. Dumbarton Oaks, 2020.

Hodell, David A., Jason H. Curtis, and Mark Brenner. "Possible Role of Climate in the Collapse of Classic Maya Civilization." *Nature* 375, no. 6530 (1995): 391-94.

Houston, Stephen D. "Appendix: Caracol Altar 21." In *Sixth Palenque Round Table, 1986*, edited by Virginia M. Fields and Merle Greene Robertson. University of Oklahoma Press, 1991.

Houston, Stephen D., ed. *Contributions to Maya Hieroglyphic Decipherment.* Human Relations Area Files, Inc., 1983.

Houston, Stephen D. *Hieroglyphs and History at Dos Pilas: Dynastic Politics of the Classic Maya.* University of Texas Press, 1993.

Houston, Stephen D. "The Phonetic Decipherment of Mayan Glyphs." *Antiquity* 62, no. 234 (1988): 126–35.

Houston, Stephen, John Robertson, and David Stuart. "The Language of Maya Inscriptions." *Current Anthropology* 41, no. 3 (2000): 321–55.

Houston, Stephen, Edwin Román Ramírez, Thomas Garrison, David Stuart, Héctor Escobedo Ayala, and Pamela Rosales. "A Teotihuacan Complex at the Classic Maya City of Tikal, Guatemala." *Antiquity* 96, no. 384 (2021): 1–9.

Houston, Stephen, David Stuart, and Karl Taube. *The Memory of Bones: Body Being and Experience Among the Classic Maya.* University of Texas Press, 1996.

Hutson, Scott R. "Urbanism, Architecture, and Internationalism in the Northern Lowlands During the Early Classic." In *The Ancient Maya of Mexico: Reinterpreting the Past of the Northern Maya Lowlands,* edited by G. Braswell. Routledge, 2014.

Iannone, Gyles, ed. *The Great Maya Droughts in Cultural Context: Case Studies in Resilience and Vulnerability.* University Press of Colorado, 2014.

Iceland, Harry B. "The Preceramic Origins of the Maya: The Results of the Colha Preceramic Project in Northern Belize." PhD diss., Department of Anthropology, University of Texas, 1997.

Inomata, Takeshi. "The Isthmian Origins of the E Group and Its Adoption in the Maya Lowlands. In *Early Maya E, Solar Calendars, and the Role of Astronomy in the Rise of Lowland Urbanism,* edited by D. A. Freidel, A. Chase, A. Dowd and J, Murdock. University Press of Florida, 2017.

Inomata, Takeshi. "Olmecs and Other Western Neighbors." In *The Maya World,* edited by S. Hutson and T. Ardren. Routledge, 2020.

Inomata, Takeshi. "Plazas, Performers and Spectators: Political Theaters of the Classic Maya. *Current Anthropology* 47, no. 5 (2006): 803–42.

Inomata, Takeshi, and Daniela Triadan, eds. *Burned Palaces and Elite Residences of Aguateca: Excavations and Ceramics.* Aguateca Archaeological Project First Phase Monograph Series, Volume 1. University of Utah Press, 2010.

Inomata, Takeshi, and Daniela Triadan, eds. *Life and Politics at the Royal Court of Aguateca: Artifacts, Analytical Data, and Synthesis.* Aguateca Archaeological Project First Phase Monograph Series, Volume 3. University of Utah Press, 2014.

Inomata, Takeshi, Daniela Triadan, and Kazuo Aoyama. "After 40 Years: Revisiting Ceibal to Investigate the Origins of Lowland Maya Civilization." *Ancient Mesoamerica* 28, no. 1 (2017): 187–201.

Inomata, Takeshi, Daniela Triadan, Kazuo Aoyama, Victor Castillo, and Hitoshi Yonenobu. "Early Ceremonial Constructions at Ceibal, Guatemala, and the Origins of Lowland Maya Civilization." *Science* 340, no. 6131 (2013): 467–71. https://doi.org/10.1126/science.1234493.

Inomata, Takeshi, Daniela Triadan, Verónica A. Vásquez López, et al. "Monumental Architecture at Aguada Fénic and the Rise of Maya Civilization." *Nature* 582 (2020): 530–33. https://doi.org/10.1038/s41586-020-2343-4.

Isendahl, Christian, and Michael E. Smith. "Sustainable Agrarian Urbanism: The Low-Density Cities of the Mayas and the Aztecs." *Cities* 31 (2013): 132–43. https://doi.org/10.1016/j.cities.2012.07.012.

Jones, Christopher, and Linton Satterthwaite. *The Monuments and Inscriptions of Tikal: The Carved Monuments. Tikal Report no. 33, Part A.* The University Museum, 1982.

Justeson, John S., and Lyle Campbell, eds. *Phoneticism in Mayan Hieroglyphic Writing*. Institute of Mesoamerican Studies Publication No. 9. State University of New York, 1984.

Kaufman, Terrence A. *Mayan Comparative Studies*. 2020. https://www.researchgate.net/publication/340925779_Mayan_Comparative_Studies_Kaufman

Kelley, David H. *Deciphering the Maya Script*. University of Texas Press, 1976.

Kelley, David H. "Kakupakal and the Itzas." *Estudios de Cultura Maya* 7 (1968): 255–68. UNAM.

Kelly, Mary Kate, David Freidel, and Olivia C. Navarro-Farr. "Waka' on the International Stage." In *El Peru-Waka': New Archaeological Perspectives on the Kingdom of the Centipede*, edited by K. Eppich, D. Marken, and D. Freidel. University Press of Florida, 2024.

Kennet, Douglas J., Sebastian F. M. Breitenbach, Valorie V. Aquino, Yemane Asmerom, Jaime Awe, James Baldini, Patrick Bartlein, et al. Development and Disintegration of Maya Political Systems in Response to Climate Change." *Science* 338.6108 (2012): 788–91.

Kennet, Douglas J., Mark Lipson, Keith M. Prufer, et al. "South-to-North Migration Preceded the Advent of Intensive Farming in the Maya Region." *Nature Communications* 13 (2022): 1530.

Kennet, Douglas J., Keith M. Prufer, Brendan J. Culleston, et al. "Early Isotopic Evidence for Maize as a Staple Grain in the Americas." *Science Advances* 6, no. 23 (2020).

Kintz, Ellen R. *Life Under the Tropical Canopy: Tradition and Change Among the Yucatec Maya*. Holt, Rinehart and Winston, 1990.

The Knickerbocker. "American Antiquities." 1833.

Knorosov, Yuriy V. "Drevnyaya Pis'mennost' Tsentralnoy Ameriki [The Ancient Script of Central America]." *Sovietskaya Etnografiya* 3 (1952): 100–118.

Kováč, Milan, Eva Jobbavá, and Guido Krempel. "The Legacy of an Early Maya King: Text, Imagery and Ritual Contexts of a Late Preclassic Cache from Structure H-XVI Sub, Uaxactun." *Mexicon* 38, no. 1 (2016): 9–29.

Kowalski, Jeff. *The House of the Governor: A Maya Palace of Uxmal, Yucatán, Mexico*. University of Oklahoma Press, 1987.

Kowalski, Jeff. "Lords of the Northern Maya: Dynastic History in the Inscriptions of Uxmal and Chichen Itza." *Expedition* 27, no. 3 (1985): 50–60.

Kowalski, Jeff, and Cynthia Kristan-Graham, eds. *Twin Tollans: Chichen Itza, Tula, and the Epiclassic to Early Postclassic Mesoamerican World*. Dumbarton Oaks, 2007.

LaFarge II, Oliver, and Douglas Byers. *The Year Bearer's People*. Department of Middle American Research, Tulane University, 1931.

Laporte, Juan Pedro, and Juan Antonio Valdés. *Tikal y Uaxactun en el Preclásico*. UNAM, 1993.

Law, Danny, and David Stuart. "Classic Mayan: An Overview of Language in Ancient Hieroglyphic Script." In *The Mayan Languages*, edited by J. Aissen, N. C. England, and R. Zavala Maldonado. Routledge, 2017.

Lentz, David L., T. L. Hamilton, N. P. Dunning, et al. "Molecular Genetic and Geochemical Assays Reveal Severe Contamination of Drinking Water Reservoirs at the Ancient Maya City of Tikal." *Scientific Reports* 10 (2020): 10316. https://doi.org/10.1038/s41598-020-67044-z.

Lizana, Bernardo de. *Historia de Yucatán*. Crónicas de America 43. Historia 16, 1988 (1633).

Lockhart, James. *The Nahuas after the Conquest: A Social and Cultural History of the Indians of Central Mexico, Sixteenth through Eighteenth Centuries*. Stanford University Press, 1992.

Lohse, Jon C., Molly Morgan, John Jones, et al. "Early Maize in the Maya Area." *Latin American Antiquity* 33, no. 4 (2022): 677–92.

Looper, Matthew. *Lightning Warrior: Maya Art and Kingship at Quirigua.* University of Texas Press, 2003.

López Austin, Alfredo, and Leonardo López Luján. "The Myth and Reality of Zuyua: The Feathered Serpent and Mesoamerican Transformations from the Classic to the Postclassic." In *Mesoamerica's Classic Heritage: From Teotihuacan to the Aztecs,* edited by Davíd Carrasco, Lindsay Jones and Scott Sessions. University Press of Colorado, 2000.

López Luján, Leonardo, and Saburo Sugiyama. "The Ritual Deposits in the Moon Pyramid at Teotihuacan." In *Teotihuacan: City of Water, City of Fire,* edited by Matthew H. Robb. Fine Arts Museum of San Francisco, 2017.

Lounsbury, Floyd. "On the Derivation and Reading of the 'Ben-Ich' Prefix." In *Mesoamerican Writing Systems,* edited by Elizabeth Benson. Dumbarton Oaks, 1973.

Lucero, Lisa. *Maya Wisdom and the Survival of Our Planet.* Oxford University Press, 2025.

Lucero, Lisa. *Water and Ritual: The Rise and Fall of Classic Maya Rulers.* University of Texas Press, 2006.

MacLellan, Jessica. "Settling Down at Ceibal and Cuello: Variation in the Transition to Sedentism Across the Maya Lowlands." *Frontiers in Human Dynamics* 6 (2024). https://doi.org/10.3389/fhumd.2024.1354725.

Macri, Martha J., and Anabel Ford, eds. *The Language of Maya Hieroglyphs.* Pre-Columbian Art Research Institute, 1997.

Magaloni-Kerpel, Diana, Megan E. O'Neil, and María Reresa Uriarte. "The Moving Image: Painted Murals and Vessels at Teotihuacan and the Maya Area." In *Teotihuacan: The World Beyond the City,* edited by Kenneth Hirth, David M. Carballo, and Barbara Arroyo. Dumbarton Oaks, 2020.

Maler, Teobert. *Explorations in the Department of Peten, Guatemala, and Adjacent Region.* Peabody Museum of Archaeology and Ethnology, 1908.

Manzanilla, Linda R. "Gobierno corporativo en Teotihuacan: una revision del concepto 'palacio' aplicado a la gran urbe prehispanica." *Anales de Antropoloogía* 35 (2002): 157–90.

Marcus, Joyce. *Emblem and State in the Classic Maya Lowlands.* Dumbarton Oaks, 1976.

Marcus, Joyce. *Mesoamerican Writing Systems: Propaganda, Myth, History in Four Ancient Civilizations.* Princeton University Press, 1992.

Marcus, Joyce. "Territorial Organization of the Lowland Classic Maya." *Science* 180 (1973): 911–16.

Martin, Simon. *Ancient Maya Politics: A Political Anthropology of the Classic Period, 150–900 CE.* Cambridge University Press, 2022.

Martin, Simon. "Caracol Altar 21 Revisited: More Data on Double Bird and Tikal's Wars of the Mid-Sixth Century." *The PARI Journal* 6, no. 1 (2005): 1–9.

Martin, Simon. "Ethnicity and Identity at Chichen Itza." In *When East Meets West: Chichen Itza, Tula, and the Postclassic Mesoamerican World,* edited by Travis Stanton, Karl Taube, and Jeremy Coltman. BAR International Series, 2023.

Martin, Simon. "In Line of the Founder: A View of Dynastic Politics at Tikal." In *Tikal: Dynasties, Foreigners, and Affairs of State,* edited by Jeremy A. Sabloff. School of American Research Press, 2003.

Martin, Simon. "The Long Twilight of the Tikal Dynasty: What Ninth Century Tikal, Zacpeten, Ixlu and Jimbal Tell Us About the Classic Maya Collapse." In *Substance and the Ancient Maya: Kingdoms and Commodities, Objects and Beings*, edited by Andrew K. Scherer and Thomas G. Garrison. University of New Mexico Press, 2024.

Martin, Simon. "Moral-Reforma y la contienda por el oriente de Tabasco." *Arqueología Mexicana* 11, no. 61 (2003): 44–77.

Martin, Simon. "Nuevos datos epigraficos sobre la guerra maya del Clasico." In *La guerra entre los antiguos mayas: memorias de la Primera Mesa Redondo de Palenque*, edited by Silvia Trejo. INAH, 2000.

Martin, Simon. "A Northern War: Coba vs. Oxkintok." *Maya Decipherment*, December 31, 2019. https://mayadecipherment.com/2019/12/31/a-northern-war-coba-vs-oxkintok/.

Martin, Simon. "The Painted King List: A Commentary on Codex-Style Dynastic Vases." In *The Maya Vase Book: A Corpus of Rollout Photographs of Maya Vases*, vol. 5, edited by Justin Kerr. Kerr Associates, 1997.

Martin, Simon. "At the Periphery: The Movement, Modification and Re-Use of Early Monuments in the Environs of Tikal." In *The Sacred and the Profane: Architecture and Identity in the Maya Lowlands*, edited by Pierre Robert Colas, Kai Delvendahl, Marcus Kuhnert, and Annette Schubart. *Acta Mesoamericana*, volume10. Verlag Anton Saurwein, 2000.

Martin, Simon. "In Search of the Serpent Kings: From Dzibanche to Calakmul." *Ancient Mesoamerica* (2024): 1–17. https://doi.org/10.1017/S095653612200030X.

Martin, Simon. "Secrets of the Painted King List: Recovering the Early History of the Snake Dynasty." *Maya Decipherment*, May 5, 2017.

Martin, Simon. "Of Snakes and Bats: Shifting Identities at Calakmul." *The PARI Journal* 6, no. 2 (2005): 5–13.

Martin, Simon, and Dmitri Beliaev. "K'ahk' Ti' Ch'ich': A New Snake King from the Early Classic Period." *The PARI Journal* 17, no. 3 (2017): 1–7.

Martin, Simon, and Nikolai Grube. *Chronicle of Maya Kings and Queens*. Thames and Hudson, 2000.

Martin, Simon, and Nikolai Grube. *Chronicle of Maya Kings and Queens*. 2nd ed. Thames and Hudson, 2008.

Martin, Simon, and Joel Skidmore. "Exploring the 584286 Correlation Between the Maya and European Calendars." *The PARI Journal* 13, no. 2 (2012): 3–16.

Martin, Simon, Vilma Fialko, Alexandre Tokovinine, and Fredy Ramírez. "Contexto y texto de la estela 47 de Naranjo-Sa'al, Petén, Guatemala." In *XXIX Simposio de Investigaciones Arqueologias en Guatemala 2015, Tomo II*. Ministerio de Cultura y Deportes, IDEAH, and Asociación Tikal, 2014.

Mathews, Peter. "Classic Emblem Glyphs." In *Classic Mayan Political History: Hieroglyphic and Archaeological Evidence*, edited by T. Patrick Culbert. Cambridge University Press, 1991.

Mathews, Peter. *La escultura de Yaxchilan*. INAH, 1997.

Mathews, Peter. "Maya Early Classic Monuments and Inscriptions." In *A Consideration of the Early Classic Period in the Maya Lowlands*, edited by Gordon Willey and Pater Mathews. Institute of Mesoamerican Studies, SUNY-Albany, 1985.

Mathews, Peter. "Notes on the Inscriptions on the Back of Dos Pilas Stela 8." In *The Decipherment of Ancient Maya Writing*, edited by Stephen D. Houston, Oswaldo Chinchilla Mazariegos, and David Stuart. University of Oklahoma Press, 2001.

Mathews, Peter, and John S. Justeson. "Patterns of Sign Substitution in Maya Hieroglyphic Writing: 'The Affix Cluster.'" In *Phoneticism in Mayan Hieroglyphic Writing*, edited by John S. Justeson and Lyle Campbell. Institute for Mesoamerican Studies, State University of New York at Albany, 1984.

Mathews, Peter, and Linda Schele. "Lords of Palenque: The Glyphic Evidence." In *Primera Mesa Redonda de Palenque, Part I*, edited by Merle Greene Robertson. Robert Louis Stevenson School, 1974.

Matsumoto, Mallory. "Cultures of Creativity: Hieroglyphic Innovation in the Classic Maya Lowlands. *Cambridge Archaeological Journal* 33, no. 1 (2022): 99–118.

Matthew, Laura E. *Memories of Conquest: Becoming Mexicano in Colonial Guatemala*. University of North Carolina Press, 2012.

Means, Philip A. *History of the Conquest of Yucatán and the Itzas*. Peabody Museum, 1917.

Miller, Jeffery. "Notes on a Stela Pair Probably from Calakmul, Campeche, Mexico." In *Primera Mesa Redonda de Palenque, Part I*, edited by Merle Greene Robertson. Robert Louis Stevenson School, 1974.

Miller, Mary Ellen. *The Murals of Bonampak*. Princeton University Press, 1986.

Miller, Mary, and Claudia Brittenham. *The Spectacle of the Late Maya Court: Reflections on the Murals of Bonampak*. University of Texas Press, 2013.

Millon, Rene. "The Last Years of Teotihuacan's Dominance." In *The Collapse of Ancient States and Civilizations*, edited by Norman Yoffee and George Cowgill. University of Arizona Press, 1988.

Morley, Sylvanus G. "Archaeology." In *Carnegie Institution of Washington, Yearbook no. 21*. Carnegie Institution of Washington, 1922.

Morley, Sylvanus G. *The Inscriptions of Peten*. 5 vols. Carnegie Institution of Washington, 1938.

Morley, Sylvanus G. "Maya Epigraphy." In *The Maya and their Neighbors: Essays in Middle American Anthropology and Archaeology*, edited by Clarence Hay, Ralph Linton, Samuel K. Lothrop, Harry L. Shapiro, and George C. Vaillant. D. Appleton-Century, 1940.

Nalda, Enrique. "Dzibanche: el contexto de los cautivos." In *Los cautivos de Dzibanche*, edited by E. Nalda. INAH, 2004.

Nalda, Enrique. "Prácticas funerarias en Dzibanché, Quintana Roo: Los entierros en el Edificio de los Cormoranes." *Arqueología* 31 (2003): 25–37.

Navarro-Farr, Olivia C., Mary Kate Kelly, Michelle Rich, and Griselda Pérez Robles. "Expanding the Canon: Lady K'abel, the Ix Kalomte' and the Political Narratives of Classic Maya Queens." *Feminist Anthropology* 1 (2020): 38–55.

Navarro-Farr, Olivia C., Juan Carlos Pérez, and Griselda Pérez Robles. "Lady K'abel and the City's Temple: Reinforcing Cosmic Order Through Sacred Architecture." In *El Peru-Waka': New Archaeological Perspectives on the Kingdom of the Centipede*, edited by K. Eppich, D. Marken, and D. Freidel. University Press of Florida, 2024.

Noguez, Xavier. "Altepetl." In *The Oxford Handbook of Mesoamerican Cultures: The Civilizations of Mexico and Central America*, edited by D. Carrasco. Oxford University Press, 2001.

O'Neil, Megan. "Object, Memory, and Materiality at Yaxchilan: The Reset Lintels of Structures 12 and 22." *Ancient Mesoamerica* 22, no. 2 (2011): 245–69.

O'Neil, Tom. "Uncovering a Maya Mural." *National Geographic Magazine* 201, no. 4 (2002): 70–75.

Pallán Gayol, Carlos. "A Glimpse from Edzna's Hieroglyphics: Middle, Late and Terminal Classic Processes of Cultural Interaction between the Southern, Northern and Western Lowlands. *Contributions in New World Archaeology* 4 (2012): 89-110.

Pasztory, Esther. *Teotihuacan: An Experiment in Living*. University of Oklahoma Press, 1997.

Pérez de Heredia, Eduardo, and Péter Biró. "K'ak'upakal K'inich K'awil and the Lords of Fire: Chichen Itza During the Ninth Century." In *Landscapes of the Itza: Archaeology and Art History at Chichen Itza and Neighboring Sites*, edited by Linnea Wren, Cynthia Kristan-Graham, Travis Nygard, and Kaylee Spencer. University Press of Florida, 2018.

Piperno, Dolores. "The Origins of Plant Cultivation and Domestication in the New World Tropics: Patterns, Process, and New Developments." *Current Anthropology* 52, no. S4 (2011): 453–70.

Ponce, Jocelyne M., Caroline A. Parris, Marcello A. Canuto, and Tomás Barrientos Q. "Voices and Narratives Beyond Texts: The Life-History a Classic Maya Building." *The Mayanist* 2, no. 2 (2021): 1–24.

Pope, Maurice. "The Story of Archaeological Decipherment: From Egyptian Hieroglyphs to Maya Script." Thames and Hudson, 1999.

Prager, Christian, and Antje Grothe. "From Fragments to Clarity: Reconstructing the Hieroglyphic Narrative of Lintel 34 from Yaxchilan." *Textdatenbank und Wörterbuch des Klassischen Maya*, Research Note 30, 2024. https://doi.org/10.20376/IDIOM-23665556.24.rn030.en.

Prager, Christian, Elizabeth Wagner, Sebastian Matteo, and Guido Krempel. "A Reading for the Xultun Toponymic Title as B'aax (Tuun) Witz 'Ajaw, Lord of the B'aax-(Stone) Hill." *Mexicon* 32, no. 4 (2010): 74–77.

Prager, Christian, Elizabeth Wagner, and Seichi Nakamura. "Stela 64: A New Epigraphic Discovery at Copan, Honduras." *Textdatenbank und Wörterbuch des Klassischen Maya*, Research Note 31, 2024. https://doi.org/10.20376/IDIOM-23665556.24.rn031.en.

Proskouriakoff, Tatiana. "The Death of a Civilization." *Scientific American* 192 (1955): 86.

Price, T. Douglas, James H. Burton, Robert J. Sharer, et al. "Kings and Commoners at Copan: Isotopic Evidence for Origins and Movement in the Classic Maya Period." *Journal of Anthropological Archaeology* 29, no. 1 (2010): 15–32.

Proskouriakoff, Tatiana. "Historical Implications of a Pattern of Dates at Piedras Negras, Guatemala." *American Antiquity* 25, no. 4 (1960): 454–75.

Proskouriakoff, Tatiana. *Jades from the Cenote of Sacrifice, Chichen Itza, Yucatán*. Peabody Museum, Harvard University, 1974.

Proskouriakoff, Tatiana. *Maya History*. University of Texas Press, 1993.

Puleston, Dennis E. "An Epistemological Pathology and the Collapse, or Why the Maya Kept the Short Count." In *Maya Archaeology and Ethnohistory*, edited by N. Hammond and G. R. Willey. University of Texas Press, 1979.

Rau, Charles. "The Palenque Tablet in the United States National Museum, Washington, D.C." In *Smithsonian Contributions to Knowledge*, vol. 22, article V. Smithsonian Institution, 1879.

Reents-Budet, Dorie. "Codex Style Ceramics: New Date Concerning Patterns of Production and Distribution." Presented at the XXIV Symposium of Archaeological Investigations in Guatemala, July 19–24, 2010.

Reents-Budet, Dorie, and Ronald L. Bishop. "Classic Maya Painted Ceramics: Artisans, Workshops, and Distribution." In *Ancient Maya Art at Dumbarton Oaks*, Joanne Pillsbury, Miriam Doutriaux, Reiko Ishihara-Brito, and Alexandre Tokovinine, eds., 288–99. Dumbarton Oaks, 2012.

Reese-Taylor, Kathryn. "Becoming Maya in Early Middle Preclassic Mesoamerica." In *Pre-Mamom Pottery Variation and the Preclassic Origins of the Lowland Maya*, edited by D. Walker. University Press of Colorado, 2023.

Reese-Taylor, Kathryn. "Founding Landscapes in the Central Karstic Uplands." In *Maya E Groups: Calendars, Astronomy, and Urbanism in the Early Lowlands*, edited by David A. Freidel, Arlen F. Chase, Anne S. Dowd, and Jerry Murdock. University of Florida Press, 2017.

Restall, Matthew. *Maya Conquistador*. Beacon Press, 1998.

Restall, Matthew. "Maya Ethnogenesis." *Journal of Latin American Anthropology* 9, no. 1 (2004): 64–89.

Restall, Matthew, and Wolfgang Gabbart. "Maya Ethnogenesis and Group Identity in Yucatán, 1500–1900." In *The Only True People: Linking Maya Identities Past and Present*, edited by Bethany J. Beyyette and Lisa J. LeCount. University Press of Colorado, 2017.

Restall, Matthew, Amara Solari, John F. Chuchiak IV, and Traci Ardren. *The Friar and the Maya: Diego de Landa and the Account of Things of Yucatán*. University Press of Colorado, 2023.

Rice, Prudence M., and Timothy W. Pugh. "Water, Centering and the Beginning of Time at Middle Preclassic Nixtun Ch'ich', Peten, Guatemala." *Journal of Anthropological Archaeology* 48 (2017): 1–16.

Robb, Matthew, ed. *Teotihuacan: City of Water, City of Fire*. Fine Arts Museum of San Francisco, 2017.

Robertson, John S., Danny Law, and Robbie A. Haertel. *Colonial Ch'olti': The Seventeenth-Century Morán Manuscript*. University of Oklahoma Press, 2010.

Robinson, Andrew. *Cracking the Egyptian Code: The Revolutionary Life of Jean-Francois Champollion*. Oxford University Press, 2012.

Robinson, Andrew. *Lost Languages: The Enigma of the World's Undeciphered Scripts*. McGraw-Hill, 2002.

Rosenswig, Robert M., Deborah M. Pearsall, Marilyn A. Masson, Brendan J. Culleton, and Douglas J. Kennet. "Archaic Period Settlement and Subsistence in the Maya Lowlands: New Starch Grain and Lithic Data from Freshwater Creek, Belize." *Journal of Archaeological Science* 41 (2014): 308–21.

Rosenswig, Robert M., Deborah M. Pearsall, Marilyn A. Masson, Brendan J. Culleton, and Douglas J. Kennet. "Middle Preclassic Nixtun Ch'ich': A Lowland Maya Primate/Ritual City." *Journal of Anthropological Archaeology* 63 (2021): 101308.

Ringle, William. "Debating Chichen Itza." *Ancient Mesoamerica* 28, no. 1 (2017): 119–36.

Ringle, William M., Tomás Gallareta Negrón, and George J. Bey III. "The Return of Quetzalcoatl: Evidence for the Spread of a World Religion in the Epiclassic Period." *Ancient Mesoamerica* 9 (1998): 183–232.

Rivera Dorado, Miguel. "Clues to the System of Power in the City of Oxkintok." In *Emergence and Change in Early Urban Societies*, edited by Linda Manzanilla. Springer, 1997.

Ruz Lhuillier, Alberto. "Mystery of the Mayan Temple." *The Saturday Evening Post* 226, no. 9 (1953): 30, 95–98.

Sachse, Frauke, and Allen J. Christenson. "Tulan and the other Side of the Sea: Unraveling a Metaphorical Concept from Colonial Highland Guatemalan Sources." Mesoweb Publications, 2005. https://www.mesoweb.com/articles/tulan/Tulan.pdf.

Sánchez de Aguilar, Pedro. "Informe contra los idólatras cultores del Obispado de Yucatán, 1639." *Anales del Instituto Nacional de Antropología e Historia* 1, no. 6 (1900): 12–122.

Sandstrom, Alan. *Corn Is Our Blood: Culture and Ethnic Identity in a Contemporary Aztec Village*. University of Oklahoma Press, 1991.

Saturno, William. "Centering the Kingdom, Centering the King: Maya Creation and Legitimization at San Bartolo." In *The Art of Urbanism: How Mesoamerican Kingdoms Represented Themselves in Architecture and Imagery*, edited by W. L. Fash and L. L. Luján. Dumbarton Oaks, 2009.

Saturno, William, David Stuart, and Boris Beltran. "Early Maya Writing at San Bartolo, Guatemala." *Science* 311, no. 5765 (2006): 1281–83.

Saturno, William, David Stuart, Anthony Aveni, and Franco Rossi. "Ancient Maya Astronomical Tables from Xultun, Guatemala." *Science* 336 (2012): 714.

Schele, Linda. "The Founders of Lineages at Copan and Other Maya Sites." *Ancient Mesoamerica* 3, no. 1 (1992): 135–44.

Schele, Linda. "A New Look at the Dynastic History of Palenque." In *Supplement to the Handbook of Middle American Indians, Vol. 5, Epigraphy*, edited by Victoria R. Bricker. University of Texas Press, 1992.

Schele, Linda. "The Tlaloc Complex in the Classic Period: War and the Interaction Between the Lowland Maya and Teotihuacan." Unpublished manuscript on file. Mesoamerica Center, University of Texas at Austin, 1986.

Schele, Linda, and David Freidel. *A Forest of Kings: The Untold Story of the Ancient Maya*. William Morrow, 1990.

Schele, Linda, and Peter Mathews. *The Code of Kings: The Language of Seven Sacred Maya Tombs and Temples*. Scribner, 1998.

Scholes, Frans V., and Ralph L. Roys. *The Maya-Chontal Indians of Acalan-Tixchel*. University of Oklahoma Press, 1968.

Seligson, Kenneth. *The Maya and Climate Change: Human and Environmental Relationships in the Classic Period Lowlands*. Oxford University Press, 2023.

Shaw, David W. *The Sea Shall Embrace Them: The Tragic Story of the Steamship Arctic*. The Free Press, 2002.

Shook, Edwin M. *Incidents in the Life of a Maya Archaeologist*. Southwestern Academy Press, 1998.

Smith, Victoria, et al. "The Magnitude and Impact of the 431 CE Tierra Blanca Joven Eruption of Ilopongo, El Salvador." *PNAS* 117, no. 42 (2020): 26062–68.

Solari, Amara. *Idolizing Mary: Maya-Catholic Icons in Yucatán, Mexico*. Penn State University Press, 2019.

Solari, Amara. *Maya Ideologies of the Sacred: The Transfiguration of Space in Colonial Yucatán*. University of Texas Press, 2013.

Sparks, Garry G. *Rewriting Maya Religion: Domingo de Vico, K'iche' Intellectuals and the* Theologia Indorum. University Press of Colorado, 2019.

Šprajc, Ivan, Takeshi Inomata, and Anthony Aveni. "Origins of Mesoamerican Astronomy and Calendar: Evidence from the Olmec and Maya Regions." *Science Advances* (2023). https://doi.org/10.1126/sciadv.abq7675.

Stanton, Travis W. "The Founding of Yaxuná: Place and Trade in Preclassic Yucatán. In *Maya E Groups: Calendars, Astronomy, and Urbanism in the Early Lowlands,* edited by David. A. Freidel, Arlen F. Chase, Anne S. Dowd, and Jerry Murdock. University of Florida Press, 2017.

Stanton, Travis, and David Freidel. "Ideological Lock-In and the Dynamics of Formative Religions in Mesoamerica." *Mayab* 16 (2003): 5–14.

Stephens, John Lloyd. *Incidents of Travel in Central America, Chiapas and Yucatán.* 2 vols. Harper and Bros., 1841.

Stephens, John Lloyd. *Incidents of Travel in Yucatán.* 2 vols. Harper and Bros, 1843.

Storey, Rebecca. "An Estimate of Mortality in a Pre-Columbian Urban Population." *American Anthropologist* 87 (1985): 519–34.

Stuart, David. "The 'Arrival of Strangers': Teotihuacan and Tollan in Classic Maya History." In *Mesoamerica's Classic Heritage: From Teotihuacan to the Aztecs,* edited by D. Carrasco, L. Jones, and S. Sessions. University Press of Colorado, 2000.

Stuart, David. "The Beginnings of the Copan Dynasty: A Review of the Hieroglyphic and Historical Evidence." In *Understanding Early Classic Copan,* edited by E. Bell, M. Canuto, and R. J. Sharer. University Museum, University of Pennsylvania, 2003.

Stuart, David. "The Decipherment of 'Directional Count Glyphs' in Maya Inscriptions." *Ancient Mesoamerica* 1, no. 2 (1990): 213–24.

Stuart, David. "A Foreign Past: The Writing and Representation of History on a Royal Ancestral Shrine at Copan." In *Copan: The History of an Ancient Maya Kingdom,* edited by E. Wyllys Andrews and William L. Fash. The School of American Research Press, 2005.

Stuart, David. "Historical Inscriptions and the Maya Collapse." In *Lowland Maya Civilization in the Eighth Century A.D.,* edited by Jeremy A. Sabloff and John S. Henderson. Dumbarton Oaks, 1993.

Stuart, David. *The Inscriptions of Temple XIX at Palenque: A Commentary.* Precolumbian Art Research Institute, 2005.

Stuart, David. "Longer Live the King: The Questionable Demise of K'inich K'an Joy Chitam of Palenque." *The PARI Journal* 4, no. 1 (2003): 1–4.

Stuart, David. "The Name of Paper: The Mythology of Crowning and Royal Nomenclature on Palenque's Palace Tablet." *Maya Archaeology* 2. Precolumbia Mesoweb Press, 2013.

Stuart, David. "A New Child-Father Relationship Glyph." *Research Reports on Ancient Maya Writing,* no. 2. Center for Maya Research, 1985.

Stuart, David. *The Order of Days: Unlocking the Secrets of the Ancient Maya.* Crown Publishers, 2012.

Stuart, David. *The Palenque Mythology.* Sourcebook for the XXX Maya Meetings. Department of Art and Art History, University of Texas at Austin, 2006.

Stuart, David. "Shining Stones: Observations on the Ritual Meaning of Early Maya Stelae." In *The Place of Stone Monuments: Context, Use and Meaning in Mesoamerica's Preclassic Tradition,* edited by Julia Guernsey, John E. Clark, and Barbara Arroyo. Dumbarton Oaks, 2010.

Stuart, David. "Some Working Notes on the Text of Tikal Stela 31." Mesoweb Publications, 2011. http://www.mesoweb.com/stuart/notes/Tikal.pdf.

Stuart, David. *Spearthrower Owl: A Teotihuacan Ruler in Maya History*. Dumbarton Oaks, 2024.

Stuart, David. "Stones of Kings: A Consideration of Stelae in Classic Maya Ritual and Representation." *RES: Anthropology and Aesthetics*, nos. 29/30 (1996): 148–71.

Stuart, David. "Ten Phonetic Syllables." *Research Reports on Ancient Maya Writing*, no. 14. Center for Maya Research, 1987.

Stuart, David. "Una guerra entre Yaxchilán y Piedras Negras?" In *Proyecto Arqueológico Piedras Negras, informe preliminar no. 2, segunda temporada, 1998*, edited by Hector Escobedo and Stephen Houston. Proyecto Arqueológico Piedras Negras, 1999.

Stuart, David. "You Go That Way, I'll Go This Way." In *Maya Archaeology: Tales from the Field*, edited by Mat Saunders and Panela Voelkel. Precolumbia Mesoweb Press, 2021.

Stuart, David, Tomás Barrientos Q., Alexandre Tokovinine, and Daniel Aquino. "La recuperación de la Estela 43 de Naranjo: Un breve acercamiento a la importancia histórica e iconográfica de un monumento Maya perdido." In *35 Simposio de Investigaciones Arqueológicas en Guatemala 2022*, edited by Barbara Arroyo, Luiz Mendez Salinas, and Gloria Ajú Álvarez, Tomo 1. Ministerio de Cultura y Deportes, 2023.

Stuart, David, Marcello A. Canuto, and Tomás Barrientos Q. "The Nomenclature of La Corona Sculpture." *La Corona Notes* 1, no. 2 (2015).

Stuart, David, Marcello Canuto, Tomás Barrientos Q., Jocelyn Ponce, and Joanne Baron. "The Death of the Defeated: New Historical Data on Block 4 of La Corona's Hieroglyphic Stairway 2." *La Corona Notes* 1, no. 3 (2015).

Stuart, David, and Stephen D. Houston. "Classic Maya Place Names." *Studies in Pre-Columbian Art and Archaeology*, no. 34. Dumbarton Oaks, 1994.

Stuart, David, Heather Hurst, Boris Beltran, and William Saturno. "An Early Maya Calendar Record from San Bartolo, Guatemala." *Science Advances* 8, no. 15 (2022). https://doi.org/10.1126/sciadv.abl9290.

Stuart, David, and George E. Stuart. *Palenque: Eternal City of the Maya*. Thames and Hudson, 2008.

Sugiyama, Nawa, William L. Fash, Barbara Fash, and Saburo Sugiyama. "The Maya at Teotihuacan: New Insights into Teotihuacan-Maya Interactions from Plaza of the Columns Complex." In *Teotihuacan: The World Beyond the City*, edited by Kenneth Hirth, Barbara Arroyo, and David Carballo. Dumbarton Oaks, 2020.

Sugiyama, Saburo. "Rulership, Warfare and Human Sacrifice at the Cuidadela: An Iconographic Study of Feathered Serpent Representations." In *Art, Ideology, and the City of Teotihuacan*, edited by J. C. Berlo. Dumbarton Oaks, 1992.

Sugiyama, Saburo, and Leonardo López Luján. "The Ritual Deposits in the Moon Pyramid at Teotihuacan." In *Teotihuacan: City of Water, City of Fire*, edited by M. Robb. Fine Arts Museum of San Francisco, 2017.

Sugiyama, Saburo, and Leonardo López Luján. *Sacrificios de consagracion en la Piramide de la Luna*. INAH, 2006.

Talaldoire, Eric. "El terretorio de Tonina, Chiapas." *Journal de la Socéité de Américanistes* 103, no. 2 (2017): 141–73.

Tate, Carolyn. "The Royal Women at Yaxchilan." In *Primer Simposio Internacional de Mayistas*. UNAM, 1987.

Taube, Karl A. "The Classic Maya Maize God: A Reappraisal." In *Palenque Round Table, 1983*, edited by M. G. Robertson and V. M. Fields. Pre-Columbian Art Research Institute, 1985.

Taube, Karl A. *The Major Gods of Ancient Yucatán. Studies in Pre-Columbian Art and Archaeology*, no. 32. Dumbarton Oaks, 1992.

Taube, Karl A. "Structure 10L-16 and Its Early Classic Antecedents: Fire and the Evocation and Resurrection of K'inich Yax K'uk' Mo." In *Understanding Early Classic Copan*, edited by E. Bell, M. Canuto, and R. J. Sharer. University Museum, University of Pennsylvania, 2004.

Taube, Karl A., Travis W. Stanton, José Francisco Osorio León, Francisco Pérez Ruiz, María Rocio González de la Mata, and Jeremy Coltman. *The Initial Series Group at Chichen Itza, Yucatán: Archaeological Investigations and Iconographic Interpretations*. Precolumbia Mesoweb Press, 2020.

Tedlock, Barbara. *Time and the Highland Maya*. Rev. ed. University of New Mexico Press, 1992.

Thompson, J. Eric S. *Maya Hieroglyphic Writing: Introduction*. Carnegie Institution of Washington Publication 589. Carnegie Institution of Washington, 1950.

Thompson, J. Eric S. *Maya Hieroglyphic Writing: An Introduction*. Rev. ed. University of Oklahoma Press, 1971.

Thompson, J. Eric S. *Maya History and Religion*. University of Oklahoma Press, 1970.

Thompson, J. Eric S. *The Rise and Fall of Maya Civilization*. Victor Gollancz, 1956.

Thompson, J. Eric S. *The Rise and Fall of Maya Civilization*. Rev. ed. University of Oklahoma Press, 1966.

Tokovinine, Alexandre. *Place and Identity in Classic Maya Narratives*. Dumbarton Oaks, 2013.

Tokovinine, Alexandre, and Vilma Fialko. "Stela 45 of Naranjo and the Early Classic Lords of Sa'al." *The PARI Journal* 7, no. 4 (2007): 1–14.

Tokovinine, Alexandre, and Marc Zender. "Lords of Windy Water: The Royal Court of Motul de San Jose in Classic Maya Inscriptions." In *Motul de San Jose: Politics, History and Economy in a Maya Polity*, edited by A. E. Foias and K. F. Emery. University Press of Florida, 2012.

Tozzer, Alfred M, trans. *Landa's Relación de las Cosas de Yucatán: A Translation*. Papers of the Peabody Museum of American Archaeology and Ethnology, vol. 28. Peabody Museum, Harvard University, 1941.

Tsukamoto, Kenichiro, and Octavio Q. Esparza Olguín. "Ajpach' Waal: The Hieroglyphic Stairway of the Guzmán Group of El Palmar, Campeche, Mexico." *Maya Archaeology* 3 (2015): 30–55.

Valdés, Juan Antonio, and Federico Fahsen. "The Reigning Dynasty of Uaxactun During the Early Classic Period: The Rulers and the Ruled." *Ancient Mesoamerica* 6 (1995): 197–220.

Vargas de la Peña, Leticia, and Victor Rogerio Castillo Borges. "Ek' Balam: Ciudad que empieza a revelar sus secretos." *Arqueología Mexicana* 37 (1999): 24–31.

Vargas de la Peña, Leticia, and Victor Rogerio Castillo Borges. "Ek' Balam y el reino de Talol. Origen y legado." *Arqueología Mexicana* 145 (2017): 38–44.

Velásquez García, Erik. "Los Escalones Jeroglíficos de Dzibanché." In *Los Cautivos de Dzibanché*, edited by Enrique Nalda. INAH, 2004.

Velásquez García, Erik. "K'áak' Upakal en Yucatán: historia de la historiografía de un personaje maya." In *De historiografía y otras pasiones Homenaje a Rosa Camelo*, edited by Álvaro Matute and Evelia Trejo. Instituto de Investigaciones Históricas, UNAM, 2016.

Velásquez García, Erik. "Los posibles alcances territoriales de la influencia política de Dzibanché durante el Clásico temprano: Nuevas alternativas para interpretar las menciones históricas sobre la entidad política de Kan." In *El Territorio Maya, Memoria de la Quinta Mesa Redonda de Palenque,* edited/coordinated by Rodrigo Liendo Stuardo. INAH, 2008.

Velásquez García, Erik, and Ana García Barrios. "Devenir hístorico y papel de los *Chatahn Winik* en la sociedad maya clásica." Mesoweb *Publications,* 2018. https://www.mesoweb.com/es/articulos/Velasquez-Garcia/Chatahn.pdf.

Villa Rojas, Alfonso. "Los quejaches: tribu olvidada del antiguo Yucatán." In *Estudios Etnologicos: Los Mayas.* UNAM, 1962.

Villagutierre Soto-Mayor, Juan de. *Historia de la Conquista de la Provincia de el Itza.* Lucas Antonio de Bedmar y Narvarez, 1701.

Vogt, Evon Z. *Tortillas for the Gods: A Symbolic Analysis of Zinacanteco Rituals.* Rev. ed. University of Oklahoma Press, 1996.

von Euw, Eric. *Corpus of Maya Hieroglyphic Inscriptions, Volume 5,* Part 1: Xultun. Peabody Museum, Harvard University, 1979.

Voorhies, Barbara, and George H. Michaels. "The Ancient Maya and Limestone." *Quaternary Environments and Humans* 2, no. 6 (2024). https://doi.org/10.1016/j.qeh.2024.100028.

Wagner, Logan, Hal Box, and Susan Kline Morehead. *Ancient Origins of the Mexican Plaza: From Primordial Sea to Public Space.* University of Texas Press, 2013.

Wahl, David, Lysanna Anderson, Francisco Estrada-Belli, and Alexander Tokovinine. "Paleoenvironmental, Epigraphic and Archaeological Evidence of Total Warfare Among the Classic Maya." *Nature Human Behavior* 3 (2019): 1049–54.

Walker, Deborah, ed. *Pre-Mamom Pottery Variation and the Preclassic Origins of the Lowland Maya.* University Press of Colorado, 2023.

Webster, David. *The Fall of the Ancient Maya: Solving the Mystery of the Maya Collapse.* Thames and Hudson, 2002.

Webster, David. "The Not So Peaceful Civilization: A Review of Maya War." *Journal of World Prehistory* 14 (2000): 65–119.

Webster, David, AnnCorinne Freter, and Nancy Gonlin. *Copán: The Rise and Fall of an Ancient Maya Kingdom.* Harcourt Brace & Company, 2000.

Wengrow, David. *What Makes a Civilization? The Ancient Near East and the Future of the West.* Oxford University Press, 2010.

Whorf, Benjamin Lee. "The Phonetic Value of Certain Characters in Maya Writing." *Papers of the Peabody Museum,* vol. 13, no. 2. Peabody Museum, Harvard University, 1933.

Wichmann, Soren. *The Linguistics of Maya Writing.* University of Utah Press, 2003.

Wilkerson, S. Jeffrey K. "The Usumacinta River: Troubles on a Wild Frontier." *National Geographic Magazine* 168, no. 4 (1985): 514–43.

Willey, Gordon R. "The Classic Maya 'Hiatus': A Rehearsal for the Collapse?" In *Mesoamerican Archaeology: New Approaches,* edited by N. Hammond. Duckworth, 1974.

Wisdom, Charles. *The Chorti Indians of Guatemala.* University of Chicago Press, 1940.

Zender, Marc. *A Study of Classic Maya Priesthood.* PhD thesis, Department of Anthropology, University of Calgary, 2004.

INDEX

UNEARTHING THE PAST

Eric H. Cline, Series Editor

The Four Heavens: A New History of the Ancient Maya, David Stuart
Native America: The Story of the First Peoples, Kenneth L. Feder